GLOBAL 2050 - A BASIS FOR SPECULATION

Cover design

QSR; Quorn Selective Repro, Loughborough, Leicestershire

About the author

John Cole was born in Sydney, Australia, in 1928 but has spent most of his life in England. He graduated in Geography and Spanish at Nottingham in 1950 where, after a period away, he joined the staff of the geography department. He has travelled extensively, visiting about 70 different countries, in some of which he has lectured and carried out research. He is the author of a number of books on various aspects of geography. He hopes that all his grandchildren will be alive in 2050 to compare the actual situation then with his alternative futures in *Global 2050*.

GLOBAL 2050 - A Basis for Speculation

J. Cole

NOTTINGHAM
University Press

Nottingham University Press
Manor Farm, Main Street, Thrumpton
Nottingham, NG11 0AX, United Kingdom

NOTTINGHAM

First published 1999
© Nottingham University Press

British Library Cataloguing in Publication Data
Global 2050 - a Basis for Speculation:
I. Cole, J

⊤ ISBN 1-897676-654   100 1664912

Typeset by Nottingham University Press, Nottingham
Printed and bound by Redwood Books, Trowbridge, Wiltshire

CONTENTS

CONVERSIONS

See *Statistical Yearbook* of the United Nations for a detailed coverage of conversion coefficients and factors.

Length (1 kilometre = 1,000 metres)

1 centimetre	=	0.394 inch
1 inch	=	2.540 cm
1 metre (m)	=	3.281 feet
1 foot	=	30.48 cm = 0.305 m
1 kilometre (km)	=	0.621 mile
1 mile	=	1609 m = 1.609 km

Area (1 square kilometre = 100 hectares, 1 hectare = 10,000 square metres)

1 hectare (ha)	=	2.471 acres
1 acre	=	0.405 hectare
1 square kilometre	=	0.386 square mile
1 square mile	=	2.590 square kilometres

Weight (tonne is the usual spelling in English for metric ton, 1 tonne = 1,000 kilograms)

1 kilogram (kg)	=	2.205 pounds
1 tonne	=	1.102 short tons
	=	0.984 long ton

Note:	1 million is	$1,000,000 \ (10^6)$
	1 billion is	$1,000,000,000 \ (10^9)$
	1 trillion is	$1,000,000,000,000 \ (10^{12})$

ACRONYMS/INITIALS

AIDS   Acquired immune deficiency syndrome

Asean   Association of South-East Asian Nations

ASSR   Autonomous Soviet Socialist Republic (in former USSR)

Benelux   Economic Union of Belgium, the Netherlands and Luxembourg

BP   The British Petroleum Company plc

CFCs   Chlorofluorocarbons, gases used in the manufacture of e.g. refrigerators, causing damage to the ozone layer in the atmosphere when released

CIS   Commonwealth of Independent States (Russia and most of the former Soviet Socialist Republics)

CMEA   Council for Mutual Economic Assistance (principally USSR and Eastern Europe), now defunct

COMECON   Earlier contraction of Council for Mutual Economic Assistance, CMEA.

EC   European Community or Communities, also the European Union

EEC   European Economic Communities

EU   European Union (formerly European Communities)

FAOPY   Food and Agriculture Organisation Production Yearbook

FAOTY   Food and Agriculture Organisation Trade Yearbook

GATT   General Agreement of Tariffs and Trade, superseded by WTO (World Trade Organisation)

GDP   Gross Domestic Product

GNP   Gross National Product

HDI   Human Development Index (of the UNDP)

HDR   *Human Development Report* of the UNDP

HIV	Human Immuno-deficiency Virus
LNG	Liquefied Natural Gas
NAFTA	North American Free Trade Agreement
NATO	North Atlantic Treaty Organisation
NGO	Non-Government Organisation
NICs	Newly Industrialised Countries
OECD	Organisation for Economic Cooperation and Development
OPEC	Organisation of Petroleum Exporting Countries
PPP	Purchasing power parity
PPS	Purchasing power standard
PRB	Population Reference Bureau (Washington, D.C.)
PRC	People's Republic of China
RSFSR	Russian Soviet Federal Socialist Republic (now Russia)
UK	United Kingdom of Great Britain and Northern Ireland
UN(O)	United Nations (Organisation)
UNDP	United Nations Development Programme
UNDYB	United Nations Demographic Yearbook
UNSYB	United Nations Statistical Yearbook
USA	United States of America
USSR	Union of Soviet Socialist Republics
WPDS	*World Population Data Sheet* of the Population Reference Bureau, annual publication
WTO	World Trade Organisation (succeeds GATT)

PREFACE

Global 2050 is not a textbook. You might set an examination paper on the future, but it would be very difficult to assess and grade the answers. This book is not an attempt to describe the world in 2050. It would be impossible to work out in detail all the changes that will take place between the late 1990s and the middle of the 21st century. The aim of the book is to provide a basis for the reader to speculate about how she or he expects the future to unfold.

In order to achieve the above goal, changes in the last fifty years have been presented, the situation in the 1990s has been described, and possible alternative futures to 2050 have been compared. Projecting past trends into the future appears to be the best known approach to speculation about future trends, but it is not the only one.

In *Megatrends*, J. Naisbitt (1984, p. 3) stresses: 'The most reliable way to anticipate the future is by understanding the present.' In the experience of the author, many people know very little about the present state of the world, its people, and its natural resources, and are ill-equipped to attempt to anticipate what could happen in the future. The reader is invited to answer the questions in the Quiz after this Preface. In their book *The Year 2000*, H. Kahn and A. J. Wiener (1967) stress the importance of considering various possible futures, alternative futures.

In the present book emphasis is not only on what has changed, but also on what has not. Some things change on much faster time scales than others. Although it is good practice to assume that nothing is certain in the future, for practical purposes some things can be assumed not to change, while other things may change either smoothly or abruptly.

A large number of topics have been selected for consideration. The hope, therefore, is that the general reader will benefit from the data and ideas in the book. Experts in each particular field may find that their specialisms have been covered only briefly. They may, however, benefit from reading about other people's fields of specialisation. A disproportionate number of examples are taken from UK situations, while certain US publications have been extensively drawn on for material.

It would not have been realistic to cite the source of every fact and idea presented in the book. There is, however, a list of references of considerable size. This doubles up with further reading, a selective coverage of major topics and issues to be found in the complete list of references. For the sake of simplicity and consistency, as far as possible United Nations sources have been used for many sets of information and the Population Reference Bureau for demographic material. In order to trace trends between 1950 and the 1990s it was necessary in many cases to build up data sets from various numbers of United Nations yearbooks.

The author makes no apology for the very large number of references made to articles in *Scientific American* but hopes that past numbers can be obtained reasonably easily by most readers. For the most up-to-date information on many issues and problems frequent reference has been made to *The Times, The Sunday Times* and *The European*, but the choice of these particular newspapers is simply one of convenience and in no way implies that the author considers them superior to any other reputable newspapers, British or non-British.

In the daily and weekly press one can hope to find the latest innovations and fashionable issues, signs of what may (or may not) develop in the future. Naisbitt (1984, pp. 6-7) found five particular bellwether (the leading sheep in a flock, with bell attached) states in the USA where most of the social invention occurs: California, Florida, Washington State, Colorado and

Connecticut. In the last few hundred years, which have been the bellwether countries of the world? Italy, Holland, the UK, France, Germany, the USA? Which will be the trend setters in the next 50 years?

I am greatly indebted to a number of people for their contributions to the writing of this book. My wife, Isabel, as with previous books, gave her support and encouragement. John Bates, Peter Mounfield, Michael Steven and Charles Watkins gave helpful advice and ideas. The manuscript was put on a wordprocessor by Rosemary Hoole with her usual efficiency. Elaine Watts and Chris Lewis kindly drew most of the diagrams and all of the maps. Finally, Sarah Keeling, Simon Robinson and Eleanor Griffiths gave invaluable advice and assistance in the preparation of this book.

QUIZ

1.   How many people were there in the world in mid-1997?

2.   What is the area (in sq. km.) of the USA?

3.   What is the distance around the equator?

4.   What is the distance from the earth to Saturn, to our nearest star (Alpha Centauri)? Give astronomic units, 1 unit being the distance between earth and the sun.

5.   Are the Arctic and Antarctic polar regions continents or oceans?

6.   What percentage of the earth's land surface is cultivated?

7.   The per capita Gross National Product of the USA in 1995 in US dollars was 27,000. What were those of India, Ethiopia?

8.   How many years would the proved oil of the world in 1996 last at the current rate of production?

Answers in Appendix I

1

INTRODUCTION

'Prediction is very difficult, especially about the future'

Niels Bohr
(quoted in Nown, 1985)

1.1 INTRODUCTION

Anyone looking in a library or bookshop for publications about the future might experience difficulty knowing where to find material on the subject. In contrast, like many other recognised topics and academic disciplines, history would probably be clearly signposted. There are, however, numerous serious and respected books, papers and articles, both learned and popular, explicitly or implicitly about aspects of the future. The basic difference between history and the future is that what may happen in the future is based entirely upon speculation, although for practical purposes many features are virtually certain, in addition to the two – taxes and death – sometimes flippantly cited as the only certain things about the future.

The past cannot be changed or re-run, although it can be reinterpreted if new information becomes available or new models are developed. On the other hand, the future can apparently be influenced to some extent by human decisions and acts. It is therefore worthwhile speculating about the future, even if the subject rarely figures explicitly in the curricula and timetables of educational establishments. As a subject, the future is difficult to examine objectively, and it does not attract much financial support for research, in spite of the existence of some centres in the USA, including the Hudson Institute (Croton-on-Hudson, New York) and the Massachusetts Institute of Technology (Cambridge), in which possible future trends have been the subject of serious speculation.

This book is concerned primarily with the future for humans, not for other species which, in their own ways, organise their activities on their own timescales (bees, ants), build for the future (beavers) or store food for future use (squirrels). Future prospects are regarded as good or bad, favourable or unfavourable mainly (if not exclusively) for the human population. A major issue facing humans now is whether the rapidly increasing use of various materials, essential for economic growth and improved living standards (for some, if not all) is compatible with the negative side of production, measured in terms of depletion of natural resources, pollution and the disposal of waste.

1.2 WHY SPECULATE ABOUT THE FUTURE?

It was proposed above that a strong argument for speculating about the future is the prospect that, at least to some extent, what lies ahead can be determined and manipulated, if not entirely controlled. It is useful to know what can happen or could be expected to happen with reasonable confidence, and to distinguish this from what might be possible, and from what could not happen at all. So who needs or wants to know what? In simple societies with basic farming economies, it is necessary to keep seeds for sowing in the next season, to store food, to ensure a supply of fuel, and to produce sufficient children to keep a community going. In more sophisticated societies, individuals need to plan for the future, institutions such as those dealing in insurance and pension funds must cover all contingencies, and manufacturers in market economies need to turn out the right quantity and type of products required by consumers. At a national level, economic growth and stability is hoped for by governments, foreign trade is monitored, and shortages of commodities at home or abroad are taken into account.

A particular area in which a realistic appreciation of the future is needed is in the preparation of projects that require a very large amount of investment, often (but not always) from the public sector, before they produce any returns. They usually take longer to complete than planned and cost much more than initially estimated. In *Great Planning Disasters*, Hall (1980) describes a number of prominent cases. One discussed is the BART (Bay Area Rapid Transport System) of San Francisco, which cost more than was first estimated and which did not subsequently capture enough traffic to pay for the cost of construction. It did not, as expected, bring the hoped for benefits to the urban scene by radically changing the car-based Californian life-style.

The world is full of tunnels and bridges that are for a long time, if ever, unlikely to cover the cost of construction, maintenance and running. In Japan, the rail tunnel between Honshu (the main island) and Hokkaido (to its north) took 21 years to complete, but carries rail tracks incapable of accommodating large road vehicles on flat trucks or of taking the Shinkansen 'bullet' train. Since 1972, when it was started, Japanese travellers between most places on Honshu and Hokkaido have preferred to fly. The experience of the Hokkaido tunnel came too late to warn the builders of the Channel Tunnel between France and England that it might never make a genuine profit either. The proposal to build by far the world's longest suspension bridge between mainland Calabria (in the 'toe' of Italy) and the island of Sicily has no doubt been carefully considered in the light of many existing transport 'white elephants'. At the time of writing, however, according to Endean (1997), the construction was about to be approved by the Italian government.

Mistakes are repeated in other spheres as well as in transportation links. In the 1930s, mechanised means were used to plough large areas of the Great Plains in the USA. In due course, aggravated by the hottest and driest summers in the first half of the 20th century, massive soil erosion resulted, with the removal or degradation of soil in large areas referred to as 'dust bowls'. Yet in the 1950s Soviet state farmers ploughed up large areas of environmentally very similar land in West Siberia and Kazakhstan to grow cereals, with, as later admitted, resulting soil erosion similar to that experienced in the USA two decades previously.

Since the Second World War (1939-1945), a number of global issues with implications for at least the next few decades have increasingly gained the attention of politicians and the public alike. These concerns existed before the Second World War, but in the different circumstances of the time they were overshadowed by political tensions, military conflicts and economic crises, and were further obscured by the continuing presence in the world of many colonies. Among such issues are the following:

- Concern over the rapid growth of population in recent decades in many parts of the world and the expected continuation of the 'population explosion' in some parts of the world at least for several more decades.

- The problem of achieving sustainable development when non-renewable (or exhaustible) natural resources, notably fossil fuels and non-fuel minerals, are being used in increasingly large quantities, and bioclimatic resources are deteriorating with the over- or mis-use of cultivated land and the clearance of forests.

• Pollution of the physical and man-made environments, especially of the atmosphere, biosphere, hydrosphere, and of large cities.

• The wide and growing gap between rich and poor countries and regions. In the last 50 years this situation has been given much publicity, but in relation to the total global economy, net transfers from rich to poor countries have been too small to contribute substantially to narrowing the gap except in the case of massive aid to a few small countries.

While there is increasing concern about the future, and in the 1990s a widespread gloomy attitude towards it exists in the more wealthy countries, there is not universal agreement that speculation about the future is worthwhile. Gould (1994), for example, questions whether there is any point in attempting to predict the size of the world's population in 2, 50 or 100 years' time. Who really cares, who goes back to check? What use is it to know that the world's population could be around 8 billion in 2020? Ferguson (1997) is disparaging about attempts to anticipate the future: 'But they (fiction writers) have no more to do with history than the books of 'futurology' which the London Library politely categorises as 'Imaginary History'. Futurologists offer guesses as to which of the plausible alternatives which confront us today will prevail in the years ahead, and usually base their predictions on the extrapolation of past trends. To judge by the accuracy of such works, however, they might as well be based on astrology or tarot cards!' Such a statement is ironic, given that it is included in a book in which the author is attempting to justify 'virtual history', using alternatives and counterfactuals to produce alternative histories, which could have happened but did not.

In principle a forecast is useful when it is made, not whether it is right or wrong according to what actually happens. Kahn and Wiener (1967) justify their framework for speculation from 1967 to 2000 as follows: 'By devoting attention to possibilities in a number of future settings it is possible to identify and study patterns and thus to become expert in the recognition of the patterns that are actually developing in the real world. Thus a series of studies like the present one (*The Year 2000*) can be of service in facilitating reaction to such patterns. As a result there may be fewer wrong decisions, fewer unpleasant surprises, and fewer missed opportunities.'

While Kahn and associates are broadly optimistic both about the value of speculating about future prospects for the world, and about their findings, Mesarovic and Pestel (1975) feel that their data to the mid-1970s, and projections from that time on, point to a state of emergency already: 'The analyses in this book extend over a period of fifty years. If, during this coming half century (1975-2025), a viable world system emerges, an organic growth pattern will have been established for mankind to follow thereafter. If a viable system does not develop, projections for the decades thereafter may be academic.' Almost half-way through the critical half-century of Mesarovic and Pestel there appears to be very little evidence of the positive change in the 'world system' regarded as essential by them.

1.3   TRADITIONS OF SPECULATION

Speculation about the future has been conducted through a number of different traditions or 'schools' that are largely mutually exclusive. In this brief history of speculation about the future, four are described.

First tradition: prophecies

The first tradition is that of prophecies. These have been made throughout history and many of them have been recorded and interpreted. Such prophecies are of no practical use since they are deemed to be 'inevitable' and therefore cannot be changed. However, it would be negligent to write a book on speculation about the future without referring to some intriguing prophecies.

- The French physician and astrologer Nostradamus (1503-1566) produced numerous quatrains (four line verses), describing future events. These are not arranged in chronological order, few have an exact date, and most of the contents are not expressed in a straightforward way. Until an event has occurred it is not possible to relate an appropriate quatrain to it. One example of many that seem to fit actual events is a reference to a great fire in sixty six in the maritime city, possibly the Great Fire of London in 1666, a hundred years after his death.

- The Italian painter, sculptor, architect, engineer and scientist Leonardo da Vinci (1452-1519) produced a large number of sketches and diagrams in which he portrayed machines that were not in existence in his lifetime but invented in the 19th and 20th centuries, including a heavier-than-air flying machine, a hand-propelled wooden tank and a submarine. Technically, it would not have been feasible in his time to make such machines and, where relevant, to power them. It could be inferred that both Nostradamus and Leonardo could somehow 'see' into the future and witness events and objects not of their own times.

- The French writer Jules Verne (1828-1905) wrote several adventure novels in which he apparently anticipated later scientific and technological developments. His *Voyage Round The Moon* (1865) showed an appreciation of the physics of space travel as applied to the launching of satellites and missions to the moon and other planets from the late 1950s. Verne's space vehicle that passed round the moon carried a dog that died on the journey and was put out of the vehicle; the dead dog duly followed the orbit of the vehicle. The space vehicle, developed and put into orbit by the French (of course), finally splashed down in the Pacific Ocean and was picked up by a US warship that conveniently happened to be nearby.

- A book that is thought-provoking and controversial is Drosnin's *The Bible Code* (1997). Embedded in the original Hebrew text of the Old Testament of

Figure 1.1. Jules Verne's lunar orbiter. See text for explanation.

the Bible are, according to Drosnin, numerous allusions to specific events, including some in the late 1990s. Only with the use of a computer could the regularly spaced letters that make up the words and phrases of the allusions be searched out. Drosnin debates whether the events 'must' happen or whether some are warnings of events that could be avoided.

If you make enough forecasts, some are likely to prove correct. Coincidence is a useful argument of the sceptical. It is not proposed here to debate the possibility that prophets such as Nostradamus could travel into the future (and why not also the past?); those who believe that some people can do so are able to accept that the future (and the past) must, therefore, be 'there' and as 'real' as the present. The problem can be, as Shakespeare's Macbeth found to his cost, that a warning (in his case from the three witches) of what is about to happen can be too obscure to save one from disaster.

Second tradition: cycles

The second tradition of speculation about the future assumes a series of stages in time through which human societies proceed, or special periods in which stages take place. In such rigid frameworks human progress or decline through time works out with inevitability. Possibly the theory of evolution, coupled with the stages of growth of human and other animal organisms, has partly stimulated historians to search for and identify stages in human history.

The Italian philosopher Giambattista Vico (1668-1744) developed a cyclical theory of history whereby societies are born, develop and duly decline. He also proposed that there are three stages of government: theocratic, heroic and human (see *The New Science of Giambattista Vico*, New York, Anchor Books, 1961). A more elaborate series of stages of history was proposed by the German philosopher and historian Karl Marx (1818-1883). As adopted, adapted and applied in the USSR, the process includes the stages of slavery, feudalism, capitalism (with several sub-stages), socialism and communism, each with particular economic and social features. The German philosopher Oswald Spengler (1880-1936) argued in *The Decline of the West* (1918) that civilisations (cultures) go through natural cycles of growth and decay in a period of roughly one thousand years. While his ideas are not taken seriously by most historians, his impact was considerable since his idea of thousand-year cycles influenced the Nazis in their assertion that following the Second World War the victorious German Third Reich would last for a thousand years. The identification of thousand-year periods is suspiciously related to our use of base 10 for counting (see later in this chapter).

Western Europe has not had a monopoly of thinkers who have produced grand designs for history. In the USA, Rostow (1960) claimed to have countered the Marxian stages of history with his book *The Stages of Economic Growth* (subtitled 'A Non-Communist Manifesto'). His model is based on the transformation of the traditional society, through its take-off and the drive to maturity, into the age of high mass-consumption and beyond. Rostow took a broader view than Marx, accepting that politics, social organisation and culture also influence human activities, although he still placed economic influences centrally in his model.

The view of the development and evolution of human societies by stages proposed by both Marx and Rostow implies that the future is in some respects inevitable, at least in a broad way, while the influence of individuals on the course of history is modest if not non-existent. Their models are tidy, appealing, and at their simplest are based on a list of half a dozen stages that can be learnt easily for the purposes of examinations. While not doubting the seriousness of the various creators of such grand designs of the evolution, and in some cases the decline, of human societies, their usefulness in forecasting events in the first half of the 21st century is questionable.

Third tradition: science fiction

In the early part of the 20th century a third tradition of speculating about the future was prominent and indeed had considerable influence in Britain, if not elsewhere. Among the numerous works of H. G. Wells (1866-1946) published early in the 20th century were several in which the future formed the central theme. In *Anticipations*, written around 1900, already armed with a knowledge of scientific and technological advances in Western Europe and North America in the 18th and 19th centuries, Wells anticipated (among other things) great advances in transportation and agriculture, and the probable diffusion of great cities. In *War in the Air* (1908) Wells anticipated aerial warfare, subsequently developed in the First and Second World Wars, while in *War of the Worlds* (1898) he contributed to science fiction with the arrival of aliens on a common in Surrey, close to his home in Bromley. His device in *The Time Machine* (1895) is a vehicle many people would like to have access to but as yet it also remains in the realm of fantasy. In *The Island of Dr Moreau* the attempt to turn animals into humans is the mirror image of efforts to prolong life in humans by organ transplants from other species.

Figure 1.2.

Like H. G. Wells, Aldous Huxley (1894-1963) and George Orwell (1903-1950) developed the concept of the scenario, an approach to speculation about the future that later became prominent in the 1960s and 1970s. Their scenarios were focused on particular aspects of social and political situations. In *Brave New World* (1932), Huxley was examining the implications of the reproduction of the human species by mass production in the laboratory. In *Nineteen Eight-Four* (first published 1949), Orwell vividly described the effects of the control of human existence by the state carried to the ultimate extent.

At this point it is appropriate to note the use in this book of certain words relating to speculation about the future. Arthur C. Clarke drew a critical distinction between fiction and fantasy. While for practical purposes at least, facts can usually be distinguished and accepted, fiction refers to an account of a situation that *could* happen, whereas fantasy refers to a situation that could not happen. In time, however, something that might have been considered fiction or fantasy may turn into fact.

Among the examples of fiction and fantasy given earlier in this chapter, the description by Jules Verne of a voyage round the moon would have been seen as fantasy by most people in his time but such journeys became fact in the 1960s. On the other hand, the time machine of H. G. Wells apparently remains an impossibility, and therefore in the realm of fantasy. In *Gulliver's Travels* (1726), the hero of the story by Jonathan Swift (1667-1745) not only visited Lilliput and Brobdingnag but also Laputa. Here a ruthless ruler kept control of his people by aerial surveillance, moving through the sky on a massive piece of rock, kept in position by magnets. Such a device combined the features of a low orbit spacecraft and a helicopter gunship. While it was possible to make an approximation of a flying machine, the moon vehicle and even the surveillance device, no one has any idea what a time machine would be like or how it would work. Various screen versions have been concocted, including a complicated device in the film *The Time Machine* and a blue police-box used by Dr Who in the television series, still fairly common in the streets of British cities in the 1950s but now no longer used.

Figure 1.3. An illustration in *Gulliver's Travels* (first published n 1726) drawn by Herbert Cole in 1899. See text for explanation.

The point of drawing attention to the devices described above is to show that fact, fiction and fantasy are not constant and are blurred where they overlap. In exploring the prospects for the first half of the 21st century it is useful to know how people at other times have seen their futures, in many cases now our past, and to appreciate how to use our imagination as well as common sense. I.F. Clarke's book *The Pattern of Expectation 1644 - 2001* (1979) provides an excellent background to the subject.

The three traditions briefly described above were limited in certain respects. The true practitioners of the art of prophecy seem to have been 'gifted' people with passive roles, privileged to foresee specific events and developments and to report on them, but not in a position to do anything about them. The protagonists of grand designs for human society have created rigid models such that if events turn out to contradict their structures or to water down their sharpness, it is argued that the events are wrong, not the models themselves. The third tradition mixes speculation with fiction to make specific points about future prospects.

Fourth tradition: analytical research

The fourth tradition of predicting and forecasting is characterised by a more professional, objective and sophisticated approach to speculation about the future. Research teams use massive sets of data and make lavish use of computers to analyse material and calculate alternative future trends, from which many different possible futures are created and appraised. The contributors to this tradition have been numerous, but for simplicity attention will focus below on certain key personalities (mostly American) and their projects. For a time, a battle of titans raged both between teams of optimists and pessimists, and between these and the detractors of any attempt to speculate about the future at all.

- *The Year 2000* by H. Kahn and A. J. Wiener was published in 1967. Its subtitle was 'A Framework for Speculation on the Next Thirty-Three Years'. Although the USA figures prominently in the book, the prospects of many other countries are also examined and a global perspective is maintained. Economic change is related to science and technology, industrialisation and the post-industrial future. Gross National Product (GNP) is extensively used as the measure of economic change and GNP per capita is forecast for various countries to the year 2000 and beyond. Alternative futures are considered, and possible 21st century nightmares examined.

- J. W. Forrester's book *World Dynamics* was first published in June 1971 and was quickly followed in March 1972 by *The Limits to Growth* by Meadows *et al.*, for the Club of Rome. The latter book provided a less technical presentation of the methods and findings of the former. The approach used to work out possible alternative futures for human society was based on the assumption that by combining the scientific method, systems analysis and the modern computer, relationships and interactions between many variables could be calculated through time. A world model was built specifically to investigate five major trends of global concern: accelerating industrialisation, rapid population growth, widespread malnutrition, depletion of non-renewable resources, and a deteriorating environment. Many alternative futures were produced, with variations in the speed of change through time of the variables; it was concluded that unless drastic changes are made in economic policies and life-styles throughout the world, the conditions of most if not all of the world's population would deteriorate drastically in a matter of decades or a century. In the late 1990s, however, economic growth in some form or other, considered to be the basic cause of many of the problems, is still the aim of almost every government in the world.

- H. S. D. Cole *et al.* (1973) were quick to publish a 'reply' to the limits to growth argument in *Thinking About the Future*, subtitled 'A Critique of The Limits to Growth'. Like other commentators they criticised the assumptions made in the world model, especially the approach to economic issues, and they questioned the usefulness of computers in assisting with the calculations. They considered political limits to development to be crucial, not physical limits, and argued that serious problems caused by such issues as food shortages and intense pollution were local rather than global.

- The second report of the Club of Rome was *Mankind at the Turning Point* by M. Mesarovic and E. Pestel (1975), already referred to on page 3. The systems approach, the creation of alternative projections (in some cases as far ahead as the year 2100) and the generally pessimistic prospects for mankind, echoed the conclusions of Meadows *et al.* (1972), but greater attention was given to regional differences, with the implication that some regions would decline more quickly than others.

- *The Global 2000 Report to the President* (of the USA), directed by G. O. Barney, was published in 1982. A massive amount of data was processed and the results interpreted at global, major region and in some cases national level. Alternative futures were worked out for the period from the late 1970s to the year 2000 for specific topics such as the availability of arable land, and energy needs. Some projections were also made as far ahead as the year 2100. The general conclusions resembled those reached in *The Limits to Growth*.

- A 'reply' to the *Global 2000 Report*, edited by J. L. Simon and H. Kahn was published in 1984. The opening paragraph is as follows: 'The original 1980 *Global 2000 Report to the President* is frightening. It received extraordinarily wide circulation, and it has influenced crucial US government policies. But it is dead wrong. Now *The Resourceful Earth*, a response to Global 2000, presents the relevant reliable trend evidence which mainly reassures rather than frightens.'

- Meadows *et al.* returned to the scene in 1992 with *Beyond the Limits*, referred to as a 'sequel to the international best-seller *The Limits to Growth*'. The by now familiar global estimates for population, resources, food, industrial output and pollution from 1900 to the time of writing (around 1990) and on as far as the year 2100, indicate that if recent trends continue, collapse will occur and disaster will strike humanity. They conclude that to achieve sustainable development, new paths will have to be followed and new attitudes will have to replace existing ones.

1.4 THE NATURE OF TIME

A dictionary definition of time is likely to leave the reader confused. For example, one use of the word time is defined in *The Shorter Oxford English Dictionary* as 'a limited stretch of space of continued existence, as the interval between two successive events or acts, or the period through which an action, condition, or state continues.' Here, time may be thought of as a 'line' on which events can be placed in a succession such that the order in which they occurred is unequivocally established. The reader who wishes to go more deeply into the subject of time might look at Nigel Calder's *Timescale: an Atlas of the Fourth Dimension* (1984) or Stephen Hawkings's *A Brief History of Time* (1988).

Conventionally, three dimensions are attributed to space, one to time. Places and objects can be uniquely located in space in relation to the earth's surface by three coordinates, or often for practical purposes on a map, by only two. Time, on the other hand, is at once more abstract than space and yet more simple, since events can be represented with a single dimension, a straight line. In space, cause and effect can take place in all directions, whereas in time the general consensus and practical experience indicate that cause and effect work only in one direction.

A working definition of the meaning of the present is essential in speculating about the future. It has been calculated that on a normal day each person has an average of more than 12,000 distinct thoughts. Although these thoughts have not been classified, it seems reasonable to distinguish three classes with regard to their relationship to time, rather than to subject or, where appropriate, to place. Some thoughts are about the past, some about the future and some about what might be called the immediate present, directly related to what one is doing at the time. For convenience, the present may be regarded as a period of time of some duration rather than a moment that is very short or even of no extent at all separating past and future. It may be thought of as a flexible, transparent 'buffer' between past and future. For some purposes the present may be a few minutes, for other purposes a few hours, for cautious historians not ready to tackle the immediate past, a matter of years or even decades. For the purposes of this book, ideally the future would start immediately, but on account of the lack of up-to-date information about many of the matters discussed, roughly the mid-to-late 1990s are regarded as the present, since at the time of writing (in 1996-98) complete data on many subjects could only be obtained for the years 1993-1995.

Since by its nature the future has not happened when one is writing about it, strictly it cannot be studied, so here the term 'studying the future' is avoided. On the other hand, it is useful to examine past statements and prophecies about the future (now the past), in order to assess with hindsight their success or lack of success, and also to study methods and approaches used to speculate about the future (see Chapter 3).

In a traditional society and economy, with little change from year to year and generation to generation, attention focuses on what does not alter, and 'more of the same' is expected. Many of us living near the end of the 20th century, on the other hand, are increasingly aware of and concerned about change, and we tend to overlook the prospect that some things are virtually certain not to alter in the next 50 or 100 years. The term 'future shock' is the title of a book by Alvin Toffler (1970) and refers to the difficulty experienced by many people in keeping up with changes. There is an tendency for those who speculate about the future to emphasise what has changed in recent decades rather than what has not changed. It can be assumed that the planets of our solar system will continue in their orbits around the sun, life will not be wiped out on the planet earth by a collision with a large asteroid, or a salvo of strategically-placed nuclear weapons, and humans, like other animals, will continue to be mortal. As George Orwell wrote in *England Your England* (1961): 'Meanwhile, England, together with the rest of the world, is changing. And like everything else it can change only in certain directions, which up to a point can be foreseen. That is not to say that the future is fixed, merely that certain alternatives are possible and others not. A seed may grow or not grow, but at any rate a turnip seed never grows into a parsnip.' (cited in Stillman, (1974)).

While it does not seem justifiable to talk about studying the future, there is no shortage of words and terms in use that refer to it. In this book, for simplicity, three categories are proposed:

- Words that appear to imply access to and the capability of observing a future event. These terms will be avoided by the author who, while not denying the possibility that future events can be foretold, does not have that ability himself. They include: 'to prophesy' and a 'prophecy', 'to foresee' and 'to foretell', 'to predict' and 'precognition'. The practical value of such forays into the future would be their correctness: to be of any use a winning horse or lottery number must be known. If predictions are incorrect or vague they lose effectiveness and credibility.

- Terms that refer to approximations of the future but do not aspire to predicting exact times, situations and places; these include 'forecasting', 'projecting' and 'conjecturing' about possible, usually probable, futures. They should help individuals or groups of people to anticipate what may happen in given circumstances, e.g. 'Hurricane Julia' is going to pass over your island in two days time', or 'country *x* is about to invade country *y*'. Projections are often made by continuing past trends into the future.

- Titles and words that refer to ideal situations rather than to specific events, and in which past and future, fact and fiction, mingle. In 1516 Thomas More (1478-1535) published *Utopia*, the description of a supposedly perfect society. *Arcadia* refers more to a simple, stress-free society but adequately provided with basic needs (in late 20th century eyes this is probably with organic farming and no tractors). *Cornucopia* could refer to the Soviet Union that was to be once the Marxian stage of Communism had been reached and everyone's (reasonable) needs and wants were satisfied. *Equalia* might be found among the crew of a spacecraft while in orbit.

In addition to the conventional words used in referring to the future, a daunting new inventory of terms has been introduced since the 1950s by the most recent generation of speculators about the future: multifold, megatrend, surprise-free scenario, alternative futures, multi-loop non-linear feedback system. Indeed there seems no limit to the different angles from which the relationship between past and future can be seen. The intriguing study of counterfactuals, 'alternative pasts', has been justified by Ferguson (1997), while Strauss and Howe (1991) have written *The History of America's Future 1584 to 2069*. Phrases such as 'back to the future', 'geography is history' (a British Telecom advertisement presumably implying that distance no longer counts) and 'geography is the history of the present' may be thought-provoking or enigmatic or both.

1.5   PROBLEMS OF SPECULATING ABOUT THE FUTURE

Anyone seriously attempting to speculate about the future is likely to meet a wide range of problems, some of which do not confront historians or scientists. Two serious problems are the absence of facts about the future, and the difficulty of carrying out and replicating experiments. An awareness of the concepts of probability and an appreciation of gambling could be advantageous. For simplicity a number of problems are listed and briefly discussed below.

Availability of data

Most speculation about the future takes into account relevant events in the past and is often based on examinations of past trends, which are projected into the future. Although in most countries of the world data on both human activities and natural events and processes for the half-century 1945-95 are plentiful, there are many shortcomings. Data for two very large and influential countries – the former USSR and communist China – were very limited outside their boundaries for long periods (from 1940 to the mid-1950s for the USSR, and longer for China). In both cases the publication of statistical yearbooks with retrospective series of data made amends to some extent, but information about many demographic, economic (particularly strategic) and social aspects is still limited.

Sheer lack of data-collecting facilities, rather than secrecy, has meant also that many important sets of data are lacking in developing countries. One reason is the failure to carry out regular censuses of population and production, another the fact that production from non-commercial agriculture is not recorded and is therefore only estimated for purposes of measuring Gross National Product (GNP) and for providing data for international organisations such as the Food and Agriculture Organisation of the United Nations (FAO). Other problems connected with GNP as a measure of development are discussed in Chapter 2.

Reliability of data

The most prestigious sources of numerical data sometimes contain errors of breath-taking proportions. The user should be aware of what, roughly, a value should be. For example, in the *Statistical Yearbook* of the United Nations horrendous slips occur as illustrated by the following two examples. In the 1979/80 *Statistical Yearbook*, the African country of Senegal was credited with only ten people per physician, not compatible with the absolute numbers of 334 physicians and a population of over 5 million. In the 1990/91 *Statistical Yearbook*, the population for Afghanistan for 1985 was given as 18,136,000 while the estimate for 1990 dropped to 1,612,000, clearly an error, rather than the effect of the internal conflict in the 1980s, however devastating that was.

Even the most carefully compiled sets of data can contain serious shortcomings. For example, careful checking of enumeration districts *after* the US census of population of 1960 was held (see Hauser (1971)) showed that the total population of the USA was undercounted by 3.1 per cent, the count having failed to reach an estimated 2.2 per cent of the white population and 9.5 per cent of the non-white population. The official figure, published before the checking, given with an admission that there had been undercounting (actually about 5.5 million), was 179,323,175, a striking example of an inaccurate number presented with spurious precision.

Unintentional errors can be no less confusing as, for example, a statement by a distinguished German scientist (who shall be nameless) who was aiming to show the dangers of a rise in world sea-level through global warming, that: '70 per cent of the population of the world settles within 50 km of the coast'. It is true that many big cities are located by the coast and that in places there are dense agricultural populations near sea-level, but the percentage is more like 20 at the outside. When questioned as to how 70 per cent was arrived at the scientist in question admitted with great honesty that in India he had noticed a lot of people living near the coast. The cavalier way in which experts in one area can make statements about another is illustrated again on the same subject by Stock (1995) in a reference to the speed at which sea level can change:

'with half the planet's population in coastal areas, ancient and modern data suggest we may be in a madhouse again.'

Even the report of the prestigious Royal Institute of International Affairs (1996), *Unsettled Times*, contains an error of horrendous proportions, not a printing error but one included through sloppiness and the lack of a demographer in the team of social scientists (billion throughout *Global 2050* means thousand million): 'There are as many people alive as have lived through human history.' To be generous, there were about 6 billion people alive in the 1990s (see Chapter 4). That contrasts with a Population Reference Bureau estimate of the number of people who have ever been alive of about 105 billion (including the 6 billion alive now). In reply to the author's query as to how such a mistake was made, a representative of RIIA admitted with frankness that the statement had been copied from a World Bank report. Lin (1985) gives examples of remarkable errors, sometimes with disastrous consequences, resulting from the miscalculation of distances, confusion over units of measurement, and faulty computer circuits or programs. With unintended errors such as those referred to above lurking in the texts and tables of even the most 'reliable' publications, how can one be confident about forecasts for the future?

The base 10 problem

A large number of units of measurement are used in the study of both natural features and human activities; some of these will be discussed where appropriate later in the book. It happens that for most purposes of counting, decimal or base 10 is used (i.e. ten digits including zero). Two other bases, also using positional counting, have some advantages over base 10 for particular purposes: base 2, otherwise referred to as binary (i.e. two digits, 1 and 0 (zero), used in computers), and base 12 (i.e. with twelve digits, including zero); the latter is divisible by the prime numbers 2 and 3, rather than by 2 and 5 in base 10. A nicely 'round' number ending in zero, such as 100 or 1000, often attracts attention and may be credited with special significance. In contrast, the number 100_{12} (one zero zero in base 12) is actually 144 in base 10.

It can be argued that the arbitrary predilection for ten, a hundred, a thousand and so on creates an artificial timescale on which events are placed and indeed may itself actually influence the order and way in which events happen. This point is made by Fernandez-Armesto (1995): 'It's always 1,000 years since sometime, and our way of counting time is simply a convention. Yet the habit of thinking in terms of decades and centuries induces a self-fulfilling delusion, and the way people behave or, at least, perceive their behaviour - really does tend to change every 10 or 100 years.' Three widely different examples may be noted. The 1000 year culture periods of Oswald Spengler, already referred to in this chapter, are decimal, while in the USSR economic planning was organised for simplicity or convenience round the famous Five-Year Plans which (apart from one interruption (1957-65) when there was a revised Seven-Year Plan) fitted years ending in 5 or 0 from 1945 to 1990. It could be argued that with a more flexible plan, different periods of time could have been used, as appropriate, for different sectors of the economy.

In a completely different situation, base 10 is about to strike again. According to Kane (1997): 'most of the timing mechanisms essential to running most computers have been programmed with only the last two digits of the date, taking the 19 prefix for granted.' Using another base our decimal year 2000 would have occurred at some 'other' time. The effect of base 10 thinking can be circular because goals may be set for attainment or completion in years with round numbers. Concern with the turn of a century, particularly when it coincides with the millennium, is a striking example; many projections during the second half of the 20th century have been taken to 2000. Apart from the arbitrary use of base 10 in the first place, there is even disagreement as to whether the new century (and millennium) begins on 1st January 2000 or 1st January 2001, while the starting point of the Christian calendar was not actually the year in which Christ was born (probably several years BC (see Gould, S.J. (1997)).

Forecasts may influence what they forecast

A problem with statements about the future is that they can alter what they predict. After the Second World War many Americans moved to California both for economic reasons and to retire in a benign climate. Forecasts of 'overpopulation', traffic congestion and pollution in cities, environmental degradation and social problems (due partly to the arrival of many foreign immigrants) may have slowed down migration into the state, at least from the rest of the USA itself (if not from Mexico), deflecting people to neighbouring Oregon, Arizona and Nevada or to more distant Florida. It was argued earlier in the 20th century that the emergence of the USSR as the world's first 'socialist' state, ready to challenge 'capitalism' and criticise conditions in capitalist countries, acted as an incentive to governments and companies to improve the situation and to avert a possible crisis in capitalist countries and the eventual downfall of the capitalist system. It has also been argued that forecasts of environmental disasters arising from the burning of fossil fuels, made with increasing frequency from the 1960s, have led to a levelling off in the use of fossil fuels in the 1970s and 1980s in the industrial countries (see Chapter 6).

Timescales

Experience of forecasting indicates that there is decay in accuracy and confidence the farther a trend extends into the future. Some subjects are, however, more robust than others since the timescale over which marked changes occur is far longer for some than for others. For example, weather conditions in many places can be accurately forecast at most over a matter of days rather than weeks. On the other hand, thanks to the reliable course of the earth round the sun, the unchanging rotation of the earth, and its tilt of 23 degrees, the seasonl changes of summer and winter can be expected to bring generally hotter and colder weather for the foreseeable future in most places outside the tropics.

While conditions of atmospheric pressure, temperature and precipitation can change by the hour, marked changes in climate are gradual and are unlikely to be detected and confirmed in less than a matter of some decades. Much longer forecasts of climatic change have been made, one for example anticipating for Britain 1000 years of warmer conditions followed by many thousands of years of colder conditions. Changes also take place in the earth's crust at different speeds, both at the surface and beneath it. Tectonic plates are pushed apart by sea floor spreading a matter of 2-3 cm a year. Related areas in which earthquakes can be expected to occur and volcanoes will erupt are mostly known, but success in predicting exact times and locations has been limited. Revelle (1982) sums up the difference between sudden and gradual change with reference to possible global warming: 'Societies have had much experience in responding to short-term environmental catastrophes: events such as hurricanes, floods, droughts, volcanic eruptions, earthquakes and forest fires. The changes that may come as a result of an increased amount of carbon dioxide in the atmosphere, however, will not be events. They will be slow, pervasive environmental shifts.'

Human activities also vary in the extent to which their future can be forecast. One way of looking at the speed of change and the consequent likely success of forecasting is to calculate the replacement rate of populations (not limited only to human ones). The times that elapse before about 90 per cent of a total population is replaced show marked contrasts. Humans live much longer than most other animals and the average generation gap is about thirty years. In a human population with an average life expectancy of 70 years and no marked difference in the size of age groups, it would take 63 years for 90 per cent to be replaced.

Examples of 90 per cent replacement show great differences. Ninety per cent of the students in an establishment of higher education would be replaced in a matter of several years, the residents of a housing estate in a modern city in about three decades. Buildings have a much slower turnover, while street patterns may last hundreds of years (although they may be renamed or modified by widening and resurfacing). Ninety per cent of the vehicles that use the roads, on the other hand, are replaced in a developed country in about fifteen years.

By comparison, movements in the equity markets occur over very brief time spans because prices of individual shares can change very sharply, while changes in the financial 'weather' may bring large reductions and occasionally increases in average share values in a matter of days or even hours. Conflicts, such as the war between Paraguay and its neighbours (ending 1871) that reduced the population of Paraguay from 530,000 to 220,000, like natural disasters, can bring sudden drastic changes in local populations. Short of a great catastrophe, however, the total population of the world for the next several decades can be expected to continue to change fairly smoothly. Some things are much more durable and much less changeable than others, with consequent effects on the task of speculating about the future and the timescales over which useful and meaningful forecasts can be made (timescales will be discussed further in Chapter 2).

1.6   EXAMPLES OF FORECASTS

It is a sad commentary on forecasting that in view of the fact that so many bad forecasts have been publicised, G. Nown (1985) considered it worth producing a collection. The dangers in making dubious off-the-cuff comments, either through lack of thought, or appreciation of an imminent situation, or taking notice simply because a person is famous or is regarded as an authority, are illustrated by the following:

*   US Congressman Orange Ferris, 1868, on the purchase of Alaska by the USA from Russia: 'The possession of this Russian territory can give us neither honour, wealth, or power, but will always be a source of weakness and expense, without any adequate return.'

*   British Prime Minister, Neville Chamberlain after the Munich Agreement with Hitler, September 1938: 'I believe it is peace for our time.'

*   Thomas Watson, IBM executive, 1958: 'I think there is a world market for about five computers.'

*   Education Minister, Margaret Thatcher on BBC-TV's 'Blue Peter' programme, 1973: 'I do not think there will be a woman prime minister in my time.' She was elected leader of the Conservative Party in 1975 and became Prime Minister in 1979.

It is well known that economists do not always agree, a characteristic well illustrated by the use of the Delphi method (see Chapter 3). *The Times* of 22 October 1971 contained two letters in adjacent columns. The first letter was as follows: 'Sir, The undersigned, being full-time teaching officers of economics in British universities, believe that the economic effects of joining the Common Market, taking both short and long-term effects into account, are more likely to be unfavourable than favourable to Britain'. It contained 155 signatures. In the second letter, identical in all other respects, and signed by 140 economists, the words unfavourable and favourable were transposed. The UK joined the Common Market in 1973, a move supported in retrospect by the result of a national referendum in 1975. To this day university economists and practising politicians alike continue to ponder and argue about the effects of joining the European Union.

It can be seen that some of the above forecasts are more specific than others. In the examples that follow, some forecasts are fairly specific while others are so open that they can never be assessed as successful or unsuccessful; they not arranged in chronological order but according to how specific they are.

- R. Kempson (1996) on 16 August 1996 at the start of the English football season predicted that Manchester United (1996 winners) would win the Premier League again in the 1996-97 season. Since there are 20 teams, he had one-in-twenty odds of being correct by chance. As of mid-November he could have been biting his nails, because Manchester United were in sixth place, with 19 points, against 27 points for the leaders and 7 for the lowest scoring club. In due course, however, he was proved correct. The main reason for including this example is to suggest that a good definition of a prediction is something on which bets can be placed since the result (in May 1997 in this case) becomes an indisputable fact.

- A. Bernoth and D. Smith (1995) writing at the year's end about prospects for the FT-SE 100 index (Financial Times Stock Exchange) cited ten forecasts for the end of 1996, ranging from 4,100 by Société Générale to 3,400 by Goldman Sachs, giving an average of 3,750, just 1.6 per cent above 3,690 for the end of December 1995. The divergence of predictions seems very considerable. It was unlikely that any of them would agree exactly with the index that materialised. The 'winner' could perhaps be deemed the prediction closest to the index on 31 December 1996, which at 4,118.5 turned out to exceed the highest prediction. The approach here is a simple example of the Delphi method of forecasting, to be described in Chapter 3.

- Halford Mackinder (1904) used the term 'Columbian epoch' (about 1500-1900) to refer to the period during which European influence expanded worldwide and compared it with the future (i.e. post-1900): 'Broadly speaking we may contrast the Columbian epoch with the age that preceded it, by describing its essential characteristic as the expansion of Europe against almost negligible resistances, whereas medieval Christendom was pent into a narrow region and threatened by external barbarism. From the present time forth (1904), in the post-Columbian age, we shall have to deal with a closed political system, and none the less that it will be one of worldwide scope. Every explosion of social forces, instead of being dissipated in a surrounding circuit of unknown space and barbaric chaos, will be sharply echoed from the far side of the globe.' A fair description of the 20th century?

- The Cuban newspaper *Granma* (1977) quoted Fidel Castro as saying: 'With the development of socialism and communism, mankind will eventually become one big family and our planet, one single country. The new generations must prepare for that world of the future.' Sweeping, and overtaken by events around 1990. However, Rhodes (1997) reports that Castro controls at least 10 per cent of the ailing Cuban economy, with investments in the sugar, nickel and other industries totalling 1.4 billion US dollars.

- Jensen *et al.* (1983) conclude their definitive work on Soviet natural resources with the following remarkable insight: 'In the longer term, after 1990, given current and prospective development efforts, Soviet natural resources could conceivably be more important in the world economy - or less.' This forecast could be adapted to apply to any situation! It is the universally safe forecast, in no way condemning the massive research effort required to compile their 700-page book on the subject.

- What to do about the environment of Europe? In a monumental book, also about 700 pages in length, by the European Environment Agency (see Stanners and Bourdeau (1995)) the authors identify twelve prominent environmental programmes, 'for which there is clear evidence for justifiable concern and for action to be taken', but they decline to find a simple answer to the question 'how healthy is Europe's Environment?' They state: 'a full analysis of responses and the state of actions to protect the environment was beyond the scope of the report.'

- Where to invest in the world? Guinness Flight (1996) states that the 21st century belongs to Asia, which in the 1990s has been experiencing explosive economic growth. Asia here does not apparently include Western Asia or Siberia, while Japan is sidelined on account of its much slower relative rate of economic growth, and what of the Pacific rim? During 1998-9 it became evident that some countries of Asia had experienced excessive economic growth, a situation resulting in severe economic crises.

- In 1986, the former Soviet leader Mikhail Gorbachev published *The Coming Century of Peace*, a statement about the future on the lines of that made by Mackinder in 1904. No-one would claim that Gorbachev is a clairvoyant. Did his insight into the future come from an appreciation of the weakening of Soviet military and/or economic power? Ahead of his time, Amalrik (1970) asked: 'Will the Soviet Union survive until 1984?' Amalrik's guess was less than a decade out.

One issue that has caused great concern and speculation has been that of world oil reserves, production and prices; two views are noted:

- In 1978 A. R. Flower wrote: 'The supply of oil will fail to meet increasing demand before the year 2000.' According to BP (1996) in 1980 world proved oil reserves were 90 billion tonnes and annual production was 3 billion. The reserves-to-production ratio at the rate of production at the time was therefore thirty years. In 1996, however, proved reserves had risen to 141 billion tonnes, annual production to 3.36 billion tonnes and the reserves-to-production ratio to about 42 years (BP (1997)). New discoveries, additions and revisions had raised reserves in spite of a continuing production of around 3 billion tonnes a year during 1980-95. Flower's statement can therefore be questioned, although the discrepancy could be related to some extent to what is meant by demand.

- Pearce (1979) stated: 'it is not really useful to make projections beyond 1990', but even so he projects the oil and natural gas outlook for the demand range of the non-communist world to the late 1990s and the possible production range to 2020. He divided the combined world oil and natural gas reserves into those already extracted (almost 100 billion tonnes of oil equivalent, (t.o.e.)), discovered reserves (another 200 billion), and undiscovered potential. Understandably there is great disparity among the estimates of undiscovered reserves made by 24 experts consulted, ranging between about 150 billion and 750 billion t.o.e., with an average of around 300 billion (from a skewed distribution). The oil industry will be discussed more fully in Chapter 6.

Even among the limited selection of forecasts given in this section it is evident that anyone can pronounce on what will happen in the future. A prediction, it seems, can be as much about what the forecaster wants to see happen as about what, objectively, the evidence may show. This situation has already been illustrated with the optimistic Kahn and pessimistic Meadows views of the global future, both using broadly the same information about the recent past. Forecasts have been made, for example, of global and regional population totals over the next few decades, the expected availability of arable land, the extent of forest clearance, especially of the tropical rain forest, and changes in total and per capita Gross National Product of various parts of the world. These and other issues will be discussed in later chapters.

1.7   WORLD VIEWS

It is not expected that all readers of this book will hold similar views about the world, the place of humans in it or the relative importance of different trends and prospects for the future. The author has tried to keep a neutral view, focusing on the prospect for material changes that affect everyone rather than on beliefs and ideologies that are specific to particular groups of people and regions.

It is difficult not to be influenced in the choice of topics by the preoccupations and priorities of the society in which one has been brought up. It is therefore appropriate to raise here two issues that will affect the reader's view of the future. The first concerns the position of Europe in the world since the 15th century; the second is the strong influence of Christianity, initially mainly in Europe and adjoining areas, then on a global scale.

The period from 1500 to 2000 has been one in which European powers came to dominate much of the rest of the world, while at the same time engaging in numerous wars among themselves at home. Figure 1.4 shows the extent of acquisition of territory outside Europe by European powers. It started with the build-up of the Spanish and Portuguese enterprise in what is now referred to as Latin America. In the 16th and 17th centuries Russia expanded eastwards into Siberia. England (then Britain), France and Holland, later joined by Germany, Italy and Belgium, occupied Canada, India, Australia, almost all of Africa, and much of Southeast Asia, while in the 19th century Russia conquered lands in Central Asia. In the end, outside the few per cent of the world's land in Europe itself, at one time or another most of the land in the world apart from China, Japan and parts of Southwest Asia had been occupied, although often loosely, by at least one European power. The period 1500-2000 might be thought of as the half-millennium of Europe. Ironically, during 1403–1433, not long before the Portuguese and Spanish navigators set out on their voyages of discovery, the Emperor of China sent out fleets to explore the seas to the south of his country and the Indian Ocean, but the prospect that China rather than Europe might have conquered much of the world was short-lived, as the project was soon abandoned. Here is a situation for a counterfactual study: what if China had conquered much of Asia and Africa?

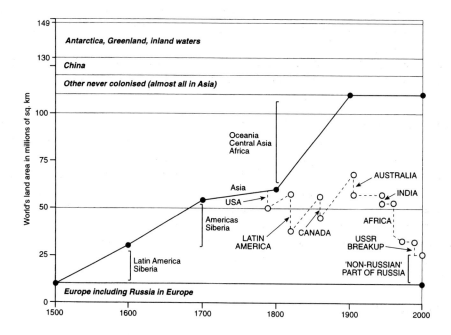

Figure 1.4 The extent of European colonisation, 1500-2000. Territorial gains and losses during Mackinder's (1904) Columbian epoch, 1500-1900, by European powers. The vertical scale corresponds to the total land area of the world; areas of land are represented only very approximately. At the bottom of the graph is Europe itself, about 10 million sq km. The continuous line shows new territory added to the empires of European powers, mainly Spain, Portugal, Russia, England/Great Britain, France. Losses, whether the result of wars of independence or through the granting of effective independence, are shown by the dashed line. At the end of the 20th century, there remain in the Russian Federation large political administrative units (formerly ASSRs) with predominantly non-Russian populations. A similar diagram representing population conquered rather than area would show considerable differences and, unlike area, the total would grow. For almost five centuries, European conquerors have changed forever the indigenous cultures of almost all of the rest of the world, affecting most profoundly many thinly populated areas, as Cocker (1998) shows in *Rivers of Blood, Rivers of Gold, Europe's Conflict with Tribal People.*

From historical examples, empires do not last for ever. The break-up of the European empires began with the Declaration of Independence (1776) by some of the British colonies in North America and continued to 1997, when the British colony of Hong Kong was returned to China. Strictly, it could be argued that many other areas occupied by Europeans during the last five centuries are still effectively colonies: for example, there are many non-Russian nationalities in the Russian Federation, and an indigenous population in much of North America, Australia and Brazil. However, the formal empires of European powers have virtually disappeared with the break-up of the Soviet Union in 1991. Coincidentally, in Europe itself, confrontation between the major European powers finally appears to have ceased with the removal of the Iron Curtain, the end of the Cold War, and the arrival at a tenuous *modus vivendi* between NATO and Russia. One reason for creating the European Common Market in 1956 was to make a new military conflict between France and Germany unlikely, if not impossible.

In the 1952 BBC Reith Lectures the historian Arnold Toynbee (1889-1979) predicted that the influence of Europe on the rest of the world was waning and that there would be a backlash (not his word) from various regions as they grew stronger economically and militarily. In 1904 Mackinder in his paper 'The Geographical Pivot of History' noted the way in which, until the

16th century the Christian world had been under pressure from Mongol and Tatar invaders from the east, and the Ottoman Turks from the southeast. Spain and Portugal were finally removing Moorish and Islamic influences in the south of Iberia. From the time of the voyages of the Portuguese and Spanish navigators and the journeys of the Russian conquerors of Siberia, various versions of Christianity, whether Orthodox, Catholic or Protestant, were spread to many parts of the world. The beliefs of Christianity have had such a great influence both within Europe itself and in many areas outside that they affect the world view of those people who have a world view at all, and their expectations for the future.

For simplicity, it is assumed that the reader will hold one of the four following views about the place of humans in the world. Several points are elaborated in the rest of this sub-section.

- The world was created by a super being – God in the case of Christians – for his own purposes. It may be deduced or assumed that human life on this earth is a means to an end, possibly a testing ground for a place in the next life or world. In *Is there a God?* Swinburne (1996) offers a powerful response to modern doubts about the existence of God. Although not so widely diffused globally as Christianity, other religions, especially Islam, Hinduism and Buddhism, also influence the beliefs and world views of large populations.

- Humans are a species apart from the rest of nature, one that has reached the highest pinnacle of evolution so far, and has a 'right' or even an 'obligation' to use the resources and other species of the world as it wishes.

- The human species is just a part of nature and on account of its greatly superior powers of using resources and other species, and in its own interest and that of other species, it should proceed with care and with consideration for nature.

- Any other views. Among other possibilities is the prospect that past, present and future are already there, the future is actually already determined, and the possession of free will to shape it is just an illusion.

Two of the principal functions of the Christian Bible have been to explain how and why the world was created, and to recommend behaviour and lifestyles for those aspiring to favourable conditions in the next 'life'. The first account has been discredited by scientific discoveries, especially in geology and biology, in the 19th century. The second function continues to raise debate. In *God is Green*, Bradley (1990b) discusses the concern of some Christians that nature was not put there just for humans to use it as they wish. *Rich Christians in an Age of Hunger* by Sider (1987) relates more to the inequality in the world and the moral side of Christianity. In the last resort, each Christian will place emphasis on what he or she expects or hopes the 21st century will be like. There could be greater concern about issues such as the development gap and the environment, or acceptance that if things go badly it is the will of God, part of his grand design. The prospect seems to be that people of the Islamic faith may increase their influence in the world in the next few decades, increasingly affecting political and economic affairs in a swathe of countries from Morocco to the Philippines. For one thing population is now growing more quickly here than in almost all the Christian countries of Europe and the Americas.

For those who profess to be atheist, agnostic or indifferent about Christianity and other religions the idea that humans are the top species, capable of taming nature and shaping conditions to their needs, is being eroded by two views. One view is that the anthropocentric position of humans should be replaced by an ecological perspective, another that life has no higher purpose than to perpetuate the survival of DNA (Dawkins (1995)).

An intermediate view is described by Kates (1994) who uses evidence from studies of opinions held in industrial and developing countries alike: 'Along with ... widespread evidence of environmental concern, more profound ideas are emerging. Witness the ongoing fundamental challenges to anthropocentrism and the more modest efforts to resolve the conflicting needs of ecosystems and economies or the conflicting claims of equity between species, places, peoples, livelihoods and generations.'

The world of Dawkins (1995) is utterly different: 'In a universe of electrons and selfish genes, blind physical forces and genetic replication, some people are going to get hurt, other people are going to get lucky, and you won't find any rhyme or reason in it, nor any justice. The universe that we observe has precisely the properties we should expect if there is at bottom, no design, no purpose, no evil and no good, nothing but pitiless indifference.' Can it be that humans themselves have created all the ideologies, rules, grand designs of human evolution, progress and moral improvement? At all events, most people will struggle on into the next century, regardless of what the thinkers say. Should an intelligent alien (by human standards) come from another planet (not a prospect the author expects to happen in the 21st century), it could be difficult to explain to it what is going on in the world and to justify the way humans have elevated themselves to such an exalted position.

Figure 1.5 is an attempt to illustrate the multi-dimensional nature of the relationships between pairs of material and/or spiritual influences on human activities. Some relationships are more prominent than others.

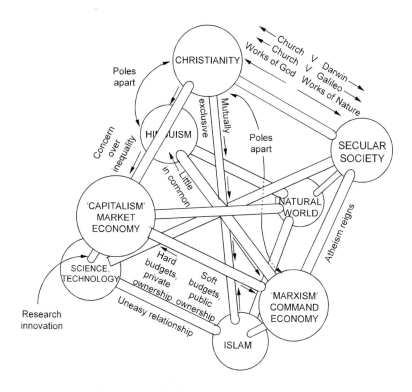

Figure 1.5 Relationships between some of the world's most influential ideologies and elements. Many pairs of ideologies are poles apart. The diagram is a two dimensional picture of a three dimensional model. The eight circles are at the eight corners of a cube. There are N(N-1)/2, i.e. (8x7)/2 or 28 possible pairs of relationships, only some of which are shown on the diagram. The reader may care to ponder as to whether there are actually eight 'dimensions' or even 28.

1.8   THE STRUCTURE AND AIMS OF THE BOOK

In their book *The Year 2000*, Kahn and Wiener (1967) discuss the problems of making projections one-third of a century ahead, as they themselves do (1967–2000). They argue that the time when you make your forecasts of the future affects your approach (see Figure 1.6).   For a European, 1900 would be a straightforward time at which to make a forecast because there were few major upheavals in the preceding half-century. In the mid-1930s there had recently been the First World War and the great economic depression, two serious upheavals. Around 1950 the Second World War was still remembered, a possible third World War was a major preoccupation, many newly independent countries had emerged, nuclear and computer power were being developed. Past trends were irregular and bumpy, and not long enough to give much help in determining how they might be expected to continue. The period from 1914 to 1945 had the most irregular trends.

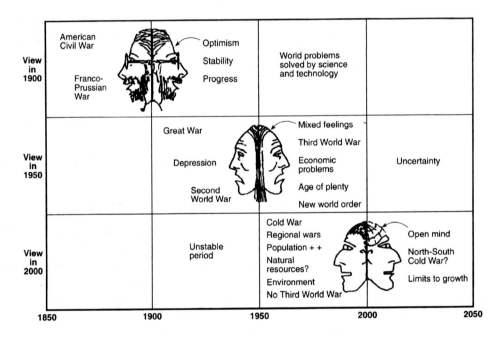

Figure 1.6 Viewpoints in time. The diagram has been inspired by the following statement in Kahn and Wiener (1967, p. 5): 'We have considered how the problem of projecting one-third century ahead might have appeared in 1933, 1900, and so on, in order to get a sense of the current and future pace of change and the likelihood of unexpected developments ...'

In *The History of America's Future 1584 to 2069*, already referred to, Strauss and Howe (1991) – clearly disappointed that college graduates give history as the academic subject whose lessons they found of least use in their daily affairs – take an approach to American life that merges past and future (p. 8): 'This book presents the "history of the future" by narrating a recurring dynamic of generational behaviour that seems to determine how and when we participate as individuals in social change - or social upheaval. We say, in effect, that the dynamic repeats itself. This is reason enough to make history important: for if the future replays the past, so too must the past anticipate the future.' They give individual people locations in history in the generational cycle in America.

In some respects the late 1990s is an easier time to make forecasts about the future than any time since the 1910s. No Third World War has taken place, although there has been no lack of regional and local conflicts, almost all between developing countries. In the view of the author, the four greatest shocks and upheavals since the Second World War have been: the break-up of West European colonial empires, the oil price rises in the 1970s, the nuclear accident at Chernobyl in 1986, and the break-up of the Soviet Union in 1991 (the latter is of special importance because the threat of a global war, as opposed to local wars, has been greatly reduced). Time will tell whether the forest fires in Indonesia in 1997, and in Brazil and Mexico in 1998 will have the same simultaneous awakening and sobering effect on the attitude of influential people with regard to the rain forests as the oil price rises and Chernobyl did in two key energy sectors.

Trends can, therefore, be more clearly discerned in the second half of the 20th century than in the first half. There is a reasonably clear perspective of 50 years from 1945 to 1995. While it is not implied that forecasting the next 50 years is now a simple matter of projecting the trends of the last 50, it is possible to get a reasonable sense of the recent and current pace of change and the likelihood of events that might alter conditions. It was this situation that persuaded the author to speculate about the next half-century, choosing the year 2050 as the target, accepting the familiar base 10 preference referred to already and avoiding the spurious precision of a more intriguing year such as 2042 or 2066.

The book has three main aims.

1. To introduce the reader to a number of features, methods and problems related to speculation about the future (mainly Chapters 1-3)

2. To provide factual material about such key features of the world as population, food, energy and regional disparities, in the second half of the 20th century.

3. To present possible alternative projections to 2050 for such key features.

After the first three introductory chapters, the main body of the book is subdivided into two parts. In Chapters 4-8 specific trends between 1950 and 1990 are examined and tentative forecasts to 2050 are made. When data availability allows and a greater time span is appropriate, some trends are traced back into the 1930s and earlier. These chapters cover population, food, energy, raw materials and industry, and links and transportation. In Chapters 9-12 more complex issues are covered, with reference to the 'development gap', environmental issues, the world political map and, finally, the overall situation in 2050 and prospects to 2100.

Several of the projections made in the 1960s and 1970s relied heavily on Gross National (or Domestic) Product as the principal measure of economic development or transformation. United Nations and World Bank reports on the state of the world have also tended to rely on GNP as a measure of success and of living standards. In the view of the author it is equally important to examine the performance and prospects of specific natural resources and levels of production of both material goods and services. Many distinct 'concrete' elements of human activity actually underlie the more notional and esoteric global measure of GNP, some of the drawbacks of which are discussed in Chapter 2.

When a book with a global perspective is produced by one author there is more freedom as to the choice of topics and the range of ideas presented than if a book is written by a team of people and edited: for this reason the present book may appear idiosyncratic. The author does not profess to forecast any changes in human nature in the next fifty years, less than two generations time. In many respects human behaviour has changed little over far longer than this. In *Life's Grandeur* S. J. Gould (see Bragg (1996)) accepts the great impact of inventions in recent centuries but argues that human nature and the creative imagination in the arts have hardly changed over millennia.

Opinions vary widely with regard to the feasibility and usefulness of speculating about the future. For example, historians generally appear to be against it while economists are more positive. In the physical and biological sciences, processes and laws tend to be independent of time and should apply equally in the past and the future, allowing continuity of many things to be expected. In the real world of farming, manufacturing and services, a failure to anticipate the future could spell disaster, especially in countries in which a market economy predominates.

A strong argument for speculating about the future is the prospect that there are choices to be made, so that it can to some extent be shaped before it happens, whereas the past cannot be changed, although it can be reinterpreted. In the preface to *Uncertain Futures*, Ayres (1979) sees the future as follows: 'I think of the future as one might think of a play sketched in outline, with the characters and their initial relationships well defined, but the script as yet unwritten.' However, there have been numerous wild forecasts in no way reflecting what has subsequently happened. Humans have a way of foreseeing what they want to happen, they are inclined to look for the unusual or the spectacular (the yeti and alien syndrome of the 20th century) and they may be restricted in how they see the future by preconceived ideas about the world that may originate in fiction, fantasy or ideological dogma.

Speculation about the future can be based on or guided by a number of different approaches (see Chapter 3), which may sometimes be combined, but there are no hard data or facts to work with. Forecasts and projections should nevertheless be feasible and responsible, not improbable or impossible. One aim is to provoke other people into thinking about issues that you consider important. The statement: 'The population of Ethiopia could increase three times in the next 50 years' may provoke indifference (so what? where *is* Ethiopia?), dismay (what can be done about it?) or disagreement (rubbish, it will be the same as now).

To end on a technical note, in this book for comparative purposes, the world has been subdivided into ten major regions. Following the example of the US Population Reference Bureau, different parts of the former USSR has been allocated to four major regions.

Developed:

1. Europe, excluding the former USSR apart from the Baltic Republics

2. Russia, Ukraine, Belarus and Moldova

3. Japan and South Korea

4. North America (Canada and USA) and Oceania (Australia, New Zealand, Papua-New Guinea, various Pacific islands)

Developing:

5. Latin America

6. Africa south of the Sahara

7. North Africa and Southwest Asia, including the former Soviet Republics of Transcaucasia

8. South Central Asia, including the former Soviet Republics of Central Asia, and Kazakhstan

9. Southeast Asia

10. China and other smaller countries

2

CHANGE

Plus ça change, plus c'est la même chose

French saying

2.1 THE NATURE OF CHANGE

In earlier centuries marked changes in human activities were exceptional rather than normal. To be sure, cyclical changes such as the regular recurrence of the seasons and the less regular succession of rulers and movements of political boundaries were part of life, but the broad features of society remained the same. In contrast, most of the population of the world now lives in countries and regions in which change of various kinds is rapid and is expected to continue and indeed its rate to increase. More 'traditional' societies do, however, still exist, especially among indigenous populations of the rainforests of Amazonia, Papua-New Guinea, and the Congo, and in arid areas of Africa and Australia.

Attitudes of both individuals and whole communities and institutions to change have varied in recent centuries. In Europe in the 16th century, the influential Catholic Church resisted change in both moral matters and evidence about the heliocentric structure of the solar system. Referring to Galileo's discoveries about the solar system, Gingerich (1982) remarks: 'Galileo was sent back to his house in Arcetri, outside Florence, where he remained under house arrest until his death in 1642. Partly as a consequence of his persecution, the center of creative science moved to the Protestant countries, notably the Netherlands and England.' More recently, around the middle of the 19th century, after some persuasion, Japan chose to adopt the technological innovations of Europe and North America. However, China resisted them, with subsequent dramatic consequences for the Far East region, when in the 1930s Japan tried to swallow up its much larger neighbour.

In the 20th century the USA and USSR have encouraged scientific research and technological change. The USSR was less innovative in its political and economic organisation while the US political system remains largely unchanged since independence. Late in the 20th century a few countries, notably Myanmar (formerly Burma) and North Korea, still resist changes in their own ways, while Islam, noted for its tolerance towards science and learning in southern Spain and elsewhere in the Middle Ages, now calls for draconian restrictions on human rights (as understood in the West) in some fundamentalist countries.

The 'process of change' is now widely accepted as normal and is often associated with progress and development, although the more neutral words transformation and modernisation might be more appropriate in many contexts. Living conditions have improved in many areas of the world during the last two centuries, but some of this progress has been at the expense of the natural world, and near the end of the 20th century many people are still below the material standards regarded as adequate by the United Nations (see Chapters 9 and 12) and presumably by themselves.

This chapter contains an informal examination of the types and features of change. It is not an exhaustive classification, but an outline for the study of situations to be discussed in the rest of the book. Changes in both time and space are of interest. In the rest of this section some aspects of change are noted: cause and effect, the nature of change itself, timescales and space scales.

Cause and effect

To appreciate probable and possible changes in the 21st century it is useful to consider four different types of cause and effect:

- Physical changes affecting physical conditions, with no human influence. Examples are: changes in the location of land masses (continents), changes in sea-level, changes in natural vegetation due to climatic change, volcanoes and flooding. Such changes have occurred long before humans came on the scene.

- Physical changes affecting human activities: climatic change, volcanoes impacting on the atmosphere and climate, earthquakes, hurricanes, flooding.

- Human activities changing physical conditions: clearance of forests, ploughing, extraction of minerals, burning of fossil fuels. The impacts from weakest to strongest are: earth's crust, hydrology, atmosphere (pollution, possible global warming), vegetation and soil. As human society progressed from simple gathering, hunting and fishing activities to the management and use of the land, water and animals, and then to the modern industrial society, the impact on the natural environment has increased rapidly.

- Human activities affecting human conditions: economic growth, political boundary changes, conflict, application of scientific discoveries, research and technology.

The nature of change itself

Two types of change may be distinguished: cyclical (modular) or repetitive change, and on-going change. Examples of cyclical change in the physical world are day and night and the seasons of the year; an example in human activities is the difference in the number of commuters in the central areas of large cities at midday and at midnight. Economists have identified cycles of human activity connected with production and business, but have not always gained universal acceptance. In 1925 a Russian economist, Kondratiev, claimed the existence of long-term cycles of 50–60 years duration. Examples of on-going change are climatic change once diurnal and seasonal variations have been smoothed out, and world population growth in the 20th century (see Figure 4.1 in Chapter 4).

Change may be smooth and gradual, or it can be sudden. The problems of using past trends as a basis for forecasting future changes and situations will be discussed in Chapter 3 (see Figure 3.5). Abrupt changes may result from the build-up of pressure or tension until a certain threshold is reached, when a 'catastrophic' change occurs. Such a change may not necessarily be negative in its impact, as the conventional use of the word catastrophic implies. Catastrophe theory has been developed (see Zeeman (1976), Woodcock and Davis (1980)) to examine different kinds of sudden event and change of state. In the natural environment, earthquakes and sudden volcanic eruptions are examples. The explosion of the atom bombs on Hiroshima and Nagasaki in Japan in August 1945 revolutionised destructive capacity in an instant. In each case one aircraft carrying a nuclear device of modest proportions did as much damage as hundreds of conventional bombers had been doing to German cities up to May 1945 and to Japanese cities in the months before the atom bombs were used. The political map can alter at 'the stroke of a pen'. In 1697, Spain ceded Haiti to France and as a result the economy of the colony was drastically transformed in the 18th century. The dissolution of the USSR in 1991 has had a momentous impact on world affairs in the 1990s. The nature of abrupt or catastrophic changes is such that the time of their occurrence cannot usually be anticipated with certainty, even if they are expected.

The extent to which past trends help in anticipating changes in the next few decades will be discussed in Chapter 3. Changes in human activities in the 19th and 20th century are near enough to offer guidance on possible changes from 2000 to 2050. Changes throughout history can also be expected to throw a general light on things to come and are worth examining. It is misguided to expect exact repetitions of past events to take place in the next few decades, but parallels can be found. In particular, the systems of political and administrative boundaries, both international and internal, illuminate longstanding cultural features of subsets of populations, and although exact shifts in the next few decades cannot be predicted, the existence of distinct cultural groups can serve as a guide to the possibilities. Whittemore Boggs (1940) showed how in Europe certain stable political boundaries between or around sovereign states (e.g. Spain and Portugal, Switzerland) have remained virtually unchanged for centuries whereas others (e.g. much of the boundary of Germany) have only come into being recently, while others have disappeared (e.g. between England and Scotland).

Timescales (see Table 2.1)

In considering the prospects for the world in the first half of the 21st century it is crucial to consider how much change is possible or likely in different sectors of the economy, in demographic situations and in the natural environment. Changes occur much more quickly in some phenomena than in others, in both the natural world and human activities. Since the timescales on which alterations occur vary greatly, it is to be expected that some features of the world in 2050 can be forecast with reasonable accuracy while others can only be very approximate efforts at speculation. Thus, for example, the continents will have changed their relative positions on the earth's surface by distances of 1-2 metres, a movement that is so small that by 2050 it will be imperceptible and for our purposes need not be taken into consideration. On the other hand, bearing in mind the shrinking of the Caspian and Aral Seas in the present century, a considerable change in world sea-level *could* occur by 2050, enough to cause serious problems in many coastal areas, whether it rises or falls. Again, without some drastic physical change or an all-out nuclear war, the total population of the world seems set to grow smoothly towards 10 billion by the year 2050, although very great demographic changes could occur at local levels. The timespan for which goals are set, plans made, and agreements reached, gives an idea of how far different people and institutions are looking ahead (see also Chapter 3).

Space scales

In considering the possible future impact of changes in both physical and human features of the world it is also necessary to look at space scales; different types of change will affect areas of different sizes. For simplicity, five scales of area are described in this book, using the terms: local, regional, national, major regional and global. The major regions of the world, the 10 groups of countries used in this book, are described at the end of Chapter 1.

Table 2.1 Selected timescales

1. *Millions of years ago*

    550 all present continents near equator
    250 long period of volcanic activity
    65 giant meteorite affects global climate

2. *Appearance of Homo sapiens, thousands of years ago*

    130 in Africa
    73 in Asia
    51 in Europe
    34, 15, 9 separate spread into Americas

    Source: Wallace (1997)

3. *Doubling time of population at 1997 rate of growth (in years)*

Global and regions		Selected individual countries	
Africa	26	Gaza (lowest)	15
All less developed	38	Nigeria	23
Latin America	38	India	36
Asia	44	Brazil	48
World	47	China	67
Oceania	63	USA	116
North America	117	Japan	289
All more developed	564	UK	433
Europe[1]	–	Russia[1]	–

    [1] Population declining in 1997
    Source: *WPDS 1997*

4. *Reserves-to-production ratio of fossil fuels at 1996 rates of production (in years)*

Coal	224
Natural gas	62
Oil	42

    Source: BP (1997)

2.2   CAUSES OF CHANGE

Changes in the natural environment are caused by forces from outside the earth's atmosphere, from below its crust, and in the biosphere in the intervening space (see Table 2.2). Changes caused by external forces include the possible influence of sunspots on the earth's atmosphere, in eleven-year cycles, and the potentially devastating impact of meteorites and comets. Sea-floor spreading, resulting from the upwelling of molten material from the earth's interior, causes tectonic plates (large areas of crust, much underlying the sea) to move (albeit very slowly by human timescales) producing continental drift.

Human activity has produced great changes in the natural environment, especially in the last few decades. The basic features of the lithosphere are not affected but, for example, the extraction of minerals and the building of transport links have made a considerable local impact on the terrain. Interference with the hydrosphere has been much more marked. Water is diverted from rivers for irrigation, dams and reservoirs help to control the flow of water, and underground (artesian) water is brought to the surface for the water supply in many areas.

Table 2.2 Causes and elements of change

External: sun's heat, sunspot cycles, seasons (increasingly marked from the Equator to Poles and resulting from the tilt of earth's axis) other heavenly bodies: moon, Mars, Jupiter, asteroids, meteorites, comets

Earth's interior: heat causing sea-floor spreading, volcanoes, earthquakes

Earth's crust/surface: lithosphere, minerals, soil, hydrosphere, atmosphere, biosphere

Natural resources: air, water, cultivable land, forest, fisheries, pasture, fossil fuels, non-fuel minerals

Human impact on natural environment: forest clearance, cultivation, soil erosion, desertification, depletion of ozone layer, possible global warming causing change in sea-level through changing quantity of ice on ice caps, species loss

Human activities: production of goods and services (agriculture, industry, services), movement of goods, passengers and information, trade

Population: change in quantity (births to deaths relationship), change in location (migration)

Organisation: political and administrative units, management of economy, support for research and technological innovation by government and/or by private companies

Individuals: it is a matter of debate and controversy as to the extent to which decisions and actions of individuals can affect the course of history.

Like the hydrosphere, the atmosphere is increasingly affected by human activities. The burning of coal, most types of which contain many impurities, has been the cause of heavy pollution locally since the 18th century, especially in the industrialised countries. The moisture in the atmosphere flushes out many of the pollutants when it rains; however, chemical compounds from the burning of all kinds of fossil fuels (see Chapter 6) remain in the air, particularly carbon dioxide. On a very short timescale of decades, the combustion of large quantities of carbon 'captured' in the vegetation of the distant past and compressed into coal deposits, as well as of the hydrocarbons oil and gas, returns carbon to the atmosphere. The increasing amount of carbon dioxide in the atmosphere is thought to be a cause of global warming. The dilemma is whether to go on burning fossil fuels and risk the consequences or to stop burning them and cause great economic upheavals. In reality they may not actually be causing global warming and climatic change, although their contribution to pollution is unquestionable.

Thanks to the proliferation of scientific discoveries, inventions and various kinds of technology, each generation of people influences the lifestyle of future generations. Most inventions can be classed under a small number of headings according to what parts of humans they enhance: the muscles, the senses, the brain. Steam driven and internal combustion engines, for example, have greatly increased the muscular power and physical capabilities of people. The enhancement of human physical strength has happened for millennia on a much smaller scale through the use of work animals, and with power from wind and falling water, and indeed other humans, whether enslaved or not. The senses have likewise been enhanced in various ways. Developments in optics led to spectacles, telescopes and microscopes, improving the sense of sight. Similarly, the telephone and radio have indirectly increased the sense of hearing.

Electronic computers have greatly increased the power of the brain by supplementing earlier devices such as encyclopaedias and dictionaries for storing (and retrieving) information, and abacuses, slide-rules and calculators for carrying out computations. Since the 1950s computers have become increasingly indispensable in numerous aspects of life, but their capabilities are not clearly appreciated by many people. It was reported in *The Times* (15 September 1967) that according to Professor Robert Kenedi, a pioneer in medical engineering, 'the time may come when an artificial man might be created with an artificial intelligence capable of taking decisions.' More practically, Nuttall (1990a) reported the view of two Australian academics that there should be 'a world-wide ban on the use of computers in sensitive areas, including intensive care wards, the nuclear power industry, air traffic control and early warning defence and strike command systems... Computers are inherently flawed and too unreliable for critical or vital tasks.' Thomas (1989) expressed the same view about the use of computers in safety-related applications. Computers can fail in applications either on account of a fault in the machine or on account of errors in the program.

Improvements in means of communication between people, and means of keeping the body in reasonable comfort with modern heating and air conditioning, are further developments passed on through the generations. The clever thing is to anticipate ways in which in the future comparable developments that could affect other parts of the human body and other human activities will be thought of and applied. Nuttall (1997c) notes one possible breakthrough expected by 2055: a machine to make us trigger emotions by stimulating the brain's mood centres – a replacement for drugs?

Until the last few centuries many inventions and innovations appear to have been the result of chance discoveries, sometimes apparently made independently in different parts of the world. Although it cannot be proved conclusively, the manufacture and use of tools with materials from animals (bones), plants (wood), and stone in the first technological revolution tens of thousands of years ago, appears to have started in many different places at different times. Again, agriculture and the domestication of animals, with the accumulation of seeds for next year's planting, irrigation in some areas, and storage facilities for food, were also developed independently, in this case for certain, in civilisations in Asia and in the Americas.

In the last few hundred years there has been a more conscious and positive drive in Europe to develop new technology, with circumstances or curiosity leading to new scientific discoveries and new inventions. In the 16th century, for example, the rapid development of Portuguese, Spanish and later other navigation across oceans over great distances required new ships of a certain minimum size and sophistication, together with improved weapons. The sudden need to know longitude required accurate timepieces and led to the development of clockwork, reflecting in miniature the spirit of modern engineering. In England in the 17th and early 18th centuries supplies of wood for fuel and construction were running out as forests became depleted (see e.g. Nef (1977)). Early in the 18th century coal was first used to smelt iron ore, the beginnings of our serious involvement with fossil fuels. Advances in Europe in mathematics, physics, chemistry, geology and biology formed the basis for modern industrial processes, medicine and other sectors of human activities.

Both world wars hastened the development of new technologies. In the First World War, for example, lorries partially replaced mules and horses in road transportation, tanks were developed, and rapid progress was made in the development of combat aircraft. In the Second World War, radar was employed, the jet engine developed and atom bombs used. It is tempting to say that without these conflicts the development of some technologies would have taken much longer, and even that some, such as nuclear weapons, might not have been developed at all (this should not be taken to imply that the author advocates war).

Comparatively recently Hamilton (1968) writing in *New Scientist* noted that technological forecasting - broadly speaking predicting changes in materials, machines and methods - was still in its infancy. Three decades later the paths of scientific research and technological development appear much more clearly defined and in the 21st century are most likely to follow fairly clearly marked directions towards particular goals. Synergism is replacing serendipity. New discoveries depend increasingly on research along known lines but, as in the past, circumstances may lead to the need for changes in production and consumption. Examples of possible areas in which changes might be expected could result from the pressure on bioclimatic resources, leading to a more vegetarian diet in countries currently with a high consumption of meat and dairy products, a less lavish approach to private motoring, and protective measures to reduce the negative effects of a rise in sea-level due to global warming (should this occur). Massive devices could be put in orbit round our planet to deflect some of the heat from the sun, should global warming become a serious problem; this is fiction at the moment (rather than fantasy) and an enormous challenge technologically and financially. The Russian attempt in 1999 to put a device in orbit to reflect sunlight onto places in the far north of Siberia in winter time marks a modest step in this direction.

Researchers in many countries of the world are following agendas to increase scientific knowledge and to develop new applications, whether supported by national governments or by privately-owned companies. Throughout the last five centuries, however, individuals or small groups of people have been responsible for making many breakthroughs in science and technology or implementing political decisions that have changed the course of history. In his book *The 100, a ranking of the most influential persons in history*, M.H. Hart (1993) examines developments resulting from the achievements of individuals and distinguishes those changes that might not have happened without a particular individual and those that would have happened anyway. Although a matter of speculation, it could be argued, for example, that if the Chinese inventor Ts'ai Lun had not invented paper (around 105 AD), no one else would have done so. In contrast, if James Watt (1736-1819) had not produced a comparatively efficient and in due course commercially viable steam engine, someone else would have done so.

While the general direction of scientific research and technological development in the next few decades can be anticipated with some confidence, it is impossible to predict which individuals, in which countries, will come up with completely new discoveries and inventions. It is even more difficult to allow for errors, hoaxes, and misunderstandings, until with hindsight they are appreciated, as the following examples from the past show. In the Middle Ages the general consensus about the form of the earth was that it was flat. Columbus, supported by Spain, correctly thought that the earth was spherical, but assumed it to be much smaller than it is. Boorstin (1975) gives the reason for the misunderstanding: China and India should not have been very far to the west across the Atlantic from Europe because in the book of *Esdras* in the Apocrypha (on which Fra Mauro's map of 1459 was based) it was stated that six-sevenths of the earth's surface is land. In reality, the Americas stood in the way of the expected short crossing to Asia and instead of immediately establishing an alternative trade route between Europe and East Asia, Columbus and other explorers opened up a continent hitherto unknown to Europeans, to conquest by Spain and later Portugal.

Science has been confused by hoaxes, a classic case being the Piltown skull and jawbone, which misled anthropologists about human evolution for several decades until radiocarbon dating showed the two parts to be of completely different ages. A Punch cartoon in 1955 showed a corridor in a university with a bin labelled: 'for your notes on the evolution of man'.

It is now being debated whether, indeed, there are any more major discoveries to be made in science. In the view of Forrester (1973): 'The industrialised world expects solutions for its problems to come from technology. Such has been possible in the past when technology was able to run ahead of population and exploit land and natural resourses faster than population grew. But technological solutions become less possible as the ultimate world limits are approached.'

2.3 PHYSICAL CHANGES

It will be shown in Chapter 3 that a systems approach can help in showing how variables are linked in such a way that a change in one may cause a change in another. Such a situation exists with regard to the relationship and interactions between different elements in the physical and natural world. It is not within the scope of this section to examine these relationships in detail. Table 2.3 is intended to indicate roughly the strength of or lack of influence of nine elements on six of them.

Table 2.3 Strength of mutual influence of basic elements of the earth's crust, rows on columns

	2a Lithosphere	2b Hydrosphere	2c Atmosphere	2d Pedosphere	2e Biosphere	3 Humans
1a Sun	L	H	H	M	H	H
1b Meteorites	M	M	H	H	H	H
1c Internal	H	L	L	L	L	L
2a Lithosphere	-	H	M	H	H	H
2b Hydrosphere	M	-	M	H	H	H
2c Atmosphere	L	H	-	M	L	H
2d Pedosphere	L	M	M	-	H	L
2e Biosphere	L	L	L	H	H	H
3 Humans	L	M	H	H	H	H

H - High, M - Medium, L - Low

The numbering below refers to the rows in Table 2.3.

1. a-c External and internal influences: The sun, meteorites and the internal heat of the earth influence one another very little if at all and only their influences on the other six elements are noted in Table 2.3.

   1.a The sun has little impact on the rocks of the earth's crust except very near the surface but is crucial in determining the state of the biosphere.

   1.b Meteorites and comets (see Grady (1997)). Most meteorites that strike the earth originate in the Asteroid Belt, located between Mars and Jupiter, but some originate in Mars or the Moon. Each year a total weight of about 40,000 tonnes of meteorite material hits the earth, but usually in very small quantities. A very large meteorite strikes the earth about once every million years. An exceptionally large meteorite, about 10km in diameter, is thought to have caused a crater 200-300 km across about 65 million years ago at Chiczabub in the Gulf of Mexico. It is considered by some that the material thrown into the earth's atmosphere caused the climate to change globally, destroying many species, including the dinosaurs.

While meteorites are known to be a potential threat to life on earth, the suspected presence of up to several thousand undetected comets in the solar system is regarded as no less of a threat (see Nuttall (1997a)). The impact of a sizeable comet could be devastating, while even a near miss could cause disaster by leaving behind comet dust that could hinder the sun's rays from reaching the earth's surface.

1.c   Internal forces are responsible for the almost imperceptible movement of tectonic plates over the earth's surface, 2-3 cm a year. They also cause sudden impacts through volcanoes and earthquakes. Earthquake damage is usually local or at most regional, but spectacular if in or close to large centres of population. There have been several serious earthquakes in the last 20 years. One of the most recent was in Kobe, Japan in 1995 (see Reid (1995)). There were about 5,500 deaths, while fires destroyed many older wooden houses and roads were damaged. The death toll was much lower than in the earthquake in the Tokyo area in 1923 when there were 143,000 deaths. Damage was heavy in two earthquakes in California (see Gore (1995)), in the San Francisco Bay area in 1989 (6 billion dollars) and Northridge, Los Angeles in 1994 (20 billion dollars). Earthquakes in densely populated areas in developing countries tend to cause greater loss of life, but less structural damage, than in developed countries.

Volcanic eruptions and subsequent outpourings of lava and ash from volcanoes may damage agricultural areas and settlements locally in the short term. Some eruptions (e.g. Krakatoa in 1883) have produced a large amount of dust, the presence of which in the atmosphere causes cooling for a time, with the same effect as the impact of a meteorite. Volcanic eruptions over several million years occurred some 250 million years ago (see Erwin (1996)) producing marked cooling of the earth's atmosphere and the end of many forms of life.

2. a-e   Elements of the earth's surface: lithosphere (rocks, geology), hydrosphere, atmosphere, pedosphere (soil) and biosphere (flora and fauna excluding humans).

3.   Humans: are considered separately from the rest of the biosphere.

On the timescale of the next 50 years, the influence of the sun and the internal heat of the earth are likely to stay roughly the same. The arrival of bodies from space on the other hand is unpredicatable and even if a meteorite or comet is observed to be heading for the earth, nothing can at present be done to deflect it. It is known broadly where earthquakes will occur and volcanoes will erupt, and on previous experience many small earthquake shocks and a few large ones can be expected before 2050 .

The relief features and configuration of the rocks of the earth's land surface greatly influence human activities, whether by altitude or by steepness of slope, for example, precluding or making the cultivation of the land or the construction of transportation links difficult and costly. Climate and vegetation are also influenced by the relief features of the surface. Since relief features mostly change on a very slow timescale their influence is not likely to change in the next few decades.

The hydrosphere is of more immediate concern for several reasons. The amount of water in the world's oceans and seas (97 per cent of the total) is unlikely to change to a great extent, although its liquid volume could be enlarged or reduced slightly by a marked change in global temperature. The supply of fresh water, whether from precipitation, rivers and lakes or in artesian basins beneath the surface of the land, is crucial to the biosphere and to human activities (see Chapter 5.2). The fact that a large proportion of the world's fresh water is at present frozen in ice sheets and glaciers in Antarctica, Greenland and many mountain areas of the world is of great concern since the melting of even a small part of the total volume could raise world sea level by 1-2 metres.

The state of the atmosphere is one of the main influences on the location and distribution of the fresh water of the world. Whether the temperature of the atmosphere will stay the same in the next few decades, get warmer or get cooler, is one of the main environmental issues debated in the 1990s. With an increase in temperature, not only is it possible that some of the water in the form of ice will melt (or more will form, lowering sea-level), but the climate could alter markedly over a few decades in various parts of the world, with impacts on agriculture over large areas. The global warming/cooling issue is examined in more detail in Chapter 10.

The biosphere and soil of the earth's surface is the part of the natural environment most influenced by human activity. The soil, vegetation and fauna of more than 10 per cent of the earth's land surface has already been completely transformed by cultivation. An even larger area has been modified by pastoral activities, which affect the natural vegetation more than the soil. Considerable areas of forest have also been cut, without the land occupied actually being brought into cultivation, again resulting in environmental change in some places, since forests do not necessarily regain their previous form once removed.

One matter of concern is that large areas of hitherto natural environment little affected by human activity are either being destroyed outright or fragmented by roads and settlements into small, often awkwardly shaped, patches. Many species of plants and animals have already disappeared, but since it is not known how many species there are altogether in the world, the proportion of the total already lost cannot be calculated. Although it does not seem to be appreciated by many politicians or economists, one thing is certain: like fossil fuels, species are non-renewable. Once extinct, they are unlikely to reappear in the same form, because evolution takes place over very long timescales. It seems ironic that there is much excitement about the prospect of life on other planets, whether in our own solar system or in others when so many of our own species are dying out through lack of concern. The loss of diversity is one issue that seems likely to be high on the world agenda of problems in the first half of the 21st century.

2.4   CHANGES IN HUMAN ATTITUDES (see Table 2.4)

For several centuries in Europe and more recently in the USA there has been a proliferation of studies offering solutions to political, economic and social problems. They include descriptions of ideal states, models of change by stages, and more specific scenarios of situations that could be expected if certain changes take place. It would be convenient to have a single model or formula that would provide the foundation for speculation about human activities in the next half-century and serve as the basis for projections to 2050 and beyond. For the purpose of this book the models of stages of economic and other kinds of development such as those of Marx, as adopted in the Soviet Union, and of Rostow, already referred to in Chapter 1, are considered to be too narrow and inflexible to allow wide-ranging speculation.

The various attempts to produce comprehensive models using systems of causally related variables are more flexible than attempts to identify stages of change in that they allow alternative

Table 2.4 Calendar of selected events with contemporary or subsequent global implications (all dates are AD)

320	The Roman Emperor Constantine is converted to Christianity
622	Muhammad settles in Medina and in 630 returns to Mecca as conqueror
1493	Columbus explores islands in the Americas
1494	Treaty of Tordesillas establishes a demarcation line dividing the tropical world into Spanish and Portuguese domains
1552	Russians capture Kazan on the Volga, opening the way to eastward expansion into Siberia
1709	First successful use of coke (from coal) to smelt iron ore, instead of charcoal (from wood), Coalbrookdale, England
1771	First water-powered cotton-spinning mill, Cromford, England
1775-83	American War of Independence
1807	First steam powered boat, *Clermont*, USA
1853	Japan forced to trade with USA
1911-12	Chinese Revolution, abdication of the boy Emperor
1914-18	Great War (later called First World War)
1917-18	Russian Revolution, Bolshevik party comes to power
1939-45	Second World War; entry of Germany, UK and France in 1939, entry of Russia, Japan and USA in 1941
1944	United Nations founded
1947	India becomes independent
1948	Berlin airlift, start of 'Cold War'
1949	Communists gain power in China
1957	Treaty of Rome, European Economic Community established
1991	Break-up of the USSR

futures to be compared. Changes in some variables can be expected to cause changes in others. In several of these models, population and natural resources have key positions. Meadows *et al.* (1972) quote a Chinese writer of around 500 BC, Han Fei Tzu on the subject: 'People at present think that five sons are not too many and each son has five sons also, and before the death of the grandfather there are already 25 descendants. Therefore people are more and wealth is less; they work hard and receive little.' Clearly the issue of the relationship between population change and natural resources is not new, but Thomas Malthus (1766-1834) is often referred to as the 'father' of the modern limits-to-growth concept. His main argument was that there should be restriction on the number of children born because while the population of humans (and other animals) can grow geometrically, production can only grow arithmetically.

The limits-to-growth of population and production, ultimately set by the availability of natural resources, can be seen to apply on various scales, from single villages to whole countries and ultimately to the whole world. Although systems models developed since the 1960s include many variables, a small number of basic elements can be isolated. The human population and the rest of the biosphere depend on what the physical world provides in the form of natural resources. In traditional villages, still numerous in developing countries, much of what is needed and consumed by the population is produced locally, even if it would now be difficult to find villages that are completely self-sufficient in their subsistence. Local natural resources usually include soil, water, heat from the sun, some woodland for fuel. These allow the production of food, clothing, shelter and tools, with or without a contribution from livestock. The more villages and larger settlements become interdependent economically, the greater the need for transport and communications. While it would be an over-simplification to say that the whole 'global village' system of human activity is simply an enlarged traditional village, the basic ingredients are similar.

The rapid growth of world population in the 19th and (especially) the 20th centuries (see Chapter 4) is itself a cause of change. The parallel rapid growth in the ability of people to use technology in various forms to enhance their own capabilities has also been a cause of change. As 'development' has taken place, the basic needs of most people in the richer countries are satisfied, but wants have proliferated, in due course some of them becoming needs. Economic growth in the last decade of the 20th century is the explicit aim of most governments in the world. As noted at the beginning of this chapter, however, there are a few countries in which conditions are different, including Myanmar, in which development is not apparently a concern, and North Korea, in which the government has lost touch with the needs of the population. In some countries, as for example in the tropical rain forest of some South American countries and in Indonesia (especially West Irian) and Papua-New Guinea, many small settlements continue to exist largely isolated from outside influences. In view of the large amount of internal and foreign trade and other transactions between various parts of the world, however, for simplicity one can generalise about a global system in which changes in the aspirations, the number and the level of consumption of the human population affect both the rest of the biosphere and the use of non-bioclimatic resources such as water, fossil fuels and non-fuel minerals. Views differ as to the extent to which natural resources can sustain a population of a given size, at what levels of consumption of goods, and for how long.

Since the end of the 15th century, much of the conflict in the world has been the result of military conquest of lands with particular natural resources and products. The Spanish colonised parts of the Americas to control the production of precious metals while the Portuguese used the coastlands of eastern Brazil to cultivate sugar cane. North America and Australia provided large areas of agricultural land for European settlers, while Russia overran an enormous area in Siberia in the 17th century (although it made little use of the resources there until the 20th century). As recently as the 1930s and the Second World War, Japan (in Manchuria), Italy (in Abyssinia), and Germany (in the USSR) occupied territory – only temporarily as it turned out – to gain control of natural resources lacking at home. Even more recently, in the 1980s, Iraq attempted first to occupy a region of southern Iran with oil reserves and then in 1990 occupied Kuwait, small in area but with about 10 per cent of the world's oil reserves. Since 1945, however, the major western industrial powers of the world that previously had empires have had to control or influence the use of natural resources and to organise production in other countries indirectly, by using economic means such as investment through transnational companies.

Without putting exact and rigid limits to eras in history it can be argued that the five centuries roughly between 1500 and 2000 were distinct from all human history that went before. Soon after the voyages of discovery late in the 15th century, Portugal and Spain, sanctioned by the Treaty of Tordesillas (1494), proceeded to occupy territory in the Americas and Africa, and

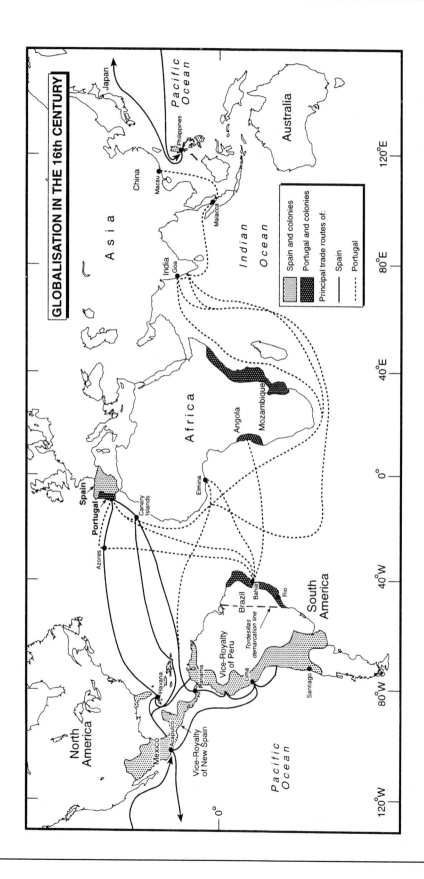

Figure 2.1 Globalisation, 16th century style. The colonies, trading posts and trade routes of Spain and Portugal towards the end of the 16th century. Each country had been 'allocated' half of the tropical world by the Pope at the end of the 15th century, according to the Tordesillas demarcation line, and each operated largely in isolation, although during 1560-1640 the two countries were united. Based on a map in Barraclough (1979).

to establish trading posts there and in Asia. Figure 2.1 shows the first global system, in which during the 16th and 17th centuries, and particularly from 1580 to 1640, when Spain and Portugal were united for a time, these two powers set up a remarkable trading system that encircled the globe, mainly in the tropics, thanks to their superior technology in military and navigation areas. Africa provided slaves, Latin America exported silver and sugar, while manufactured goods such as silk and china, not made extensively in Europe, were imported from Asia. In due course other European powers, notably England, France, Holland and Russia, built up their own empires outside Europe and much later Germany, Belgium and Italy did so too.

In the last two centuries the USA and Japan have also, in their own ways, extended their existing territories by acquiring new ones either by conquest or by purchase. By the 1990s, the powers of Western Europe had finally lost or given independence to virtually all their colonies outside Europe (see Figure 1.4). The Japanese Empire had already collapsed in 1945. However, the USA, China and Russia (even after losing 14 republics) still hold territories well beyond the limits of the areas in which they originated as states (see Chapter 11).

The point of describing the main territorial gains and losses of Mackinder's Columbian era is to argue that the first half of the 21st century will be different in the sense that no further conventional colonisation is likely to occur. On numerous occasions in the last 500 years the countries of Europe were in conflict among themselves as power shifted from Spain to France then to Germany and finally to Russia. The end of the Cold War and the expansion of NATO may finally mean that all Europe will be at peace, although events in the former Yugoslavia in the 1990s and especially Kosovo in 1999 suggest that there may still be some way to go. The political scene will be reconsidered in greater depth in Chapter 11. In view of the above global situation it may be argued that the 1490s and the 1990s mark respectively the beginning and the end of European domination of much of the world. Fernandez-Armesto (1995) asks us to: 'Imagine looking at the history of the world from AD 1000 to 2000 from a very distant point in the future. Suddenly the great moments of the past seem insignificant.' For the purposes of speculating about the next 50 years, however, it is crucial to take into account the impact of the Europeans on the rest of the world, positive and negative alike.

In addition to global models of development and limits-to-growth, there are numerous more specialised models focusing on such issues as population change, economic development and global inequality. This section concludes with a brief account of three demographic models to illustrate the scope and limitations of models of human activity in forecasting possible trends to 2050.

- Population change itself has been fitted to the Demographic Transition Model (see Figure 2.2), in which countries and regions go through three stages, starting with high birthrates and deathrates, the result of low life-expectancy, and living conditions at the limits of subsistence. The second stage is observed as improvements in healthcare and hygiene lead to a fall in the deathrate, while the birthrate stays high for a time. Subsequently the birthrate also falls, to 'catch down' with the deathrate, giving a stable population with high life-expectancy. The gap between birthrate and deathrate has been much wider among most of the countries of the present developing world in the later decades of the 20th century than it was in the present developed countries in the 19th century. Moreover countries do not all take exactly the same length of time to pass through the period in which birthrate and deathrate differ, which means the model can only give an approximate forecast of future population.

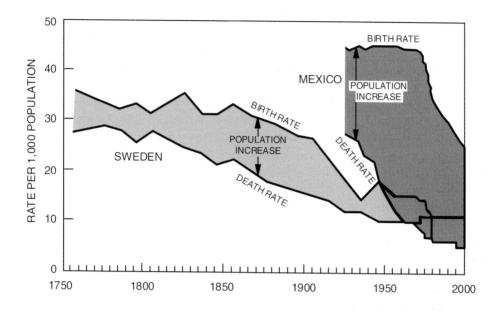

Figure 2.2 The Demographic Transition Model, illustrated by Sweden and Mexico. Updated from van der Tak *et al.* (1979). The gap between birthrate and deathrate is much greater in most developing countries in the 20th century than it was in most current developed countries in the 19th century, indicating a more rapid growth of population in the developing countries.

- The Epidemiological Transition Model runs broadly in parallel with the Demographic Transition Model. Initially environmentally-caused infectious, contagious and parasitic illnesses produce many deaths among young and old alike. As these are reduced, people live longer and are then at risk from degenerative illnesses such as cancer and heart attacks. Other afflictions such as diabetes, common in the developed countries are also spreading to the developing world. For example, cancer is widespread in China and many varieties have been mapped in a special atlas published by the China Map Press (1979).

- There is no straightforward model for international migration which, unlike most internal migration, is subject to severe controls and quotas. The decision to migrate to another country may be the result of pressure at home, as with refugees, or it may be more economic, with the prospect of better economic conditions in another country. In the 19th and early 20th centuries opportunities were seen by Europeans in North America, southern South America and Australia, regions with plentiful land and other natural resources, thinly populated and ready to be developed. In the second half of the 20th century, this kind of migration has been limited; now migration is generally up the GNP 'ladder' from poorer, predominantly agricultural countries, to richer industrial ones. In the first half of the 21st century such migration is likely to be severely restricted as the rich countries keep entry quotas for immigrants very low, or close their doors altogether. Much internal migration in developing countries is from rural to urban areas, and so the total fertility rate is likely to decline gradually. Again, when immigrants from developing countries manage to enter developed countries their total fertility rate also tends to decline. This issue will be discussed further in Chapters 4 and 12.

2.5   MEASURING CHANGE

One of the most commonly used means of measuring production and consumption and changes in these has been Gross National Product (GNP) or Gross Domestic Product (GDP). The use of GNP or GDP has the advantage that in theory all goods and services are covered, although in both developed and developing countries there are problems. As well as this comprehensive indicator, in developed economies it is common to find a substantial black or grey economy, in which transactions are not officially recorded. In addition, housekeeping (largely performed by the wife or female partner) and other unpaid work are not counted as the production of a service. One estimate for Germany (see *The Week in Germany*, 1995) puts unpaid (and therefore non-GNP) work as equal to half of all paid work, thereby implying that GNP greatly understates the economy. In developing economies, much of the production of both goods and services in rural and urban settlements alike is not officially recorded and has to be estimated. For example, de Soto (1989) estimates that 'informals', the black marketeers who work outside the law, represent 60 per cent of the Peruvian economy.

GNP has been widely used in World Bank publications as a key indicator of economic change and development. In *The Year 2000*, Kahn and Wiener (1967) project GDP into the future. In one table they have estimates of how many years it would take for a selection of countries to reach the equivalent of the 1965 United States GNP of 3,600 dollars per capita. For Sweden it would take eleven years, for Canada, twelve; on the other hand Nigeria would need 339 years and Indonesia 539. The concept of GNP is so abstract and detached from the real goods and services it measures that it gives little idea of what is happening on the ground. Comparisons of GNP data among countries at any given moment in time is confused by exchange rates, while comparisons through time are complicated by varying inflation rates in different countries.

The usefulness of using GNP alone to measure human development has been questioned for a long time. For example, Morris (1979) has for more than 20 years used a Physical Quality of Life Index (PQLI) to compare how well (or badly) societies satisfy certain specific life-serving characteristics: life-expectancy at age one, infant mortality, and literacy. The criteria are available for almost every country in the world and can be compared through time (see Doyle (1996) for a recent account of PQLI). For the first time in 1990, then with subsequent yearly adjustments, the United Nations Development Programme (UNDP) has combined life expectancy, duration of enrolment in education and real GNP per capita (virtually truncated above 6,000 dollars) to give a Human Development Index (HDI); this index will be discussed in Chapter 9.

In questioning the value of the indicators used to compare countries and to measure change, Thomas, R. (1997) is particularly critical of GNP. She notes that 'sales of the anti-depressant Prozac alone add more than $1.2 billion to GNP, as people try to feel better amid all the 'progress'. In the view of the author, much of the 'value added' in production is 'candy floss'. Table 2.5 shows various 1997 UK prices for a kilogram of potatoes (in different forms), anything from about 12p to over £6. The nutritional value of the crisps can only be marginally higher than that of the original potatoes.

When using experience of the past to speculate about change in the future it is common to focus on what *has* changed, and to ignore or overlook what has *not* changed. It is difficult, if not impossible, to quantify many kinds of change. It may be useful to compare how much change is theoretically possible with what, if any, is taking place. A rough idea of how some situations may be expected to change, or could change, can be achieved by taking into account how long it

Table 2.5 How much is a kilogram of potatoes?

	Type/form of potato	*Price (pence per kilogram)*
From farm shop	25kg bag	12p
From standard retailer	Economy	18p
Special for baking	Large potatoes	49p
New potatoes	Tinned	68p
Crisps (no frills)	Salted	265p
Crisps (top class)	Various flavours	680p

Source: author's research, Nottingham, May 1997

takes for all of the members of different sets of objects, or a large percentage of them, to be replaced (see p. 15).

It is useful to distinguish between changes that are on-going and those that are cyclical. The movement of tectonic plates, the process of erosion, world population growth in the last few hundred years, have all proceeded in one direction. By contrast, the seasons are cyclical as, it may be argued by economists, are some economic changes. Again, some changes are generally gradual, while others are sudden. In the physical world, the erosion of the land surface is usually a gradual process whereas the advent and impact of an earthquake, a volcanic eruption or a hurricane is sudden, as can be financial changes, and a new arrangement of political boundaries simply after the signing of a treaty.

An appreciation of the timescales on which different phenomena are likely to alter is crucial in speculating about the future. The popular view is that things have changed more quickly in the 20th century than previously, two causes of which being the many new discoveries and inventions in science and technology, and new ways of organising and managing society and the various enterprises in it. Experience seems to show, however, that projects, especially big ones, often take at least twice as long to complete as originally planned and cost twice as much (or more) to build or produce as originally estimated (e.g. the Anglo-French Concorde, the Channel Tunnel, the Honshu-Hokkaido Tunnel). A remarkable exception was the erection of the Empire State Building, New York, which was built roughly a storey a day, in about three months (contrasting with the Cathedral of St John the Divine, further up Manhattan, which was not even completed in the form originally intended).

Change may lead to conformity, as with the virtually worldwide use of the clockwise direction on circular clocks, of decimal representation (except for time), Greenwich Mean Time (although Mussolini tried to replace this with the meridian of Rome as the base) and the gradual expansion of English as the second language, if not the first, in many countries of the world. Change may also lead to diversity as, in the past, languages have spread widely, and have then 'evolved' differently as they became relatively isolated in different areas, as with the transformation of Latin into Italian, Spanish, Portuguese, French and Romanian.

3

METHODOLOGY OF SPECULATING ABOUT THE FUTURE

'... the heart of the present future studies, whether of domestic or international affairs, is the effort to chart "alternative futures" as the condition for policy choices'

H. Kahn and N. Wiener (1967)

3.1   GOOD PRACTICES

Since the appearance of the tradition of 'professional' speculation about the future (see Chapter 1) many writers on the subject have described and justified the approaches they have used and have proposed sound guidelines: among those concerned about the methodology of forecasting are Kahn and Wiener (1967), Forrester (1973) and Naisbitt (1984). This introduction to Chapter 3 is about some of the problems and pitfalls of forecasting, while the remaining sections of the Chapter are about five different approaches. For simplicity the various points in this section are numbered, although it is not claimed that the list is exhaustive or that the points are mutually exclusive.

1.   The propensity of people to fail sometimes to distinguish fact from fiction, reality from fantasy was discussed in Chapter 1. It may also be helpful to attempt to distinguish between fact (which may not be true or correct at a given time), speculation (which can be about the past, present or future), and opinion. For example, it is a fact that in the mid-1990s the total population of the world was approaching 6 billion. It is a matter of speculation as to the extent to which this already unprecedentedly large population will grow in the next fifty years. It is a matter of opinion whether or not, assuming the continuing increase of population is expected to cause or aggravate global problems, attempts should be made to limit further growth.

One of the most popular television programmes in the USA and UK has been *Star Trek*. Everyone who watches it knows it is fantasy, however convincing some of the events may be. On the other hand, it may lead many people to believe that in the not too distant future spacecraft and even people will be able to land on and return from planets outside our own solar system. The distance from the earth to the sun is about 150 million kilometres, eight light minutes, or one astronomic unit of distance. The nearest star, which of course may not have any planets in orbit round it, is about four light years away. A spacecraft travelling at the speed of the vehicle that landed on Mars in July 1997, after a six month journey, would need about 90,000 *years* to reach the nearest star (see Chapter 12.9).

At a more down-to-earth level, ever since the end of the Second World War it has been the practice for politicians and people of influence in world bodies to profess that the gap between rich and poor countries would narrow substantially, if not close, as the 'developing' countries catch up economically with the 'developed' ones. Is this expectation fiction or fantasy?

2.   In speculating about the future it is to be expected that many practitioners will tend to choose evidence that supports the view that the outcome they want to happen *will* happen. It is a common human characteristic that people want to be right and to win in a speculation 'match', an example being the continuing divergence of emphasis between the optimists and the pessimists over the limits to growth issue, referred to in Chapter 1. The situation is illustrated by views on the controversial question of the consumption of alcohol. In a paper on the subject by Musto (1996) the attitude to alcohol in the USA is summarised succinctly as follows: 'In the US, attitudes toward alcohol and drinking seem to oscillate between approval and condemnation over intervals of about 60 years, according to this historian. The medical research cited to defend each point of view tends to reflect the prevailing social opinion of the times.' Similarly, the role of women in society, particularly whether it is appropriate for women with small children to work outside the home, has had varied support depending upon the economic circumstances of the time, with sociologists and psychologists eager to substantiate or contradict the prevailing trends. On a more sombre note, in 1941 Japanese leaders assessed the possibility of destroying US naval capacity in the Pacific by a surprise attack. Their simulations of the situation invariably showed that their goal could not be achieved; in spite of the negative evidence they went ahead with their attack on the US fleet in Pearl Harbour, Hawaii. Their initial victory turned into a disastrous defeat four years later.

3.   Rather than make forecasts about the future 'in a vacuum' it is advisable to take into account what is 'in the pipeline' already. This point is put succinctly by Stillman (1974): 'One can make serious remarks about the near future for the simple reason that it is implicit in decisions, events and tendencies discernible in the present.' In the case of population, for example, over a third of the population in developing countries is under the age of 15 and average life expectancy is about 65 years. Therefore roughly a third of the present population of the developing world should still be alive around 2045 unless a conflict, mass genocide, a disease (such as AIDS), or mass starvation strikes globally before then. In the mid-1990s many projects are being started, the construction of which may last several years. When completed, factories, transportation links and service establishments should have a life of at least several decades.

During the Soviet period the economy of the USSR was run for some six decades on the directives of Five-Year Plans (with two interruptions). The exact quantity of such products as steel, cement, nails, and jars of jam could in theory be forecast with certainty for some time ahead, whether or not people wanted to consume them, and assuming targets were achieved. National production plans are now out of fashion in almost every country in the world, although large companies in the industrial sector have to commit themselves to lines of products for a considerable time ahead, while pension funds and life insurance policies are calculated and accumulated on the basis of assumptions about the life expectancy of people not expected to die for decades ahead.

4.   Forecasts should not be set in stone. They should be flexible, be constantly monitored and if necessary revised to take into account what is actually happening if, as is usually the case, this is not exactly consistent with the forecast. There is no point in arguing that something

different *should have* happened. George Orwell (1961) deplored the approach: 'what if history had followed a different path. Every nationalist is haunted by the belief that the past can be altered. He spends part of his time in a fantasy world in which things happen as they should - in which, for example, the Spanish Armada was a success or the Russian Revolution was crushed in 1918 - and he will transfer fragments of this world to the history books whenever possible.'

5. Although for most practical purposes some things are certain for a few decades ahead, it is unsound to say that a particular thing *will* happen. Certainty should be avoided and *will* usually replaced by *could*. Speculation should be plausible and the changes expected feasible, unless a deliberately outlandish forecast is made to shock people.

6. Until the 1960s it was common to attempt to 'discover' or construct what would happen in the future with as much precision as possible. Kahn and Wiener (1967), Forrester (1970), Meadows *et al.* (1972), Mesarovic and Pestel (1975), and Barney (1982) have all preferred to map out and compare a wide range of alternative futures. The application of electronic computers has made possible the enormous amount of calculations needed, although much of the data itself has not changed greatly in quantity and quality (with exceptions such as information from satellite images). However, the assumptions made may not necessarily be any more valid than those made by earlier explorers of the future.

Figure 3.1 shows a simple example of three alternative futures for the population of China between 1980 and 2080, the first two being of a mechanical nature, showing what would happen if on average each woman had 2 children and 1.5 children respectively throughout that period. In the third projection, demographic 'engineering' is assumed, with two goals set for 2080, firstly to reach about 700 million and secondly to have the same number of people in each cohort (ten-year age group in this case). The number of births allowed each year (or decade) is strictly regulated and rationed. The spirit of alternative futures is illustrated in this example by the fact that the projections are not intended to answer the question 'how many people will there be in China in 2080?' but are made to show that if this and this happen, then that is the result to be expected.

In contrast to the alternative futures illustrated above, Ferguson (1997) and his collaborators create alternative pasts in *Virtual History Alternatives and Counterfactuals* in which it was asked: 'What if there had been no English Civil War? What if there had been no American War of Independence? ... 'The obvious objection to such hypothetical or 'counterfactual' questions is simple: why bother asking them?... Of course we know perfectly well that we cannot travel back in time and do these things differently. But the business of imagining such counterfactuals is a vital part of the way in which we learn. Because decisions about the future are - usually - based on weighing up the potential consequences of alternative courses of action, it makes sense to compare the actual outcomes of what we did in the past with the conceivable outcomes of what we might have done.'

In considering *alternative futures*, asking; 'will China or India break up politically?' 'will the tropical rain forests disappear?' 'will oil run out in the next 50 years?' one is doing at the present moment what Ferguson and his collaborators have done at particular moments in the past. Is this a way in which the study of *alternative pasts* by historians can contribute to speculation about the future?

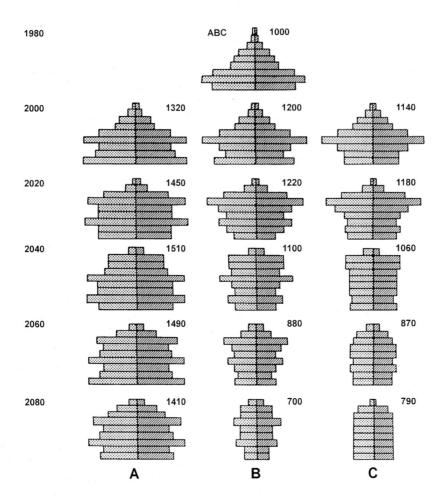

Figure 3.1 Alternative futures for the population of China. Population is in ten-year age groups, males to the left, females to the right, youngest to oldest from bottom to top of each diagram. All three projections start with the situation in 1980. Population in millions is shown at the top right of each diagram. For simplicity, mortality rates stay the same throughout. In Projection A, each female has an average of two children. In Projection B, each has an average of 1.5 children. In Projection C, the number of births is 'manipulated' every 10 years to produce in 2080 a smooth, 'rectangular' structure rather in excess of Liu Zheng's (1981) optimum population for China in 2080. See Cole (1996) for further details.

7.   The need for a holistic approach to speculation about the future is stressed in the publications of the last 30 years. It is usually unsatisfactory to project one thing into the future without considering expected trends in related things. For example, a projection of the future number of cars in use in a given country or region should be accompanied by or should take into account the supply of fuel, presumably mainly from oil products for some years if not decades to come, and the accompanying road building programme, if any. Other changes and developments may be difficult to forecast, as happened in the period between the two World Wars when there was concern that with the widespread use of aircraft, the privacy of one's territory could easily be violated because of the flexibility of air travel and the

prospect that aircraft could easily cross frontiers and land anywhere with ease. In the event air traffic control and the deployment of radar largely removed the earlier perceived risk of such penetration.

Doubletalk and doublethink are widespread in a sloppy rather than a malicious sense. Politicians in most developed countries lament the existence of high levels of unemployment and hope that levels will duly fall. At the same time, greater efficiency is expected and applauded in all areas of production, whether of goods or services, and efficiency is achieved by greater productivity of workers and mergers of companies, often leading to job losses.

8.   Projections should make sense. Two simple examples will serve to illustrate the point. In a projection of the population of Venezuela it was possible for the population of the capital, Greater Caracas to reach a total that exceeded the population of the whole country. This was because the rate of growth of Caracas at the start of the projection was much faster than the rate of growth of Venezuela as a whole on account of internal migration. In the second example, a computer program run in the early 1980s projected the fish catch of Chile, which had declined in the 1970s, into the future. It continued to decline into the 1990s when it became negative, a reminder that computer programs need 'safety nets' to prevent absurd results being produced. Such errors are easily spotted because they defy commonsense, but in much more elaborate projections they could have devastating results, a point made by Lin (1985) with reference to the Ballistic Missile Defence (BMD) system ('Star Wars'), thought up in the USA in the 1980s which, it was estimated, would need a computer program 6 million lines long that could never be properly tested except in an actual missile attack.

9.   Many projections include a quantitative element. When production and consumption are being considered it is important to distinguish between total amounts and amounts per capita in a given country or region. Thus, for example, India has about as many passenger cars in use as Switzerland, but it has more than 130 times as many inhabitants and therefore a vastly smaller number per 1,000 population. Again, the difference between relative and absolute change needs to be underlined. For example, during a certain period after the Second World War the per capita income of two Italian provinces, A and B, increased in A from 1,000 to 3,000 units but in B from 2,500 to 5,000. The threefold increase in A was greater relatively than the doubling in B, but in absolute terms the increase of 2,500 in B exceeded that of 2,000 in A. When considering trends in production in the world in the last fifty years it is crucial to take into account the fact that between 1950 and 1990 alone, the total population of the world more than doubled. Particular attention is given in Chapters 4-8 to this feature of global change.

In the sections that follow, five approaches to speculation about the future are described. They are not mutually exclusive and indeed they all have in common the need to examine past trends and situations, since most if not all future developments have their roots in the past.

3.2   PROJECTING PAST TRENDS

It is widely considered that a knowledge of past events and a study of past trends can contribute positively to speculation about the future. Historians may be too modest, cautious or simply unconcerned to claim that one of the practical functions of the study of the past is to provide lessons for the future. Whatever the merits and drawbacks of launching into the future from a past trend, this method is widely practised. It is appreciated, however, that the further ahead a trend is projected, the wider the band in which in terms of a given probability a future trend may fall. Figure 3.2 shows, for example, that for inflation in the UK, in a matter of two years the 90 per cent probability of being correct, according to the assessment of the authors of the projection, is so wide that it is of little use as a policy guideline. It is as unhelpful as saying that the 1997 UK population of about 59 million should be somewhere between 20 and 100 million in twenty years' time. As will be shown below, some trends can more meaningfully be projected further into the future than others.

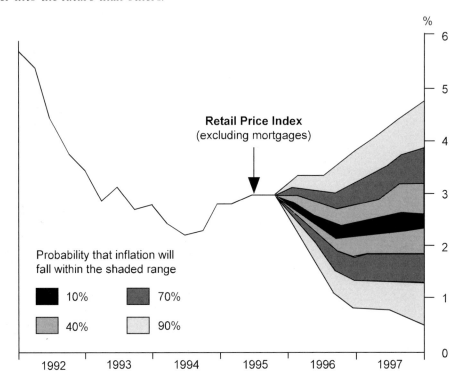

Figure 3.2 Inflation forecasts, based on Kaletsky (1996).

If past experience is to be used to assist in speculating about the future it should be chosen with care. Individuals and indeed whole countries appear to be caught in time warps, fighting past battles. A striking case in the 1990s was the conflict in Bosnia between Serbs and Muslims, the former drawing inspiration from battles lost six centuries ago during the invasion of the Balkans by the Ottoman Turks. No less incongruous to non-Israelis is the claim that Palestine should be Jewish because it was Israeli 3,000 years ago. Italy might with equal justification claim sovereignty over Britain because much of it was a Roman colony for several centuries. In the 20th century, conflict in Ireland has revolved around members of two branches of the same Christian religion, Catholics and Protestants, who have learned to co-exist peacefully in many other parts of Western Europe for more than two centuries.

It is illuminating to compare trends with an appropriate time lag if it is assumed that countries or regions are following certain 'paths' through time. Figure 3.3 shows infant mortality rates for a selection of countries over varying lengths of time depending on the availability of data. The level in Japan dropped from around 150 per thousand to 10 per thousand twice as quickly as it did in Sweden.

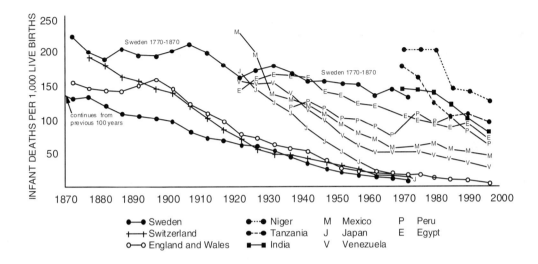

Figure 3.3 Examples of 'time lags' between selected countries in infant mortality rates. Note that data for Sweden are available from the 18th century; Sweden has therefore been shown for two centuries, 1770 to 1870 and 1870 to 1996. Infant mortality in Switzerland and in England and Wales gradually converge with Sweden. On the other hand, Sweden dropped below 150 in the 1850s, whereas Japan only did so in the 1920s, yet in four decades Japan had dropped to the level of Sweden. After 1973 the four developed countries have rates below 20 and drop to around 5 in the 1990s. Only the UK is shown after 1973. Mexico and Venezuela were around 150 in 1930 and had dropped sharply to around 50 in 1970. The situation in Peru is included because it shows the probable influence of inconsistencies and inaccuracies in the estimates of infant mortality over several decades, a frequent problem with demographic data. The levels in India and Tanzania have both fallen sharply since 1970 but still remain far above the levels of the developed countries. The possible great time lag between developed and developing countries is exemplified by Niger's score of (at least) 200 in 1980, a level below which Sweden dropped after 1810, a time lag of 170 years.

At a given point in time, one country's past can therefore be another country's future. For example, in the 1950s the leaders of China's Communist Party, which came to power in mainland China in 1949, quickly modelled their economic development on that of the USSR, with technical and financial support from their ally to speed up progress. Cole (1987) studied the per capita production of a range of goods in the two countries, comparing change in China not only with contemporary change in the USSR from 1950 on, but also with that of the USSR 25 years previously, since it was considered that the year 1953 in China compared with the year 1928 in the USSR. It was found that much faster per capita economic growth took place in the USSR between 1925 and 1960 than in China between 1950 and 1985, in spite of the devastating impact of the Second World War on the Soviet economy during 1941-45. One factor contributing to the slower growth in China could have been the much greater per capita availability of natural resources in the USSR than in China, each of which was largely self-contained economically.

Concerned at the time about the professed aim of Soviet leaders to overtake the USA, Cole (1963) earlier compared US and Soviet per capita pig iron production, using a time lag of 55 years, 1858-1908 for the USA and 1913-1963 for Russia/USSR. During that period US output increased fairly smoothly from 25 kgs per inhabitant to 270, while that of Russia/USSR increased from 26 to 266, in spite of the interruptions of both World Wars and the Revolution, when levels temporarily dropped. The point of referring to these two earlier studies by the author is not to draw any conclusions but to argue that such comparisons can at least be thought-provoking.

On a subject that would have been an academic exercise until the 1990s, but is now more topical, it would be interesting to speculate what Russia would be like now if it had not been under Soviet Communist rule for some 70 years. The diagram in Figure 3.4 and the message it carries may seem simple, even simplistic, but it shows how on one criterion, the proportion of the economy (or more precisely the means of production) held by the state in Russia/USSR changed dramatically in the 1920s and early 1930s from private to state ownership, only to return towards what it *might have been* if Russia had remained an empire, with or without a popularly elected government. Obsessed with the idea of stages of economic and social development, Russians now see themselves in the 'next' (painful) stage, the transition back to capitalism. They are going backwards into the future, at least in the Marxian sense, where socialism and communism should *follow* capitalism.

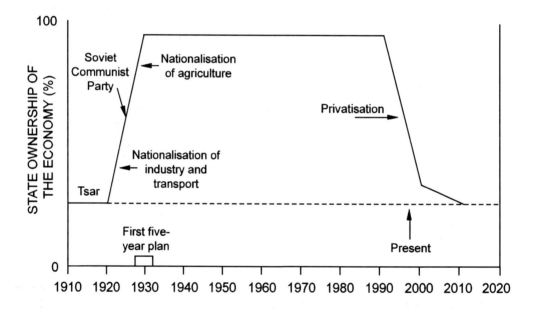

Figure 3.4 What if Russia had not been Communist? Are changes in the ownership of the means of production leading Russia towards a future it might have had if the Communist Party had never controlled the Soviet economy, an idea inspired by Ferguson's (1997) *Virtual Histories, Alternatives and Counterfactuals.*

Various past trends will be examined in Chapters 4–8, and it is therefore appropriate here to look briefly at some examples. Clearly changes take place on enormously different timescales and, for this reason alone, over a period of a few decades some are more 'projectable' than others. On a global scale, population changes smoothly (see Figure 4.1), although considerable disparities occur in actual estimates from year to year in, for example, publications of the United Nations and the Population Reference Bureau. A number of broad types of curve can represent different types of trend, each presenting problems when projected into the future (see Figure 3.5). These will be noted in turn and real world cases that broadly fit them will be noted. Time is on the horizontal axis, frequency or quantity on the vertical axis.

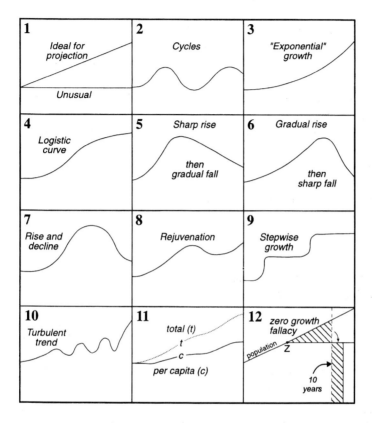

Figure 3.5 Types of trend. See text for explanation.

The numbers in the text that follows refer to the graphs in Figure 3.5.

1. A straight line ('curve') is ideal since it can be uniquely projected, but it is unlikely in the real world except where 'mechanically' determined as, for example, the conversion between Celsius and Fahrenheit.

2. A reasonably regular series of peaks and troughs, exemplified by the US view on alcohol, already referred to (Musto (1996)). In extra-tropical latitudes, changes in temperature reflect the distinct seasons and broadly follow the cycles in the diagram.

3. Exponential growth, in which the total grows by an increasing amount in each time span of equal duration. It is a characteristic of the total population of the world during most of the 20th century (see Figure 4.1); incidentally, if the same rate of increase were to continue throughout the 21st century the total population of the world would be well in excess of 20 billion by the year 2100. Much of the controversy over the limits to growth models in the early 1970s revolved round both the meaning of exponential growth and its application to given past situations and future trends.

4. If saturation is approached in a given context, increase may slow down and cease. Car ownership has risen fairly steadily in the developed countries of the world, since the 1920s in North America and since the 1940s in the countries of Western Europe. Eventually, saturation should be reached.

5. In the oil industry, for example, once oil reserves have been discovered and the necessary equipment installed, the level of extraction increases rapidly in a matter of months or a few years to a peak, after which it tends to fall gradually until all the commercially extractable oil has been taken out.

6. A catastrophe can arrest a gradual increase in output and lead to a sudden drop. Such was the experience of the Peruvian fishing industry in the 1960s and early 1970s (see Figure 3.6). On a shorter timescale, share prices sometimes build up gradually then fall dramatically in a few days.

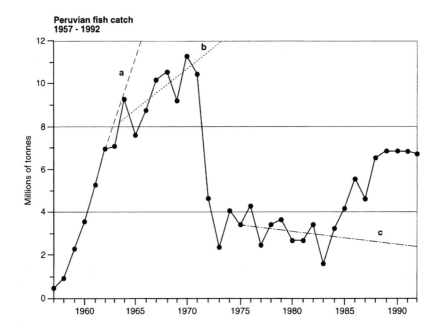

Figure 3.6 The Peruvian fish catch, 1957 to 1992. Lines a, b and c show futures that might have been anticipated by projecting past trends in 1964, 1970-71 and 1983-84 respectively. Fish catches are restricted by the Peruvian government as far as possible but there is no control over the dreaded El Niño warm current, which reduces the quantity of food available for the fish themselves. See Idyll (1973). See also Figure 1.6 on viewpoints in time.

7. The rise and fall of empires, transportation modes and the production of many goods can extend over a few decades or several centuries. Over different periods in the last 500 years the empires of Spain, England/Britain and Russia each expanded to reach a peak of about 20 million sq km (or almost one sixth of the world's land area), Spain when united with Portugal during 1580-1640, Britain and Russia near the end of the 19th century. Between about 1830 and about 1920 the length of route in the railroad system of the USA continued to grow, after which the closure of lines reduced the total to about half by the mid-1990s (see Figure 3.7).

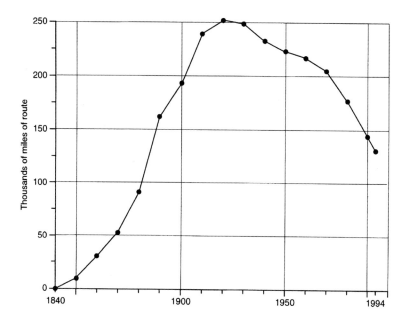

Figure 3.7 The mileage of railroad route in use in the USA, 1840-1994. Source of data: *Historical Statistics of the United States, Colonial Times to 1957*, US Dept of Commerce, Bureau of the Census, Washington 1960 and *Statistical Abstract of the United States*, various numbers.

8. A setback, rather than a catastrophe, can slow down growth but can then be followed by the rejuvenation of a trend. The growth of world coal production was slowing down in the 1960s but picked up for a time after the rise in oil prices in the 1970s.

9. In some situations a major innovation can produce a sharp increase, followed by a 'plateau'. A succession of such 'steps' may be experienced in various situations. The commercial maximum speed of passenger travel (ignoring such exceptions as Dick Turpin's horse, Concorde and space shuttles) has risen in the last two centuries by 10 times each time: horse drawn carriage 5 m.p.h. until the 1830s/40s, rail travel 50 m.p.h. until the 1950s, jet air travel (courtesy of the Boeing 707) 500 m.p.h. (with around 250 m.p.h. for propeller planes before this). It is expected that some time early in the 21st century travel at 5,000 m.p.h. may be possible. At a much more down to earth level, such stepped increases were experienced in the production of copper ore in Peru, which stayed at a moderate level until a large new mine came into operation in 1958 and another one in 1976.

10. The two world wars and the economic depression during the interval between them produced a very turbulent period for graphs of production, exemplified in Figure 3.8 by Italian steel output and generalised in Figure 12.1.

11. The two curves here are found in many graphs in Chapters 5-8. The line *t* represents the world total of some item of production. This is shadowed by the lower line, which reduces the total by the extent to which population has grown, specifically between 1950 and 1990 in many of the trends studied in Chapters 5-8 (e.g. Figure 5.1).

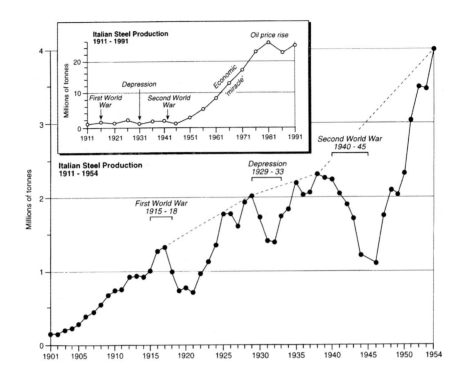

Figure 3.8 Italian steel production, like numerous other types of production, reflects the four big setbacks to smooth economic growth in 20th century Europe. The main graph shows the steep sided hills and valleys of production from 1917 to around 1950. These pale into insignificance, becoming just undulations in a plain compared with the surge in steel production between 1950 and the late 1970s, the 'mountainside' in the inset graph. Ironically, Italy has almost no deposits of iron ore or coking coal. The opening of several steel works in the Mezzogiorno in the 1960s left 'cathedrals in the desert'.

12. It is often assumed that once a situation is reached in which world population ceases to grow and per capita consumption remains the same, the problems of the world will be solved. In practice a state of zero growth merely delays the attainment of a specified situation or quantity and indeed not usually by all that much time. In the year z (indicated by the dot on the graph) population growth improbably ceases suddenly. Thus all the consumption in the shaded triangle is 'saved' when the population remains stationary instead of continuing to grow. But in this example, the same amount is consumed by the stationary population in 50 years instead of in 40 years by the growing one. Buying or borrowing time comes to mind as an apt description of this situation.

Provided data are available it is not difficult to plot past trends between the 1920s and the 1990s. It may be illuminating and it is sometimes revealing to examine earlier trends, when data are available, but in the scope of this book 1950-1990 makes a reasonable springboard for looking ahead to around 2050. It has already been stressed that in making projections from past trends into the future it would be simplistic to 'continue' the trends, even if that were possible. In Figure 3.5, curves 1-7 appear easier to project than curves 8-10 since the latter contain big irregularities, more of which may (or may not) occur at some time in the future.

3.3　PROBABILITY

Many decisions about the future, whether about something expected to happen in the next few minutes, the next few years or even further ahead, are based on the probability of some event happening. Bergamini (1965) describes succinctly the difference between the two related branches of mathematics, probability and statistics: 'Probability and its helpmate statistics are, in a sense, like two people approaching the same house from opposite ends of the street. In probability the contributing factors are known, but a likely result can only be predicted. In statistics the end product is known but the causes are in doubt.' Mosteller *et al.* (1961) highlight two extreme positions regarding the level of interpretation and use of probability theory. The *objective* position holds that probability is applicable only to events that can be repeated over and over again under much the same conditions, such as with the tossing of a coin (heads and tails each have a theoretical probability of 0.5 out of 1 of falling), the manufacture of mass produced items, or a large number of people with life insurance policies. At the other extreme, the *personalistic* approach accepts that probability statements can be made about unique or rare events, for example that there will be an African-American or Hispanic president of the USA before 2030. Both approaches can be useful in helping to explore the future.

The use of the *objective* position on probability as a guide to the future is more appropriate and practical when applied to events and situations of a local nature expected in the relatively near future than as a basis for speculating about the world in 2050 or 2100. In the case, for example, of insurance coverage, it is assumed that on previous experience a given number of deaths or accidents will occur during a given time span, which ensures that adequate premiums are collected. In this respect, then, the use of probability differs from the method of explicitly projecting past trends into the future in that it is based on a consensus of past experiences and situations rather than changes through time.

Probability statements of a *personalistic* nature made about unusual events may be thought-provoking rather than the basis for decisions about the future. Stix (1995) gives examples of risks of dying *in a year* in the USA from various causes from: a 1 in 20 million chance of dying from an aeroplane crashing on you, through 1 in 10,000 of becoming a murder victim, to 1 in 300 of dying from some form of cancer. On a global rather than an individual scale, a tentative probability scale can be applied to events with dire consequences for the future of humanity. Figure 3.9 shows the prospects if certain events occur. The reader is as well informed as anyone else to arrive at the probability of the events in the diagram occurring or not.

When a large number of elements combine to contribute to a future trend and prospect, the concept of probability can be helpful in showing the reason why a 'central' or average future is more likely than an extreme one. Figure 3.10 shows the example of the foreign trade of a fictitious developing country which, for simplicity, exports ten commodities of roughly equal value. While it would be ideal for economic development and government revenues if every export sector did well, and disastrous if every sector did badly, the probability is that some sectors will do well (G), some will have average success (A), and some will do badly (B) over a given period in the future. If for simplicity it is assumed that G, A, and B all have an equal probability of occurring, then the probability that all ten export sectors will be G is only 1 in 3^{10} or about 1 in 59,000, the same being the probability of all being B. The number of combinations giving roughly equal numbers of G, A and B is far greater. This is one reason why in very general terms 'more of the same' is the most likely future for the next few decades rather than a future in which either all the world's problems are solved (if particular policies are implemented) or the world sinks into a disastrous state (if particular policies are not implemented).

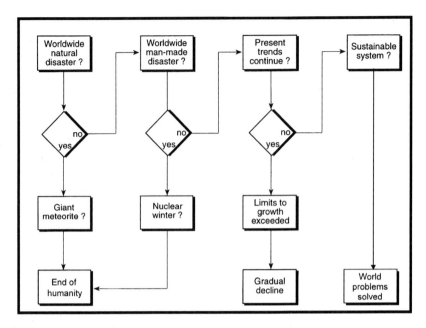

Figure 3.9 Paths to alternative futures.

Futures for exports of a fictitious developing country

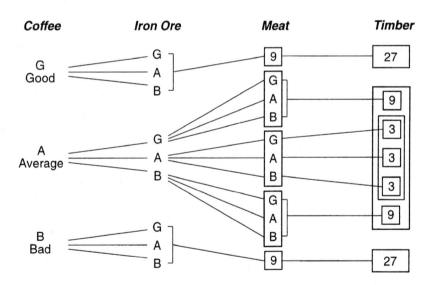

Figure 3.10 Combinations of Good, Average and Bad futures. A great simplification of the real world in which a combination of roughly equal numbers of Good, Average and Bad futures is far more probable to occur than an all Good or all Bad package, in spite of the promises of politicians. The diagram shows the possible combinations of Good, Average and Bad for four products. For coffee there are three possible futures, G,A and B. Each of these can combine with each of three possible futures for iron-ore, giving nine pairs: GG, GA, GB, AG, AA, AB, BG, BA, BB. When each of these pairs is combined with the three possible futures for meat there are 27 combinations, GGG, GGA, GGB, GAG and so on. For 10 products there are about 60,000 possible combinations, of which only one is 10 Goods and only one 10 Bads. See text for further explanation and discussion.

It is appropriate to add here a note about chaos theory. Franks (1990) refers to the book *Chaos* by James Gleick, the 'sole constant is seeming randomness, and its seeming ability to thwart projections by even the most credible scientific models. In meteorology and weather forecasting any prediction deteriorates rapidly. Errors and uncertainties multiply, cascading upward through a chain of turbulent features... This realisation has led to the abandonment of long-range weather forecasting.'

McGinty (1997) reports on a study that looks at probability from the point of view of individuals: 'Luck is a lady who understands all the odds. People on whom fortune always smiles have a greater understanding of the laws of probability, a new study claims.' The experiences of samples of people who believed themselves to be lucky and those who did not were compared, the former emerging as better able to work out the odds of a situation and to understand probability questions.

3.4   TARGETS AND GOALS

The purpose of speculation about the future, based on the projection of past trends as discussed in section 3.2, is to show that, given certain assumptions, a particular future is likely to occur or a range of futures is possible. The approach using the examination of goals, on the other hand, shows that if a given goal is wanted, then various things must happen or be done to achieve it. The difference can be illustrated by comparing approaches to the future population of China. The projection of trends in recent decades leads to the conclusion that the population of China might peak at about 1.5 billion around 2020-30 and then gradually decline, reaching 1.2 billion by 2080. For a goal of 0.7 billion to be reached in 2080 (see Figure 3.1), as proposed by Liu Zheng (1981, see Chapter 4), fertility would have to drop to a very low level and mortality might have to rise.

Throughout the 20th century targets and goals have been proposed by political leaders and international bodies, with very different prospects of success. The goal of Hitler to create a Europe dominated by Germany with a life span of a thousand years is an example of a political goal. A target was set by the Soviet leader Nikita Khrushchev (1894-1971) in the late 1950s of overtaking the USA in total production and a short time later in per capita production; it had an economic basis. The World Health Organisation established a goal of eradicating smallpox globally and this was achieved (see Henderson (1976)), whereas the hope rather than goal that malaria could be eradicated globally has defied attempts so far. In 1996 a target was set to eradicate polio in India by the year 2000: in one day in December 1996, 120 million children aged 5 to 14 were immunised. The goal is clear and the success of the campaign will be known in the near future.

In 1990 the United Nations Development Programme (UNDP) published its first Report (*Human Development Report 1990*). The aim of the UNDP is to improve living conditions and standards for the poorest sectors of the world's population. The point is made that: 'The global targets that the international community sets at world conferences and during UN Assembly debates must be seen more as desirable objectives ... than as carefully calculated projections of what is feasible and realistic.' It is stressed that, to be useful, global target setting should be feasible. Examples of quantified global targets set for the year 2000 do exist. In the view of the authors of the Report, even these targets are either very unlikely to be reached or their achievement will be impossible to verify with precision:

- Complete immunisation of all children.
- Reduction of the under-five child mortality rate by half or to 70 per 1,000 live births, whichever is less.
- Elimination of severe malnutrition, and a 50 per cent reduction in moderate malnutrition.
- Universal enrolment of all children of primary school age.
- Reduction of the 1990 adult illiteracy rate by half, with the female illiteracy rate to be no higher than the male.
- Universal access to safe water.

These goals are above all of a social nature. Their implementation would be helped by appropriate assistance from the developed countries, but a target established for the latter to contribute annually 0.7 per cent of GNP to assist developing countries (actually not enough to make much of an impact) had lapsed by the 1990s (see Chapter 9). The United Nations itself is in a position to recommend goals but unable to provide more than minimal practical support.

While the provision of such basic needs as those shown above is largely, if not entirely, a problem for the developing countries, environmental damage and pollution, especially of the atmosphere, potentially affect all countries equally. A number of goals have been proposed to stabilise or reduce the emission of various gases and in particular to control the level of consumption of fossil fuels in the industrial countries, since with only 20 per cent of the population of the world, these consume about 70 per cent of the fossil fuels burnt. Politicians in many countries have found it expedient when looking for votes to play the environmental card. They and their advisers do not always think clearly. One common mis-statement is to say that cutting the consumption of fossil fuels will *reduce* global warming. They should really say that it will *slow down the rate of increase* of global warming.

The year 2050 is too far off to be chosen for goals and targets by most politicians and policy makers. Even the next decade is full of uncertainties and problems, sufficient in most situations to keep them busy. Quick returns are often needed from economic developments, and specific goals for decades ahead are either meaningless or must be reached along routes fraught with unknowns and uncertainties.

One way in which an examination of goals can help to assess the likelihood or feasibility of possible changes in the decades to come is to plot graphically total production or consumption against total population. In Figure 3.11 total population and total energy consumption of individual large countries and of the EU are plotted on the graph in various years. Neither scale shows time, but the path through time of each country can be followed. The lines radiating from the point of origin of the two axes at zero, lower left, show different levels of per capita consumption of energy. With the help of the graph it is easy to see what path a country would have to follow to achieve a given level of consumption.

The graph in Figure 3.11 clearly shows the massive gap between developed and developing countries (see also Chapter 9). The amount of energy consumed is expressed here in millions of tonnes of coal equivalent (t.c.e.), a measure devised to allow comparability between different primary sources of energy such as coal, oil and hydro-electric power. In the 1990s, per capita energy consumption in China was about 750 kilograms of coal equivalent. To double the level of consumption per capita in China by 2010, consumption would have to grow from about 900 million to 2,100 million t.c.e., given the expected increase in population. For China to reach the 1990 US level of consumption per capita by, say, 2050, when it could have 1.5 billion inhabitants, it would have to consume annually about 15 billion t.c.e., much more than the whole world consumed annually in the 1990s.

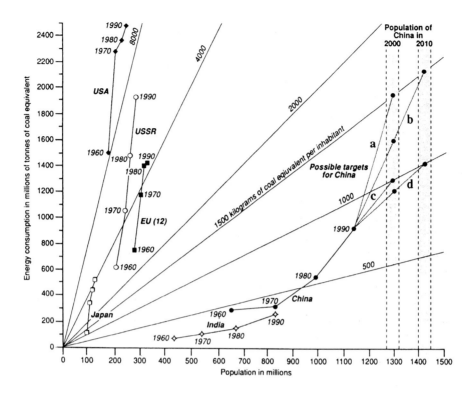

Figure 3.11 A method of examining and comparing future goals and targets. Note that neither axis is a time scale. The path of countries (or other entities) through time can however be followed on the graph.

3.5   THE USE OF SYSTEMS MODELS

The term system can be applied to a situation in which two or more variables interact, in some cases one influencing the other, in others with influences working in both directions. A simple example is a central heating system in a building: the temperature inside the building is affected by that outside and is maintained by a thermostat which activates the heating device. A number of technical terms, such as feedback and homeostasis, are used in systems research; other terms such as political system, economic system and social system are all also widely used, often in a loose sense. More specifically, as noted already in Chapter 1, Forrester, and soon after him Meadows, and Mesarovic and Pestel, used a systems approach to link large numbers of variables measuring economic, demographic, environmental and other elements that influence human activities.

Before the 1960s, speculation about the future tended to focus on single features such as population, economic growth or particular social and political scenarios. In the 1960s it was appreciated that few things can be projected in isolation. Population growth, for example, is related to the supply of food, the quality of hygiene and medical provision, government policy, religious and social demands and customs, and many other influences. Even climatic change can increasingly be affected by human activities.

Figure 3.12 shows the agricultural system in a region of China, the loess plateau of the north. In this model population growth increases pressure on the land for food and fuel. Eventually productivity declines through soil erosion, and either fertilisers have to be imported into the region to increase yields, food has to be imported, population has to decline, or more land (if there is any) has to be brought into agricultural use. Figure 3.13 shows an example of a system working at global level and having a more comprehensive set of variables than those in the loess plateau model. Natural resources in the loess model are represented by land as also in the simplified world model.

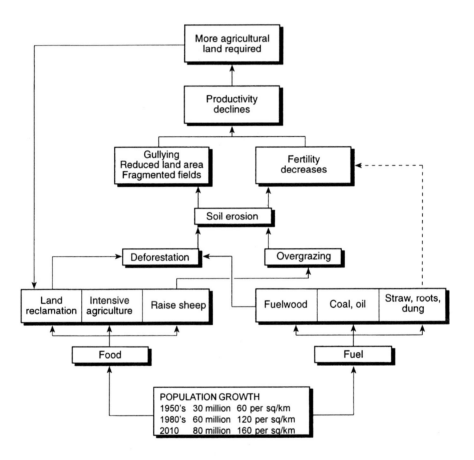

Figure 3.12 A system of cause and effect in a region of China that still depends heavily on agriculture, the loess plateau in the Huang-he basin. The diagram was provided by a Chinese geographer, Huang Runhua of Peking University, Beijing. With appropriate minor modifications this diagram could be applied to situations in many rural areas of the developing world.

A criticism of elaborate global models with tens or even hundreds of variables, rather than the few in Figure 3.13, is that it is difficult to know the exact intensity of mutual influence among the variables because in the area of human activities perfect correlations are rare and tendencies rather than mechanical laws are all that can be expected. The graph in Figure 3.14 shows the relationship between real GDP per capita (the horizontal axis) and total fertility rate (the vertical axis) for 50 countries, including the 24 largest in population in the world (the black dots) and 26 others, chosen randomly. There is a fairly strong negative correlation between per capita GDP and fertility rate among the countries with under about 6,000 dollars per capita, but above this level there is no correlation. With the exception of Israel and the United Arab Emirates in this sample, every country with over 6,000 dollars per capita has a total fertility rate of less than 2. This example shows how difficult it would be to accommodate meaningfully a very important relationship like the one in this example into a systems model, when the situation is so complex at national level. In spite of the increasingly global nature of the world economy in terms of trade and links, the global total is still made up of a large number of countries, each following its own interests and agendas as it plays its own game in world affairs.

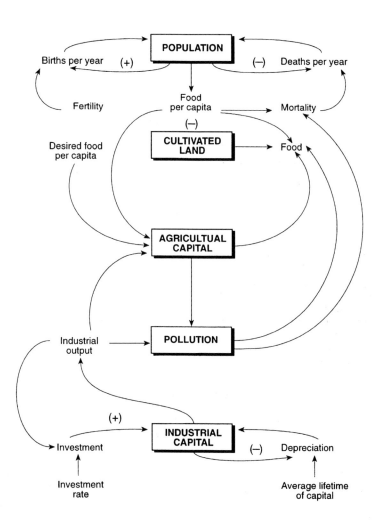

Figure 3.13 A rudimentary system diagram for the global economy showing feedback loops of population, capital, agriculture and pollution, after Meadows *et al.* (1972).

3.6   THE DELPHI APPROACH

For hundreds of years people of distinction and ordinary people alike in Ancient Greece went to consult the oracle at Delphi. The place is now a ruin, but enough remains of the structures to

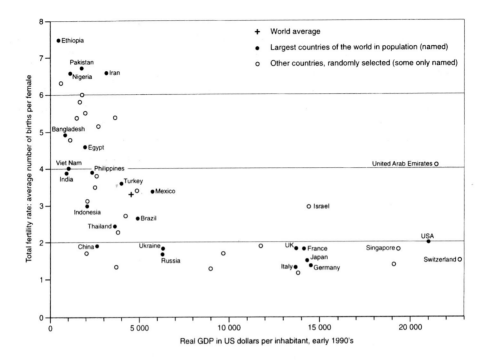

Figure 3.14 The relationship between Gross Domestic Product and total fertility rate. Up to about 6,000 dollars per capita there is a rough negative correlation between per capita production and fertility but above 6,000 there is no correlation. This example underlines the difficulty of using one variable to predict another in a system of interlinked variables.

show what an impressive setting and atmosphere the people running the oracle worked in. The impression is now given to visitors to the ruins that there was a good deal of fixing of prophecies to please clients, if not downright fraud. The term Delphi is now used to refer to one possible approach to speculation about the future, often seriously used to forecast events of particular interest. Unlike the four approaches already described it may have little or no bearing on or reference to past trends. The modern use of the Delphi technique was pioneered by Dr Olaf Helmer at the United States Airforce, RAND Corporation.

The Delphi approach is usually used to elicit the views about a future event from a team of experts, consulted independently. They may be asked when they expect a specified event to occur or how big a given quantity may be at a specific time in the future. The average of the answers given may be taken as a reasonable consensus, somewhere near what is likely to happen (or not). The approach can be applied both to events of great moment and to more humdrum occurrences. The answer 'never', where appropriate, is usually permitted, but arithmetically it would have a devastating effect when the average or consensus of the team is calculated and would have to be ignored. Experts are asked questions such as: when will electricity first be produced commercially by nuclear fusion (rather than fission)? when will the population of the world exceed 10 billion? when will the first human land on Mars? or what will a given share index be a year from now? Three examples will suffice at this point to give an idea of the approach.

1. How large are the total world oil and natural gas reserves? Pearce (1979) plotted the average of 24 estimates made in 1977 in answer to this question. The estimates are shown

in Figure 3.15 in billions of tonnes of oil equivalent (t.o.e.). Together with some established statistics of petroleum reserves, they gave 300 billion t.o.e. of undiscovered potential in addition to 300 billion tonnes already extracted or in discovered reserves. Since exploration for reserves of oil and natural gas continues worldwide, including in many areas hardly explored yet, the last word has not been said on the subject of the size of reserves, but production of oil and gas between 1977 and 1995 was roughly 80 billion t.o.e., a sizeable slice of the reserves estimated in 1977. However, more reserves were discovered between 1977 and 1995 than the amount extracted during that time and they stood at about 250 billion t.o.e. in the latter year. This subject will be discussed in more detail in Chapter 6.

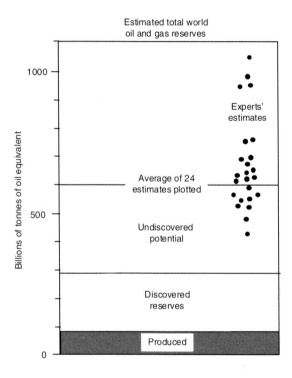

Figure 3.15 Estimated oil and gas reserves according to a number of experts, an example of the Delphi approach. The diagram is from Pearce (1979). See text for explanation.

2. A much less ambitious example of the Delphi approach is given by Bernoth and Smith (1995) and illustrated in Figure 3.16. At the end of 1995 the FT-SE (Financial Times-Stock Exchange) 100 share index stood at 3,690. It can be seen in Figure 3.16 that the average forecast for the end of 1996 was 3,750, the consensus of ten experts representing prestigious financial companies. To the uninitiated, the gap between the extremes may seem considerable, 4,100 being more than 20 per cent higher than 3,400. The preference for base 10 round numbers may be noted. It is often advisable to use well rounded numbers to avoid giving the impression of unjustified precision. In the event, at the close of trading on 31 December 1996 the FT-SE 100 index turned out to be 4,118.5. People who sold shares during 1996 on the advice of Goldman Sachs could be cursing. Bernoth (1996) cites the forecasts for the ten companies for the end of 1997, the average being 4,315, already exceeded by April

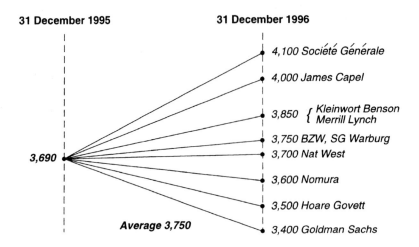

31 December 1995   **31 December 1996**

4,100 *Société Générale*

4,000 *James Capel*

3,850 { *Kleinwort Benson*
         Merrill Lynch

3,750 *BZW, SG Warburg*
3,700 *Nat West*

3,690

3,600 *Nomura*

3,500 *Hoare Govett*

Average 3,750   3,400 *Goldman Sachs*

Figure 3.16 Estimates made at the end of 1995 of the share index (FT-SE 100) at the end of 1996. In the event it was slightly above the highest estimate. From Bernoth and Smith (1995).

1997; in October 1997 they passed 5,300 for a few days. On 1 January 1998 the index stood at 5,136, 19 per cent above the 4,315 forecast. For a time in the early months of 1998 the FT-SE 100 index reached above 6,000. On 10 June 1998 it was 6,019, so far above the forecast for the end of 1997 that one cannot escape the conclusion that share prices are not something that can realistically be forecast for 2050!

3. Smith, M. (1974) describes the results of a questionnaire on the future of psychology given to a panel of 50 experts connected in various ways with the subject, his concern being to find when and in what ways the subject would 'grow up'. The predictions were made in the early 1970s and the average dates for developments to take place included some as soon as the 1980s when, among other things, improved techniques for behaviour manipulation would be used. The panel were in universal agreement that the first reliable application of Extra-Sensory Perception and the first convincing demonstration of thought transference with animals would be later than 2040, or never. A cosy even rosy future was predicted for psychology in school education, eclipsing geography among other traditional subjects, by the year 2000, a forecast for which in 1997 there seemed little supporting evidence. The number of British sixth-formers (in thousands) taking the following subjects in summer 1997 was: English 94, Mathematics 69, Biology 59, Geography 44, History 42, Physics 34, Sociology 30, Psychology 27. Most other subjects were taken for several years, Psychology only in the sixth form (*The Times*, 14 August 1997). The study described above contains at least two warnings for forecasters: first there is a constant danger that predictions will show what forecasters want to happen, and second, never say never.

In many people's minds speculation about the future is either about projecting past trends or working out probabilities. In this chapter it has been shown that other ways can be used where appropriate. In the end it may be useful to use more than one approach to speculate about a complicated issue. For many purposes it is more useful to compare reasonable alternative futures than to seek to produce an exact prediction of what a situation will be like after a given length of time. Flexibility is needed, an acceptance that usually it is not possible to work out precisely what will happen, especially since, in the words of Mesarovic and Pestel (1975): 'We are indeed living in a very dynamic world in which we have to look decades ahead when making decisions concerning many vital issues.'

Kahn and Wiener (1967) depend heavily on a study of past trends in their book *The Year 2000*: 'By selecting extrapolations of current or emerging tendencies that grow continuously out of today's world and reflect the multifold trend and our current expectations, we create a "surprise-free" projection, one that seems less surprising than any other specific possibility.' They have produced a checklist of 13 long-term multifold trends, which cover most human activities.

This chapter concludes with three thoughts:

- Your past was once your future and was someone else's future too, while your future will be your past and will be someone else's past.

- Don't judge the standards of the past by your own or your country's present standards; slavery was widely accepted in past civilisations. 20th century Western views on human rights, needs and wants may not be those widely held in the world in 2050.

- A survey of women's first names in England shows that twice as many Margarets remained unmarried as Susans. You are keen to have grandchildren. Your own first baby daughter has just been born. Would you call her Susan?

4

POPULATION

'John Maynard Keynes, the English economist, said: "In the long term we're all dead". But we're taking a long time dying. Europe's aging population is leading governments to realise that the state can no longer cope with everybody's pension needs. Four workers used to support every pensioner; by 2040 it will be down to two workers.'

M. Bien (1997)

4.1   POPULATION IN THE MID-1990s

According to the Population Reference Bureau, the mid-1997 population of the world was estimated to be 5,840 million. Whether that number of people is large or small, excessive, adequate or too limited for a particular goal (if indeed the world has a goal) is difficult to judge without some context in which to place it. The fact that the population of the world has doubled in the last forty years and has increased more than three times since the beginning of the 20th century, within the lifetime of the oldest people in the world today, indicates that we have been living in an exceptional period of demographic change. There is a broad consensus, to be discussed later in this chapter, that the population could approach 10,000 million by 2050, cause for satisfaction, concern or alarm, depending on one's viewpoint. At this point it is appropriate to note the emergence of a new view of the global demographic situation, that the population 'explosion' is no longer an issue. Ridley (1997) points out that the real global threat is 'population implosion' in view of the prospect that the world's population approaches a cycle of decline.

Estimates of the total population of the world at any given time vary considerably among different sources and may be revised with hindsight as new information becomes available about past numbers and as new data are published, mostly following censuses held at the end of each decade. Three main sources of demographic data are used in this book, the *Demographic Yearbook* of the United Nations *(UNDYB)*, the *Production Yearbook* of the Food and Agriculture Organisation to the United Nations *(FAOPY)*, and the *World Population Data Sheet (WPDS)* of the Population Reference Bureau. The basis for population data and projections used in this chapter has been *WPDS 1996*, but in this first section it has been possible to update figures by one year, using *WPDS 1997*. The population of the world can be divided into various subsets, three of which will now be described.

- Of the total population in the world of 5,840 million in mid-1997, 1,175 million (20.1 per cent) lived in the 'more developed' countries, 4,666 (79.9 per cent) in the 'less developed' ones. The more developed countries are the USA, Canada, Australia, New Zealand, Japan, and all of Europe including Russia and other former European Soviet Republics. A complete definition of the major regions used in this book is given at the end of Chapter 1. The population of the more developed countries is only growing by about 0.1 per cent a year. In contrast, the population of the less developed countries is growing by about 1.8 per cent a year. If such a rate continues, the population of the less developed group would double in less than 40 years.

- Another basic subdivision of the population of the world is into agricultural and non-agricultural. According to the 1995 *Production Yearbook* of the Food and Agriculture Organisation of the United Nations, out of a total world population of 5,716 million in 1995, 2,591 million (45.3 per cent) lived in agricultural communities. Broadly similar proportions are found when only the economically active part of the population is considered. Altogether 2,738 million people (47.9 per cent) of the total population were defined as economically active, and of these 1,301 million (47.5 per cent) worked in the agricultural sector. The world average is however made up of countries with vastly different proportions of their economically active population in the agricultural sector, ranging from Burundi and Rwanda in Africa, and Nepal in Asia, with more than 90 per cent, to Belgium, the UK and the USA, with less than 3 per cent and Singapore with a mere 0.2 per cent.

- A third subdivision of population is into rural and urban. While it is possible to obtain a reasonably consistent definition of the economically active population in agriculture and in non-agricultural activities in the countries of the world, already discussed, the definition of urban is far less consistent. In most countries one of the three following criteria is used: the size of a settlement, its function, or its definition according to administrative status. Data for the percentage of urban population in individual countries are therefore only broadly comparable. In 1997 (*WPDS*), 43 per cent of the total population of the world (2,511 million) was defined as urban, 57 per cent as rural. There was a marked contrast between the average of 74 per cent urban in the more developed countries of the world and 36 per cent in the less developed ones. At the level of individual countries, the global contrast is enormous, ranging from a mere 5 and 6 per cent urban respectively in Rwanda and Burundi to 100 per cent in Singapore, in effect an island city.

A further feature of the demographic situation in the world, the great disparity in the total population size of countries, should also be noted at this stage (see Table 4.1). Due to the very large population size of China and India, the five largest countries of the world have almost half the world total, the ten largest almost 60 per cent. When considering future prospects for the countries of the world, demographic trends and policies in the largest countries can usually be assumed to have a greater impact on total world population than trends and policies in small countries.

Table 4.1 The largest countries of the world in population in 1996

	(millions)	Population Individual (per cent)	Cumulative (per cent)		(millions)	Population Individual (per cent)	Cumulative (per cent)
China	1,218	21.1	21.1	Russia	148	2.6	51.1
India	950	16.5	37.6	Pakistan	134	2.3	53.4
USA	265	4.6	42.2	Japan	126	2.2	55.6
Indonesia	201	3.5	45.7	Bangladesh	120	2.1	57.7
Brazil	161	2.8	48.5	Nigeria	104	1.8	59.5

Source of data: *WPDS 1996*

4.2   PAST POPULATIONS

In their *Atlas of World Population History*, McEvedy and Jones (1978) have published detailed material on the population of different regions of the world, and in some cases of individual countries, in the last 2,000 years. For the world as a whole they estimate 170 million in AD 1, 265 million in AD 1000, 425 million in AD 1500, and 900 million in AD 1800. The 'magic' first time there were 1,000 million was reached around 1820 and there were 1,625 million people in the world around 1900.

Haub (1995) gives broadly similar estimates of population at different times and then attempts to answer the question 'How many people have ever lived on earth?' He calculates the number of people who have ever been born, arriving at a total of about 105,000 million, of which 5.5 per cent, or 5,760 million were alive in mid-1995. One reason for making this calculation was to refute a statement made in the 1970s that at that time 75 per cent of the people who had ever been born were alive. The level of material consumption of many of the 9,000 million people born in the world in the 20th century has been far higher than the level of consumption among the predominantly agricultural population characteristic of earlier times.

Estimates of the population of individual countries and of the world as a whole before the 20th century diverge considerably. Even in the 20th century, during which many countries have held regular or occasional censuses of population, it is not possible to give an accurate figure for population, as shown in examples in Chapter 1. For the purposes of this book the author has produced a 'definitive' population for the world at five year intervals. The population for every fifth year has been calculated by taking the average (in effect a running mean) for five individual years, as for example for 1988, 1989, 1990, 1991, 1992, and attributing the average to the middle year, in this case 1990. For the crucial period from 1950 to 1990 some licence has been used to smooth the growth curve produced. The resulting population totals are shown in Table 4.2 for the period 1920-2000; they will not necessarily agree exactly with other versions because as explained they are averages for five year periods. The total in Table 4.2 for 2000 is of course a projection. Figure 4.1, based on the data in Table 4.2, shows the growth of world population during the 20th century.

Table 4.2 Population of the world, 1920-2000 at five-yearly intervals

	Total (millions)	Gain (millions)	Change (per cent)		Total (millions)	Gain (millions)	Change (per cent)
1920	1,810	20	1.1	1965	3,300	320	10.7
1925	1,920	110	6.1	1970	3,650	350	10.6
1930	2,070	150	7.8	1975	4,020	370	10.1
1935	2,160	90	4.3	1980	4,420	400	10.0
1940	2,250	90	4.2	1985	4,850	430	9.7
1945	2,370	120	5.3	1990	5,300	450	9.3
1950	2,520	150	6.3	1995	5,710	410	7.7
1955	2,720	200	7.9	2000	6,100	390	6.8
1960	2,980	260	9.6				

Note: Estimates have been made by the author after comparing data in different sources and applying some appropriate smoothing. Populations are averages for five year periods.

The data in Table 4.2 show that the highest *relative* percentage increases of world population over five year periods were in the 1960s and 1970s, whereas the largest *absolute* gain occurred around 1990, when births exceeded deaths by about 90 million. It appears that globally the rate of population increase is now gradually slowing down. A simple if not simplistic 'top down' method of arriving at a population for 2050 would be to project the curve in Figure 4.1, continuing

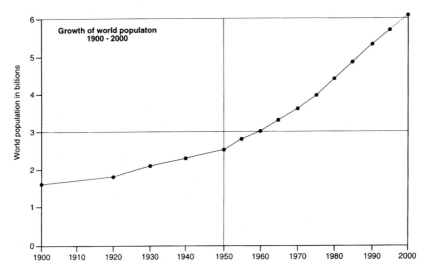

Figure 4.1 World population growth in the 20th century. Estimates are 5-year running means for every 5th year after 1950.

its 'logistic' form, and moving towards a state of no change late in the 21st century. Consideration should however be given to an appraisal of 'bottom up' trends, since the global total is made up of regions with vastly different rates of change, ranging from some European countries in which a decrease in population is already occurring or is imminent to some countries in Africa and Southwest Asia in which a further doubling in three decades or even less seems inevitable. This matter will be expanded upon in section 4.4.

A trend of great significance, referred to already in section 4.1, has been the continuing absolute growth of agricultural population in the second half of the 20th century in almost every country in the developing world. In 1950, the agricultural population of the world, including dependents as well as the economically active, numbered 1,380 million, about 55 per cent of the world total. In 1990 it had grown to 2,380 million, although then it was only 45 per cent of the world total. Therefore, during the period 1950-1990, the agricultural population of the world grew by over 70 per cent whereas the area of arable and permanent crops in the world only increased by about 10 per cent (see Chapter 5). In many parts of the developing world there are now more people working a given area of cultivated land than there were half a century ago. The almost universal increase in agricultural population in the developing countries in the second half of the 20th century has produced a 'surplus', from which some of the population have moved to non-agricultural/urban areas, and some to areas newly brought into cultivation by, for example, forest clearance and irrigation works, while some have stayed locally in the area of their birth, thereby increasing pressure on jobs in the agricultural sector.

During the 20th century the total population of the world will have almost quadrupled from 1,625 million to about 6,100 million. The growth of the world's urban population has, however, been even faster, rising from about 500 million in 1900 to an expected 2,750 million in the year 2000, an increase of 5.5 times. In particular, in recent decades the growth of the population in large cities in developing countries has been rapid. For example, the population of what will probably be the two largest cities in the world by the year 2000, Mexico City and São Paulo (Brazil), could grow from 9.2 and 8.2 million respectively in 1970, to 26 and 24 million by

2000. Not far behind are India's three largest cities, expected to grow between 1975 and 2015 as follows (in millions): Bombay (now Mumbai) 7 to 27, Calcutta 8 to 17.6, Delhi 4.5 to 17.5.

4.3   POPULATION CHANGE

At its most basic the arithmetic of population change is very simple. In any given region or country of the world change in population during a given time period will be the difference between the number of births and the number of deaths plus the difference between the number of immigrants and the number of emigrants. For the world as a whole there is no migration element, apart from the future possibility of settlement on the moon or on another planet.

It is common to use a standard measure for expressing births and deaths in a given region or in the world as a whole, the number per 1,000 total population in a chosen period, usually a year. These give the birthrate and deathrate, the difference between which is referred to as the natural increase. Table 4.3 shows the birthrate, deathrate and natural increase in selected countries. Assuming no change in the rate of natural increase it is possible to calculate future population by using the annual rate as a percentage by which the total increases (or decreases), in a similar manner to the calculation of compound interest. From the data in Table 4.3 it can be seen that the population of the world was increasing annually in the mid-1990s by about 1.5 per cent per year or by about 86 million. The rate of increase varies greatly between the more and less developed major regions of the world and, in particular, among different countries of the world, as seen in the contrast between the examples of Italy and Kenya. Most African countries even have a somewhat higher rate of natural increase than that of Kenya, while in 1996 Latvia was estimated to have a birthrate of 9 per 1,000 but a deathrate of 16, giving a negative annual natural increase rate (a decrease!) of -0.7 per cent, almost unknown in the world this century in peace time.

Table 4.3 Birthrate, deathrate and natural increase per year in selected countries in the mid-1990s

	(1) *Births* *(per 1000 population)*	*(2)* *Deaths*	*(3)* *Natural increase (per cent)*	*(4)* *Total fertility rate*
Italy	9	10	0.0	1.2
USA	15	9	0.6	2.0
China	17	7	1.1	1.8
India	29	10	1.9	3.4
Colombia	27	6	2.1	3.0
Kenya	40	13	2.7	5.4
More developed	12	10	0.1	1.6
Less developed	27	9	1.9	3.4
World	24	9	1.5	3.0

Source: *WPDS 1996*

In the 20th century the rate of natural increase of population has changed considerably in most parts of the world. Due to declining deathrates it has increased for up to several decades in many of the present developing countries but due to declining birthrates has decreased in the developed countries. This situation fits the Demographic Transition Model, referred to in Chapter 2. The rate of natural increase cannot therefore be used to project mechanically a given population into the future. A more useful guide to possible future trends is the total fertility rate (TFR). This is the average number of births per female during her child-bearing years. The average covers a range from 0 births for some women to over 20 in extreme cases.

Total fertility rate for selected countries is shown in column (4) of Table 4.3. Depending on mortality rates in the female population up to age 50 (after which child bearing virtually ceases), an average rate of slightly more than two children per female is needed to keep a population stable, given that some females can be expected to die before they reach child-bearing age or pass completely through it. A TFR of about 2.1 is therefore regarded as the number of births needed to maintain a population at a given level in the developed countries, but a higher rate is needed in developing countries, where mortality rates of young females are higher. The TFR has the disadvantage that it is actually calculated with hindsight because, strictly speaking, it asks women at the end of their child-bearing period how many children they have had but cannot anticipate how many children women will have in the future. Alternatively, young women can be asked how many children they intend, expect or hope to have. Both natural increase and TFR can change (or be changed) at any time in the future and neither can therefore be used with certainty to predict future population. The TFR has the advantage, however, that it can be set in the context of the total population structure of a region or a country (see Figure 4.2), and the number of potential future mothers already in the total population is known.

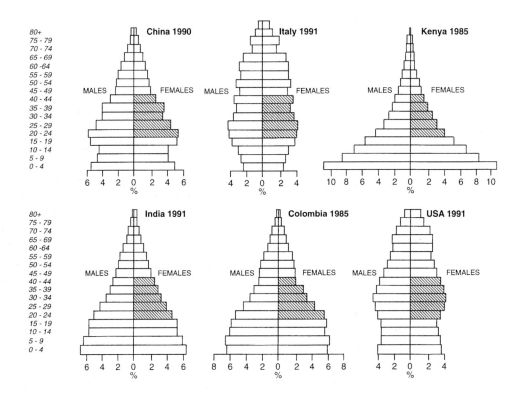

Figure 4.2 The population age-sex structures of six selected countries. Cohorts of women aged 20-44 are shaded in all diagrams. To ensure comparability of the shape of the six structures, all the scales are percentages of the total population, regardless of the absolute number of people in the population.

Figure 4.2 shows the population structure of six selected countries. China, India and the USA are shown because they are the three largest countries of the world in population. The other three represent different major regions of the world. In order to stress the structure of the population, shown by the shape of the diagrams, the bar for each age group (cohort) is drawn in length according to its percentage share of the total population, rather than in proportion to the total size of the population. The shaded bars are females between the ages of 20 and 44, those most likely to be bearing children in the years that the diagrams represent.

A population structure diagram with a rectangular shape is characteristic of a population that is changing slowly, if at all. A wide based triangular or pyramidal shape has the potential to grow fast for some decades to come unless a drastic change takes place over a very short period to reduce the TFR. All population age-sex diagrams are popularly referred to as population pyramids.

Among the larger countries of the world in population, in the 1990s, Italy and Spain had the lowest TFRs. Between 1980 and 1996 alone their TFRs dropped from 1.9 and 2.6 respectively to 1.2. Should Italy's TFR remain at 1.2 (or even drop below that level), the number of births in each successive five-year cohort (the lowest in the diagram in Figure 4.2) would continue to diminish, producing eventually an upside down pyramid (a cornetto?). On the other hand, an increase in TFR to well above 2.0 would in due course produce for Italy a form with a slim waist (a power station cooling tower?).

At the other extreme from Italy, the population structure of Kenya is broadly similar to that of most African countries. In Kenya there are more than twice as many females under the age of 20 destined to be mothers of the future, as there are women aged 20-39. Even if Kenya's TFR for some reason dropped from over 5.0 to around 2.5, in the next 20 years there would still be about the same number of births.

Latin America was the first major developing region in which a population 'explosion' was recognised when, four decades ago, Cook (1958) entitled a paper on the subject 'The "Fountain of Youth" Overflows'. Several more fountains have overflowed since then. Among Latin American countries there are now very marked differences in TFR, but Colombia (see Figure 4.2) is broadly representative. It shows the effect even as long ago as 1985 of a reduction of TFR, but even so there are considerably more females aged 0-19 than 20-39. Population is therefore expected to continue to grow for some decades.

In spite of various national and regional programmes to encourage a reduction in the number of babies born per female, in India the pyramidal shape of the population structure is still evident. China, on the other hand, has a more irregular population structure, reflecting an excess of deaths over births during a short period of famines in the early 1960s, a pro-natal policy following the Cultural Revolution in 1966, and later the introduction of drastic family planning measures following the death of Mao Zedong in 1976. The 1990 population structure of China shows among other things the effect of its baby boom of the late 1960s on the number of births (see the longer bar of 20-24 year olds). China's experience is of particular importance globally because the country has over one fifth of the total population of the world.

The USA has a faster growing population than Japan or any of the larger countries of Western Europe. The post-Second World War baby boom (born roughly during 1945-60) can be seen in the diagram, but some of the continuing growth in the USA, as in Canada and Australia, is the result of net in-migration of mainly young people, recently in the US case from Latin America and East Asia in particular.

The examples in Figure 4.2 illustrate and underline the complexity of the world demographic situation and the dangers of generalising at global level about possible future population trends.

It is nevertheless proposed to make projections of the population of the world to 2050. These will be based on an examination of the prospects for each of the ten major world regions. The relationship between fertility and mortality must be kept in mind when projections are made. A number of states of change can be experienced in a given country or region: these fit the Demographic Transition Model discussed in Chapter 2.

- Fertility and mortality are both high, common in societies with low average life expectancy, the result of precarious supplies of food and other materials, and of frequent outbreaks of infectious diseases.

- Fertility is higher than mortality, in which case population will be growing. Conventionally this situation is subdivided into two stages, the first during which birthrate and deathrate diverge, the second in which they converge.

- Fertility and mortality are both low, as in most developed countries.

- Mortality exceeds fertility, a situation apparently already experienced in parts of Europe, in which case population will decline unless offset by immigration.

Changes in the level of mortality are broadly related to the availability of food and other basic needs and the quantity and quality of diet, as well as to the availability of healthcare facilities and the quality of hygiene. Except in cases of conflict, ethnic cleansing and genocide, government policy is to lower mortality. No political party concerned about popular feeling could contemplate taking measures that would explicitly raise mortality. Sen (1993) may be referred to for a discussion of the relationship between mortality data and economic performance. Prolonging life expectancy by lowering mortality levels especially in both very young and very elderly age groups contributes to an increase in population (or delays a decrease in the rate of increase). The prospect that a more pleasurable and active old age may be in store for the elderly is discussed by Perls (1995). Olshansky *et al.* (1993) argue that the human species has modified the evolutionary forces that have always limited life expectancy. Policy makers should be prepared for the presence of a far larger proportion of elderly people in the future, sooner in the developed countries, later in the developing countries. The issue of pensions has become prominent in the developed countries only in the last two decades.

As fertility is related to the number of children born to each female it is the result of large numbers of parental decisions. Early in the 20th century the size of families was normally determined by biological factors until the widespread introduction of contraceptives. In developed countries, the pro-natal policies of governments have in some cases encouraged relatively high fertility rates. More commonly in developed and developing countries alike, however, in the second half of the 20th century population growth has been regarded by governments as the cause of various problems, and family planning methods have been publicised, contraceptives made available and efforts made to persuade or even coerce people into having fewer children. Marked differences in fertility levels are found within the larger individual countries at regional level (e.g. in China in the 1980s), among groups of employment (also in China), between urban and rural areas, and between different religious groups (e.g. Catholic and Protestant, as in some West European countries).

Views differ on the scale of population growth to be expected in the developing countries in the next few decades. May (1989), a biologist viewing population growth as the cause of many current problems, wonders: 'Pre-eminent among the still unanswered questions about our own past is how were human numbers maintained roughly constant with overall rates of population growth being imperceptible over hundreds of thousands of years before the advent of the Agricultural Revolution some 10,000 years or so ago? An increasing amount of evidence suggests the explanation lies not primarily in high deathrates among infants and adults, but rather in longer intervals between births than is characteristic of rapidly growing populations in many developing countries today.'

Robey *et al.* (1993) give evidence of a faster than expected decline in fertility rates in many developing countries in the last decades of the 20th century: 'Recent evidence suggests that birthrates in the developing world have fallen even in the absence of improved living conditions. The decrease has also proceeded with remarkable speed. Developing countries appear to have benefited from the growing influence and scope of family planning programs, from new contraceptive technologies and from the educational power of mass media.'

Before world population projections to 2050 are discussed in the next three sections it is appropriate to refer to influences that could produce subtle if not catastrophic changes in population trends in the next few decades. By the mid-1960s in a number of Asian countries governments were already supporting family planning and slower population growth (Donaldson and Tsui (1990)), among them India (1951), Pakistan, South Korea and China. By 1989, 47 per cent of all developing countries had specific government policies to lower fertility. Assuming such policies continue and are effectively implemented, the rate of world population increase should continue to diminish.

A smaller and arguably less desirable way of limiting population growth could be a failure to reduce infectious and parasitic diseases. Olshansky *et al.* (1997) caution that there is no cause for complacency either towards older diseases such as cholera, diphtheria and malaria, or towards 'new' or previously unrecognised disease-causing microbes (about 30 have been identified since 1973 alone).

Neither family planning nor infectious and parasitic diseases are likely to change drastically the rate of growth of population for some decades to come. An analogy with a large ship moving at a considerable speed comes to mind. There is no way it can be brought to a halt until it has continued a good distance after measures to stop it have first been applied. The term population momentum refers to the tendency for population growth to continue beyond the time that replacement level fertility has been achieved because of a relatively high concentration of people in their child-bearing ages.

4.4 THE POPULATION OF THE WORLD AROUND 2050

Before the world population is projected to 2050 some assumptions must be noted. It is assumed that there will not be a global disaster such as the impact of a large meteorite or the occurrence of an all-out nuclear war. Less obviously, it is also assumed that human 'demographic' practices and biological features will not change drastically. People will not suddenly stop having children, there will not be mass suicide, and the number of female and male births will continue to be approximately equal.

The Population Reference Bureau (PRB) has included projections of populations in its *World Population Data Sheet* (*WPDS*) since the 1970s. In the *1996 World Population Data Sheet* the population of the world is projected to rise from 5,771 million in 1996 to 8,193 million in 2025, an increase of 2,422 million or of 42 per cent in 29 years. In this projection a gradual decrease is assumed in the global rate of natural increase between 1996 and 2025, which was 1.5 per cent per year in 1996. If the global rate of natural increase continues its gradual decline after 2025 then a 'tidy' figure of 10 billion (10,000 million) would be near the total population of the world in the year 2050. In this section the evidence for such a total is examined on a regional basis. In the following section projections from other sources are described for comparison. In the final section of this chapter, events that might result in a markedly lower population for the world in 2050 are discussed. On the other hand, should there be a marked change upwards in fertility, then the prospect would be a total in excess of 10 billion.

Columns (1)-(7) in Table 4.4 show the author's estimates of the total population of the world, subdivided into ten major regions, for 1965, 1980 and 1995, and projections into the 21st century (note the intervals are 15 years except for 2040-2050). Projections for 1995-2010 and 2010-2025 are based on projections of the Population Reference Bureau. Those for 2025-2040 and 2040-2050 are based on assumptions made by the author about rates of natural increase, which broadly follow previous trends. Columns (8)-(10) show the percentage of the total population of the world observed or expected in each of the major regions in the selected years.

Figures 4.3 and 4.4 show the population of the ten major regions of the world during the period 1965-2050. Figure 4.3 shows the absolute number, Figure 4.4 the percentage share. In Figure 4.3, alternative futures after 2025 are shown for three regions, South Central Asia (mostly India), China and its neighbours, and Africa south of the Sahara. Whereas trend 'a' continues the trend over preceding decades, trend 'b' is the result of a fairly sharp drop in fertility rates (and/or an increase in mortality rates), a projection within the realm of possibility, but requiring a marked change in attitudes to family size to arise either spontaneously or through government family planning policy, or both. Figure 4.5 shows the changing size and distribution of population for major regions from 1965 to 2050, each major region being drawn proportional to its population size.

It must once again be stressed that the projections of regional and world population given in Tables 4.4 and 4.5 and shown graphically in Figures 4.3 and 4.4 are not claimed by the author to be precisely what will happen. At best they are a reasonable approximation of what might be expected in the decades to come, given no drastic changes in trends observed in the decades up to 1995. The reader who considers the projections to be either too high or too low can make adjustments accordingly, but for consistency and convenience these will be the projections used in the rest of the book against which projections of natural resource availability, production and consumption will be compared and measured. Some salient features of the projections will now be noted.

Table 4.5 World population 1965-2050

	1965	1980	1995	2010	2025	2040	2050
			(population in millions)				
Developed	993	1,119	1,220	1,290	1,331	1,338	1,320
Developing	2,301	3,296	4,481	5,686	6,862	7,879	8,660
World	3,294	4,415	5,701	6,976	8,193	9,217	9,980
			(population percentage)				
Developed	30.1	25.3	21.4	18.5	16.2	14.5	13.2
Developing	69.9	74.7	78.6	81.5	83.8	85.5	86.8

Author's estimates and projections

Table 4.4 Population trends and projections for the ten major regions of the world, 1965 to 2050 (see list of regions at the end of Chapter 1).

		(1) 1965	*(2)* 1980	*(3)* 1995	*(4)* 2010	*(5)* 2025	*(6)* 2040	*(7)* 2050	*(8)* 1965	*(9)* 1995	*(10)* 2050
		(population in millions)							(percentage)		
1	Europe	451	491	515	527	520	491	460	13.7	9.0	4.7
2	Russia	184	203	214	218	223	227	230	5.6	3.8	2.3
3	Japan	126	155	170	180	177	168	160	3.8	3.0	1.6
4	North America	232	270	321	365	411	452	470	7.0	5.6	4.8
5	Latin America	245	360	481	584	678	759	800	7.4	8.4	8.1
6	Africa S. of Sahara	250	381	558	828	1,190	1,655	2,190	7.6	9.8	22.2
7	N. Africa, W. Asia	139	203	330	458	600	740	810	4.2	5.8	8.2
8	South C. Asia	694	980	1,355	1,752	2,105	2,316	2,360	21.2	23.8	23.8
9	Southeast Asia	248	354	485	614	727	800	810	7.5	8.5	8.2
10	China	725	1,018	1,272	1,450	1,562	1,609	1,590	22.0	22.3	16.1
	World	3,294	4,415	5,701	6,976	8,193	9,217	9,880	100.0	100.0	100.0

Sources: Various years of *WPDS*, *UNDYB* plus author's estimates

Notes on the membership of the regions:
1 All Europe excluding former USSR
2 Russia, Ukraine, Belarus, Moldova
3 Japan plus South Korea
4 USA, Canada and Oceania
6 Excludes Morocco, Algeria, Tunisia, Libya, Egypt and Sudan
8 India and its neighbours in South Asia, Afghanistan, Iran, former Soviet Republics of Central Asia and Kazakhstan
10 China plus Hong Kong, Taiwan, North Korea, Mongolia

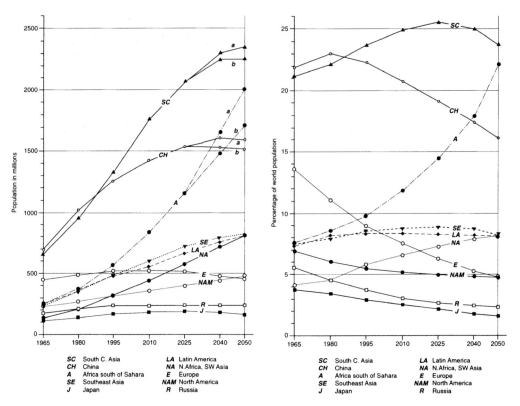

SC South C. Asia · LA Latin America
CH China · NA N.Africa, SW Asia
A Africa south of Sahara · E Europe
SE Southeast Asia · NAM North America
J Japan · R Russia

Figure 4.3 The expected absolute growth of population in ten major regions, 1965 to 2050, according to projections made by the Population Reference Bureau to 2025 and by the author after that. North America includes Australia and New Zealand. Europe includes all countries in the continent which are not parts of the former USSR (except the three Baltic Republics which are included). Alternative population futures after 2025 are given for the three most populous regions.

Figure 4.4 The expected changing share of world population in each of ten major world regions, 1965 to 2050. For details of the composition of certain regions see Figure 4.3.

1. If the alternative '*b*' projections for the three largest regions of the world in population in 2025 do occur, then in 2050 there would be about 400 million people fewer in Africa south of the Sahara than in the '*a*' projections, and 80 million fewer each in South Central Asia and in China. The world total would therefore be 9,320 million in 2050 rather than 9,880 million, a 'saving' (or 'loss' in the eyes of those who favour population growth) of 560 million. Such adjustments could also be made, as appropriate, for other major regions.

2. The data in Tables 4.4 and 4.5 show the shares of the world's population in the developed countries and in the developing countries, as so defined in the 1990s. It is possible, indeed likely, that some of the present developing countries (e.g. Argentina, Chile, Mexico, Turkey, Malaysia) might in due course transfer to the status of developed during the decades to come. Indeed the author has taken the liberty of adding South Korea to the list already. Whatever transfers there are in the future, the fact remains that between 1965 and the year 2000 the percentage of the world's population in the traditional developed countries will have dropped from about 30 per cent to about 20 per cent. Without new recruits to the

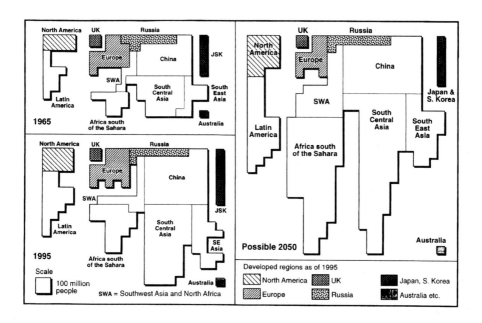

Figure 4.5 The population of the world in 1965 and 1995 and the expected population in 2050. For clarity, the UK has been detached from the rest of Europe, Australia and New Zealand from North America. The area of each region is proportional in size to the population of the region.

developed world it could be as low as 13 per cent by 2050. The already increasingly reluctant donors of development assistance (see Chapter 9) are therefore a shrinking breed, smaller still with the sudden transfer, since 1990, of resources to Central Europe and the former USSR, themselves previously net donors of assistance to developing regions. In the context of the demographic history of the world since about 1500, the relative and indeed imminent absolute decline in the population size of Europe in the 20th century has been one of the outstanding features. Europe's shrinking share of total world population should contribute to what Keens-Soper (1996) regards as its increasing susceptibility to pressures from other power blocs in a 21st century world, in which it has itself renounced power politics, echoing the forecast of Mackinder (1904) quoted in Chapter 1.

3. The data in Figure 4.3 show remarkable differences in population change among the ten major regions of the world. Of the four developed regions, little change is expected between 1995 and 2050 in three of them: Europe, Russia and Japan. Only in North America with Oceania is population growth expected to continue, rising from about 250 million in 1965 to 450 in 2050. Of the six developing regions, three (Latin America, Southeast Asia and China), appear to be moving towards a situation of relatively slow growth after 2050, but South Central Asia is more problematic, while in all of Africa and in Western Asia fast growth seems likely to continue after 2050.

4. The agricultural part of the total world population seems likely to remain in the first half of the 21st century at somewhere between 2,500 and 3,000 million (25-30 per cent of the total population by 2050). The implications of this will be discussed in Chapter 5. In anticipation, it may be noted that such a situation would mean the area of cultivated land farmed per

farm worker could decrease in many parts of the developing world and that each farm worker would also have to support a larger total population.

5. In 1996 the percentage of population defined as urban was estimated to be 43, or about 2,480 million people. The percentage in the developed countries was however 74, compared with only 36 in the developing countries. If it is assumed that these percentages will be 80 and 50 respectively in 2050, then there would be an increase of urban dwellers in the developed countries from 915 million in 1995 to 1,055 million in 2050, a change of such modest magnitude compared with other demographic changes in the world that in itself it should not create serious problems except locally. By comparison, the increase expected in the urban population of developing countries could be from 1,570 million in 1995 to 4,300 million in 2050.

The 'urban revolution' has already affected many parts of the developing world, particularly Latin America, where about 70 per cent of the population is now defined as urban, but its impact on South Central Asia and China has been more recent, while in Africa, still with only about 30 per cent of its population urban, the main impact is still to come. While numerous problems afflict most developing world cities, including the maintenance of a supply of basic needs such as water and sewerage, energy and housing, there is one positive feature if the rate of population growth is to be reduced in the developing world: fertility rates are generally considerably lower in urban areas than in rural, predominantly agricultural, areas. Such was the experience, for example, in the USSR earlier this century, when rapid urban growth was occurring. More recently, the same has happened in China, if only because rigorous family planning measures could be applied in larger urban centres, but were less effective in rural areas. Recent census data for Latin American countries shows that here, also, even among the poorer sections of the community, family size is generally smaller in urban than in rural areas. The dampening effect of urban life on family size has been accounted for by a number of influences, including the sheer constraints of space, a reduction in infant/child mortality, giving parents an assurance that they do not 'need' an unlimited number of children, and the generally greater access to education in general and family planning advice in particular.

4.5   OTHER PROJECTIONS OF POPULATION

In this section, three projections of world population have been chosen from many possible ones to provide a comparison with those of the author. In addition, population projections or goals for a number of individual countries are briefly described.

Frejka (1973) considered the prospects for a stationary world population. Starting from 1970, when the population of the world was 3.6 billion, he made five alternative projections with different fertility rates and considered that 'an extrapolation of present world demographic trends that lie somewhere between two extreme projections shows it levelling off at some 8.4 billion by the year 2100.' For 2050 they range between extremes of 5.6 and 13.0 billion. His five alternative futures are summarised in Table 4.6. Frejka's study serves to illustrate two points:

1. Projections 1 and 2 are no longer relevant unless improbably large changes in fertility and/ or mortality occur. In the view of the author, Projection 4 is the closest to what will happen. The first point to reiterate is that any projections should be abandoned or revised as soon as 'reality' shows them to be erroneous or improbable.

2. Frejka assumes that at some stage there will be a stable 'zero growth' situation that will last indefinitely. Figure 4.6 shows the improbable stability once a given population size is reached. Rejuvenation of growth, continuing decline or a roller coaster effect are not considered. Frejka's are not the only projections giving or implying a stable population extending over future centuries. In van der Tak (1974), the United Nations, the World Bank and Bogue and Tsui (1979) show stable world populations at 11.0, 9.8 and 8.1 billion respectively. There seems no reason to expect that somehow such a state of perfect stability would be maintained at least without a very powerful world government to control and adjust fertility rates universally.

Table 4.6 Alternative futures for world population according to Frejka, starting in 1970

Projection	1970 Population (billions)	TFR 1965-70	2000 Population (billions)	TFR required 1970-2005	2050 Population (billions)	No growth after
1	3.6	4.7	4.7	2.5 to 2.2	5.6	2060
2	3.6	4.7	5.1	3.9 to 2.2	6.3	2070
3	3.6	4.7	5.9	4.4 to 2.2	8.2	2080
4	3.6	4.7	6.4	4.5 to 3.1	10.5	2100
5	3.6	4.7	6.7	4.6 to 3.5	13.0	2110

Source: Based on Frejka (1973).
Notes: TFR - Total Fertility Rate

In Figure 4.6 two projections of the present author are shown by broken lines. Starting at A in the year 2000, B and C assume growth until after 2100, followed not by an exactly stable (zero growth) trend but a decline. Moreover, given the absence of a widely accepted consensus as to how many people there should be at any given time, there is no way of knowing how big or small a stationary population should be. In the event, at the level of billions of individuals, people are not all going to cooperate to maintain a particular world population size of no immediate or obvious relevance to themselves.

Lutz (1994) has edited a comprehensive volume on the future population of the world, with material on the situation at national, regional and global level. The alternative projections for the world in his study are based on various assumptions about migration, mortality and fertility in major world regions. Nine different global totals are given for 2030, and extrapolations are made to 2050 (see Table 4.7). Lutz's Projections 3, 4 and 5 are fairly close to the author's projections of about 10 billion in 2050. Two features of such projections are illustrated by Lutz's study. First, changes in fertility rates usually make a greater impact on population growth (or decline) than mortality rates or international migration. Secondly, the degree of divergence between the highest and lowest extremes, a gap of 1.1 billion between 7.9 and 9.0 billion in 2020 is much smaller, relatively, than that between the extremes in 2050, a gap of 6.7 billion between 8.3 and 15 billion. In 2020, 7.9 billion is 87 per cent of 9.0 billion, whereas in 2050, 8.3 billion is only 55 per cent of 15 billion.

Demographers at the United Nations have made numerous projections for the population of the world and for parts of it. The two most recent revisions at the time of writing were made in 1994 and 1996 and are discussed by Haub (1997). The UN projections to 2050 are shown in Table 4.8: for 1994 only the medium projection is included, but the low, medium and high projections are given for 1996. The 1994 medium projections for the world of 9,833

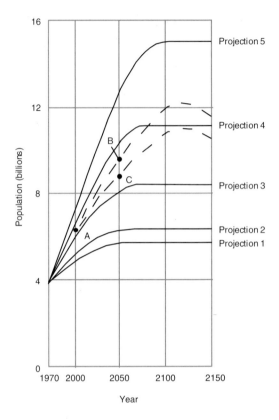

Figure 4.6 Alternative future world populations depending on different assumptions as to when a net reproduction rate of 1 might be achieved. The remarkable assumption, made by many people who talk about future population, is that once a reproduction rate of 1 (or a replacement rate of around 2.1) is reached, a zero-growth situation will be maintained indefinitely, as in these projections for 60 to 100 years. Already in Europe total fertility rate has dropped far below 2.1, as also in Japan. Why should it remain above this level in some other regions just to compensate for the fall in Europe? To Frejka's (1973) projections the author has added his two (the broken lines), starting in 2000, when the actual population should be about 6.1 billion, and continuing to 2150 with a decline starting after about 2130.

Table 4.7 Alternative futures for world population according to Lutz, starting in 1990

Projection	Migration	Mortality	Fertility	1990	2020	2050
1	Low	High	Low	5,291	7,868	8,307
2	High	High	Low	5,291	7,866	8,323
3	High	Low	Low	5,291	8,195	9,823
4	Low	Low	Low	5,291	8,208	9,840
5	Central	Central	Central	5,291	8,428	11,307
6	High	High	High	5,291	8,624	12,691
7	Low	High	High	5,291	8,630	12,713
8	High	Low	High	5,291	8,983	14,957
9	Low	Low	High	5,291	9,005	15,015

Based on Lutz (1994)

Note: the order in which the nine projections are listed in this table has been changed from the order given by Lutz in order to rank the Projections according to population size in 2050.

Table 4.8 United Nations population projections by region, 1994 and 1996, in millions

	1994 Revision medium		*1996 Revision*	low	medium	high
	1995	*2050*	*1995*	*2050*	*2050*	*2050*
World	5,716	9,833	5,687	7,662	9,367	11,156
More Developed Regions	1,167	1,208	1,171	959	1,162	1,352
Less Developed Regions	4,550	8,626	4,516	6,703	8,205	9,805
LDR excluding China	3,328	7,020	3,296	5,505	6,688	8,039
China	1,222	1,606	1,220	1,198	1,517	1,766
North Africa	132	256	131	208	257	312
Sub-Saharan Africa	596	1,885	588	1,523	1,789	2,096
Asia	3,458	5,741	3,438	4,405	5,443	6,501
Latin America and Caribbean	482	839	477	650	810	1,001
Northern America	293	389	297	301	384	452
Europe	727	678	728	538	638	742
Oceania	29	46	28	37	46	53

Source: Haub (1997), based on *World Population Prospects: The 1994 and 1996 revisions*, UN Population Division

million in 2050 is very close to that used by the author in this book, but the 1996 revision, 9,367 is considerably lower. Although several 'expert' projections of world population in 2050 fall between 9 and 10 billion, that does not mean that the actual figure will necessarily be within that range.

According to a forecast made in 1992 (see Nippon (1993)), Japan's present population of 125.8 million would peak around 2010 at 130 million and would drop to 114 million by 2045, a projection compatible with that made by the author for the population of Japan (without South Korea). What has been referred to as the '1.53 shock' (see Yanagishita (1992)) hit Japan around 1990, the realisation that fertility was far below replacement rate. Concern over the growing population of elderly people in the country gave rise to a novel and bizarre way of coping with excessive numbers of old people (see Alexander (1991)): that is that they should be housed cheaply in retirement homes in Senegal, West Africa.

In contrast, it is expected that the population of the USA will continue to rise, growing from 265.2 million in 1996 to 335 million in 2025 and about 385 million in 2050. As in Japan there is already concern in the USA about the ageing of the population. On the other hand, in contrast to Japan, the ethnic composition of the US population also worries at least the citizens of European origin (the non-Hispanic whites) and, according to Stix (1996), by 2056 they could make up less than half of the US population. In the European Union there is less concern about the exact population size or ethnic composition than in Japan or the USA, but an absolute decline and an ageing population are by now widely anticipated in the next few decades, and measures to cope with the problem are being contemplated.

It is more difficult in the developing countries than in the developed ones to make projections for several decades ahead, but three examples will be noted briefly. The total population of China in 1995 according to *China Statistical Yearbook 1996* was 1,211 million, at which time it was growing by about 1 per cent per year. According to Liu Zheng *et al.* (1981), the 'desirable population for China one hundred years from now [1981] should be between 650 million and 700 million in view of the availability in particular of fresh water and cultivated land.' In 1962

China's population total passed 700 million. To reduce it to that level from over 1,200 million in the mid-1990s, even in eight decades, would be a task of mind-boggling proportions for demographic policy makers (see Figure 3.1).

Brazil has frequently been described by both Brazilians and outsiders as a country of enormous potential in terms of natural resources. Writing in 1969, a Brazilian economist, Simonsen (1969), irritated by the projection of Kahn and associates (1967) already referred to, about the poor prospects for real GNP per inhabitant in Brazil, matched alternative futures for total population and total GNP in his country. The population of 80 million in 1965 could grow to somewhere between 142 and 212 million by the year 2000, total GNP to between 107 and 246 billion US dollars. The extremes would be a mere 506 dollars per capita with the highest population growth and lowest economic growth, contrasting with 1,725 with the reverse, a clear indication, calculated with a minimum of effort, of the advantage of keeping population growth down. In the event, the population of Brazil (160.5 million in 1996) should reach 171.7 million by the year 2000, while the per capita GNP in 1996 was 3,370 US dollars, to be adjusted (before comparability can be achieved) to take into account the reduction in the value of the US dollar since 1965, as well as fluctuations in Brazil-US exchange rates. In the 1990s population policy in Brazil remains ambiguous; so much of the country still has a very low density of population that it is difficult to make a strong case for reducing the rate of population growth.

An Argentinian economist, Raymundo (1969), also writing in 1969, took a different view of the future of his country, expressing concern about the small total population and low density of population. He argued that in the considerable cultivated area of Argentina a much greater agricultural population was needed and that large agricultural holdings, currently giving low yields, should be broken up and re-allocated. Contrary to his expectations, or at least proposals, according to *FAOPY* (1995) the agricultural labour force in Argentina has dropped from 18 per cent of the economically active population in 1965 to 9.4 per cent in 1995, while remaining around 1.5 million.

It is intended that the examples of concern about future population in the countries referred to above should illustrate the great variety of issues and problems foreseen for future populations. The USA, Japan and China are among the countries in which medium- to long-term demographic problems have been the subject of considerable thought and research. In most developing countries population change is very rapid and demographic data are very approximate, so concern is more likely to be about the next few years than about the next few decades. In contrast, in most developed countries there is growing concern about the ageing of the population as fertility declines and life expectancy increases. The possibility of accepting young immigrants from developing countries is one solution that has been proposed.

4.6 CONSTRAINTS ON FURTHER POPULATION GROWTH

The surprise-free or 'central' population trend for the population of the world and for the major regions could be substantially or drastically different if certain events occur before 2050. They are listed in this section for consideration, but are not regarded by the author as likely to occur on a large scale. Their geographical impact can be global, regional or local. Only global level impacts could seriously alter the world population growth trend postulated in section 4.4. Massive migration between major regions, initially at least, would alter the spatial distribution of population but would constitute a near 'zero-sum game' affecting only slightly the total population of the world. Most of the prospects noted below have the effect of raising mortality or at least of slowing the decline of mortality.

Natural events that would have disastrous effects for the human species

- A meteorite big enough to cause a large amount of debris/dust to enter the earth's atmosphere, blocking out the sun's rays for some years, lowering temperature and, most critically, lowering agricultural yields, could lead in due course to starvation of a large part of the world's population (see Chapter 5).

- A massive volcanic eruption, much larger than that at Krakatoa in 1883. The effect would be similar to the impact of a large meteorite but less drastic. Even so, adverse weather conditions could cut food production.

- In the next half-century numerous deaths can be expected locally from earthquakes (e.g. Tangshan in China in 1976 when some 240,000 people died), hurricanes, droughts and other natural hazards, but there is no reason to expect that they should occur with much greater frequency in the next half-century than previously, although damage could be greater due to the fact that per given area there are on average more people to be affected.

- As a result of sudden climatic change, through the heating of the atmosphere rather than a drop in temperature, some or all of the ice now covering most of Antarctica and Greenland, could melt, raising sea-level by a few metres or even a few tens of metres. Such a process is likely to take decades rather than years and theoretically there need not be any direct loss of human life, since evacuation of the population from areas about to be flooded could be undertaken. In the longer term, the loss of some of the world's most productive agricultural land could affect population growth in many areas, while in more general terms the economic loss of buildings and transport links would be great because many of the world's largest cities would be permanently flooded.

- Infectious diseases that could not be checked immediately could, over a short period, affect large populations, as occurred during 1348-49, when the bubonic plague (referred to as the Black Death) wiped out a quarter of the population of Europe, and hit London again in 1665. There has been a much greater amount of travel between different regions of the globe in the last decades of the 20th century than ever before and a corresponding increase in the potential for the international transfer of diseases. An example is the HIV/AIDS epidemic (see *Population Today* (1998)). Acquired immune deficiency syndrome (AIDS), the impact of which has as yet been very small on world population, could increase in a matter of decades if not checked, particularly in parts of Africa. Anderson and May (1992) consider that the rates at which the human immunodeficiency virus (HIV) is spreading reveal an alarming picture in Sub-Saharan Africa, and rates are increasing in India and parts of Southeast Asia. One forecast puts the total number of deaths expected from AIDS in Africa by about 2020 at 20 million. The spread of HIV infection is not confined to developing countries; there are sharp contrasts in AIDS cases per 100,000 people in other countries (*HDR 1996*, 1994 data). The USA has the highest level among developed countries, at 22.7 (per 100,000); Japan the lowest at 0.2. Spain, France and Italy have the highest levels in the European Union. Its incidence is spreading in the former USSR. van der Laan (1996) reports that in one city in Belarus (the former Belorussian SSR), one person in fifteen is affected; the spread of AIDS here is closely related to the sharing of needles and the reselling of syringes. Hawkes (1997b) reports that a century after the discovery of how it is spread by mosquitoes, malaria (a parasitic-infectious rather than contagious disease) still kills 2 million people a year and, unlike smallpox, it is virtually impossible to eradicate.

Man-made events that could affect the size of global population

- A military conflict of global proportions – the Third World War – a prospect that has preoccupied many people since 1945. If nuclear weapons were used in large numbers, whether locally or at many places around the world, the effect on world population would take two forms. Firstly, assuming many large cities would be targeted, there would be immediate deaths, possibly of 5-10 per cent of the population of the world, followed by later deaths from radiation sickness. Secondly, a large number of people would later die directly as a result of fires started in both man-made structures and natural vegetation. In the words of the British Medical Association (1986): 'Fires resulting from a nuclear exchange would be quite different from those which occur from agricultural burning, fossil fuel combustion and wildfires. They would be burning simultaneously over enormous areas of land; they would emit a relatively large amount of smoke because of their uncontrolled nature; and that smoke would be relatively high graphitic carbon with great capacity for absorbing sunlight.' Agricultural output would fall inevitably, as with a meteorite impact, on account of cooling of the atmosphere. If an all-out nuclear war, with the aftermath of a nuclear winter, does occur, then current projections of population to 2050 will be academic. A civilian nuclear accident of the type experienced at Chernobyl in Ukraine in 1986 would have to be on a much greater scale to make a similar impact on global population, but deaths would be from nuclear contamination rather than food shortage.

- A global population policy either to restrict population growth, as in the case of China, or to increase fertility (and lower mortality) would make a considerable difference to population change to 2050, possibly cutting population size or increasing it by a billion or more. An effective global policy, with enforcement and sanctions strong enough to alter population trends markedly is possible, but seems highly unlikely. It can, nevertheless, be argued than since about 1970 China's population policy has kept the total to around 1,200 million in the mid-1990s compared with the possibility of 1,400 million if fertility rates experienced in the late 1960s had been maintained. Much 'evidence' has been produced in the Chinese foreign language publication *Beijing Review* to prove the advantage of having one child or at most two (e.g. Li Rongxia (1996)).

Specific economic situations and change

In most of the attempts to forecast global futures for the human population it is accepted that a change in one element can affect and be affected by changes in other elements. Water and food supply are two of the most obvious factors to influence population size and change in given regions. The prospect of increasing the availability of fresh water and food to levels compatible with a growth of population from around 6 billion in the late 1990s to around 10 billion in 2050 will be assessed in Chapter 5. Energy and raw materials will be considered in chapters 6 and 7. The question of how many people the earth can support, at what given economic level, and for how long, will be discussed in Chapter 12.

4.7   MIGRATION

International migration, like ageing, is an issue widely discussed in the 1990s. The largest absolute number of migrants moving between continents in modern times took place after the widespread introduction of steamship services and railways around the middle of the 19th century. Tens of millions of people migrated, mainly out of Europe, between about 1850 and 1930, settling principally in areas in which the indigenous population was small in number and lacked the technology or weaponry to resist the occupation of their lands by Europeans. North America was the largest recipient of migrants from Europe, but Australia and New Zealand, southern South America, southern Africa, and Siberia (settled by Russians and Ukrainians) also attracted new settlers from Europe. Since the Second World War this type of migration has been greatly reduced. In contrast, a new type of migration has been growing in significance in the last decades of the 20th century.

Western Europe, North America and to a small extent Australia have attracted people from developing countries. The flow of migrants, many illegal, has been from poorer to richer countries, a 'South-North' flow, which as yet has not markedly affected Russia or Japan. Thanks to the widespread availability of air services it is relatively easy for people to move between continents, but their flow can largely be monitored and controlled at airports. There are also interfaces between developing and developed countries, the international land boundary in the case of Mexico and the USA, and the Mediterranean between North Africa and Europe, neither of which is completely controlled and policed at present (see Figure 12.10). For example, according to Tremlett (1997) increasing numbers of West Africans pass through Morocco and into Spain across a narrow sea to breach 'Fortress Europe' illegally. The combined effect of a very steep economic 'gradient' from developing countries to nearby developed countries, and the continuing growth of the population of most Latin American and African countries, is making the flow likely to increase as time goes on.

Since the break-up of the Soviet bloc in 1990-91, the European Union has been faced with the additional problem of greatly increased immigration from Central Europe and the former USSR in addition to the traditional flow of immigrants, especially from former colonies in the Caribbean, Africa and southern Asia. As yet there is little appreciation of the pressure that could build up in developing countries to move into the more affluent parts of Europe. In the USA, on the other hand, it is now appreciated that some eventual benefit might be derived from allowing large numbers of immigrants to enter the country, given that their average age is roughly six years younger than that of US residents. They would help to offset the ageing process among existing US citizens, the elderly in 1990 making up 12.5 per cent of the population, but expected in 2050 to be 22.3 per cent. Espenshade and Gurcak (1996) conclude: 'To keep the dependency ratio [of persons age 65 and over plus persons under 18 to those aged 18 to 64] at 1990 levels requires 2 million migrants per year by 2020 and 10 million per year by 2080 - numbers the American public is unlikely to tolerate.' Surely this must be the demographic understatement of the year!

While most Americans are only indirectly affected by the influx of illegal Mexican immigrants, Whittell (1997b) describes the bizarre situation on the ground at Campo in the extreme south of California. Owners of ranches along the actual international border have organised themselves into patrols of armed vigilantes. In 1996 no fewer than 78,000 immigrants were arrested in the Campo area, compared with 2,300 in 1994. How soon will the USA erect an immigrant-proof barrier along its southern frontier?

Whether 1 million or 10 million people migrate permanently each year from developing to developed countries, the impact on the population of the developing countries would be small. In a hypothetical (but highly unlikely) situation in which Australia agreed in a one-off deal to allow the entry of one Indian into the country per one Australian, the 18 million Indians immigrating to match the 18 million population of Australia would be just one year's increase of India's population.

Population growth in the developing countries in the decades to 2050 is likely almost entirely to be absorbed internally, with potential problems of some magnitude. The prospect is illustrated by the situation in China described by Li Tan (1994). Of the six major developing regions in the world, China has the lowest rate of natural increase, about 1.0 per cent per year: 'At present [1994] there are an estimated 120 million surplus laborers in China. By 2000, there will be 490 to 540 million farmers in the rural areas, about 200 million of whom will have to find new jobs outside the agricultural sector. Supposing that 10 million, a generous estimate, can find a new job each year as the country's economy develops, by the turn of this century at least 140 million laborers will remain jobless.'

Migration into cities from rural areas has proceeded more rapidly in many developing countries than in China, and has resulted in the presence of enormous numbers of poorly paid, underemployed or unemployed people living in squatter settlements or in slums (see Figure 12.9). Such people could be seen as economic refugees from their own rural areas. An extreme case is the Gaza strip between Egypt and Israel, in which unemployment is very high and material conditions are poor, yet the highest total fertility rate in the world is recorded there. In the next few decades an increasing proportion of the population of the developing world can be expected to be living in the 'Gaza strip' type of settlement, more a threat to the better-off citizens in their own countries than to the developed countries.

4.8   ON THE NEXT FOUR CHAPTERS

Now that the author's projection of the future population of the world for the next five decades has been explained it is possible to make projections for various aspects of world production and consumption, indicating both total amounts and amounts per capita. A standard approach has been used for almost all the aspects covered in the next four chapters. A past trend from 1950 to 1990 or in some cases from the 1930s to 1990 is worked out and plotted graphically. Whatever the natural resource or item of production or consumption considered (e.g. area under forest, natural gas production, passenger cars in circulation) the absolute amounts are first given and the per capita amounts are then calculated.

In order to make immediate comparisons between various items possible, 1990 always has an index of 100, whatever the absolute quantity involved. As with population (see Section 4.2), five-year running means are used in order to smooth out year-to-year fluctuations. The amounts are attributed to each year ending in 0. The figures may therefore not be exactly the same as the figures for the actual year itself in the source(s) of the data.

Three alternative futures are then projected to the year 2050. In each case, two of these are always the same. In one projection the 1990 total stays unchanged to the year 2050, in which case the per capita level drops to about 55 per cent between 1990 and 2050 on account of expected population growth. In another projection, the per capita level stays the same and the total amount therefore has to increase by more than 85 per cent to allow for the expected increase in population. A third alternative projection, calculated by the author, is also shown. It is explained and justified in the text. It may simply be a continuation of the 1950-1990 trend or it may reflect what could happen given changing circumstances expected in the future. The repetition of showing the same first two projections on every graph is justified on the grounds that each set of projections can then be considered in its own right. The alternative would have been to refer the reader to a particular graph somewhere in the text to see what the 'no change' projections for total and per capita amounts look like.

At this point it is appropriate to warn the reader of a possible reason for confusion in the chapters that follow as to the different figures given for expected total world population growth. The following are mentioned:

Period in question	World population	Amount of increase
1990-2050	5,300 to 9,880 million	86 per cent
1995-2050	5,720 to 9,880 million	73 per cent
2000-2050	6,130 to 9,880 million	61 per cent

The expected increase in the present developing countries only is

1990-2050	4,100 to 8,660 million	111 per cent

The main purpose of the procedure used is twofold. First, the reader can quickly compare past trends with future prospects, judging which future trend of the three, if any, seems nearest to what he or she expects to happen. Second, past trends and future prospects for different items can quickly be compared. The projections for oil in Chapter 6 should be referred to first because the actual data from which the projections are made, before their conversion to an index of 100 for the year 1990, are shown in Table 6.6. The tables in Appendix II show the raw data for each of the other projections in Chapters 5-8.

The items projected in the next four chapters are of two main kinds, natural resources and products. Natural resources are things that have been in the natural world before humans came on the scene. Products, derived from natural resources, are the result of the application of means of production (capital resources) to provide goods and services. Instead of considering first the natural resources of the world and then moving on to production, the two aspects of the economy are examined together. For example, in Chapter 5, cultivated land, fertilisers and cereal output are grouped together, in Chapter 7, raw materials and industrial production. Natural resources and their uses are listed below with examples. In addition to the natural resources listed, the author would include space, time and air, all three taken very much for granted.

1. Water: beverages, domestic uses, hydro-electric power, processing, irrigation.

2. Bioclimatic resources: food, fuelwood, raw materials, e.g. cotton, timber, wool.

3. Fossil fuels: energy, raw materials.

4. Non-fuel minerals: e.g. iron ore, phosphates.

The above list covers most conventional resources. Almost all are processed in some way before being consumed. Conventionally two of the three sectors of economic activity, agriculture and industry, are concerned with the production of goods, as opposed to the third 'non-goods' sector, services. The boundaries between the three sectors are becoming increasingly blurred. The author wonders if in the future a different classification of economic activities will be preferred, but space does not allow a justification, and data are not readily available under the headings proposed:

1. Production: farmers, miners, factory workers, healthcare staff, teachers, entertainers.

2. Distribution: transport workers, communications, wholesalers and retailers.

3. Redistribution: banks, financial houses, charities, gambling, tax, insurance.

By the year 2000 the population of the world will probably reach 6.1 billion and will therefore have grown almost four times in the 20th century, a cause for alarm or satisfaction, depending on one's views. At the same time, the total consumption of non-renewable natural resources is at least ten times as high in the 1990s as it was in the 1890s.

Population is changing at very different rates in different regions and countries of the world. In some countries of Central Europe it is now slowly declining, whereas on average it is increasing by about 2.6 per cent annually in Africa, a 'compound interest' rate that would result in a doubling of population in 26 years. In Europe and North America the reduction of fertility in recent decades has largely been spontaneous whereas in China draconian measures have been applied since the 1970s to achieve as many one-child families as possible. In India birth control methods have been less drastic and less effective, while in most Muslim countries and in most of non-Muslim Africa family planning is either seen as unfavourable ideologically or is not widely available.

In mid-1997 the population of the world was about 5,840 million (5.84 billion) and each year there are about 140 million live births but only about 50 million deaths, giving an increase of about 90 million (*1997 WPDS*). Since population change is determined by tens of millions of 'decisions' each year to have children it is unlikely that anything other than a devastating natural or man-made disaster could suddenly change the present trend. A total world population of around 10 billion is anticipated by the author for 2050, a figure that falls within the range of several other projections. There will be a much smaller share of the total population in the present developed countries in 2050 than now, a situation affected in only a very limited way by international migration.

In 2050 the global demographic picture will be characterised by two outstanding features: the presence of a very large rural, predominantly agricultural, population on a correspondingly very limited area of farmland, and the presence of numerous very large cities, many of them the capitals of larger developing countries (see Chapter 12).

5

WATER AND FOOD

'Many men are inclined ... to predict that the day has at last come when the human race must cease to expand its numbers, or else face inevitable hunger'

National Geographic, January 1916

5.1   INTRODUCTION

Since 1916, when the statement at the head of the chapter was made, the total population of the world has increased more than three times, from about 1.8 billion then to 5.8 billion in 1997. In his contribution to 'How the World is Fed', Showalter (1916) expressed concern about world cereal production, but expected a much greater contribution of wheat from Russia in the future. In 'Can the World Feed its People?' Canby (1975) found greatly varying prospects for future food supplies in different regions of the world and concluded that continuing action was needed to feed the growing population.

Brown *et al.* (1997) have monitored the performance of world food production and the loss of cropland since the 1960s. In his latest contribution at the time of writing he noted: 'During the nineties, the growth of world grain production has slowed dramatically, while demand has continued to climb, driven by the addition of nearly 90 million people a year and an unprecedented rise in Asia, led by China. Part of this widening gap has been filled in recent years by drawing down carryover stocks - the amount left in the world's grain bins at the start of each new harvest. By 1996, these had fallen to 50 days of consumption, the lowest on record.' Among factors contributing to a slowdown in food production in relation to population in the 1990s Brown included cessation of growth of the world fish catch, an increasing scarcity of water for irrigation, and the failure of existing varieties of grain to use more fertilisers than the amounts already being applied. Elsewhere, 20 years ago, Brown (1978) was already drawing attention to and providing examples of the worldwide loss of cropland.

Bender and Smith (1997b) took a cautious view of prospects for the world food supply in the 21st century, comparing the concern of Brown with the confidence of the following World Bank forecast (D. O. Mitchell and M. D. Ingco, 1993): 'The world food situation has improved dramatically during the past 30 years and the prospects are very good that the 20-year period from 1990 to 2010 will see further gains... If Malthus is ultimately to be correct in his warning that population will outstrip food production, then at least we can say: "Malthus Must Wait".

As with so many other cases of speculation about the future, concern, complacency or confidence about the future of food production seem to some extent to reflect what the person speculating wants to happen, in order to prove themselves correct. The background of those expressing views also appears to affect their opinions, as already noted in Chapter 1. Bongaarts (1994) observes: 'How will the environment and humanity respond to this unprecedented growth [of population]? Expert opinion divides into two camps. Environmentalists and ecologists, whose views have widely been disseminated by the electronic and print media, regard the situation as a catastrophe in the making ... The optimists, on the other hand, comprising many economists, as well as some agricultural scientists, assert that the earth can readily produce more than enough food for the expected population in 2050.' The credibility gap may to some extent be attributed to the contrast between the more pragmatic view of the pessimists, expecting future organisational failures, military conflicts, droughts and other negative impacts on agriculture similar to those experienced in the past, and the more theoretical, idealistic view of the optimists, speculating about what could happen in a perfect world.

Whatever the experts forecast, in November 1996 the Food and Agriculture Organisation of the United Nations (FAO) organised a World Food Summit in Rome. It was attended by representatives from 194 countries, only 50 of them actually heads of state or government. At the summit it was resolved that the number of hungry people in the world, estimated to be some 840 million (14–15 per cent of the world's population in 1996), should be halved by 2015. Owen (1996) remarked: 'Officials at the FAO do not much like to be reminded of the last United Nations food summit 22 years ago (1974), when Henry Kissinger rose to his feet and vowed with a rhetorical flourish that world hunger would be eradicated "within ten years".'To digress from food, but to keep to Kissinger and forecasting, there is a story that Kissinger was asked what would have happened if Khrushchev had been assassinated in 1963 instead of Kennedy. After some thought he said: 'Onassis would not have married Mrs Khrushchev.' According to the FAO, in the late 1970s almost 700 million people, 16 per cent of the population of the world at that time, lived in absolute poverty in rural areas of developing countries, and were therefore exposed to high risk of malnutrition. It was assumed at the Summit referred to above that there would be a 70 per cent increase in population by 2050. Scommegna (1996) reports that the FAO has estimated that Africa will need to step up food production by 300 per cent, Latin America by 80 per cent, Asia by 69 per cent and North America by 30 per cent by that date.

In a United Nations (1962) study *Population and Food Supply* there is a familiar conclusion: 'Time is too precious to be wasted in futile arguments over what steps should be taken first to deal with the problem of population and food supply. Nothing less than an "all out" attack on all major aspects of the problem can bring success. To banish hunger and achieve a minimal diet for all people in the face of rapid population growth will at best take time. To check population growth in those countries where such is the desire of the people and their governments will also take time. And time is of the essence.'

In Chapter 3.1 it was stressed that it is not realistic to speculate about the future of any one aspect of the world without taking into account other aspects. It may be useful to think of a system, the elements of which make up a whole. In this chapter a number of the elements and variables most closely related to food production form a cluster. Beyond this cluster are other clusters of variables, which are discussed in Chapters 6-8. Although water supply is a crucial influence in many human activities it is discussed in this chapter together with bioclimatic resources, from which virtually all the world's food supply is derived. The availability of the following four natural resources is described in sections 5.2 and 5.3: fresh water, cultivable land, forest and woodland, and permanent pasture. Each of these natural resources has a number of uses and provides a number of products, most of which may be classed as food, energy and raw materials:

1. Water: land resources, industrial and domestic processes and uses, fishing (food, fertiliser), hydro-electric power, navigation

2. Cultivable land: food for humans, fodder for livestock, raw materials (e.g. cotton), fuel (limited)

3. Natural pasture: livestock (food, raw materials)

4. Forest: food (limited), fuelwood, raw materials for construction and industrial products (e.g. paper)

5.2 WATER RESOURCES AND SUPPLY

Concern and conflict over water resources are not new. With the growth of the world population and increasing per capita consumption of water, especially in the developed countries, however, there is a growing awareness of a global problem of availability of adequate water supply and of the particular features of water itself. The total amount of water in the world has remained virtually unchanged for thousands of years. Unlike fossil fuels and non-fuel minerals it is renewable, albeit fixed in quantity. Of all the water in the world, 97.3 per cent is in the ocean and adjoining seas, and is saline, some 1,350 million cubic kilometres. Of the remaining 2.7 per cent, most (29 million cubic kilometres) is in the form of ice in icecaps and glaciers, some 8.4 million cubic kilometres is under the ground, 0.2 million in lakes and rivers, 0.001 per cent in the atmosphere at any given time.

Water in the form of ice is almost all on the Antarctic continent and in Greenland, with much smaller quantities in glaciers on the land, or on the sea in pack ice in the Arctic Ocean and around Antarctica. Although water in the form of ice is of little immediate importance in terms of the world's water supply, the quantity is so great that if it all melted the level of the world's ocean surface would rise about 60 metres (see Peixoto and Ali Kettani (1973)). Even the melting of a modest amount of ice from the surface of the ice caps, and from land glaciers mostly in mountain areas, could produce a rise of sea level of 1-2 metres (see Chapter 10).

With regard to the total quantity of water in the world, only a tiny fraction is easily available for human consumption or for irrigation. Of the water that evaporates into the atmosphere from the surface of the oceans, and in smaller quantities from the surface of the land, 113,000 cubic kilometres falls on the land in the form of rain, snow or hail (referred to collectively as precipitation). It falls very unevenly, with some areas of desert having on average a few centimetres a year, other areas receiving a hundred times as much.

The precipitation that falls on a given region or country is described as endogenous. Some of it evaporates from the surface of the ground or from plants, while some sinks into the ground and some runs off in streams and rivers. In addition, some countries or regions receive exogenous water, carried from elsewhere by rivers over the surface or moved underground in ground water systems, referred to as aquifers, in the underlying rock where this is of porous material such as sandstone. In the 20th century much water has been extracted from wells in such aquifers even in areas in which precipitation is low, but the renewal rate of aquifers is very slow and supplies can quickly be depleted. Of the world's four hundred largest river systems, over three quarters are situated in more than one country. As, for example, with the Nile in Africa and the Amazon in South America, rivers transfer water from one country to another, often causing problems of supply and pollution as they cross international boundaries. Within the USA, individual states have fought and continue to litigate over water rights in the arid Southwest.

The amount of precipitation falling on land areas is highest in a zone either side of the equator, much lower in a zone extending either side of the tropics, high in mid-latitudes and low in the northern hemisphere around the Arctic Ocean, but regional and local exceptions are numerous. In terms of water supply, the effectiveness of a given amount of precipitation for agricultural purposes increases from the tropics to the poles as average temperature and therefore evaporation diminish.

The world's water is used for a large number of purposes, some more important than others. Conventionally water is measured in cubic kilometres for very large quantities, cubic metres for domestic consumption (there are 1 billion cubic metres in one cubic kilometre) and in litres for day-to-day use (there are 1000 litres in 1 cubic metre).

Agriculture

The irrigation of crops takes nearly 70 per cent of all the water used in the world, accounting for about 80 per cent of that used in Asia but only 30 per cent in Europe. In large areas of dry permanent pasture, water from wells sunk into aquifers may be needed to support livestock. About 270 million hectares of cultivated land, more than a sixth of the total cultivated area of the world, is irrigated, half of it in developing countries. Somewhere between 70 and 80 per cent of irrigation water is actually lost through evaporation or seepage into the ground without being used by crops.

Industry

Industry takes about 23 per cent of the water used and is the second largest user of water in the world, and in some developed countries is the largest user. Many branches of refining, processing and manufacturing require large quantities, for example, metallurgical, chemical and pulp and paper branches, oil refining, and for cooling in thermal electric power stations.

Domestic consumption

Domestic consumption accounts for about 8 per cent of all water used but the amount per capita varies enormously from one country to another. Each person needs a minimum of about 100 litres per day to have adequate amounts for drinking, cooking and washing, or 36-37 cubic metres per year (Falkenmark and Widstrand (1992)). Domestic supply falls far short of this level in many parts of the developing world.

Other uses of water

Navigation on the world's oceans, seas and inland waterways. The generation of hydro-electric power may conflict with the supply of water for irrigation at a local level since by definition the feeding of water to generators may lower the water below a level at which it could have been used to irrigate adjoining farmland. Sea water is also evaporated to leave deposits of salt (sodium chloride) in saltpans in the coastal areas of many countries.

One of the first comprehensive estimates of the distribution of world water availability was published in Barney (1982) and was based on data calculated by Soviet hydrologists. Those data have been simplified in Table 5.1 to show the broad distribution of water availability by major world regions. Column (1) shows the percentage of the total population of the world in each region, column (2) the percentage of the world's available water attributed to it. The index in column (3) is the percentage of water divided by the percentage of population multiplied by 100,

Table 5.1 The distribution of the world's water availability by major regions (world average index = 100)

	(1) *Population*[1]	*(2)* *Water*[2]	*(3)* *Index*[3]
Oceania	0.5	2.0	400
North America	5.2	11.7	225
Former USSR	5.2	10.6	204
Western Europe	6.9	4.6	67
Japan/S.Korea	3.1	1.1	35
Central Europe	2.4	0.7	29
Latin America	8.4	27.6	328
Africa S. of Sahara	10.0	14.9	149
Southeast Asia	8.4	10.2	121
China plus	22.3	9.7	43
South Asia	21.2	5.4	25
N. Africa/SW Asia	6.4	1.5	23

Based on Cole (1996), data from Barney (1982)

1 Regional percentage of world population
2 Regional percentage of world's available water
3 (2) ÷ (1) x 100

the mean for the world as a whole. The six developed and six developing regions are each ranked according to their scores in column (3).

Oceania emerges as the best endowed region of the twelve, but within Oceania, Papua-New Guinea and New Zealand have far more water per capita than Australia. Of the developing regions, Latin America is the most generously endowed, but most of the precipitation falls in the region of tropical rain forest where there are few people, while in dry or desert areas such as Northeast Brazil and the Pacific coastal desert of South America, water is in very short supply. At the other extreme, many European countries, together with Japan, while not desperately short of water, have problems of water supply, as do China, India and some other parts of southern and eastern Asia. North Africa and Southwest Asia, which consist mostly of the semi-desert or desert areas of the Sahara and Arabia are, however, the regions with the most serious water problems. Three rivers, the Nile in Africa and the Tigris and Euphrates in Southwest Asia, carry water through Egypt, Iraq and other countries and are vital for their water supply. In the former Soviet Union, the desert areas of the newly independent countries of Uzbekistan, Kazakhstan and Turkmenistan also depend heavily on rivers to supply water for agriculture.

The issue of water supply will be so crucial in the first half of the 21st century that it is worth showing a second assessment of the water resources of the world in relation to population. The version of Falkenmark and Widstrand (1992), shown in Table 5.2, has estimates for 1990 and 2025 and therefore shows the mounting pressure on water resources in developing regions due to population growth. The major regions differ from those used in Table 5.1, making exact comparison difficult, but there is broad agreement as to the order in which the regions come in water resources per capita. The disparity between Oceania on the one hand and North Africa/ Southwest Asia on the other hand differs for around 1990 in the two estimates. It is 400:23 or 17:1 in Table 5.1 but 74,480:1,200 (the average for the two regions) or 62:1 in Table 5.2, one of many possible ways in which different data sources give different figures for the same thing. The data in Table 5.2 show the effect of expected population growth between 1990 and 2025 on

Table 5.2 Population and water resources by major world regions

		Population (millions)		Water (billion cubic metres)	Water per person (cubic metres)	
		1990	2025		1990	2025
1	North Africa	140	280	85	610	310
2	Western Asia	132	286	253	1,920	880
3	Southern Asia	1,191	2,100	3,980	3,340	1,900
4	Africa S. of Sahara	492	1,276	3,575	7,270	2,800
5	Other Asia[1]	1,794	2,476	8,737	4,870	3,530
6	Europe[2]	509	542	2,321	4,560	4,280
7	C. America and Caribbean[3]	147	250	1,330	9,050	5,320
8	Former USSR	276	360	5,379	19,490	14,940
9	North America	281	344	4,384	15,600	12,740
10	South America	294	452	10,377	35,300	22,960
11	Oceania	27	41	2,011	74,480	49,050

Source: based on Falkenmark and Widstrand (1992)

Notes: 1   China, Japan and Southeast Asia
            2   Excluding former USSR countries
            3   Includes Mexico and Central America

per capita resources, particularly in all of Africa and in Southwest Asia, the regions in which the fastest population growth in the world is currently being experienced and where it seems likely to continue.

Since irrigation for agricultural purposes is by far the largest user of water in many countries Table 5.3 has been compiled to show the countries with the largest areas of irrigated land in the world. In China about half of the cultivated land is irrigated, in India almost a third. In several smaller countries the proportion is much higher, as for example in Egypt, where it is almost 100 per cent, and in the former Soviet Republic of Uzbekistan, where it is over 90 per cent. The world's twelve largest users of water for irrigation (in Table 5.3) account for 70 per cent of all water consumed for irrigation, while Asia uses about 64 per cent of the total.

Table 5.3 The twelve largest users of water for irrigation

		(1) Irrigated area (millions of sq km)	(2) Percentage of world total			(1) Irrigated area (millions of sq km)	(2) Percentage of world total
1	China	49.4	19.8	7	Russia	5.4	2.2
2	India	48.0	19.2	8	Thailand	4.8	1.9
3	USA	21.4	8.6	9	Turkey	4.2	1.7
4	Pakistan	17.2	6.9	10	Uzbekistan	4.0	1.6
5	Indonesia	7.3	2.9	11	Spain	3.7	1.5
6	Mexico	6.1	2.4	12	Egypt	3.5	1.4
					World	249.5	100.0

Source: *FAOPY* Vol 49

Some form of irrigation is practised in many countries of the world, but there is still the potential in many places both to make greater use of water from rivers, and to use the present supply more efficiently. The distribution of water to plants along ditches and furrows can be particularly wasteful, and the modern method of irrigating with sprinklers or by drip irrigation to individual plants is more efficient, albeit more costly to install and operate, than conventional systems.

The remaining natural resources of the world will be discussed in section 5.3 of this chapter and in Chapters 6 and 7. None of the world's main natural resources is distributed evenly in per capita terms among the countries of the world. There is however a crucial difference between water resources on the one hand and bioclimatic resources, fossil fuels and most non-fuel minerals on the other. In relation to its volume (or weight), water is very cheap at present, but costly to transport. Agricultural products, fossil fuels and non-fuel minerals, often with the help of weight and volume reduction at source thanks to processing and refining, can generally be transported, relatively, much more cheaply than fresh water, as the trade in such products as cereals, oil and iron ore shows. A comparison of the value of a cubic metre (1000 litres) of petrol and of water in the UK in 1997 was about £600 against £2; also the retail price of beer is about £2,000, milk about £500.

Most of the water used, apart from precipitation falling directly on plants, is moved some distance from where it falls to where it is consumed. Since the amount of water in the world is finite and fixed, any movement of water from one place to another is like a zero-sum game. For example, the technique of cloud seeding has been used with limited success to cause rain to fall on a given agricultural area, but somewhere else may be deprived of that rain. Similarly, if Ethiopia increased the amount of water it takes for irrigation from one of the headwaters of the Nile originating in its mountains, it would reduce the amount available in Sudan and Egypt, through which the river flows before reaching the Mediterranean Sea. The headwaters of the Tigris and Euphrates originate in Turkey, where new works have been installed to take more water from these rivers, thus reducing water available in other places downstream, mainly in Iraq and Syria.

Theoretically enough fresh water falls on the earth's land surface to satisfy the needs of a possible population of around 10 billion in the year 2050. Falkenmark and Widstrand (1992) estimate, however, that already in the early 1990s a third of the countries of the world had severe water problems. There is abundant fresh water, but much of it is too far from places that need it. For example, Alaska has a large amount of water but this water could only be transferred to the rest of the USA at great cost. The Congo basin in Africa has an abundance of water, but the cost of transporting it over a great distance to the Sahara Desert would be far too high for such a project to be initiated at present. Water, like electricity, is lost during 'transportation'.

Table 5.4 shows internal renewable water resources per capita in a selection of countries. The countries have been selected to show the extremes of availability as well as the situation in some of the largest countries of the world in population terms. The enormous disparity is shown by the fact that per capita Iceland has more than 6,000 times as much water available as Saudi Arabia. Among the selection of countries exemplifying very low per capita water resources, Hungary is the only country in which population is not growing fast.

In the view of the author, the evidence presented so far in this section points to a growing concern about water supply and the application of various measures to prevent water problems from getting worse. Water supply is likely to be a great problem particularly in a large number of developing countries in which population is expected to grow; greater use of irrigation would be an asset in the agricultural sector, industrialisation is proceeding, and United Nations

Table 5.4 Internal renewable water sources per capita in thousands of cubic metres per year, 1992

	Largest resources		*Selected large countries*		*Selected smallest resources*	
1	Iceland	645	Brazil	33.7	Algeria	0.7
2	Suriname	457	Russia	27.1	Hungary	0.6
3	Guyana	298	Indonesia	13.2	Uzbekistan	0.4
4	Papua-New Guinea	197	USA	9.7	Israel	0.3
5	Gabon	131	Japan	4.4	Jordan	0.2
6	New Zealand	115	China	2.4	Egypt	0.1
7	Canada	106	India	2.1	Saudi Arabia	0.1
8	Norway	95	UK	2.1	Libya	0.1

Source: *HDR 1996* (1996)

reports express the need for a decent minimum domestic supply. A number of strategies and tactics are possible, some appropriate or relevant in developed countries, some in developing ones.

It is possible to enhance the existing capacity of rivers and aquifers to transfer water over large distances by river diversions. A successful scheme was completed in the extreme southeast of Australia to divert the headwaters of the Snowy River through a tunnel into the Murray-Murrumbidgee basin. Very large scale schemes have been discussed elsewhere in the world, including proposed diversions southwards of rivers (currently flowing into the Arctic Ocean), into dry areas in the former Soviet Union , the NAWAPA project to transfer water from Alaska to California (see Micklin (1977)), and the diversion at some point or points along its course of water from China's largest river, the Chang Jiang, to dry lands to the north.

Such projects require much time and investment in the construction of dams, canals and pipelines before the water is moved. Large amounts of water leak from pipes even over short distances. Water evaporates from or seeps out of irrigation canals, as has occurred in the Karakum Canal, which runs through Turkmenistan (formerly in the USSR). Of the eight very generously endowed countries in Table 5.4, only Canada could pipe its surplus water to another country (the USA), although Norway seems set to supply fresh water to other countries bordering the North Sea by tanker, and experiments have already been carried out with giant water carrying containers (see Leake (1997b)). More locally, the movement of water by rail and road over more than very short distances is prohibitive and likely to be used only in emergencies.

More exotic ways of moving or producing fresh water include the towing of icebergs from Antarctica or the shores of Greenland to coastal sites in dry regions of the world, and the desalination of salt water in such arid coastal regions as the coastlands of Saudi Arabia and desert areas in California and Nevada, USA. There is a limit to the number of suitable icebergs, and the distribution of water from them once they reach their destination is complicated. The traditional method of extracting salt from sea water by evaporation in saltpans is simple, but the fresh water is therefore lost. A large amount of energy, presumably mainly from fossil fuels, is needed to produce the reverse effect, a modest amount of fresh water from sea water. Leake (1997a) points out a contradiction in the derivation of fresh water from salinated with reference to the plans of water companies in southeast England to set up desalination plants: 'The prospect of a string of energy-guzzling "water factories" around Britain's shores has appalled environmentalists. Matt Phillips, the water and wildlife campaigner for Friends of the Earth, said overproduction of global warming gases, such as carbon dioxide, had *caused* water shortages.'

Two other changes could influence water supply in the future. The lavish consumption of water in the developed countries for domestic purposes could be reduced by measures such as the development of machines that are more economical in their performance of household tasks, and flushing toilets that use less water. In the total water supply situation, however, such measures are 'drops in the ocean', critical only in very large urban areas such as New York. A more serious problem of domestic water supply and the removal of sewage concerns the large cities in developing countries. French and British firms have been prominent in winning water-supply and waste-treatment contracts in cities as far apart as Buenos Aires, Cairo, Bangkok and Manila (see Wright (1997)). The second change could affect agriculture in particular and water availability in general. A shift of a few hundred kilometres northwards or in some other direction of the world's climatic belts could bring considerable changes in temperature and/or precipitation over large areas. Prospects for various regions have been modelled and forecast (see e.g. Hulme and Barrow (1997)), but the whole thing has an element of luck in it, a kind of climatic lottery.

Hutchings (1997) reports: 'In June world leaders at the United Nations' Earth Summit II ... were told that unless urgent conservation action was taken in the developing world, wars over the world's dwindling water reserves would be likely in the next 10 years. The situation was so serious, they were told, that it threatened to put global food supplies in jeopardy, limit economic and social development, and trigger local and regional water crises. The latest UN report on freshwater supplies estimates that two-thirds of the world population will be affected by "severe water stress" by 2025.'

5.3 WORLD LAND USE

Less than 30 per cent of the earth's surface is land. If Antarctica and Greenland, land areas almost entirely covered by ice caps, are not counted, then little more than a quarter is land. In the *Production Yearbook (FAOPY)* of the Food and Agriculture Organisation of the United Nations, the land area, roughly 134 million square kilometres. (13,400 million hectares) is subdivided into five categories, three of which are used for cultivation and livestock raising or are forest covered. Table 5.5 shows a breakdown of the uses. Like so many other data sets with global totals, differences will be found between sources.

Table 5.5 World land use in the early 1990s

	Area (thousands of sq km)	Percentage of all surface	land only
Total earth's surface	509,920	100.0	
All sea	360,650	70.7	
All land	149,270	29.3	
Antarctica and Greenland	15,050	3.0	
All other land	134,220	26.3	100.0
Inland water	3,050	0.6	2.3
Arable and permanent crops	14,480	2.8	10.8
Permanent pasture	33,620	6.6	25.0
Forest and woodland	41,800	8.2	31.1
Other land	41,270	8.1	30.8

Source: Food and Agriculture Organisation *Production Yearbook 1994*

Worse, however, is the lack of consistency from country to country in the definition of uses, particularly of permanent pasture and of forest. Each of the five categories will now be discussed.

1. Inland water bodies (lakes and rivers) cover about 3 million square kilometres. Their exact extent is difficult to measure precisely at any given time because the levels of lakes may change, while new reservoirs appear from time to time in connection with hydro-electric projects and water supply. There are great contrasts in the proportion of total area occupied by inland waters, from 10 per cent in Finland and 7.6 per cent in Canada to zero in Saudi Arabia and in Libya.

2. Land described as 'other' consists mainly of natural environments with little or no vegetation such as hot deserts, high mountain areas and Arctic wastes. It also includes built-up areas, such as residential or industrial buildings and their surroundings, mines and quarries, and transportation links. Although man-made elements of the 'other land' category still only occupy a minute fraction of the total land area of the world, their presence, particularly that of roads and ribbon developments along them, breaks up the continuity of farmland and locally may affect agriculture adversely. The proportion of the category 'other land' varies greatly among countries accounting, for example, for 97 per cent of the area of the United Arab Emirates, almost all of it desert and contrasting with a mere 9 per cent in the former Czechoslovakia.

3. Forest and woodland consists of some vegetation still hardly modified by human activity, forest in which interference has taken place over the centuries through the felling of trees for fuel and construction materials, and areas that have been re-forested. Areas planted with specific tree crops, such as oil palm in the tropics and fruit orchards in cooler latitudes are counted as permanent crops, not as forest. Over 90 per cent of the area of Suriname (South America) is classed as forest, compared with less than 1 per cent in Libya.

4. Permanent pasture varies greatly in the value of production per unit of area. In many parts of the world, areas with a very sparse vegetation, supporting only a very low density of livestock, are classed as pasture, including, for example, much of the Sahara Desert, the interior of Australia and the reindeer herding lands around the Arctic Ocean in the Nordic countries of Europe and in Russia. More locally, permanent pastures and meadows support comparatively high densities of livestock. There remains a 'grey' area in which trees and bushes occur sporadically in areas of grassland, referred to as savanna or scrub, but in some places regarded as forest, in others as pasture. Almost 80 per cent of the area of Mongolia is classed as permanent pasture, contrasting with a mere 2 per cent in Japan.

5. Virtually all the crops grown in the world come from no more than 2.8 per cent of the total surface of the earth, or less than 11 per cent of the earth's land surface. Almost 100 million hectares out of 1,450 million of land under crops in the early 1990s was classed as permanent crops (trees, bushes) as opposed to field crops (e.g. cereals, sugar cane) and fallow, which make up the remainder. Part of the area under field crops is used to produce fodder for livestock and some is used to produce raw materials (e.g. cotton, sunflower oil), but most is for consumption by humans after appropriate processing.

Arable and permanent crops

Around 1959 the total area in the world under arable and permanent crops was about 1,310 million hectares. By 1970 it had risen to about 1,460 million, since which time it has not changed markedly. A source of possible confusion should be noted here. The area sown and harvested in the world is about 100 million hectares larger than the arable area because, mainly in southern and eastern Asia, double and even triple cropping can be practised thanks to high temperatures, an all-year growing season, and abundant rain or irrigation water.

Figure 5.1 shows the total area of arable and permanent crops and the per capita amount at ten year intervals from 1950 to 1990 and projections to 2050. The left hand part of the graph shows the modest rise in total amount (t) to 1970 and little change after that, but the population of the world more than doubled during 1950-90, from 2,520 million to 5,300 million. As a result, the area of arable and permanent crops per capita in the world as a whole dropped from 0.52 hectares in 1950 to 0.27 in 1990. In *The Global 2000*, Barney (1982) projected 0.32 for 1985 against the actual amount of 0.30 for that year, and 0.25 for the year 2000 compared with Projection Cp in Figure 5.1 of 0.23 per capita in that year.

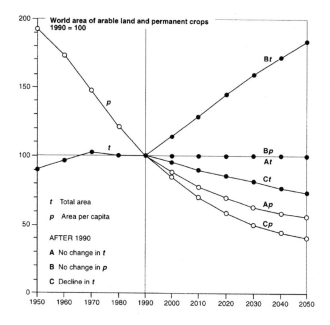

Figure 5.1 The area of arable land and permanent crops in the world as a whole, 1950-2050. See text for explanation. ● = total amount or total amount and per capita where ● and ○ coincide; ○ = per capita.

- In Projection A it is assumed that there will be no change after 1990 in the area of arable and permanent crops in the world. Straight lines rarely occur in the real economic world, but to put plausible fluctuations on the At line would give an unjustified impression of accuracy. The stark prospect is that whereas in 1950 there was an average 0.52 of a hectare to support each person, in 2050 there would be only 0.15.

- Projection B shows what would have to happen between 1990 and 2050 to achieve the goal of maintaining the 1990 level of about 0.27 of a hectare per person of arable and permanent crops (see line Bp). The total area (see line Bt) would have to increase from 1,450 million hectares to 2,670 million, an increase of over 80 per cent. The extra area under crops would have to be taken from land under forest and/or permanent pasture and/or land with no bioclimatic use at present. It seems optimistic to assume that much of the land not already under cultivation in the world is of suitable quality to be converted to cropland, at least without costly reclamation work.

• Projection C shows what would happen if for a number of possible reasons the area under arable and permanent crops diminishes at the rate of 5 per cent every 10 years between 1990 and 2050 (C*t*). Reasons for the loss of cropland could include the spread of the built-up area, loss of land through soil erosion, desertification or salinisation, set aside policies in the developed countries, and neglect of the agricultural sector, for example, in Russia.

The three possible futures discussed above do not take into account a number of facts about the world's arable and permanent crops, two of which are noted here. Firstly, even before chemical fertilisers and other modern means of production for increasing yields are applied, some areas are much more productive than others on account of differences in the inherent fertility of the soil and in moisture (rain, irrigation) and thermal resources (accumulated temperature). Secondly, as can be seen in Table 5.6, the amount of land under arable and permanent crops available per person in the total population varies enormously among the major regions of the world, which implies that shortage of land for cultivation is and will continue to be a problem in some regions but not in others.

Since the area of the earth's land surface is known and is unlikely to change more than minutely, if at all, between 1990 and 2050, it is obvious that any gain in the area under one use would have to be at the expense of another use or of the unused portion. The situation is shown diagrammatically in Figure 5.2. Projection B in Figure 5.1 requires a large increase in the area of cropland in the world. As noted above, some of that increase, if it takes place, is likely to be at the expense of the forest and woodland area. This use will be examined next.

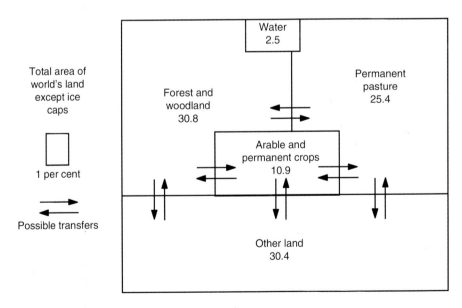

Figure 5.2 Competition for a finite land area. The diagram shows the proportion of the world's land area other than that covered by ice used for different purposes or not used at all. Possible changes of use are indicated by arrows, but since the total is finite, a gain in area by one use must be at the expense of one or more of the other uses. Here, potentially, is a case of oversubscription or over-booking, a zero-sum game in game theory.

Table 5.6 Cropland in millions of hectares and hectares per capita

	Cropland (millions of hectares)	1995 Population (millions)	Cropland per capita (hectares)	2025 Population (millions)	Cropland per capita (hectares)	2050 Population (millions)	Cropland per capita (hectares)
Europe	141.0	515	0.27	520	0.27	460	0.31
Russia	176.8	214	0.83	223	0.79	230	0.77
Japan	6.5	170	0.04	177	0.04	160	0.04
North America	283.5	321	0.88	411	0.69	470	0.60
Latin America	140.9	481	0.29	678	0.21	800	0.18
Africa S. of Sahara	147.2	558	0.26	1,190	0.12	2,190	0.07
N. Africa, SW Asia	83.7	330	0.25	600	0.14	810	0.10
South C. Asia	279.7	1,355	0.21	2,105	0.13	2,360	0.12
Southeast Asia	85.9	485	0.18	727	0.12	810	0.11
China	101.4	1,272	0.08	1,562	0.06	1,590	0.06
Developed	607.8	1,220	0.50	1,331	0.46	1,320	0.46
Developing	838.8	4,481	0.19	6,862	0.12	8,560	0.10
World	1,446.6	5,701	0.25	8,193	0.18	9,880	0.15

Table 5.7 The possible future availability of arable and permanent crops in hectares per inhabitant by major world regions.

	1995	*2025*	*2050*
Former USSR	0.83	0.79	0.77
North America-Oceania	0.88	0.69	0.60
ALL DEVELOPED	0.50	0.46	0.46
Europe	0.27	0.27	0.31
Latin America	0.29	0.21	0.18
WORLD AVERAGE	0.25	0.18	0.15
South Central Asia	0.21	0.13	0.12
Southeast Asia	0.18	0.12	0.11
N. Africa-SW Asia	0.25	0.14	0.10
ALL DEVELOPING	0.19	0.12	0.10
Africa S. of Sahara	0.26	0.12	0.07
China	0.08	0.06	0.06
Japan-S. Korea	0.04	0.04	0.04

The countries are ranked in descending order of expected land availability per person in 2050
Source: author's estimates

Forest and Woodland

The *Production Yearbooks* of the Food and Agriculture Organisation have contained data since the Second World War on the area of forest in most countries of the world, but much of the data consists of rough estimates. Abrupt changes due to re-definition are common, making the whole picture unsatisfactory. Nevertheless, the broad evidence is that there has been little change in the area between 1950, when there were 3,900 million hectares of forest in the world, and 1990, when there were 4,030 million hectares. By contrast the population of the world doubled during that time. In 1950 there were on average 1.55 hectares of forest per person, in 1990 only 0.76. Three alternative projections for the area of forest are shown in Figure 5.3.

- In Projection A little change occurs in the area of forest in the world during 1990-2050 (A*t*). Given the expected increase in the population of the world, however, the area of forest per person would decline from 0.76 hectares in 1990 to 0.41 in 2050 (A*p*).

- Projection B shows what would happen between 1990 and 2050 if the average per capita area of forest for the world remains at 0.76 hectares in the latter year, as it was in 1990. An increase of over 85 per cent would be needed in the area of forest in the world, an increase from 4,030 million hectares in 1990 to about 7,500 million in 2050. The actual cost and logistics of planting enough trees that would grow into something worthy of being described as forest is daunting. More importantly, the forested area of the earth's land surface would have to increase from about 31 per cent in 1990 to more than 55 per cent in 2050. The projections for cropland show that very little could be spared from this use. The alternatives are to grow trees in areas of permanent pasture or of waste, neither of which is likely to be suitable except locally, even with great outlays on the preparation of land for tree growth.

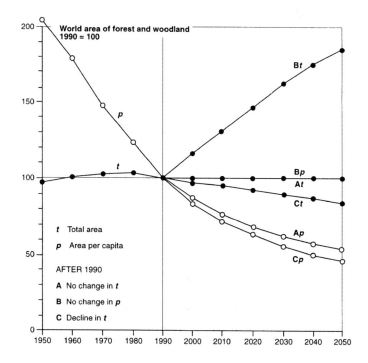

Figure 5.3 The area of forest and woodland in the world as a whole, 1950-2050. ● = total amount or total amount and per capita where ● and ○ coincide; ○ = per capita.

Ironically, some areas that are now permanent pasture or waste were once forested and have been degraded. The idea that vegetation can change climate was behind the planting of trees in large areas of dry steppe and semi-desert in the USSR in the 1950s, one of many 'white elephant' campaigns more characteristic of state capitalism than private capitalism. Many of the trees planted failed to grow.

- Projection C is linked to Projection B for cropland in Figure 5.1. It is assumed that two per cent of the area of forest in the world is lost every decade between 1990 and 2050, 600 million hectares altogether, about half of the area by which the cropland in Projection B in Figure 5.1 would have to increase in order to maintain the 1990 per capita level of cropland for the following sixty years.

According to the United Nations *Human Development Report 1996*, in 1993 some 31.3 per cent of the world's land area was forested. In the industrial countries the percentage was 35.1, in the developing countries 28.7. Given these differences and also the big differences in total population, the industrial countries have about six times as much forest per capita as the developing countries. The annual rate of forest clearance averaged 1.1 per cent during 1980-89 in the developing countries whereas there was little change in the industrial countries, thanks to reforestation.

The annual percentage rate of deforestation (1980-89) varied greatly among developing countries, ranging from over 5 per cent in Ivory Coast (West Africa) to very little change in Papua-New Guinea, Bolivia and Gabon. Among the largest developing countries, India was losing 2.3 per cent of its forest a year, Indonesia 0.8 per cent and Brazil 0.7 per cent. In China reforestation was apparently roughly in step with deforestation. In most industrial countries the forest area was roughly stable (Canada, Europe, the former USSR, Australia) but in the USA and Japan deforestation exceeded reforestation (Population Reference Bureau (1997)). Ellis (1988) gives a vivid account of changes in Rondônia, one of the Amazonian states of Brazil, as settlers move into the rain forest environment.

Permanent pasture

No attempt has been made to project the area of permanent pasture into the next century. Some of the 'other land' may be redefined as permanent pasture either thanks to improvements, especially in water supply for livestock, or through political decisions aimed at giving the impression or reassurance that conditions have somehow improved when in reality they have not. Figure 5.4 shows that there was apparently a sharp increase in permanent pasture during 1960-1965 but after that only a gradual increase. In 1950 the total area was 2,370 million hectares, in 1990 it had risen to 3,360 million hectares, 25 per cent of the land area of the world excluding Antarctica and Greenland. In spite of the increase in total area during 1950-1990, the average area of permanent pasture per capita worldwide dropped from 0.94 hectares to 0.63 hectares on account of the increase in population of over 100 per cent.

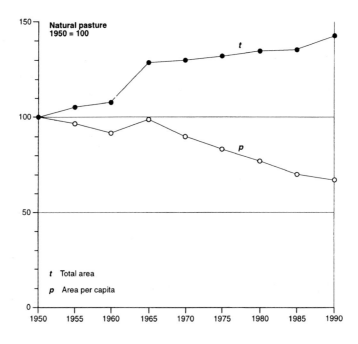

Figure 5.4 Natural pasture in the world as a whole, 1950-1990. ● = total amount or total amount and per capita where ● and ○ coincide; ○ = per capita.

In view of the expected large growth of world population between the 1990s and 2050 it is reasonable to expect that more cultivated land will be needed, especially in many parts of the developing world, even if crop yields can be raised. At the same time, in view of the value of forests, both as a source of products and as a means of keeping carbon dioxide from the atmosphere, it is desirable that the present extent of forest should at least be retained, if not expanded. The total land area is fixed, and any gain by one use of land, such as an increase in cultivated land from 11 to 15 per cent, or of built-up land (in the broad sense) from 1 to 2 per cent would mean a reduction in other uses. The use of the world's land surface is potentially oversubscribed (see Figure 5.2).

5.4   CROPS, LIVESTOCK AND FISHING

Almost all the food consumed by humans, numerous raw materials, and a small quantity of fuel and of energy (work animals) are provided by cultivation, livestock raising and fishing. These bioclimatic products are considered together in this section. Changes in total and per capita production will be traced from 1950 to 1990 and projected to 2050. In section 5.5 the means by which production has increased since the Second World War will be studied.

Cereals

In the early 1990s, more than half of the area of the world devoted to the cultivation of field crops was used to grow cereals. Space does not allow speculation about the possible mix of different crops in 2050. For simplicity, therefore, the performance and prospect of cereal cultivation is taken to represent all arable farming. Between 1950 and 1990 the world production of cereals increased almost three times, from 686 million tonnes in 1950 to 1,970 million in 1990 (see *t* in Figure 5.5a). As a result, in per capita terms the level rose from 272 kilograms in 1950 to 345 kilograms in 1990. It should be appreciated, however, that a considerable quantity of cereals, especially grain maize, is fed to livestock, not directly to humans.

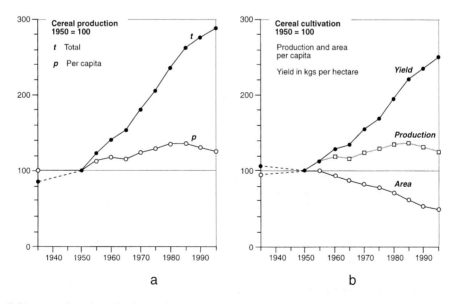

Figure 5.5   a   Cereal production in the world as a whole, 1935-1995. ● = total; ○ = per capita.
            b   Cereal yield, area and production per capita, 1935-1995

The area under cereals increased from 500 million hectares in 1935 to 600 million in 1950, and peaked at 740 million around 1975. Since then it has fallen to about 685 million in 1995. Even during 1959-75, therefore, most of the increase in cereal production was achieved through higher yields. Since 1975 the area under cereals has gradually diminished, while world population has continued to grow.

Figure 5.5a shows the growth of cereal production from 1935 to 1995 in relation to 1950=100. Since about 1985 there has been a slight decline in per capita production. Figure 5.5b shows that per capita production was about 15 per cent higher in 1995 than in 1950 but the per capita area under cereals was only about half as great in 1995 as in 1950. Most of the increase in production came from an increase in yield which, in kilograms per hectare, has risen from 1,140 in 1950 to 2,850 in 1995. There are however very great differences in yield between regions of the world. For example, the average in kilograms per hectare for 1992-94 was only 1,160 for the whole of Africa, 2,480 for South America, but 5,590 for Japan and 6,520 for France. Yields depend on a number of factors, including weather and climate, inherent soil fertility, the type of cereal grown and the application of fertilisers and other means of production of the crops.

In theory there is scope for greatly increasing cereal production if the world average could be raised to the level achieved in Northwest Europe or Japan. In practice such a view is simplistic, at least in the short term, while over the next few decades the enormous amount of fertilisers needed would have to be related to the reserves and the production of the main fertiliser minerals. There are several basic types of cereal, each cultivated within the constraints set by particular environmental conditions. For convenience the total production is plotted in Figure 5.6 to show three alternative futures. The left hand part of the graph shows the large increase in total production (*t*) between 1950 and 1990 (=100) and the accompanying more limited increase in per capita production.

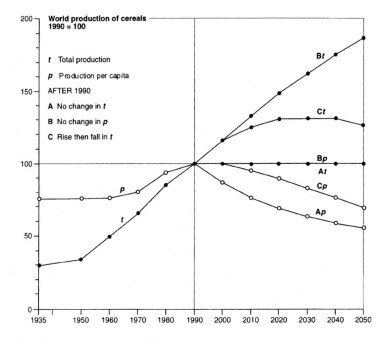

Figure 5.6 World production of cereals 1935-2050.

- In Projection A it is assumed that no further increase is achieved in production (At). Per capita production therefore declines so that by 2050 it is little more than half what it was in 1990 (Ap). Such a future would bring shortages of cereals in many parts of the world, unless other sectors of agriculture could compensate.

- Projection B shows the increase in production (Bt) that would be needed merely to keep world per capita production of cereals (Bp) at the 1990 level for the following sixty years.

- Projection C comes closest to the author's own expectation for the future, given the growing constraints on the availability of arable land, diminishing returns on the application of fertilisers, environmental protection, and the technical and political difficulties of achieving a sudden increase in yields in many developing countries. The following changes are assumed each decade: 1990-2000-2010, 8 per cent increase; 2010-2020, 4 per cent increase; 2020-2030-2040 no change; 2040-2050 a 4 per cent drop. In this projection, therefore, the production of cereals per capita would be reduced in 2050 to about two thirds what it was in 1990. Some of the reduction could be compensated for by reducing the amount of cereals used to raise livestock, whether for the production of meat and dairy products in developed countries, or as work animals in developing ones.

Livestock

The United Nations publishes data for six types of livestock. For comparative purposes these have been weighted so that horses and cows are each equal to 1 unit, mules and asses to ½ a unit, pigs and sheep to ⅙ of a unit. The size and 'productivity' or 'yield' of animals, especially in developed countries, has increased considerably since the 1940s so strictly allowance for this change should be made in the trend and possible futures discussed below.

In 1950 the total number of livestock units in the world was 923 million, giving 366 units per 1,000 people. A peak of about 430 units per 1,000 people was reached around 1955, after which the number declined to 320 in 1990, when there were about 1,700 million livestock units in the world. The situation is shown graphically on the left hand side of Figure 5.7, with 1990=100. Three alternative projections are shown from 1990 to 2050.

- In Projection A it is assumed that there is no change in the total number of livestock units (At) in the world between 1990 and 2050. On account of population growth, the per capita number (Ap) is almost halved by 2050.

- Projection B shows the extent to which the total (Bt) needs to grow in order to maintain the 1990 per capita level (Bp) of livestock units up to 2050. This projection would put great pressure on arable production and at the same time would require a considerable improvement in the yield per unit of area of the permanent pasture of the world.

- Projection C roughly continues the trend from 1950 to 1990. There is a small increase of 5 per cent in the total number of livestock units from 1990 to 2000, no change from 2000 to 2010 and a drop of 5 per cent per decade after that. The number of livestock units per thousand population drops drastically from 320 in 1990 to 148 in 2050, the latter little over one third of the peak level in the late 1950s of about 430. This projection shows what could lie ahead unless there are drastic changes in the livestock industry. A gradual decline in the production/consumption of meat and dairy products in the developed countries could be

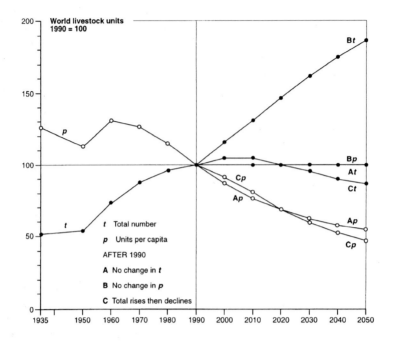

Figure 5.7 World livestock units, 1935-2050.

expected. The use of work animals for transport, ploughing and other duties would have to be reduced in developing countries, accompanied by an increase in the use of mechanisation, itself a potential cause of job losses in the agricultural sector and a certain cause of considerable increase in fuel consumption for the machines

Life for most people was difficult in Stalin's Soviet Union. Soviet statistics show, however, that horses had a much worse time. The subject of work animals does not have a prominent place in the study of agricultural performance and prospects, so the Soviet experience is worth noting. The population of horses in the boundaries of post-1945 USSR dropped from over 38 million in 1916 to 6 million in the late 1970s, presumably releasing considerable quantities of fodder for other livestock (*NkhSSSR v 1958 godu* and *NkhSSSR 1922-1982*). During the process of collectivisation between 1928 and 1935, the total number of horses dropped from 36 million to 15 million largely, presumably, because many were eaten during famines, but also as part of the plan to mechanise agriculture. Between 1941 and 1946 the number again fell, from 21 million to less than 11 million, the result of the German invasion.

Fishing

The fishing industry has been a major source of food and other products for some countries of the world, and is widely assumed to have a great future potential. Compared with the land, however, the sea offers only a very limited 'pasture', and in most areas sustains a low density of 'fishstock'. Like hunting, fishing remains largely a gathering of wild species, in spite of the development of fish farming. Between 1930 and 1990 the world fish catch has increased about ten times as fishing vessels and equipment have grown in sophistication. Many countries have expanded their fishing fleets and extended their fishing grounds, sometimes reaching places far from their own parts of the world. At the same time, concern over the intensity of fishing has grown, especially since the sudden collapse of the large Peruvian fishing industry in the early 1970s (see Figure 3.6). Stocks of certain species of fish are being depleted as excessive quantities of young fish are caught and sustainability is not maintained.

In 1939 the world fish catch was about 10 million tonnes, compared with about 100 million tonnes in 1990 (see *t* in Figure 5.8). During that time the per capita catch increased from 4.6 kilograms to 18.6 (see *p*). Three alternative futures for the fish catch are shown in Figure 5.8, related to the index of 100 for 1990.

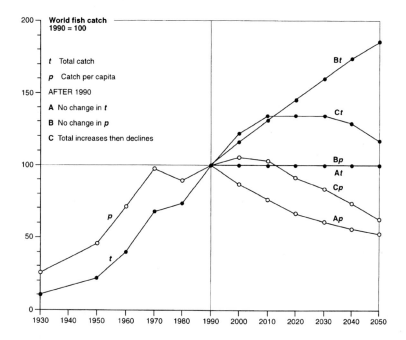

Figure 5.8 World fish catch 1930-2050.

- Projection A shows a future in which the total fish catch (A*t*)remains unchanged between 1990 and 2050. The per capita catch (A*p*) drops almost to half during that time.

- In Projection B it is assumed that the per capita fish catch (B*p*) remains the same and the total catch therefore rises (B*t*). While B*t* roughly continues the trend of 1950-1990 (*t*), there is now a consensus that some sea and ocean areas are already being overfished, while the limit has been reached in others. The oceans off Antarctica are probably the most extensive area still capable of yielding larger catches, although the logistics involved in doing so are considerable. In one of many publications on the prospects for the world fishing industry Safina (1995) argues that: 'Wild fish cannot survive the onslaught of modern industrial fishing. The collapse of fisheries in many regions shows the danger plainly' and see also Parfit (1995). More than two decades ago Idyll (1973) described the collapse of the anchovy fishing industry of Peru around 1970. The causes were a periodic ecological disturbance and heavy fishing (see Figure 3.6).

• Projection C shows an increase in total fish catch for about two decades after 1990 then a levelling out for about two decades, followed by a gradual decline. The increase 1990-2000 is 22 per cent, that between 2000 and 2010 is 11 per cent. During 2030-40 there is a 5 per cent decline, during 2040-50 a 10 per cent decline. The per capita level in 2050 is less than two thirds that of 1990.

It is of course a matter of speculation as to how the production of cereals and other crops, livestock farming and fishing will change in the next fifty years. The expected 86 per cent increase in the population of the world between the late 1990s and 2050 will no doubt somehow be fed, but with difficulty, possibly with a commitment from developed countries with a comparatively generous endowment of cultivated land and good pasture to supply areas of the present developing countries unable to cope with population growth. In 2050, the expected per capita arable land gap between developed and developing contries of 0.46 and 0.10 hectares per person (see Table 5.6) will be discussed further in Chapter 9.

5.5   THE USE OF FERTILISERS

One of the outstanding changes in the second half of the 20th century in the agricultural sector of the developed countries, and to a lesser extent of the developing countries, has been the enormous increase in the production and use of chemical fertilisers and other means of increasing yields. The combined weight of nitrate, phosphate and potash fertilisers produced worlwide (*t* in Figure 5.9) rose from 10 million tonnes in 1940 to 13 million in 1950 and to over 150 million in 1990 (*UNSYB*). The absolute increase was parallelled by more than a fivefold per capita increase (*p*). As might be expected the level of application of fertilisers per unit of cultivated area is far higher in most developed countries than in most developing ones. For simplicity, the use of fertilisers is assumed in this section to represent all means of increasing yields in agriculture, including the contribution of, for example, pesticides and fungicides, and improvements in strains of plant.

The world consumption of three main types of fertiliser, nitrogenous, phosphate and potash is shown in Figure 5.9 in relation to the 1990 total of 100 units, 151 million tonnes. The sharp rise in the production of fertilisers up to 1990 is shown on the left hand side of the graph and the corresponding per capita increase can also be seen. Three projections are made from 1990 to 2050. For simplicity, production and consumption are taken to be the same quantity.

• Projection A shows in A*t* a situation in which total fertiliser production is assumed to level out after 1990. Per capita production (A*p*) would decline to a little more than half by 2050.

• Projection B shows in B*t* the increase in total production needed to keep per capita production (B*p*) uniform after 1990.

• Projection C shows in C*t* a threefold increase in total fertiliser production from about 150 million tonnes in 1990 to 450 million tonnes in 2050. Per capita production would then rise by 60 per cent between 1990 and 2050, enough to allow for a considerable increase in the use of fertilisers in developing countries, assuming little change in their application in the developed ones.

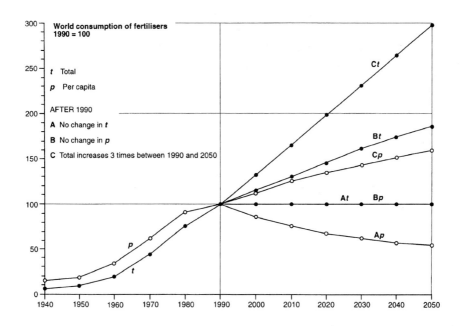

Figure 5.9 World consumption of fertilisers, 1940-2050.

Whether the reserves of phosphate and potash minerals can sustain such a big increase in production as far ahead as 2050 is dubious. Unlike phosphate and potash fertilisers, nitrogen-based fertiliser is produced from the synthesis of ammonia, the basic ingredient of which is nitrogen; it can be obtained from the atmosphere, where it is plentiful (see Smil (1997)). The heavy use of fertilisers would be expected to continue beyond 2050. Again, such intensive use of chemical fertilisers for so long could cause environmental problems, as for example with the heavy use of nitrate fertilisers in northern France. Smil (1997) points out: 'Massive introduction of reactive nitrogen into soils and waters has deleterious consequences for the environment. Problems range from local health to global changes and, quite literally, extend from deep underground to high in the stratosphere.'

Although the application of appropriate amounts of chemical fertiliser to crops growing in areas with reasonably good bioclimatic conditions does influence yields, it would be simplistic to assume a very high correlation. The data in Table 5.8 shows the level of application of fertiliser and of wheat yields in selected developed and developing countries. The Netherlands is one of the countries with the highest application of fertiliser per hectare in the world, and achieves wheat yields of around 8,000 kilograms per hectare which, however, the UK approaches while using half as much fertiliser.

Unfortunately the comparability of yields in all the three-year averages for the early 1990s is affected by at least two factors. First, although all the countries produce wheat, it is not possible to say how much of the fertiliser is actually applied to the area under wheat. Again, fertiliser is not used to any great extent in Argentina, Algeria or Morocco but the bioclimatic conditions under which wheat is grown in Argentina are on average much more favourable than those under which it is grown in Northwest Africa. In the cases of Canada and Australia the cultivated area per inhabitant is very large by world standards and there is less urgency to increase yields than in the European Union, China or India. Again, rice is the principal cereal

Table 5.8 The use of fertilisers and wheat yields in selected countries, early 1990s

| | | *Fertiliser* | *Wheat* | | | *Fertiliser* | *Wheat* |
		(kilograms per hectares)				*(kilograms per hectare)*	
1	UK	323	7,510	8	Russia	77	1,490
2	France	251	6,520	9	Iran	69	1,520
3	Italy	207	3,490	10	India	57	2,390
4	China	181	3,500	11	Brazil	57	1,500
5	USA	102	2,580	12	Canada	46	2,200
6	Spain	101	2,190	13	Morocco	35	1,060
				14	Australia	25	1,590
	WORLD average	95	2,470	15	Algeria	13	880
				16	Ethiopia	8	1,270
7	Turkey	78	2,010	17	Argentina	6	2,050

Sources: *FAOPY, UNSYB*

grown in both China and India, with wheat mainly grown in drier areas in which conditions do not favour or allow the growing of rice.

Smil (1997) points out that even in areas of cultivation with very favourable soil, moisture and temperature conditions, until the use of chemical fertilisers, only about five people could be supported per hectare of cultivated land before the 20th century in China, Japan and Northwest Europe. At present there are about four people supported per hectare of cultivated land worldwide, but by 2050 there could be seven. World agriculture is increasingly dependent on chemical fertilisers, whatever the problems of increasing supply and environmental damage. Between 1950 and 1990 the total amount of nitrogen fertiliser consumed in the world rose from about 5 million tonnes a year to almost 80 million.

Hornsby (1997b) notes that incentives to farmers in the European Union to convert to organic methods are now generous, but prices of products are higher than when chemical fertilisers are used. Because world food production has kept up with population growth in the second half of the 20th century that does not mean that the process can be repeated in the next five decades. Organic farming may be more friendly in environmental terms but could not support the present population of the world, given the constraints faced by traditional farmers on the amount of crop residues, and animal and human wastes available to restore nitrogen to the soil.

Attention has been drawn to regional differences in environmental conditions for agriculture as well as different levels of use of fertilisers in order to raise and question a rather naïve view of world agriculture. It is argued that sooner or later everywhere or at least in many areas yields could be raised to the level currently achieved in the countries with the highest yields. If world wheat yields could be raised to levels achieved in Northwest Europe, rice yields to those achieved in Japan and maize yields to the US level then, assuming comparable increases in other crops, a world population of 10 billion could easily be provided with enough food. By then, however, the great disparity expected in the amount of cultivated land per inhabitant between the developed and developing countries would be presenting a massive problem of distribution, a problem that already exists in the 1990s. From time to time food may be given to countries or regions by world bodies or by individual rich countries to provide famine relief, but it is considered that regular shipments of free food supplies to poor agricultural areas would undermine attempts to improve agricultural practices and yields, leaving many people living off food charity.

5.6   MECHANISATION IN AGRICULTURE

During the 20th century the use of farm machinery, like the use of chemical fertilisers and other means of increasing yields, has expanded enormously. One of the main consequences of mechanisation has been a great reduction in the labour force needed to farm a given area of land in some parts of the world. The use of mechanisation has also allowed the cultivation of some areas not hitherto used, but is of little use in other areas, such as terraced hillsides, still cultivated by hand or with the help of work animals. With deeper ploughing possible by machines, some increase in yields can be credited to mechanisation. Much of the increase in yields noted in the previous section has resulted, however, from the great increase in the use of fertilisers and other means of production, such as pesticides and the development of new strains of plant that are able, for example, to mature more quickly in areas with a short growing season.

For simplicity tractors have been taken to represent all forms of the mechanisation of agriculture. Tractors themselves vary in size, capacity and intensity of use from region to region, however, which makes comparisons between regions only approximate. Before the Second World War, the mechanisation of agriculture was largely restricted to North America, Australia and Western Europe, and to a lesser extent the USSR. In 1950 there were about 6 million tractors in use in the world, but between then and 1990 there was a steady increase to bring the total number to about 26 million by 1990. In view of the growth of population, however, the number per 1,000 total world population only doubled, from 2.4 to 4.9. By the 1990s there was roughly one tractor per person economically active in farming in North America, Australia and much of Europe. In contrast, in most developing countries there was still very little mechanisation in the agricultural sector. In Figure 5.10, the number of tractors is considered in relation to total population to allow a comparison with similar trends and projections in other activities in Chapters 5-8. On the graph 1990=100 and the fourfold increase in the total number of tractors (t) between 1950 and 1990 can be seen alongside the doubling in per capita terms (p).

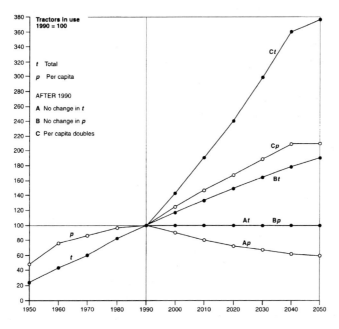

Figure 5.10 Tractors in use in the world, 1950-2050. ● = total amount or total amount and per capita where ● and ○ coincide; ○ = per capita.

- Projection A shows what would happen after 1990 as saturation in the developed world is reached and there is no increase in the use of tractors in the developing world (At). The number of tractors per capita (Ap) would drop almost to half by 2050. Such a prospect would be possible if the total number of people working in the agricultural sector does not diminish and the area cultivated does not change.

- In Projection B it is assumed that the per capita level (Bp) remains the same. In such a situation the total number of tractors in use (Bt) would have to increase by more than 80 per cent. Assuming little change occurs in the total number of tractors used in the developed countries, there would be scope for further mechanisation in some parts of the developing world.

- Projection C is wildly extravagant in the number of tractors in use, adequate to mechanise agriculture in developing countries broadly to the level achieved in developed ones around 1990. The area under line t (before 1990) is however less than a third of the area under line Ct between 1990 and 2030. In terms of 'tractor-years' there would be three times as much activity during 1990-2030 as during 1950-1990. Among others, two consequences of note would be the great increase in the consumption of tractor fuel and the vast number of jobs that would be lost in the agricultural sector of the developing countries. The second issue is discussed in the next section.

5.7   THE AGRICULTURAL WORKFORCE

Until the 19th century the overwhelming proportion of the economically active population in almost every country of the world was engaged in agriculture and associated activities, notably forestry and fishing (see Bairoch *et al.*).   Even among the present developed countries of the world, as recently as 1850 over half of the economically active population of France and of the USA worked in agriculture, about 75 per cent in Japan. Britain, however, only had 25 per cent of its work force in agriculture early in the 19th century.

In the 20th century, and especially since the 1940s, the proportion of the economically active population accounted for by agriculture has been diminishing almost everywhere in the world. In most parts of the developing world, however, the absolute number has been increasing in spite of the relative decline. In many countries it has been increasing more quickly than the area cultivated. There has therefore been a marked increase in the number of people working a given area of land, what can be termed the density of labour to agricultural land. Before the situation is described and the implications for the world in the first half of the 21st century are assessed, some problems regarding the availability of data on the subject must be noted.

1.   Almost all of the 'agricultural' population of the world is employed in the cultivation of arable and permanent crops or in the raising of livestock, only a very small number in forestry and fishing. In some countries permanent pasture is very extensive (e.g. Australia), in some it is virtually non-existent (e.g. Egypt). For simplicity, it is assumed in this section that a given area of permanent pasture employs only a tenth as many people as the same area of cultivated land.

2.   The main source of data in this section has been the Yearbooks of the Food and Agriculture Organization of the United Nations (FAO). A revision of the data for employment in agriculture in the 1995 Yearbook, taken back to 1990, has produced some potential confusion

resulting from a considerable increase in numbers compared with those given in the 1994 Yearbook. Thus the 1994 Yearbook gives a world total of 1,127 million people engaged in agriculture in 1994, whereas the 1995 Yearbook gives 1,287 million for the same year, a difference of 160 million, an 'increase' of 11.4 per cent. The new estimates for 1995, 'backdated' to 1990, show differences in the degree of revision among developing regions and countries. The unfortunate result of the new calculations is that the new estimates for the years 1990 to 1995 are not compatible with figures for earlier years, which however can be raised appropriately, if not necessarily entirely accurately, according to the new version giving the 11.4 per cent increase for the world as a whole.

3.   The break-up of the USSR in 1991 has made comparisons through time particularly difficult for that region. Since 1991, United Nations sources have given data for each of the 15 former Soviet Socialist Republics of the USSR, so the 1990s totals for the former USSR can be calculated, but they cannot be traced back by Republics before 1990 as data were not available even in official Soviet statistical sources for employment in agriculture. No less confusing and depressing is the great disparity in the number employed in agriculture in China in the 1990s, 513 million in 1994 in *FAOPY 1995* compared with 334 million in the same year in 'primary industry' in the *China Statistical Yearbook, 1996*, the latter only 54 per cent of all employment.

According to *FAOPY 1995*, 1,301 million people in the world were economically active in agriculture in 1995 (the total agricultural population, including dependents, was 2,591 million). The 1,301 million engaged in agriculture accounted for 47.5 per cent of the total economically active population of the world, 2,738 million. A spectre faces the world in the 21st century: the growing labour force in agriculture in the developing world. The awesome arithmetic of the situation is a little difficult to tie down satisfactorily, but is so important in any assessment of possible futures in the 21st century that it will be discussed in some detail, with the help of a number of tables. As with spectres in general, most people do not see them. Murphy (1983, p. 5) has drawn attention to the continuing growth of the agricultural labour force in developing countries in spite of its relative decline but does not explicitly relate it to the stagnation in the area cultivated.

The data in Table 5.9 are from various *FAO Production Yearbooks* published prior to the revisions in the *1995 Yearbook*. The data for 2010 are projections made by Cole (1996). To allow for increases made in the *1995 Yearbook*, the figures for developing countries should be raised 11-12 per cent. The numbers engaged in agriculture in developing countries according to the *1995 Yearbook* are 1,032 million in 1980 (replacing 923 million) and 1,176 (replacing 1,051) for 1990. The number engaged in agriculture in developing countries grew by 144 million between 1980 and 1990, an average annual increase of over 14 million. Between 1990 and 1995 the total grew from 1,176 million to 1,250 million, giving a similar annual increase. As noted earlier in this chapter, the cultivated area hardly changed during that time.

A comparison of the data for developed and developing countries between 1965 and 1990 shows two strikingly different trends. The developed countries experienced not only a sharp relative decline in the agricultural labour force in relation to total employment (from 23 per cent to 8 per cent) but also an absolute decline, from 108 million to 50 million. In contrast, while developing countries also experienced a relative decline (69 per cent to 59 per cent), the absolute number rose from 646 million to 1,051 million, an increase of over 60 per cent, although less than the 75 per cent increase in the total population of all developing countries.

Table 5.9 The economically active population in agriculture in developed and developing countries, 1965-2010

Year	Total population (millions)			Total economically active (millions)		In agriculture (millions)		In agriculture (percentage)	
	world	developed	developing	developed	developing	developed	developing	developed	developing
1965	3,276	1,023	2,253	461	931	108	646	23.4	69.4
1970	3,694	1,072	2,622	484	1,100 [1]	90	750 [1]	18.6	68.2
1975	4,079	1,124	2,955	519	1,244	80	851	15.4	68.4
1980	4,448	1,168	3,280	552	1,404	70	923	12.7	65.7
1985	4,851	1,209	3,642	579	1,584	60	993	10.4	62.7
1990	5,205	1,251	3,954	601	1,765	50	1,051	8.3	59.5
2010	7,040	1,320	5,720	650	2,545	35	1,240	5.4	48.7

Note: [1] Adjustment to total made by author

Source: *FAOP**, various numbers, based on a table in Cole (1996)

Table 5.10 The economically active population in agriculture in millions and as a percentage of all economically active population in four developing regions/countries

Year	Latin America		Africa		India		China	
	millions	per cent	millions	per cent	millions	per cent	millions	per cent
1965	34	43	91	74	143	72	–	–
1970	36	41	97	72	151	69	336	78
1975	38	36	119	76	172	71	368	76
1980	39	32	130	74	185	70	406	74
1985	41	29	141	71	200	68	439	71
1990	41	26	154	68	215	67	458	68
1990 (revised)	45	26	168	63	232	64	494	72
1995	44	22	186	60	249	62	517	71

Note: - = no data

Source: *FAOP**, various years, based on a table in Cole (1996)

Table 5.10 shows how the agricultural population has grown in four regions of the developing world during 1965-1990. Together the four regions have about 75 per cent of the population of the developing world, but Southwest and Southeast Asia are excluded, together with other areas of the developing world with small populations. In Latin America the absolute number peaked around 1990 but numbers continue to grow in the other regions. There are big differences among countries within Latin America and Africa, and also among major administrative divisions within India and China.

Table 5.11 shows how between 1980 and 1995 the average number of people working 100 hectares of agricultural land in the world as a whole has actually risen considerably, although it has gone down sharply in most developed countries. The data for 1980 are calculated by the author, taking into account the revision of the economically active population in agriculture in the *1995 FAO Yearbook* already referred to.

Table 5.11 Relationship of employment in agriculture to cultivated land and permanent pasture

	(1)	(2)	(3)	(4)	(5)	(6)	(7)
	Economically active population			*Cultivated land, plus permanent pasture divided by 10 (millions of hectares)*			*Workers per 100 hectares*
	Total (millions)	*In agriculture (millions)*	*(percentage)*	*Cultivated*	*Pasture*	*Total*	
1980	2,076.3	1,110.4	53.5	1,426.6	326.5	1,753.1	63
1990	2,509.7	1,230.9	49.0	1,458.5	339.3	1,797.8	68
1995	2,738.8	1,301.3	47.5	1,450.8	339.5	1,790.3	73

The economically active population in agriculture (col 2) is divided by agricultural area (col 6) then multiplied by 100 to give the number of workers per 100 hectares (col 7).

Table 5.12 shows the great differences in the average number of people working 100 hectares of agricultural land. The area of permanent pasture has been reduced to a tenth compared with that under arable and permanent crops, to which it has then been added. Every country in the world is included in the table, but the notes should be consulted in order to find the composition of the various regions. The eleven regions are ranked in descending order of the percentage of economically active population in agriculture. Average yields of relevant crops and of livestock products vary greatly among the countries of the world, but no attempt has been made in Table 5.12 to weight the 100 hectares of each region. Even at the level of major regions, the contrast in the amount of workers per 100 hectares is enormous: 185 for Asia compared with 0.6 for Australia and New Zealand, roughly a 300-fold gap. Although yields for some crops are 2-3 times as high in much of Asia as in Australia, the productivity per worker in agriculture in Australia and North America is still 50-100 times higher than that per worker in most of Asia and Africa.

The productivity gap in the agricultural workforce is so important for the future of the world in the next few decades, that the situation is shown in more detail in Table 5.13, with 12 countries including the largest three in population in the world (China, India and the USA) and nine others, selected from different continents and from both developed and developing countries. The countries are ranked in descending order of the average number of people working 100 hectares. In this table permanent pasture is ignored altogether.

Table 5.12 Labour-to-land relationship in agriculture in 1995 by regions and countries

		Economically active population in agriculture (percentage)	Agricultural workers per 100 hectares[6]
1	Oceania [1]	67	166
2	Asia [2]	63	185
3	Africa	60	68
4	N. and C. America [3]	27	36
5	South America	20	17
6	Central Europe	20	25
7	Former USSR [4]	14	9
8	Japan	6	82
9	Australia and New Zealand	5	0.6
10	Western Europe [5]	5	10
11	USA and Canada	3	1.5

1 Without Australia and New Zealand
2 Without Japan, Russian Federation
3 Without USA and Canada
4 Excluding Southern Republics
5 European Union, Norway, Switzerland
6 Hectares of land under arable and permanent crops plus permanent pasture divided by 10

Table 5.13 Labour-to-land relationship in agriculture in selected countries in 1995

	(1) Total (millions)	(2) Economically active population In agriculture (millions)	(3) (percentage)	(4) Cultivated area (millions of hectares)	(5) Agricultural workers per 100 hectares
China	725.4	517.2	71	95.8	540
Ethiopia	24.2	20.7	86	13.9	149
India	404.2	249.1	62	169.7	147
Nigeria	44.5	16.8	38	32.7	51
Poland	19.3	5.0	26	14.6	34
Brazil	72.7	13.6	19	50.7	27
UK	29.3	0.6	2.1	6.0	10
Russia	77.6	9.6	12	132.3	7
France	25.8	1.1	4.2	19.5	6
USA	133.4	3.5	2.6	187.8	1.9
Australia	9.0	0.4	4.5	47.2	0.9
Canada	15.6	0.4	2.5	45.5	0.8

For what they are worth, the data in column (5) of Table 5.13 show that there are about 600 times as many people working a unit of cultivated land in China as in Australia or Canada and about 300 times as many as in the USA. To be sure, some of the cultivated land in China is so intensively cultivated that it can be considered small-holding, market garden or allotment land. The 'density' of workers per area cultivated in China appears to be exceptionally high even compared with India, but very high densities can be found in other countries: Bangladesh 384 per 100 hectares, Haiti 230, Egypt 217. A report on Haiti in the 1940s (United Nations (1949) *Mission to Haiti*) noted that the system of cultivation was such that often so many people were working a given piece of land that they got in each other's way. A number of implications of the situation may now be noted:

- Without the prospect of being able either to increase the cultivated area greatly or to reduce the labour force in agriculture drastically over a short period, the agricultural workers virtually everywhere in Asia and Africa and also in many parts of Latin America cannot possibly produce enough to reach material levels comparable to those experienced by most people in agriculture in the developed countries, even if these latter tend to have lower incomes than most people working in industry or services in their own countries.

- For China to reduce its density of agricultural workers per unit of cultivated area to the level in the UK, it would only need 1 in 50 of its present labour force. To reduce it to even half its present size would release 250 million workers (plus dependents) from the land, either to find other employment locally, or to move into urban centres. Until the 1980s, the central government of China kept a relatively tight control on internal migration. Almost everywhere else in the developing world, migration from agricultural areas to cities, especially the largest ones, has proceeded with increasing rapidity since the Second World War.

- The spectre for 2050: in 1995, about 1,250 million people were engaged in agriculture in developing countries compared with under 50 million in developed ones. They worked very roughly the same total areas of land. With continuing loss of jobs in agriculture in the southern countries of the European Union and throughout Central Europe and the former USSR there could be a mere 20-30 million people in agriculture in the present developed countries in 2050. In contrast, the total population of the present developing countries could almost double between 1990 and 2050. The percentage of the economically active population working in agriculture in developing countries dropped from 69.4 per cent in 1965 to 59.5 per cent in 1990. If the percentage drops to 35 per cent in 2050 there would still be 1.2-1.3 billion people employed in the agricultural sector, in other words little change in the number compared with that in the 1990s.

5.8   PROSPECTS FOR WATER AND FOOD

Water

The need for water seems likely to increase with the growth of the world population expected in the next 50-60 years. Even if global warming modifies the climate by 2050 it is unlikely that the broad picture of the distribution of fresh water would change greatly. Therefore the existing water sources have to be used more intensively; three futures for water can be contrasted: Good, Average and Bad (see Chapter 3, section 3.3, probability).

- Good. The population of the world increases to only 9 billion (or less) in 2050. Extensive transfers of fresh water by canal or pipeline move water into areas where cultivation is at present precluded or yields are low through lack of precipitation: for example, Uzbekistan, parts of western USA, northern China. Water supply in growing urban areas in developing countries is improved. Water use, especially for domestic purposes, is reduced in developed countries, possibly through some form of rationing, such as a surcharge on water consumed over a certain level. Desalination is practised on a much larger scale than now. While such developments would improve water supply in various parts of the world in the next few decades, the environment could be adversely affected, both by construction works and by emissions from the fossil fuels used to desalinate water, at least until enough solar power or power from nuclear fusion becomes widely available.

- Average. Recent trends continue.

- Bad. The population of the world increases to around 11 billion. Little is done to facilitate new transfers of water, to use irrigation water more efficiently, or to economise on water use in developed countries. Aquifers are used up more quickly than at replacement rate, a widespread feature now in India.

Given the present and prospective water supply problems facing many parts of the world it makes a welcome diversion to speculate on whether there is water under the surface of the moon or on Mars. If there is not, then the cost of transporting enough water there from the earth to support even one respectable sized settlement could appropriately be described as astronomical. There is a challenge here: to find a way of reducing the weight and volume of water for transfer purposes, dehydration clearly not being an option!

Food in particular and arable products in general

Good, Average and Bad prospects for food production are so described only with reference to food since a future that may be favourable for food production may be unfavourable for other users of the land. Four sets of Good, Average and Bad futures can be combined to give 81 different possible outcomes.

- World population grows as follows by 2050:

  Good: to 9 billion, 50% above the level of the late-1990s

  Average: to 10 billion, 67% above the level of the late-1990s

  Bad: to 11 billion, 83% above the level of the late-1990s

  Assuming there is already pressure on cropland, then the above use of Good, Average and Bad is valid.

- The area under arable and permanent crops in the world changes as follows:

  Good: the area increases at least as quickly as population (Projection B in Figure 5.1), but this is at the expense of forest and/or pasture, or is achieved by reclamation of land with no bioclimatic use at present. Of the three main types of forest in the world, only the mid-latitude broadleaf forest, mainly found in Europe and eastern North America, is generally suitable for clearance for cultivation. The northern coniferous forest (mainly Russia and Canada) is mostly unsuitable, the tropical rain forest problematic, and only fertile in limited areas. In the USA much of the remaining coniferous forest is already owned either by lumber companies or by the federal government.

Average: only a slight increase in the area of cropland is achieved.

Bad: the area of cropland decreases by 10-20 per cent as a result of encroachment by non-agricultural uses, soil loss and/or the 'cultivation' of trees for fuel or timber on present arable land.

- Yields change as follows:

Good: an all round increase is achieved, with the greatest increase in those countries with low yields at present; production grows more quickly than population provided that population and cultivated area are also Good.

Average: some increase in yields, but not enough to match population growth. The Green Revolution card has now been played in many developing countries.

Bad: yields change very little in most countries.

- Trade in food products and the distribution of food in cases of emergency become:

Good: more flexible, in particular enabling poor countries to obtain food at low prices.

Average: continuation of the present situation.

Bad: countries with a large surplus (relative to population) of food products take extensive areas of arable land out of cultivation into set aside or soil conservation.

From 81 possible combinations of Good, Average and Bad, and assuming equal probabilities for each, there is only a 1:81 probability of getting four Goods. Such a future would be characterised by only a 50 per cent increase in the number of people to be fed, an increase in the area under cultivation of 70-80 per cent, a widespread increase in yields, and an organisation in place to ensure flexible transfers of food as and when needed. Fortunately there is also only a 1:81 probability of getting four Bads. Such a future would result in a desperate food situation by 2050, with an 80-90 per cent increase in the number of people to be fed, rather less land to cultivate, little change in yields, and each major region or country largely left to feed its own population, a situation consciously chosen by the leaders of North Korea and Cuba in the 1990s, and one arrived at through internal conflicts in the former Belgian colonies of Africa, Congo (formerly Zaire), Rwanda and Burundi.

The probability for the future of food production is that there will be one of the many combinations of Good, Average and Bad, in which all three are represented. Whatever that future, one prospect is as certain as anything can be: the developed countries hold virtually all the cards and will continue to do so. They now have about 2½ times as much cropland per inhabitant as the developing countries (see Table 5.6) and in 2050 could have about 4½ times as much. They have better research facilities and technologies to improve production methods than most developing countries. For example, according to Stafford (1997) the ability to monitor within-field spatial variability in soil, crops and environmental factors makes it possible to target inputs to field crops according to very locally determined requirements. Such technology-led innovations in agriculture could benefit developed and developing countries equally, but the cost of setting up such a system makes it more likely to be used in developed regions (see also Durisch (1997)).

In the last resort the consumption of animal products in developed countries can be reduced, thereby releasing more land for the cultivation of crops destined for direct human consumption.

According to Bender and Smith (1997): 'grain provides at least twice as much food energy when it is consumed directly by humans as when it is fed to livestock that produce meat and dairy products.' Typically, there are big disparities in estimates of the saving of food by giving up meat and dairy products. In contrast to the above estimate, Spedding (1988) writes: 'In terms of economics, it *ought* to be cheaper to use crops to produce edible products industrially than to use animals. This does vary with the terrain, the level of crop productivity and the resources available but, basically, it takes about 10 times as much land to feed people on animal products as it does to feed them on crops.'

There are further possible future strategies for food production that the developed countries are better placed to use. For example, Canby (1975) refers to: 'SCP - single-cell protein - (which) can be grown as a fortifier for human and livestock food by 'planting' yeast in a mixture containing a petroleum derivative. A 250-acre area devoted to such 'food from crude' could yield as much protein as a million acres of soybeans.' Where, then, is there a future food problem at all? A more likely solution to the impending world food crisis would be for some multi-national organisation on the lines of NATO or the EU to buy cheap grain and other agricultural commodities and send them to appropriate developing countries, where it would be obtainable on rations at artificially low prices, a potential problem as already noted, however, for the farmers in such developing countries.

Views differ widely as to the prospects for the expansion of agricultural production in the next century. For example, Brown (1995) writes: 'As the world progresses (sic) through the nineties, each year brings additional evidence that we are entering a new era, one quite different from the last four decades. An age of relative food abundance is being replaced by one of scarcity.' Prosterman *et al.* (1996), referring specifically to China, regard aspects of organisation, particularly land ownership, as crucial in raising food production, concluding: 'The Chinese government appears willing to give people greater control over the land they farm; only if it succeeds in implementing these reforms will China be assured of its ability to feed itself in the next century.' In their book *The Hunger Machine*, Bennett and George (1987) express the view that we actually live in an age of plenty but that on account of inequalities both in the world as a whole and within individual developing countries, more than a billion people are chronically hungry (Preface): 'People are dying, not because there is not enough food [in the world] but because they are too poor to buy it and have no land where they could grow it.'

In an ideal world, in which agriculture is managed everywhere at the most efficient possible level and the food needs of every citizen are catered for, the quantity of food produced could be changed in two ways: either the area of agricultural land could be extended, or yields could be increased, or both. Since the total land surface of the world is likely to change only fractionally in the next half century, any increase in the area used for agricultural purposes would be at the expense of other uses. For example, a 'Good' future for agriculture could mean a 'Bad' future for the world's forests. The increase in yields needed could not be achieved exclusively by organic farming and would therefore require, among other changes, a greater application of chemical fertilisers, with implications for the environment.

As far back as 1973, Brown (1973) referred to the then recently initiated 'Green Revolution', which brought increases in cereal production in parts of the developing world, mainly thanks to the use of new seeds, as follows: 'Many of those working closely with the Green Revolution ... have stressed from the beginning that the new technologies embodied in the Green Revolution did not represent a solution to the food problem. Rather we noted that it was a means of *buying time* (author's italics), perhaps an additional 15 or 20 years during which the brakes could be applied to population.'

To feed some 10 billion people in 2050 will require fuller use to be made of water and land resources, together with improved means of production and management. The main victims will be much of the present agricultural population of developing countries, the excessive number of whom needs to be reduced by anything from half to a tenth, depending on which parts of the world are considered.

6

ENERGY

'The energy problem now faced by the United States began to be recognized 10 years or more ago. Still, the occasional symptoms (the oil embargo of 1973, the natural gas shortage of 1976-77, and the gasoline lines of the summer of 1979) are frequently mistaken for the problem itself. As each symptom is relieved, the public sense of crisis fades. The seeds of future crisis, however, remain.'

National Academy of Sciences, Washington D.C. 1979

6.1   INTRODUCTION

The word energy conventionally refers, in an economic sense, to fossil fuels, as well as to non-fuel sources of power such as hydro-electricity and wind power. If the goal of food production is to keep humans and animals alive, the goal of energy production is to fuel heating and cooking appliances, to process materials and, above all, to drive machines. A shortage of food is likely to have a greater impact on human activities in the short term than a shortage of energy. Nevertheless, the availability of energy reserves and the pollution caused by the use of three of the main sources - the fossil fuels coal, oil and natural gas - have given rise to widespread concern over the consumption of energy in the last three decades. A serious reduction in the amount of energy available would have grave worldwide consequences for the industrial sector as well as for the lifestyles of most people in the developed countries and unfavourable consequences for many in the developing countries.

For convenience, energy sources are often subdivided into two types: commercial and non-commercial. Fuelwood is the main source of non-commercial energy, although some of it is marketed in the formal economy. Other traditional sources, including water and wind power and, by a flexible definition, fodder given to work animals, are also widely used in some parts of the world. The burning of wood and the use of work animals both contribute to pollution of the atmosphere, but wind and water power are clean.

There are five main sources of primary commercial energy in the world, the three fossil fuels coal (and lignite), oil and natural gas, together with nuclear power and hydro-electric power. None is entirely free of problems. One of the main sources of atmospheric pollution is the burning of fossil fuels. The generation of electricity by nuclear power and hydro-power is clean, but the disposal of nuclear waste and the decommissioning of nuclear power stations are becoming major concerns. Many hydro-electric stations are affected by the silting of reservoirs, while the development of new sites often threatens existing land use and settlements or wildlife.

Fossil fuels have been formed gradually over very long geological timescales covering millions of years. The rate at which they have been extracted and consumed in the last 150 years has been so great that already considerable proportions of the known reserves of fossil fuels have been extracted, including many of those most easily reached and those located in areas that are most convenient and accessible to markets.

Coal was the first of the fossil fuels to be extracted in large quantities, and well into the 20th century it formed the basis of fuel consumption in most of the industrial countries. Now less important relatively than in the past in producing steam power, it is still used in the generation of thermal electricity, the processing of mineral raw materials, and for domestic heating. Seepages of oil have been known for centuries, but the invention of the kerosene lamp in 1854 was one reason for the exploitation of oil reserves beneath the surface. The first well specially sunk to extract oil was by E. L. Drake near Titusville, Pennsylvania, USA, in 1859; it reached a depth of 69 feet. In the 20th century oil has in general been cheaper to extract and transport than coal, and production has risen sharply since the 1920s once oil had become the main source of energy in the transport sector. It is generally more versatile in its application than coal. The use (in quantity) of natural gas as a fuel dates from the 1930s, although the first large natural gas well was sunk at Murrysville, Pennsylvania in 1878; 'town gas' had been extracted from coal well before that. Natural gas is cleaner than coal, cheaper to extract, and easy to transport on both land (by pipeline) and by sea in liquefied form (LNG). All three fossil fuels are also used as raw materials for industrial purposes and all three can be used to generate electricity. Oil was derived from coal in Germany during the Second World War and in South Africa since then, but the process is costly.

Hydro-electricity and nuclear electricity both count as primary sources of energy, but in the assessment of world energy production and consumption, electricity generated from fossil fuels is not counted as a primary source; to do so would be double-counting. Other 'clean' sources of energy for generating electricity, apart from nuclear and hydro-electric power already referred to, are wind, tidal and solar power, the first two being modern versions of traditional sources. In the mid-1990s their contribution to total energy consumption was negligible. In spite of several decades of research and a number of false claims, the generation of electricity through nuclear fusion (rather than fission) seems to be only a remote prospect still.

Arguably, world energy consumption is likely to rise substantially between 2000 and 2050 unless demand is deliberately curbed by the international community through, for example, heavy taxes on use, artificially high prices, or formal rationing. There should therefore be continuing concern over the use of fossil fuels on account of both the availability of reserves and the emission of carbon dioxide, which accumulates in the atmosphere. Table 6.1 shows the contribution of each of the main commercial primary sources of energy to total world energy consumption in 1995. Table 6.2 shows that the total amount of commercial energy consumed in the world has risen from 5.2 billion tonnes of oil equivalent (t.o.e.) in 1970 to over 8.1 billion in 1995, but as a result of the growth of population during that time the per capita amount used in 1995 was almost the same as that used in 1970. Table 6.3 shows the distribution of energy consumption by major world regions. One of the most striking features is the fact that in 1995 the four developed regions (1-4) consumed 68.5 per cent of the total yet they had only 21.4 per cent of the population, almost exactly eight times as much per capita as was used in the developing regions.

While there is no immediate prospect of fossil fuels running out in the world, when the future for energy is considered as far ahead as 2050, then there is cause for concern. In 1996 (see BP (1997)), proved reserves of oil were 141 billion tonnes, enough to last 42 years at the 1996 level of production. Proved reserves of natural gas, 141 trillion cubic metres, were sufficient to last 62 years at the 1996 level of production. In contrast, all coal reserves, 1,032 billion tonnes, would last 224 years at 1996 rates of production. There are limits to the total capacity of sites in suitable locations at which hydro-electric power could be generated commercially, while the reserves of uranium for the nuclear power industry are finite, although abundant at present. No meaningful specific size can be attributed to these sources of energy as can be done for proved reserves of fossil fuels.

Table 6.1 World consumption of commercial sources of primary energy in 1995

	Consumption (millions t.o.e)	(percentage)
Oil	3,227	39.6
Natural gas	1,884	23.2
Coal	2,211	27.2
Nuclear energy [1]	596	7.3
Hydro-electricity [2]	219	2.7
Total	8,136	100.0

Source: BP (1996)

[1] Converted on the basis of the average thermal efficiency of a modern nuclear power plant (i.e. 33 per cent efficiency)

[2] Converted to t.o.e on the basis of the energy content of the electricity generated

Table 6.2 World primary energy consumption 1970 - 1995

	Consumption (millions t.o.e)	Population (millions)	Kilograms per inhabitant
1970	5,171	3,650	1,417
1975	5,965	4,020	1,484
1980	6,883	4,420	1,557
1985	6,949	4,850	1,433
1990	7,855	5,300	1,482
1995	8,136	5,720	1,422

Source of data: BP (1996)

Table 6.3 Distribution of world primary energy consumption by major regions 1995

		Consumption (millions t.o.e.)	(percentage)
1	Europe[1]	1,725	21.3
2	North America[2]	2,404	29.6
3	Japan	490	6.0
4	Former USSR	943	11.6
5	China	833	10.2
6	Latin America	433	5.3
7	Middle East	312	3.8
8	Africa	238	2.9
9	Rest of Asia	758	9.3
	World	8,136	100.0

[1] Includes Turkey

[2] Includes Australia, New Zealand, excludes Mexico

Source: BP (1996)

It has already been noted that between 1970 and 1995 world energy consumption rose roughly in accordance with population growth. It was shown in Chapter 4 that a world population of almost 10 billion could be expected in 2050. If the production of oil and natural gas continues to increase merely at the rate of expected population growth, and if no new reserves are found, oil reserves would run out by about 2020, those of natural gas by about 2035. Given the drive to industrialise in many developing countries, average world per capita energy consumption is actually likely to rise. In reality, many promising areas of the world for oil and gas reserves remain hardly explored, including deep sea gas deposits, but the cost of exploration and extraction is likely to be much higher here than in the Middle East.

6.2   COAL AND LIGNITE

Coal reserves are conventionally divided into two types, both solid fuels, bituminous and anthracite (sometimes referred to as hard coal), and lignite and brown (sub-bituminous) coal. A tonne of lignite has only about half the heating value of a tonne of hard coal. Table 6.4 includes the countries with the largest proved reserves in the world of anthracite and bituminous coal at the end of 1995. The 519 billion tonnes of hard coal would last 156 years at the 1995 level of production of 3,317 million tonnes. In addition, there are estimated to be 512 billion tonnes of sub-bituminous coal and lignite, with a life of about 420 years at the 1995 level of production of 1,214 million tonnes. Five countries, the USA (134 billion tonnes), China (52), Australia (47), Germany (43) and Indonesia (31) have about 60 per cent of all the proved reserves of lignite. For environmental reasons as much as economic ones, lignite and brown coal are out of favour and production is unlikely to increase. Even so, coal production could continue well beyond 2050, even with some increase in output.

Table 6.4 The ten countries with the largest proved reserves of anthracite and bituminous coal at the end of 1995

		(billion tonnes)	*Coal reserves (percentage)*	*(cumulative percentage)*
1	USA	107	20.6	20.6
2	USSR	104	20.0	40.6
3	India	68	13.1	53.7
4	China	62	11.9	65.6
5	South Africa	55	10.6	76.2
6	Australia	45	8.7	84.9
7	Poland	29	5.6	90.5
8	Germany	24	4.6	95.1
9	Canada	5	1.0	96.1
10	Colombia	4	0.8	96.9
	World	519	100.0	100.0

Source: BP (1996)

Figure 6.1 shows possible futures for world hard coal production. To allow comparison with graphs showing other forms of energy, the production for 1990 (actually the mean for 1988-92) has a score of 100. The average annual amount produced during 1988-92 was 3,510 million tonnes, 662 kilograms per capita. The following points may be noted:

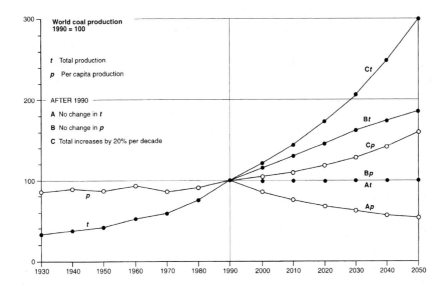

Figure 6.1 World coal production 1930-2050.

- Projection A shows what would happen during 1990-2050 if coal production stays at the 1990 level (A*t*). On account of expected population growth from 5.3 billion in 1990 to almost 10 billion in 2050, in the latter year the per capita level would drop almost to half (A*p*). Such a situation would arise either through pressure to protect the environment or as a result of a rapid increase in the production of other sources of energy. Both China and India, with almost 40 per cent of the world's population between them, have large coal reserves, but little oil and natural gas, and their future economic growth for some decades is therefore likely to require an increase in coal production. Indeed, during 1990-95 alone China's hard coal production rose from 916 to 1,253 million tonnes (up 37 per cent), India's from 185 to 264 (up 43 per cent). In 1995 China and India together accounted for 46 per cent of total world production.

- Projection B. Per capita coal production (B*p*) continues to 2050 at the 1990 level. Production (B*t*) therefore almost doubles.

- Projection C. Coal production increases by 20 per cent per decade to 2050, requiring a threefold increase in the 1990 level of production by 2050.

During 1930-90 world hard coal production increased almost threefold, but on account of population growth the per capita average only increased slightly.

How much coal has been extracted up to 1990 in the world altogether and how much would have to be extracted by 2050 according to projections A-C? Roughly between 1830 and 1930, 40 billion tonnes of coal were extracted. Between 1930 and 1990 the amount was about 120 billion (the area under *t* on the left hand half of the graph in Figure 6.1). According to projections A, B and C (see the area on the graph under the *t* curves), the amounts required would be 210 billion for A, 305 for B and 385 for C. In other words, merely to keep the same per capita level of production as that in 1990 (projection B), almost twice as much coal would have to be extracted during 1990-2050 as during 1830-1990.

The speed with which fortunes can change in an industry is illustrated by the decline of coal production in the Europan Union (EU) and most vividly by the decline in the workforce. Between 1980 and 1994 alone, in the four largest EU producers of coal, Germany, the UK, Spain and France, the number of miners declined from 570,000 to 170,000. Such a trend would hardly have been anticipated in the 1970s and serves as a caution on making forecasts about economic activities over a decade or two, let alone to 2050.

6.3   OIL

Oil production is usually measured either in tonnes or in barrels: roughly seven barrels are equivalent to one tonne. Both are usually expressed in production per year, but production in barrels per day is also used. For simplicity, oil will be measured in tonnes of crude oil in this chapter, roughly one tonne of oil being equivalent to 1.5 tonnes of hard coal.

Table 6.5 shows the location of the proved reserves of oil at the end of 1995. The 138 billion tonnes of oil would last 43 years at the 1995 level of production of 3,252 million tonnes. The Middle East has 65 per cent of the reserves and the countries with the main oil reserves in that region have many decades of oil left, whereas the USA had about ten years left in 1995 and Europe (excluding Russia) seven years.

Table 6.5 The ten countries with the largest proved reserves of oil at the end of 1995

	Oil reserves (billion tonnes)	(percentage)	(cumulative percentage)	*R/P ratio*[1] (years)
Saudi Arabia	35.7	25.8	25.8	84
Iraq	13.4	9.7	35.5	over 100
Kuwait	13.3	9.6	45.1	over 100
United Arab Emirates	12.7	9.2	54.3	over 100
Iran	12.0	8.7	63.0	66
Venezuela	9.3	6.7	69.7	64
Former USSR	7.8	5.6	75.3	22
Mexico	7.1	5.1	80.4	47
Libya	3.9	2.8	83.2	58
USA	3.7	2.7	85.9	10
World	138.3	100.0	100.0	43

Source: BP (1996)

[1] Reserves to production ratio. i.e. life expectancy of reserves at current rate of production.

From the evidence so far it is clear that the oil industry is much more vulnerable than the coal industry in terms of quantity of proved reserves and prospects for future production. In tonnes of oil equivalent, the reserves of hard coal are more than twice as large as those of oil. Politically, also, the situation is more problematic for oil because such a large share of reserves is in the relatively unstable Middle East, while the three industrial regions, Western Europe, North America and Japan are large importers of oil. Forecasting the future of the oil industry, the possibility of discovering new reserves, and the fluctuation in oil prices, have been the subject of widespread speculation and controversy for several decades. In this section it is intended only to show the implications of a number of different possible futures. Table 6.6 shows the data on which the trends and projections are based. Figure 6.2 shows total and per capita production of oil in relation to the 1990 output of 3,140 million tonnes (592 kgs per capita).

Table 6.6 Three possible projections of world oil production

Year	P	C	1930 - 1990 trend T	Cr	Tr	Year	P	C	Projection A T	Cr	Tr
1930	2,070	92	190	16	6	2000	6,130	512	3,140	86	100
1940	2,250	127	285	21	9	2010	6,950	452	3,140	76	100
1950	2,520	212	535	36	17	2020	7,770	404	3,140	68	100
1960	2,980	356	1,060	60	34	2030	8,560	367	3,140	62	100
1970	3,650	614	2,240	104	71	2040	9,260	339	3,140	57	100
1980	4,420	682	3,015	115	96	2050	9,880	318	3,140	54	100
1990	5,300	592	3,140	100	100						

Year	P	C	Projection B T	Cr	Tr	Year	P	C	Projection C T	Cr	Tr
2000	6,130	592	3,630	100	116	2000	6,130	692	4,240	117	135
2010	6,950	592	4,110	100	131	2010	6,950	823	5,720	139	182
2020	7,770	592	4,600	100	146	2020	7,770	995	7,730	168	246
2030	8,560	592	5,070	100	161	2030	8,560	1,220	10,440	206	332
2040	9,260	592	5,480	100	175	2040	9,260	1,520	14,090	257	449
2050	9,880	592	5,850	100	186	2050	9,880	1,926	19,030	325	606

Note: P = total population in millions
         C = per capita oil production in kilograms
         T = total oil production in millions of tonnes
         Cr = per capita oil production in relation to 1990
         Tr = total oil production in relation to 1990

Columns 1-3 are totals, columns 4 and 5 show columns 2 and 3 in relation to the 1990 figure =100

Between 1950 and 1980 total annual world oil production rose from 535 million tonnes to 3,015 million. After that, the rate of increase slowed down dramatically and between 1980 and 1990 per capita production actually fell. Oil price rises in 1973-74 and in 1979 put a brake on consumption and production, and in the 1980s new emphasis was put on coal and natural gas as well as alternative energy sources. In Figure 6.2 three projections for oil are shown for the period 1990-2050.

- Projection A shows what would happen if oil production remained at the 1990 level throughout the following six decades (A*t*). By 2050 per capita production would drop to little over half the 1990 level (A*p*). Such a future would of course only be possible if extensive new reserves of oil are discovered.

- Projection B shows what would happen if oil production is such that the 1990 per capita level is maintained (B*p*). By 2050 production would have to be at almost twice the 1990 level (B*t*).

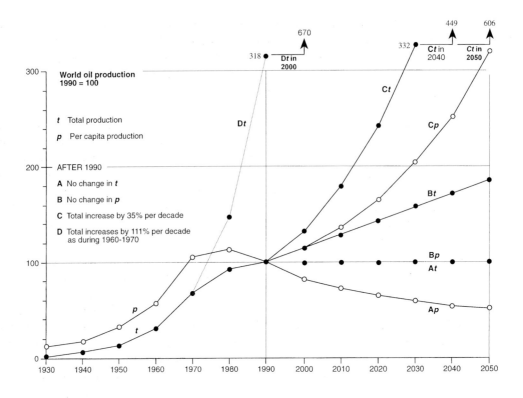

Figure 6.2 World oil production 1930-1950. See text for explanation.

- Projection C assumes a decade by decade increase in production of 35 per cent, similar to that experienced between 1970 and 1980, the result of a rejuvenation of the expansion of the oil industry. Total production would be six times as high in 2050 as in 1990 (C*t*), per capita production more than three times as high (C*p*).

- Projection D shows the continuation after 1970 of the increase of 111 per cent experienced during the decade 1960-1970, the future that seemed to lie ahead before the oil price rises of the 1970s, a future that never was.

The Baku area in Russia, Romania, Mexico, and various places in the USA saw the earliest comparatively large scale oil operations before the First World War. As recently as the eve of the Second World War in the late 1930s, however, only about 250 million tonnes of oil were being extracted annually. The recent growth of oil production has been so rapid that between 1870 and 1970 only about 32 billion tonnes of oil were produced, compared with 56 billion tonnes between 1970 and 1990, in spite of oil price rises. Expressed in a different way, more oil was extracted between 1973 and 1990 than in all the time the industry existed before 1973. Up to 1990 some 88 billion tonnes of oil had been extracted in the world, compared with 188 billion required between 1990 and 2050 merely to keep production at the 1990 level (Projection A), and 274 billion to keep per capita production at the 1990 level (Projection B). The proved oil reserves of 1995 would last 43 years in Projection A but only 30 in Projection B and little more than 20 in Projection C.

During 1970-1986 new discoveries of oil roughly matched oil production. In both 1987 and 1989 new discoveries and revisions of existing deposits pushed up the reserves by over 40 per cent. Between 1989 and 1996 new discoveries, additions and revisions have again broadly matched the world's production, leaving total reserves virtually unchanged. Between 1986 and 1996 world oil production has risen from 2,940 million tonnes to 3,361 million a year, an increase of 11.4 per cent, while world population has grown by about 18 per cent during that time.

The future scale of the world's oil industry depends initially on the discovery of new reserves and, depending on the extent of these, on the rate of extraction. Given the many advantages of oil as a source of energy, it will still be valued and used in preference to coal and natural gas by many consumers unless environmental considerations outweigh the advantages of using oil at all, in which case the use of coal and to a lesser extent natural gas should be curtailed for the same reason. In '*The End of Cheap Oil*', Campbell and Laherrère (1998) consider that: 'Forecasts about the abundance of oil are usually warped by inconsistent definitions of "reserves". In truth, every year of the past two decades the industry has pumped more oil than it has discovered, and production will soon be unable to keep up with rising demand.'

Until the end of the Second World War the discovery of oil reserves depended largely upon the occurrence of oil seepages, most easily found in areas of sparse vegetation, less easy to detect in forested areas, and impossible in the sea except in very shallow areas (e.g. the Caspian Sea in Azerbaijan, the Gulf of Maracaibo in Venezuela). New techniques of exploration and more sophisticated types of equipment now make it possible to detect oil in deeper sea areas and even at depths of more than 200 metres, beyond the limits of the continental shelf. For example (see Beardsley (1997)), the study and detection of types of rock formation most likely to have trapped worthwhile reserves of oil can be helped by a pair of molecules that apparently reveals how far the oil has migrated from its site of origin.

Many land and sea areas have so far hardly been explored for oil. They include the ground beneath the extensive tropical rain forest of the Amazon basin, the cold coastlands and offshore areas of the Arctic Ocean held by Russia, Canada and the USA (Alaska), the South China Sea, the Gulf of Mexico and the South Atlantic, especially around the Falkland Islands. One problem with these areas is that production costs would be much higher than in the highly favoured Middle East region. Brierley (1995) describes the capacity of the newly developed floating production, storage and offloading system (FPSO), which operates from a special ship rather than a platform and is capable of reaching the sea-bed at a depth of about 600 metres (2000 feet), three times the depth of the continental shelf, the practical limit for conventional drilling rigs.

With regard to the distribution of oil consumption in the future, in 1995 the developed regions of the world consumed 66 per cent of the world total, compared with 75 per cent in 1985. The change in distribution was mainly due firstly to a very sharp drop in consumption in the former USSR and secondly to a rapid increase in consumption in China, India and many smaller newly industrialising countries of Southeast and East Asia.

With reference to Figure 6.2, four broad alternative futures for the oil industry may be proposed:

1. Few new reserves are found. Oil consumption declines over the next few decades in the developed countries, while most parts of the developing world never partake in the oil dominated life and lifestyle experienced by people in the rich countries in the second half of the 20th century.

2.   Some new reserves are found, enough to maintain world production at around the 1990 level to 2050 and beyond (Projection A). Average world per capita production/consumption would drop, and again the level of consumption in many developing countries would remain minimal.

3.   Considerable new reserves are found, enough to allow the world per capita level to remain roughly unchanged (Projection B) through almost a doubling of annual production between 1990 and 2050 (but what after 2050?). There would be a shift in the distribution of consumption such that by 2050 the present developed regions, with only an eighth of the total population of the world by then, might only consume one third of the total.

4.   Vast new reserves are found, in which case Projection C would ensure abundant oil to the middle of the 21st century for many parts of the world. One negative aspect of this future would be the huge amount of pollution and carbon dioxide emissions produced.

Of the four alternative futures briefly described above the author anticipates Projection A. Even in this future more than twice as much oil would be produced during 1990-2050 as during the preceding 12 decades, and as new discoveries became increasingly rare in the 2020s or 2030s, thought would have to be given to gradually reducing and phasing out the oil industry to allow a reasonably gradual decline in the second half of the 21st century.

Even when large new oil reserves *are* discovered, as in Azerbaijan and Turkmenistan, both former Soviet Socialist Republics, where a century-old oil industry is being rejuvenated, there is no guarantee that production will start at once or distribution will be straightforward. Williams (1997) compares three possible routes for pipelines out of Azerbaijan, itself with a coast only on the inland Caspian Sea. All three run through regions of recent, current or likely future ethnic conflict. Georgia, Armenia, Russia, Turkey and Iran could all argue that parts of the pipelines should cross their territories.

Very large quantities of oil are also located in shales and in tar sands. The cost of extracting petroleum products from these and also from coal are comparatively high. Some oils are currently refined from shales in Russia and Estonia, while Venezuela produces and exports fuel oil, orimulsion from its tar sands. The refining and combustion of these fuels have been criticised for the pollution they cause.

6.4   NATURAL GAS

The natural gas industry is similar in many respects to the oil industry, but its rise has been even more recent. Geographically there is much similarity in the broad distribution of the deposits of the two fossil fuels, but proved reserves of gas are even more concentrated than reserves of oil insofar as Russia and Iran together have almost half. In contrast to oil, as yet natural gas makes only a minor contribution to transportation. In 1995 oil accounted for 39.6 per cent of world primary energy consumption, natural gas for 23.2 per cent.

Table 6.7 shows the location of the proved natural gas reserves at the end of 1995. Russia and the Middle East each have about a third of all reserves. The 140 trillion (million million) cubic metres of reserves of natural gas would last about 65 years at the 1995 level of production. Until the 1970s natural gas was transported almost exclusively by pipeline, but the development of liquefied natural gas transport by sea, now safe and cheap, has greatly extended the scope for international trade. For several decades the USA was by far the largest producer

Table 6.7 Proved natural gas reserves

		Natural gas reserves (trillion cubic metres)	(percentage)	(cumulative)	R/P ratio[1] (years)
1	Russian Federation	48.1	34.5	34.5	82
2	Iran	21.0	15.0	49.5	over 100
3	Qatar	7.1	5.1	54.6	over 100
4	United Arab Emirates	5.8	4.1	58.7	over 100
5	Saudi Arabia	5.3	3.8	62.5	over 100
6	USA	4.6	3.3	65.8	9
7	Venezuela	4.0	2.8	68.6	over 100
8	Algeria	3.6	2.6	71.2	60
9	Nigeria	3.1	2.2	73.4	over 100
10	Iraq	3.1	2.2	75.6	over 100
	World	139.7	100.0	100.0	65

Source: BP (1996), p. 20

[1] Reserves/production ratio, i.e. life expectancy of reserves at current rate of production.

and consumer of natural gas in the world but in the 1950s Soviet planners made a change in policy to favour oil and natural gas rather than the more traditional coal, and in Western Europe natural gas has been used locally since the Second World War and more extensively thanks to production from North Sea reserves since the late 1960s.

In 1995 the USA still produced over 25 per cent of the world's natural gas but consumed almost 30 per cent. The former USSR consumed 25 per cent but produced over 31 per cent. In 1995 the developed countries consumed over 80 per cent of the world total (about 15 times the amount per capita consumed in the developing countries) compared with 87 per cent as recently as 1985.

Figure 6.3 shows total and per capita production of natural gas in relation to the 1990 (1988-1992 five-year average) output of 2,120 billion cubic metres (2.1 trillion). Between 1930 and 1990 about 52 trillion cubic metres of natural gas were extracted. By comparison, to maintain the 1990 level of production until 2050 (Projection A), about 127 trillion cubic metres would have to be produced, compared with total reserves as of 1995 of 140 trillion. Even then, per capita production would be reduced by 2050 to little over half what it was in 1990 on account of the growth of population.

Assuming large new reserves of natural gas are found in the decades to come, then there is no reason why Projection B could not be achieved; even this increase would only allow per capita production/consumption to stay at the 1990 level. With projections A and even B it seems likely that the consumption of natural gas would be at a very low level in most developing countries, assuming no change in consumption in the developed countries.

In Projection C, an increase each decade of 27 per cent from 1990 to 2050 is assumed, the rate achieved during 1985-95. This trend would require about twice as much natural gas as the total reserves of 140 trillion cubic metres estimated in 1995. It would lead to a doubling of per capita natural gas production by 2050 and to the prospect that the developing countries could share to some extent in the consumption of the fuel in the first half of the 21st century.

It was shown in section 6.3 that there is no justification for complacency about the future of the oil industry. The natural gas industry is roughly 20 years behind the oil industry in development, so by the same reckoning there should be concern in a decade or two about natural

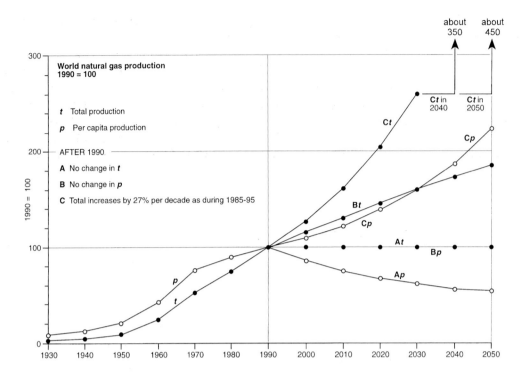

Figure 6.3 World natural gas production 1930-2050.

gas. There is, however, evidence that very large deposits of gas hydrates have formed in deep ocean and permafrost areas. With appropriate technology these could be extracted, thus greatly extending reserves from potential to accessible, although to extract the trapped methane is at present prohibitively expensive. De Koker (1995) describes the deposits of crystallized natural gas and water, estimated to contain twice as much energy as the reserves of all other forms of fossil fuel combined. Japan imports 99 per cent of all the oil it consumes and 96 per cent of all the natural gas. Not surprisingly, therefore, the Japan National Oil Corporation is planning to gather hydrates from the Sea of Japan to assess the prospects for developing an indigenous supply of energy. Off the coast of North Carolina, USA, a hydrate field estimated to have 350 times the amount of energy consumed in the USA in 1989 is to be explored and the feasibility of extracting the methane without destabilising the ocean floor is to be assessed.

6.5   ELECTRICITY

The position of electricity in the energy industry is complicated by the fact that it can either be generated in thermal power stations by fossil fuels, which have alternative uses, or by hydro-power or nuclear fuels, which are almost exclusively used to generate electricity. Hydro- and nuclear electricity are both therefore primary energy sources. During 1988-92, 64 per cent of all electricity generated in the world was produced from the burning of fossil fuels, 19 per cent from hydro-power and 17 per cent from nuclear fuels. Very small amounts were generated from geothermal, tidal, wind and solar sources of power.

As well as counting as a source of primary energy when generated from hydro- and nuclear sources, all electricity is a means of distributing power in a flexible way to innumerable consumers, albeit wastefully, on account of the great loss of energy during generation by fuels, and in transmission. The world production of electricity increased about 12 times between 1950 and 1990, but on account of population growth, the increase was less than six times in per capita terms. Figure 6.4 shows the growth of electricity generation during 1950-1990 in relation to 1990, when 11.7 trillion kWh were generated, giving an average of 2,205 kWh per capita. Very little nuclear electricity was generated before 1970. The generation of hydro-electricity increased by little more than five times during 1950-90, that of thermal electricity by almost 12 times.

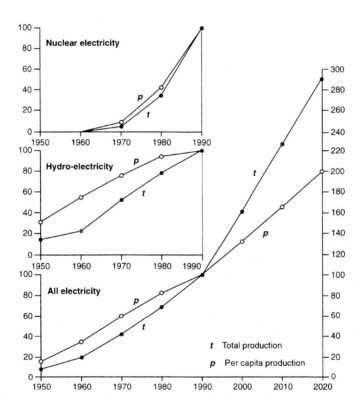

Figure 6.4 World electricity production 1950-2020, nuclear electricity and hydro-electricity 1950-1990. 1990 = 100 in all three graphs.

No attempt is made to plot alternative projections into the future from 1990, but one goal is shown in Figure 6.4, that of doubling per capita electricity production by the year 2020. To achieve such a goal it would be necessary to generate more than four times as much electricity during 1990-2020 as was generated during the preceding thirty years (compare the areas on the main graph in Figure 6.4 under the *t* line for 1960-90 and 1990-2020).

The generation of electricity should increase greatly in the next 2-3 decades if the 1950-90 trend is to continue. The share of the sources of energy used to generate it is, however, likely to change. Ideally, clean sources should replace polluting sources. If they do not, then an ever increasing amount of fossil fuels will have to be consumed each year. Alternative sources are now considered.

Nuclear energy

The development of this industry since the 1950s has not been smooth. While there is no immediate problem over reserves of nuclear fuel, two negative aspects of the generation of electricity in nuclear-fission plants have gained prominence and received increasing publicity: the danger of a serious accident in a nuclear power station (in a repetition of Chernobyl 1986, or worse), and the cost of decommissioning nuclear power stations and of disposing of nuclear waste safely. Several European countries, including Italy, Denmark and Austria, have no nuclear power stations, although all three depend heavily on imported sources of energy. On the other hand, several developing countries, including South Korea, Taiwan, China and Argentina produce nuclear electricity. The world consumption of nuclear electricity increased between 1985 and 1995 by 56 per cent, the increase accounted for largely by a growth of capacity in the USA, Japan, France and other market economy industrial countries.

Several serious nuclear accidents have occurred since the end of the Second World War. On 29 September 1957 an explosion in the Ural region of the USSR released radioactive waste, contaminating about 15,000 square kilometres. Some 10,000 people were evacuated, farmland was withdrawn from use, a river was contaminated and later contaminated dust was blown by the wind over a large area. The worst known nuclear accident in the USA was at Three Mile Island, Pennsylvania in 1979, the result of a reactor failure in a nuclear power station; there were no deaths, but 200,000 people were evacuated from the area. The Chernobyl nuclear accident in 1986 (see Shcherbak (1996)), is estimated to have caused 32,000 deaths. There have also been problems in the UK and France; the costly Superphénix nuclear power station at Morestel (east of Lyon), Europe's largest fast-breeder reactor, is to be closed after just one year of production (Brierley (1997)). Meanwhile (see Rollnick (1997b)), beaches and fishing grounds near the world's largest nuclear waste processing plant at La Hague in Normandy, France, have been closed to the public on account of high levels of contamination from nuclear waste.

A foretaste of things to come in the nuclear industry is given by the problems in the USA in both military and civilian establishments. According to Zorpette (1996), the USA is expecting to spend over 50 billion dollars to clean up one of its nuclear weapons complexes, in a desert area in southeast Washington State: 'What there will be, mostly, is radioactive detritus, millions of tons of it, ranging from contaminated soil to entire nuclear reactors. It will all be on a large plateau or stashed away in a collection of nondescript buildings. And there it will stay, probably for thousands of years to come.' Here, at least, is something that can be predicted with certainty for 2050. The timescale for actually preparing a site at Yucca Mountain in southern Nevada to receive nuclear waste from both military and civilian sources is itself considerable: about 20 years. According to Whipple (1996), even with regard to the caverns excavated in the rock deep underground no unequivocal conclusions have been reached as to the safety of storing waste there.

Hydro-electricity and other sources of clean energy

The bad news for the environment is that the share of clean hydro-electric power to total electricity generated has diminished in recent decades. For various reasons its share seems unlikely to increase and indeed may continue to decrease. One reason is that much of the hydro-electric potential is in areas such as Siberia, the Amazon and Congo river basins and the mountains in the interior of China, far from centres of population, with the prospect of excessive losses in transmission if harnessed. Another reason is that hydro-electric power stations usually require areas to be flooded to provide reservoirs of water to release through the generators. Useful land and human settlements may be put out of use and destroyed. For example, the controversial Three Gorges project on the Chang Jiang River in China would require about a million people to be re-settled and much useful land to be flooded. Tidal and wave generated electricity can also be regarded as hydro-power. The world tidal potential is minute and is restricted to inlets of a certain form in coastal areas with a large tidal range. The technology for harnessing wave power is not far advanced and is unlikely to be commercially viable for some decades, if at all, although the potential power there is considerable.

Other sources of clean energy to generate electricity include wind power and solar heat. Both forms are already used quite widely, but neither seems likely to make a major contribution to total electricity supplies for some decades, if at all, in spite of the widely accepted advantages. To generate large amounts of electricity, both processes need types of equipment that occupy large areas and each needs particular sites. Wind farms usually do best on elevated sites, often forming conspicuous eyesores in areas of scenic beauty. Solar panels are most effective in areas with long hours of sunshine, which may be at great distances from centres of population.

6.6   A COMPARISON OF SOURCES OF ENERGY

It is more difficult to anticipate the future of the energy industry than to project food production. Whatever the population in the world in 2050, that many mouths have to be fed, and in spite of marked differences in the composition of the human diet in various parts of the world, people need roughly the same amount of food. In contrast, there is an enormous difference in the average per capita consumption of commercial sources of energy between countries at the highest and lowest levels: almost 8,000 kilograms of oil equivalent annually in the USA, a mere 16 kilograms in Burkina Faso and Chad, both in Africa. The meagre amount of commercial sources of energy used in many developing countries is supplemented by 'non-commercial' fuelwood and animal dung, collected locally, but there is still an 'energy gap' of around 100:1 or more. Any projection for energy production and consumption in 2050 will be affected first of all by the scale of the gap at that time.

The energy situation is further complicated by the wide variety of uses of fuel and power, including domestic cooking and heating, the of use household appliances, agriculture, industry and transport. Figure 6.5 shows the main users of energy in the USA. In other industrial regions, notably Western Europe and Japan, the situation is broadly similar but the transport sector is somewhat less prominent while the amount per capita is appreciably less. A further complication is the fact that there are five different major commercial sources of energy, together with other commercial sources of limited importance at present, and non-commercial sources. The difficulty of using past trends to forecast future ones is illustrated by the great fluctuations in the level of Venezuelan oil production in Figure 6.6. Trends in energy production and consumption in the first half of the 21st century are likely to be influenced by a number of contradictory considerations of policy and priority, as well as by political forces and changes, especially in the oil producing countries of Southwest Asia.

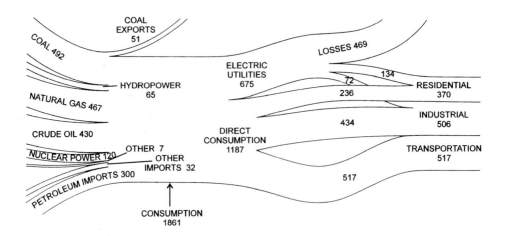

Figure 6.5 The energy flow of the USA in 1987. Quantities are in millions of tonnes of oil equivalent. The sources of energy are shown on the left, the users on the right. The width of the flows is proportional to their size, as indicated by the quantities. The contribution of different sources is broadly similar for the USA in the late 1990s, as are the uses. Western Europe and Japan depend much more heavily on imports than the USA. Based on Gibbons *et al.* (1989).

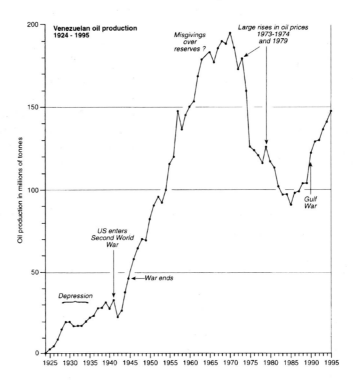

Figure 6.6 Venezuelan oil production 1924 to 1995. The impacts of the world economic depression and the Second World War can be seen in the early decades of the industry. The oil price rises enabled Venezuela to export less oil for a time, while obtaining roughly the same revenue.

World population can be expected to increase by about 86 per cent between 1990 and 2050, and even if there is no increase in the world per capita consumption of energy, a large increase in total energy production will still be needed. Even if per capita consumption remains roughly the same in the developed countries up to 2050, in many developing countries, particularly the newly industrialising and the very poor countries, it is expected that per capita levels will rise.

Exhaustible sources of energy will not last indefinitely, even if further discoveries of oil and especially of natural gas can be expected. A full assessment of possible reserves of coal in some parts of the world, including Siberia, should also increase proved reserves. Even so, if extracted and consumed at present rates in the next century, oil and gas might only last a few decades. Fossil fuels also provide raw materials, as, for example, for the manufacture of synthetic materials, and in a very long-term perspective it seems more useful to conserve them for industrial use than for them to go up in smoke.

As a source of fuel, forests are exhaustible unless properly managed and replanted. Of all types of forest in the world, at present the tropical forests are most at risk. Once they have been cut, even if only part of the timber is removed, the delicate ecological balance may be disturbed or destroyed. Although fuelwood accounts for less than 10 per cent of the energy obtained from all sources, commercial and non-commercial, the increase in its use in developing countries is a matter of concern because forests supply timber for construction purposes and as a raw material (e.g. for newsprint) in addition to fuelwood. The Population Reference Bureau (1987) contains a map of areas with an acute shortage of fuelwood in 1980. Deficits are worst in the arid and semi-arid regions of Africa, in South Asia and in mountainous regions of Latin America.

As well as being cleared for their timber, forests are being burned directly for conversion to arable farming, permanent crops and pasture in various parts of the world, especially in the tropics. Between 1980 and 1993 there was a 15 per cent increase in fuelwood consumption worldwide although population actually increased by about 25 per cent and the amount consumed per inhabitant therefore dropped. Since there is no concerted effort globally to discourage or prevent the use of fuelwood in developing countries, cutting seems likely to continue unabated until a strict policy is adopted and applied at international level to manage the world's forests. Table 6.8 shows the regional distribution and the recent growth in the extraction of fuelwood in the world.

Table 6.8 Consumption of fuelwood in millions of cubic metres in selected years

	1980	1990	1993
World	1,584	1,719	1,829
Africa	392	456	494
North America	136	146	165
South America	211	178	170
Asia	690	790	867
Europe	63	60	125[1]
Oceania	12	9	9
USSR	79	81	n.a.

[1] No explanation is forthcoming in the source for the sudden apparent increase, but it may be the result of adding consumption in the countries of Central Europe.

n.a. = not available

Source: *Energy Statistics Yearbook 1983*, Table 14 (p. 143) and *1993*, New York: United Nations

In addition to the harm done to the natural vegetation of the world by the cutting of fuelwood, the extraction and to a lesser extent the transportation of fossil fuels (especially the open-cast production of coal and lignite) is also a direct cause of local environmental damage. The combustion of fossil fuels and fuelwood causes pollution and adds carbon dioxide to the atmosphere. As noted in the previous section, the development and production of nuclear power has also caused serious environmental pollution in the former USSR, the USA and the UK, among other countries, by contaminating soil, vegetation and water. The construction of hydro-electric stations may adversely affect river systems. Much is said about converting to clean or cleaner sources of energy, but in practice for governments and for state and private companies in the energy sector alike it is simpler and more profitable to continue producing energy the way it has been produced up to now. Attempts to transform the energy industry can be expected, but there are snags and complications.

The generation of electricity, regarded as a clean form of energy, is central in the development of several new forms of energy. It is not, however, suitable for every kind of energy use. Almost all the electricity generated at present comes from one of the five main commercial sources of energy, fossil fuels, hydro- and nuclear power, the shortcomings of which have been described in this chapter. Pollution from motor vehicle exhausts is a serious problem in many cities of the world, not only the very large ones. The use of electric trains and eventually motor vehicles powered by electric batteries would reduce such pollution. The electricity that would replace the petroleum products currently used by motor vehicles would, however, still have to be generated somewhere, and if from fossil fuels, would transfer the pollution to other areas, presumably more rural ones, with fewer people to suffer and object. Similarly (see Gregory (1973)) electricity can be used to produce hydrogen, a clean fuel, which can be moved cheaply by pipeline, but the means used to generate the electricity in the first place will still cause pollution if derived from fossil fuels. Cleaner methods of generating electricity are needed.

Solar power is now beyond the experimental stage and is widely used in individual homes and commercial buildings. For it to contribute enough electricity to reduce substantially the need for fossil fuels or nuclear energy, while also catering for the expected increase in the need for electricity, is unlikely in the next few decades. Solar energy is cheapest where average sunshine hours are longest and temperatures high. There is no shortage of places in, for example, the interior of Australia or the Sahara Desert, where electricity could be generated in huge quantities, but it is lost in transmission. There is no way electricity generated in this way could, for example, be transmitted from Australia to Japan, where there are few convenient places to set up large areas of solar panels.

Wind power is no less problematic than solar power. Wind above a given speed is needed to be effective in generating electricity. The frequency of such wind varies greatly from place to place in the world. The occurrence of wind, even more than that of sunshine, is very unpredictable. As yet, only minute amounts of electricity are generated by wind power, even in parts of the world with a good 'supply' of wind, for example, in Western Europe in Denmark, northern Germany, and the UK, and in California in the USA. Typically it is not possible to please everyone with a new project. In England and Wales, areas of high wind speed are mostly in coastal and mountain areas. A plan to build the largest wind farm in Europe in northern England has been opposed by conservationists: 'the proposal underlines the growing threat to scenic countryside by a technology that will never make more than a tiny contribution to the production of cleaner energy' (see Hornsby (1997a)).

Immense amounts of energy are produced by wave power, but as with solar and wind power, there are technical and to a lesser extent aesthetic obstacles to the question of harnessing the energy. Nuttall (1999) reports that: 'The cost of electricity generated from wave power is down to about 7p a unit. From wind it is down to about 2p, in some cases, making it as competitive as gas.' New technology currently being developed could greatly reduce the cost of wave generated electricity but many countries of the world are land-locked, while some with a coastline do not experience suitable conditions for harnessing wave power.

One of the remaining hopes for abundant cheap and clean energy is the development of fusion power, which has all the advantages of fission power without, it is assumed, the disadvantages. Unlike solar, wind and wave power, plants for generating electricity by nuclear fusion could be located near to areas of high consumption.

6.7   ENERGY PROJECTIONS

The amount of energy that would be needed in the world up to the year 2050 was estimated by Ridker and Watson (1980) and is shown in Figure 6.7 and in Tables 6.9 and 6.10. This is one of many energy futures produced in recent decades. Although made in the late 1970s the estimate does not seem to take into account either the oil price rise of 1973 or the growing concern over the impact of the use of fossil fuels on the environment. Ridker and Watson forecast a ninefold increase in annual energy consumption in the world between 1975 and 2050, with an almost fourfold increase during 2000-2050. Table 6.9 shows what actually happened between 1975 and 1995, an increase of 36 per cent, contrasting with an increase of 108 per cent expected by Ridker and Watson. Their energy consumption 'target' was not, therefore, reached: the total was 8,140 million tonnes of oil equivalent instead of 12,250.

Table 6.9 Two energy futures, 1995-2050 in millions of tonnes of oil equivalent

	BP to 1995 *Cole to 2050*	*Ridker and* *Watson*
1975	5,970	5,880
1980	6,890	6,810
1985	6,950	8,160
1990	7,860	9,970
1995	8,140	12,250
2000	9,000	14,000
2025	13,000	29,400
2050	17,500	54,880

Table 6.10 Estimates of sources of world energy, 2050, according to Ridker and Watson (1980)

Source	*1995* *(millions t.o.e)*	*2050* *(millions t.o.e)*	*(percentage)*	*Increase between* *1995-2050*
Coal	2,210	19,600	35.7	Almost 9 times
Nuclear	596	15,860	28.9	Almost 27 times
Shale oil and tar sands	negligible	9,530	17.4	Huge
Solar	negligible	5,900	10.8	Huge
Oil and gas	5,110	3,990	7.2	Decline
Total	8,136	54,880	100.0	

Based on Ridker and Watson (1980), reproduced in Murphy (1983)

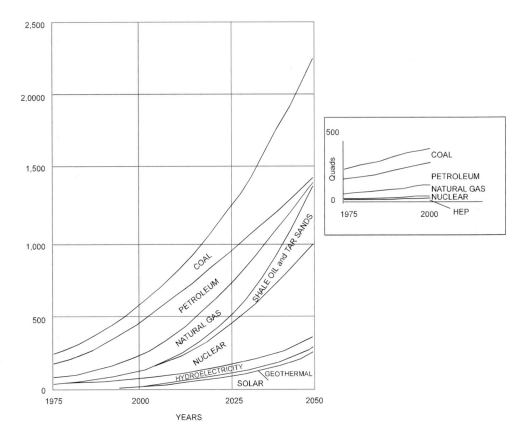

Figure 6.7 Sources of world energy consumption projected from 1975 to 2050 by Ridker and Watson (1980). The unit of measurement of energy used in the original is QUADS, one QUAD being equivalent to the energy provided by about 23.5 million tonnes of oil. The separate graph shows what actually happened between 1975 and 2000.

Table 6.10 shows the sources of the energy consumption expected by Ridker and Watson in 2050. Oil and natural gas would largely be exhausted, while the contribution of hydro-electricity would be small. On the other hand, in 2050 almost nine times as much coal and almost 27 times as much nuclear power would be needed as was consumed in 1975. The exploitation of shale oil and tar sands, most of the deposits of which are in North America (Colorado and Athabaska), Venezuela (Orinoco) and the former Soviet Union, would have to be developed from a very small base now, while nuclear and solar power would provide most of the electricity needed. Many questions can be raised about such an energy future. Among them one might ask how much investment and innovation can be made available over a period of 50 years or so to achieve such high levels of production for comparatively new types of energy supply. Could coal production and nuclear power be expanded to the extent they anticipate, and would the use of such large amounts of fossil fuels be a matter for environmental concern? No regional distribution of energy production or consumption is given by Ridker and Watson.

The author has calculated what he considers to be a plausible alternative future, whereby only a third as much energy is consumed in the world in 2050 as in the projection of Ridker and Watson. Table 6.11 shows a projection for the consumption of energy by major world regions.

Table 6.11 A possible future for world energy consumption in 2050 by major world regions

	1995			(4) Change in per capita level 1995–2050	2050		
	(1) Energy consumption millions t.o.e.	(2) Population in millions	(3) t.o.e. in kgs per capita		(5) Population in millions	(6) t.o.e. in kgs per capita	(7) Energy consumption needed millions t.o.e
Europe	1,725	576	3,000	None	540	3,000	1,620
North America	2,404	321	7,490	None	470	7,500	3,520
Japan	490	125	3,920	None	120	4,000	480
Former USSR	943	293	3,220	Small	350	3,500	1,220
China	833	1,219	680	×2	1,500	1,400	2,100
Latin America	433	481	900	×2	800	1,800	1,440
Middle East	312	150	2,080	×2	300	4,200	1,260
All Africa	238	720	330	×3	2,600	1,000	2,600
Rest of Asia	758	1,816	417	×2.4	3,200	1,000	3,200
World	**8,136**	**5,701**	**1,427**		**9,880**	**1,765**	**17,440**

Columns (1) to (7) in Table 6.11 are arranged in the order in which they are considered: (1) and (2) show the total consumption of energy and the total population in 1995. (3) shows the amount consumed per capita in each region. In (4) and (5) two sets of assumptions are made about 2050: in (4) the change in per capita level of energy consumption between 1995 and 2050 and in (5) the expected population in 2050. In (6) the resulting per capita consumption is calculated and in (7) the amount of energy needed in 2050 to reach that level given the expected population in (5).

It is assumed that there will be no change in the level of per capita energy consumption in Europe (excluding the former USSR), North America and Oceania, and Japan, and only a modest increase in the former USSR. In those developing regions with a comparatively high level of energy consumption, China, Latin America and the Middle East, the per capita level of consumption would double, but in Africa and the rest of Asia, where most needed, it would increase three and 2.4 times respectively. Figure 6.8 compares the world maps of energy consumption in 1995 and 2050 according to the data in Table 6.11. In Figure 6.9 the distribution of energy consumption among nine major regions is shown by a Lorenz curve for 1995; a similar curve is shown for a possible distribution in 2050. The respective gini coefficients of concentration are 0.544 and 0.346 (0.0 indicates a perfectly even distribution, 1.0 a total concentration in one place). Thus there would be some reduction of concentration between the 1990s and 2050, but an increase of total consumption from 8.1 billion t.o.e. in 1995 to 17.4 in 2050 and little change in per capita consumption in the developed regions.

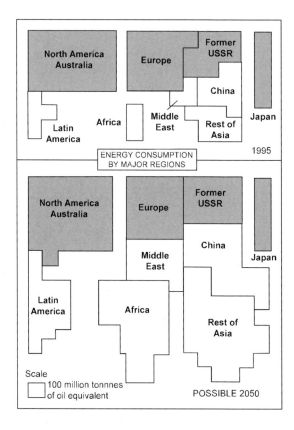

Figure 6.8 Present (1995) and future (2050) levels of energy consumption by major world regions. The area of each region is proportional to its total energy consumption, that for 2050 being based on a projection by the author.

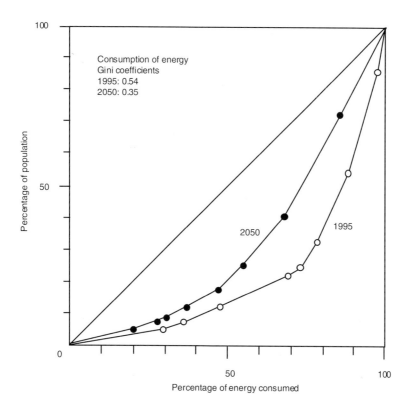

Figure 6.9 The distribution of energy consumption by nine major regions in 1995 and 2050. The further the curves are from the diagonal, the greater the degree of concentration in certain regions. The gini coefficients are calculated by dividing the area between each curve and the diagonal by the area of the lower right hand triangle, conventionally equal to one unit of area.

Environmentalists are concerned about any increase in the consumption of energy, on account primarily of damage to the natural and human environments. Political leaders and governments are almost universally committed to achieving economic growth, itself related to growth of GDP, at least in developing countries. A compromise is difficult to envisage. Figure 6.10 shows the difference in the level of energy consumption per capita between countries on the horizontal axis. It also shows, however, that there is only a rough correlation between per capita energy consumption and per capita GDP. Therefore GDP is only an approximate guide to living standards. It is, however, clear that insofar as energy contributes to GDP there is a large disparity in the amount of GDP 'produced' by given amounts of energy, as for example between Ukraine and Italy, at less than one dollar and about seven dollars per kilogram respectively.

6.8   ALTERNATIVE FUTURES FOR ENERGY

To conclude this chapter, the concept of Good, Average and Bad futures is applied to the world energy situation as it was to the world food situation in Chapter 5.

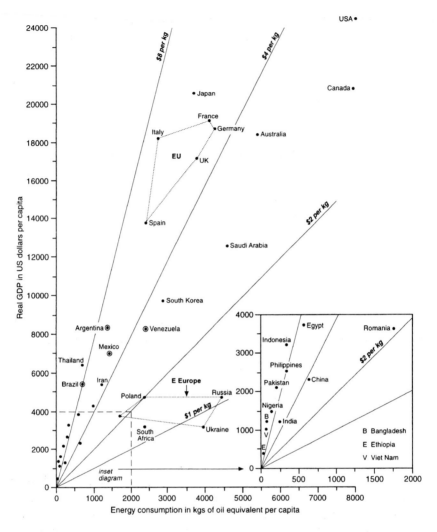

Figure 6.10 The relationship between energy consumption per capita and real GDP per capita in the largest countries of the world in population in the mid-1990s. Four countries of Latin America are distinguished by a special symbol (⊙)

1. Population by 2050:

    Good: reaches about 9 billion

    Average: reaches about 10 billion

    Bad: reaches about 11 billion.

2. Global warming and pollution:

    Good: it emerges that very little, if any global warming occurs on account of the burning of fossil fuels. In addition, efforts have been made to cut pollution. This problem will be further discussed in Chapter 10.

Average: global warming from fossil fuel combustion causes a rise of sea level of a metre by 2050, the positive and negative effects of climatic change cancel out, and pollution levels remain the same as in the 1990s.

Bad: sea level rises 2-3 metres, climatic change has an overall negative effect on agriculture, and pollution levels continue to rise.

3. The discovery of more fossil fuels:

    Good: consumption of oil and natural gas can continue to rise without shortages disrupting the world economy thanks to large discoveries. This could however have an adverse effect on global warming.

    Average: sufficient new reserves of oil and natural gas are discovered to allow present consumption to be maintained until 2050.

    Bad: very few new reserves of oil and natural gas are discovered, in which case if current levels of energy consumption are to be maintained, alternative sources of energy will have to be developed very quickly.

4. Progress in the production of clean, renewable sources of energy (i.e. including hydro-electric power but excluding fossil fuels, wood, and nuclear fission power):

    Good: by 2050 they provide at least half of all energy consumed.

    Average: by 2050 at least a quarter

    Bad: by 2050 no more than a few per cent.

5. The use of fuelwood:

    Good: the level of consumption is reduced so that forests and other natural vegetation such as scrub and savanna are not depleted or damaged. Greater efficiency is achieved in the use of fuelwood for cooking and heating (see e.g. Kammen (1995)), for example, with the use of more efficient stoves or the replacement of fuelwood in developing countries where forests are threatened, fuelwood could be saved by the use of kerosene stoves and solar heated ovens.

    Average: fuelwood consumption remains roughly at the same level as at present.

    Bad: fuelwood consumption continues to increase to keep up with population growth in developing countries.

6. Political prospects:

    Good: no big increase in oil and natural gas prices (but Bad for producers)

    Average: a big increase in prices

    Bad: for reasons of conservation of reserves or political conditions or both, oil and gas exports from the Organisation of Petroleum Exporting Countries and/or from Russia to industrial and developing countries alike are reduced.

7. World energy agreement:

Good: a global energy policy is introduced and the consumption of energy is rationed. Much of the bargaining would be about reducing the great disparity in the per capita consumption of energy between the developed and developing countries of the world.

Average: to cut down pollution in densely populated areas in developed countries, private motoring and the domestic use of fuel and power would have to be cut. Restrictions on speed of vehicles, and the use of car pools and other measures in developed countries, make little impact.

Bad: there is no global energy policy.

Taxing energy may reduce consumption marginally in some situations, but using it more efficiently seems likely to buy more time. De Cicco and Ross (1994) refer to a historic partnership in the US auto industry 'to develop vehicles having three times the fuel economy of today's fleet, while providing the same comfort, safety and performance. Possible options include electric vehicles powered by batteries or fuel cells, and hybrid vehicles combining an electric drive train with a combustion engine that might use a variety of fuels.' In their view, however, gasoline and diesel cars and trucks will most likely dominate the roads for decades to come.

The European Union imports about half of its energy needs and at the same time has some of the biggest concentrations of urban population in the developed countries. Officials of the EU Commission attempted to introduce an EU-wide tax on the carbon content of fuel in 1994 but the proposal was rejected by member states. In 1996 the Commission planned to tax energy products through the excise system. According to Snape (1996), carbon dioxide emissions would be cut by between two and four per cent by 2005, nitrogen oxide and sulphur dioxide emissions by 0.8 and 1.3 per cent respectively by 2010, small beginnings, if indeed they are introduced, with the effect of buying a little time. At the Rio 2 Earth Summit, June 1997, in New York, European nations pressed for a tax on aviation fuel. Predictably, airlines, oil companies and tourism firms objected strongly. In the European Union there are proposals to introduce a 100 km/h (62 mph) speed limit on motorways (Conradi (1997)), following the examples of the USA and Japan.

It has been pointed out in Chapter 3.1 that often different people have mutually exclusive priorities. One such inconsistency is illustrated by solutions that cancel each other out. Hall, D. (1981) proposes: 'When oil is so scarce that the cost of diesel fuel is prohibitive, one may have to grow plants to produce vegetable oils as fuels.' In fact, sugar has been grown for some time in Brazil for processing into alcohol to fuel cars. At the same time it has been proposed that when agricultural land is insufficient to feed the world's population it will be possible to obtain food from hydrocarbons (see Chapter 5).

An even more bizarre proposal to combat global warming (assuming it is happening), while avoiding punitive taxes aimed at cutting car use, is to plant trees to absorb emissions of carbon gases. Nuttall (1997b) describes the arithmetic of the proposal of Formula One racing's governing body to pay to plant trees in a community forest in Mexico. Each year 5,500 tonnes of carbon are emitted as a result of racing, testing and transport to races. It would be necessary to plant 25,000 trees to offset those emissions. However, trees do not add much volume in the first decade or two of growth, depending on the species, and the Current Annual Increment (CAI) tends to be highest between the ages of about 30 and 50 years. According to Nuttall: 'the world is producing 6 billion tonnes of carbon annually from burning fossil fuels ... an estimated

Table 6.12 Checklist of attributes of major sources of fuel and power

	(1) Coal, lignite	(2) Oil	(3) Natural gas	(4) Hydro-electricity	(5) Nuclear electricity	(6) Fuelwood	(7) Sun, wind, waves
Development of new technology	Low	Deep offshore drilling		Low	Medium	Near zero	High
Cost of extraction/production	Medium	Low	Low	Low	Medium	Near zero	High
Cost of movement	Medium	Low	Low	Distance limit[1]		High	Local
Loss of useful land	Low	Low	Low	Medium	Low	Mixed[2]	Low
Pollution, contamination	High	High	Medium	None	Low	High	None
Global warming	High	High	High	None	None	High	None
Political implications	Low	High	High	Local	Small	Mixed[2]	None

[1] There is a commercial limit to the distance over which electricity can be transmitted.

[2] The burning of fuelwood is usually for local use. Forest cleared for fuelwood may become arable or pasture land or it may be replanted (or allowed to regenerate), while arable land and pasture may be planted with trees. The uncontrolled burning of forest may give rise to political problems, as the spread of smoke from the burning of forest in Jambi province Indonesia to other countries in Southeast Asia in 1997.

40-100 billion tonnes of carbon could be absorbed by planting new forests, the equivalent of up to 16 years of carbon pollution at current levels.'

Often the implications of solutions that are theoretically possible are not carefully thought out. Depending on local conditions and species of tree, one hectare of trees could yield roughly 15 cubic metres of wood once every 25 years (see e.g. Hart (1991)). In a year each car emits about a tonne of carbon. Since there are about 500 million motor vehicles in the world, each year 50 million hectares of new forest would be needed. Where would such a large amount of suitable land be found? Either from present arable land or permanent pasture, or from waste land. Even then, motor vehicles only account for a small part of all carbon emissions. Furthermore, it is unlikely that such measures would make a significant contribution for up to 50 years.

If one assumes a population in 2050 of around 10 billion, give or take a billion, it is not difficult accordingly to work out approximately how much food would be needed to feed that number of people, although producing the food and/or distributing it equably could be a problem. More energy is consumed at present in the world than is actually needed, much of it being used to satisfy wants rather than needs in the developed countries. Energy production is more difficult to plan and to project to 2050 than food production in both the above respect and on account of the considerable variety and varied merits of different energy sources.

Table 6.12 is a checklist of relative advantages and disadvantages of different sources of energy. The reader may feel that some of the descriptions need changing. What certainly needs changing is the imprecise way in which politicians and their advisers often talk about pollution from energy sources. For example, much is said about taxing one thing and discouraging another 'to reduce global warming'. Strictly such measures only reduce the rate of accumulation of emissions that increase global warming.

If there is much uncertainty at the end of the 20th century about the future production of different sources of energy there is no doubt about the energy prospects for different regions of the world in the next few decades, given reserves, population size and per capita consumption. Oceania's future is the best, the former USSR and the Middle East are very well placed; North America and Latin America are not too bad. On the other hand, the energy situation in Western Europe is precarious, while in South Asia, Southeast Asia, China and Africa (except the extreme north and south) it is desperate, and Japan defies description. Japan and Western Europe can, however, afford to import fossil fuels from other regions while these sources last.

In the end, so much in the energy sector revolves round the price of oil. According to BP (1997), at 1996 prices the price of a barrel jumped from less than 10 constant US cents in 1970 to over 30 in the mid-1970s and over 50 in the early 1980s, only to fall quickly and in the mid-1990s to dip below 20. Stelzer (1994) wrote: 'Just when the economic landscape looked bright, domestic political pressures facing King Fahd of Saudi Arabia and his family may lead to the price of oil being tripled ... this will spin the world into another deep depression.' The reader will appreciate the difficulties of making forecasts about energy in the next decade, let alone the next half century.

7

MATERIALS AND MANUFACTURING

---

*'Wealth is created by people who make things and grow things,
not by people who push pieces of paper around'*

An industrialist interviewed on BBC Breakfast News, 11 October 1991

7.1 INTRODUCTION

In spite of the dream of achieving sustainable development, or even a sustainable economy without further development, most productive sectors of the economy use some non-renewable natural resources. Cultivation gradually removes nutrients from the soil, fossil fuels literally go up in smoke when burnt, and non-fuel minerals usually end up after processing and manufacturing in a new, unalterable form, although some re-cycling is possible. It is unrealistic to expect many radical changes in the way development takes place and economies are run in the first half of the 21st century in spite of the continuing expansion of the use of automation, robots and other means of increasing the efficiency of production and improving the quality of products. It is therefore relevant to examine the possible uses of materials to the year 2050. There are two principal, distinct sources of raw materials, bioclimatic resources on the land and in the sea, and mineral resources, mostly either quarried or mined.

Changes in the use of the world's total land are a zero-sum game in which if the area under one type of use increases, then that under other types has to decrease. If the extent of the cultivated land and natural pasture used to produce food is increased, that increase could be at the expense of land currently used to grow such raw materials as fibres and oils. Again, the greater the amount of forest cut for fuelwood, the less is available to supply timber for construction and as a raw material, although in developing countries much of the material collected for cooking and heating is actually of little use as quality timber, being from shrubs and even cactus plants.

The situation is in some respects similar in the case of fossil fuels, since at any given time an increase in the extraction of one fuel may, if only briefly, be parallelled by a reduction in the extraction of another, either absolutely or relatively. On the other hand most sources of mineral raw materials are non-renewable or exhaustible, or are replaced naturally but at a much slower rate than that at which they are now being extracted. In the 1990s almost all of the fossil fuels extracted are being used for combustion to produce heating or energy. In the longer term the importance of fossil fuels as sources of raw materials for the production of goods such as synthetic materials should grow in relative importance.

While agriculture, forestry and fossil fuels supply numerous raw materials, at present many of the principal materials used in manufacturing are obtained from non-fuel minerals. By definition such minerals do not contribute to food supply or to energy supply. After processing they are destined for use in construction, manufacturing, for increasing crop yields, and in numerous other sectors of production. Non-fuels minerals are conventionally subdivided initially into non-metallic (e.g. phosphate rock, limestone) and metallic (e.g. iron ore, copper ore). Metallic minerals may be broadly subdivided into iron ore and associated alloy metals (ferro-alloys), base metals (e.g. copper, lead, zinc), light metals (e.g. aluminium) and precious metals (e.g. gold, silver) (see e.g. Alexandersson and Ivar Klevebring (1978)).

The use of materials for building dwellings, for clothing and for the making of tools dates back to times long before cultivation started in a systematic way. Even at the end of the 20th century simple tools are still being made in remote communities, exemplified by the stone axe makers of New Guinea (see Toth *et al.* (1992)) and by one of the last undisturbed communities in the world, the Korabo, in the as yet untouched forests of northwest Brazil (see Rayment (1997)). Metals have been used extensively for tools, arms and ornaments in Asia, Africa and Europe for several millennia, but mainly for ornaments in the Americas, before the 16th century. Fibres, wood, non-fuel minerals and metals are still the basis for many branches of industry in the 20th century. As a result of innovations in technology combined with the rapid growth of population, the quantities used have been far greater than previously (especially since the 17th century) and particularly in the developed countries, which with only about 20 per cent of the total population of the world now consume about 70 per cent of the fuel and raw materials used in the world.

The increasing use of wood in parts of Western Europe in the 17th century led to concern over supplies (see Nef (1977)). In the 18th century wood was increasingly supplemented by coal, initially in Britain (which around 1800 accounted for about 90 per cent of all coal extracted in the world) then in other countries of Western Europe with coalfields, and in the USA. During the 19th century the amount of fuel and materials used in the world increased about ten times, while population only doubled. During the 20th century roughly a tenfold increase in the use of fuel and materials has again occurred, involving a far greater *absolute* amount than in the 19th century; population has increased about four times. Even in the 1990s, however, the level of consumption of energy and raw materials by a large part of the population of the world was still low. One of the challenges of speculating about conditions in the year 2050 is to calculate what would be needed to allow the much larger expected population of the present developing countries to consume energy and raw materials at a level closer to that reached in present-day developed countries.

In a paper entitled 'Beyond the Era of Materials' Larson *et al.* (1986) point out that in the latter part of the 20th century the industrial countries are facing a historic change. Economic growth is no longer accompanied by increased consumption of basic materials. They argue that in North America, Western Europe and Japan economic expansion continues, but that the demand for many basic materials has levelled off. These regions are now leaving the 'Era of Materials'. Larson *et al.* identify four main trends to support their view: 'Substitution of one material for another has slowed down the growth of demand for particular materials. So have design changes in products that increase the efficiency of materials used. Perhaps more important, the markets that expanded rapidly during the Era of Materials are by and large saturated. And new markets tend to involve products that have a low materials content.' They provide numerous examples of the impressive way in which energy and materials are being used with increasing efficiency as time passes, at least in the industrial countries.

In a paper entitled 'Advanced Materials and the Economy' Clark and Flemings (1986) focus on the rapid progress being made in materials science and engineering. According to their view: 'A fundamental reversal in the relationship between human beings and materials is taking place … it is only recently that advances in the theoretical understanding of the structure of physical and biological matter, in experimental technique, and in processing technology, have made it possible to start with a need and then develop a material to meet it, atom by atom.'

One positive message is that there is now great flexibility in the choice and use of sources of energy and materials, and economies will not depend so heavily and sometimes exclusively on one particular product. On the other hand, two reservations should be borne in mind about the trends noted. First, there will still be a need to use materials in the developed countries, even if not at per capita levels of the present. We may be entering the Era of Information, and computers greatly assist in the production and diffusion of information, but they cannot produce food, metals, or cement. Second, the progress made in using basic materials more sparingly and efficiently is a characteristic of the developed countries, the most sophisticated of which, North America, Australia, New Zealand, Western Europe and Japan, had about 840 million inhabitants in 1996 out of at total world population of 5,770 million, a mere 15 per cent. About another 340 million (6 per cent) live in Central and Eastern Europe and the more developed parts of the former USSR. After a spectacular rise in the use of materials the former Soviet bloc between the late 1940s and the 1980s, consumption has actually been diminishing, but on account of drastic economic changes rather than the more efficient use of materials. That leaves almost 80 per cent of the population of the world, where in many countries the consumption of energy and materials is rising rapidly.

7.2   RAW MATERIALS FROM BIOCLIMATIC RESOURCES

Crops grown as sources of raw materials occupy only a small part of the total cultivated area of the world. They mostly fall into two broad categories, those used to manufacture textiles and allied products, and those used in chemical and pharmaceutical products. The most prominent among the former include cotton (referred to as lint, as distinct from cotton seed), flax and hemp fibres, jute, hard fibres such as agaves, and natural rubber (the last two being permanent crops). Among the latter are such trees as the palm oil and olive trees, and field crops such as the sunflower. There is unlikely to be a global crisis in the next few decades caused by failure to grow these crops in sufficient quantity. Local problems affecting the production of particular items in specific areas may arise, but substitution of one material by another and the capability of producing synthetic materials such as, for example, rubber from fossil fuels, are widespread, as discussed in the previous section.

Raw materials from livestock, whether raised on feed from the world's cropland or from natural pasture, form an important element in the inventory of raw materials. Among the chief materials are wool, hides and skins, and raw silk. In view of the gradual decline in the number of livestock units in the world in relation to total human population (see Chapter 5), raw materials from livestock may become increasingly scarce. As with raw materials from plants, such a decline should happen on a slow timescale and in a way unlikely to set off a global crisis. In addition, materials from fossil fuels have widely replaced such natural materials as silk and leather.

The other main source of raw materials from the land is wood. Data for the area of land in the world under trees are very unsatisfactory due both to inconsistencies in the definition of forest and woodland, and to the lack of accurate measurements of areas involved (see also Chapter 5). This situation is being partly remedied by the use of satellite images. The increasing consumption of fuelwood in developing countries was noted in Chapter 6 and the use of roundwood (the term for timber before processing) will be discussed below.

Finally, reference should be made to the use of part of the world's fishing catch for the production of fertiliser. Fishes such as anchovies may be processed into fishmeal rather than providing human food. Given the doubts expressed in Chapter 5 about the possibility of greatly expanding the world fish catch, only a small proportion of the materials for the production of fertilisers can be expected from this source. Two products, raw cotton and roundwood, will now be discussed briefly to illustrate the fortunes of bioclimatic raw materials between 1950 and 1990.

Between 1948-52 and 1970 the area in the world under cotton grown for the textile industry, as opposed to oilseeds, fluctuated between 30 and 33 million hectares, during which time the yield rose from 2.15 to 3.5 tonnes per hectare. That trend has continued since 1970, with little change in the area cultivated, but with a further increase in yield. During 1930-1990, world production of cotton grew from just under 6 million tonnes a year to 18.5 million tonnes. Production per capita was 2.8 kilograms in 1930, 3.1 in 1950 and 3.5 in 1990. Figure 7.1 shows that there has been little change in per capita production between the mid-1950s and 1990s, the growth in total production closely matching the growth in total population. The prospect for this particular raw material seems to be more of the same, although yields per unit of area may be moving towards the maximum commercially possible and some extra cropland would therefore be needed to cater for population growth.

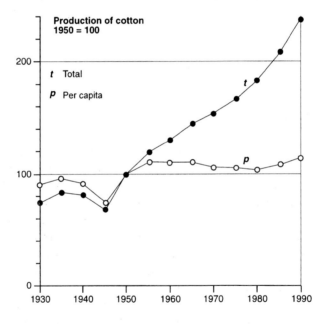

Figure 7.1   Production of raw cotton (lint), 1930-1990.

The situation with roundwood (see Figure 7.2) is different from that of cotton, although trends from 1950 to 1990 are remarkably similar. Between 1950 and 1990, roundwood cut from the world's forests rose from almost 1,500 million cubic metres to almost 3,500 million. The amount cut per inhabitant was, however, only 10 per cent higher in 1990 than in 1950, from 0.59 cubic metres in 1950 to 0.65 in 1990. The difference between plant raw materials produced from field or tree crops, and roundwood, is that in many parts of the world trees are not being replanted at the rate at which they are being cut, and unless the replacement rate exceeds the rate of extraction (to allow for the increase in population), the world's forestry industry is not sustainable and timber may therefore be deemed a non-renewable natural resource.

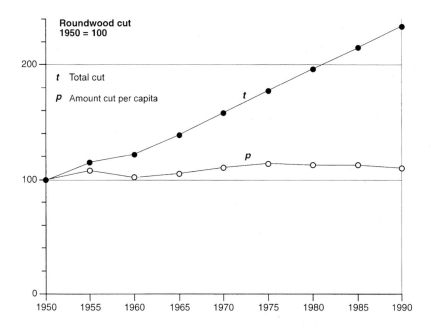

Figure 7.2 World production of roundwood, 1950-1990.

7.3   NON-FUEL MINERALS

Modern industry is largely based on the use of fossil fuels as a source of energy and on a wide range of non-fuel minerals as raw materials. While there are only three main typs of fossil fuels, 76 different non-fuel minerals are covered in US Bureau of Mines (1985), about 20 of them familiar household names, many hardly ever referred to outside industry.

For various reasons, data on the precise size of the reserves of many non-fuel minerals are not readily available. One reason is that in the Western industrial countries most reserves are controlled and worked by large private companies, reluctant to give exact quantities of their reserves, or able only to make approximate estimates. Another reason, presumably less influential now than during the Cold War, is the strategic nature of many minerals, particularly metals. Now that Russia and other Republics of the former USSR are becoming more integrated into the world economy, additional data should be forthcoming from these important sources of minerals. In addition, until the 1990s South Africa was not free to trade with the rest of the world, but sanctions have now been dropped.

Table 7.1 shows the reserves of 16 minerals prominent in the world economy and considered to be commercially extractable by the two sources given at the foot of Table 7.1. Further reserves, usually roughly equal to those shown, are considered to exist for the 11 non-fuel minerals listed. Five fuels (see also Chapter 6) are included for comparison. Annual production (column 2) around 1990 or in the early 1990s is shown against total reserves (column 1). The reserves to production ratio (R/P), the 'life expectancy' of reserves at the rate of production of the time, is shown in column (3). The 16 minerals have been ranked from high to low in the Table according to their R/P ratios.

Table 7.1 Reserves to production ratio of selected minerals around 1990 ranked in descending order of life expectancy at current rates of production

		(1) Reserves	*(2)* Annual production (year)	*(3)* R/P years[1]
1	Lignite and brown coal	512.3 bnt	1,214 mnt (1995)	420
2	Potash	9.1 bnt	24 mnt (90-94)	380
3	Bauxite	21.0 bnt	108 mnt (88-94)	190
4	Anthracite and bituminous coal	519.4 bnt	3.32 bnt (1995)	157
5	Iron ore (metal content)	72.0 bnt	565 mnt (88-94)	140
6	Manganese (metal content)	1.0 bnt	8 mnt (90-94)	125
7	Chromite (metal content)	1,165 mnt	11 mnt (90-94)	105
8	Phosphate rock	14.0 bnt	146 mnt (88-94)	95
9	Natural gas	139.7 tcm	2.12 tcm (1995)	65
10	Nickel (metal content)	58 mnt	900,000 t (90-94)	60
11	Uranium	2.6 mnt	46,000 t (88-92)	55
12	Oil	138.3 bnt	3.25 bnt (1995)	43
13	Copper (metal content)	340 mnt	9.2 mnt (90-94)	35
14	Lead (metal content)	95 mnt	3.1 mnt (90-94)	30
15	Zinc (metal content)	170 mnt	7.0 mnt (90-94)	24
16	Tin (metal content)	3.1 mnt	187,000 t (90-94)	16

t = metric tonnes
mn = million metric tonnes
bn = billion metric tonnes
tcm = trillion cubic metres
[1] reserves to production ratio

Main sources of data;

Reserves:	U.S. Bureau of Mines, *Mineral Facts and Problems*, 1985 edition, Bulletin 675, Washington: U.S. Government Printing Office
Production:	U.S. Bureau of Census, *Statistical Abstract of the United States: 1995*, 115th edition Washington DC, 1995 *Calendario Atlante de Agostini*, 1995, Novara

While it cannot be expected that the extraction levels of the early 1990s will continue indefinitely, a very marked disparity can be seen in present R/P ratios. The extraction of the first ten minerals listed could continue at early 1990s levels as far ahead as 2050 without the discovery of new reserves, whereas the extraction of the remaining six would not be possible that far ahead without the discovery of more reserves. Aluminium (from bauxite) and iron are two of the most widely found elements in the earth's crust, while the three ferro-alloys, manganese, chrome and nickel appear to be in reasonably good supply.

Of the last six minerals in Table 7.1, uranium is unlikely to be a problem in view of the slowing down of expansion of the nuclear power industry, the possibility of obtaining nuclear fuel in other ways, and the prospect that nuclear fusion power could be developed within a few decades. The oil industry has been discussed in Chapter 6. There remain four non-ferrous metals, of which copper is the highest in value of production; none has a long term future unless new reserves are found.

The distribution of reserves of some non-fuel minerals is very uneven over the earth's surface, in effect the land surface, since estimates of minerals on and beneath the floor of the seas and oceans are only very approximate. Table 7.2 shows the three countries with the largest reserves of each of 11 non-fuel minerals. Some non-fuel mineral reserves are widely distributed over the world while others, among them chromite, phosphates (see Sheldon (1982)) and potash, are highly concentrated.

Table 7.2 The three largest reserves of 11 major non-fuel minerals in percentages of the world total

		First		*Second*		*Third*	
1	Iron ore	USSR	34.7	Brazil	15.0	Australia	14.0
2	Chromite	S. Africa	78.4	USSR	12.2	Finland	1.6
3	Manganese	S. Africa	40.7	USSR	36.5	Australia	7.5
4	Nickel	Cuba	34.5	Canada	13.6	USSR	12.6
5	Bauxite	Guinea	26.7	Australia	21.1	Brazil	10.7
6	Copper	Chile	23.2	USA	16.8	Zambia	8.8
7	Lead	USA	22.1	Australia	16.8	Canada	12.6
8	Tin	Malaysia	35.9	Indonesia	22.2	Thailand	8.8
9	Zinc	Canada	15.3	USA	12.9	Australia	10.6
10	Phosphate rock	Morocco	49.3	S. Africa	18.6	USA	10.0
11	Potash	Canada	48.4	USSR	33.0	Germany	14.3

Note: USSR means former USSR
Source: Bureau of Mines (1985)

Table 7.3 shows the share of the world total of 27 mineral reserves held by five countries, the USA, Canada, Australia, South Africa and the former USSR. With only 11.3 per cent of the total population of the world (but 37.2 per cent of the area), these five countries together have more than their 'share' of 24 out of the 27 minerals listed. Four of the countries are regarded as part of the developed world, while arguably South Africa could also be included, at least with regard to its high level of mining and heavy industrial activities. All the developed countries together consume 70-80 per cent of most minerals so the presence in Table 7.2 of only two West European countries and the complete absence of Japan underline the very weak non-fuel mineral resource base of these two leading developed regions of the world. Together with the USA, they import minerals from developed regions (e.g. Canada, Australia, Russia) and developing ones (e.g. South America, southern Africa). Reserves of some minerals, for example phosphates, tin and nickel, are highly concentrated in one or a few developing countries, but so far there has not been a concerted effort by producers of non-fuel minerals to raise prices similar to that made by oil exporters and OPEC. Several non-metallic non-fuel minerals have prominent places in the world economy, notably limestone, clays, sand and gravel, and other building materials, as well as salt and gypsum, but they are widely available in large quantities and are mostly used near to where they occur.

The life expectancy of fossil fuels and non-fuel materials, calculated with various assumptions about rates of extraction, has received attention in many publications in the last thirty years. There is some inter-reference of data and estimates, as researchers and authors quote the same original data sources and each other. A number of examples are:

- Cloud (1968). Projections from 1964 show an end to recoverable world reserves of lead, zinc, tin, gold, silver and platinum *before* the year 2000, crude oil, natural gas, uranium, tungsten and copper before 2050 (quoted in Ehrlich and Ehrlich (1972)).

Table 7.3 Mineral reserves of five major sources of minerals as percentages of world totals.

		USA	*Canada*	*Australia*	*S. Africa*	*Former USSR*	*Combined percentage share*
1	Platinum	–	0.9	–	85.6	13.3	99.8
2	Chromite	–	–	–	78.4	12.2	90.6
3	Gold	6.3	3.3	1.8	59.4	15.6	86.4
4	Manganese	–	–	7.5	40.7	35.5	84.7
5	Potash	1.0	48.4	–	–	33.0	82.4
6	Diamonds[1]	–	–	57.3	7.1	8.2	72.6
7	Asbestos	3.6	36.4	–	5.2	27.3	72.5
8	Uranium	5.2	7.4	23.8	12.5	23.6	72.5
9	Lead	22.1	12.6	16.8	4.2	12.6	68.3
10	Molybdenum	50.0	8.3	–	–	8.3	64.6
11	Iron	5.1	6.3	14.0	4.0	34.7	64.1
12	Lignite[2]	26.2	0.8	8.9	–	26.8	62.7
13	Hard coal[3]	20.5	0.9	8.7	10.7	20.0	60.8
14	Silver	11.7	14.8	10.0	1.3	17.9	55.7
15	Zinc	12.9	15.3	10.6	6.5	6.5	51.8
16	Sulphur	12.0	11.6	–	–	27.1	50.7
17	Natural gas	3.3	1.4	0.4	–	40.0	45.1
18	Phosphate rock	10.0	–	–	18.6	9.3	37.9
	AREA	6.9	7.3	5.7	0.9	16.4	37.2
19	Tungsten	5.4	17.1	4.6	–	10.0	37.1
20	Nickel	–	13.8	4.0	4.8	12.6	35.2
21	Copper	16.8	5.0	2.4	–	7.3	31.5
22	Bauxite	–	–	21.1	–	5.0	26.1
23	Antimony	2.0	1.5	2.2	5.7	6.5	17.9
24	Tin	0.7	2.0	5.9	1.0	2.6	12.2
	POPULATION	4.7	0.5	0.3	0.4	5.4	11.3
25	Mercury	3.5	–	–	–	7.5	11.0
26	Oil	2.9	0.7	0.2	–	5.5	9.3
27	Cobalt	–	1.3	0.6	0.5	3.8	6.2

The percentages of area and population in the five countries are shown for comparison

[1]   Natural industrial
[2]   Including sub-bituminous
[3]   Anthracite and bituminous

Main sources:

BP Statistical Review of World Energy 1996 for fuels
US Bureau of Mines (1985) for non-fuel minerals

- Meadows *et al.* (1972) as from around 1970 give gold, mercury, silver and zinc the shortest life expectancies, together with oil and natural gas.

- In 'Blueprint for Survival', out of 16 metals considered, Goldsmith *et al.* (1972) give only iron and chromium a life expectancy beyond 2050.

- Barney (1982) starts with 1976 reserves of 17 non-fuel minerals (four non-metallic) and compares life expectancy if there is no change in the 1976 level of production with that resulting from projected demand growth rate for each mineral. Only 8 of the 17 would last to the year 2000 in the first instance and only 2 in the second instance (chromium and potash).

The above examples of potential futures for the life expectancy of mineral deposits, both fossil fuel and non-fuel mineral, highlight the difficulty of making projections for non-renewable resources largely located beneath the surface of the land or of the sea, much of it as yet unexplored. In contrast, the land (and sea) surface of the earth is virtually fixed, and projecting the level of food and raw materials from cultivated land, pasture and forest depends on what use is made of known areas, allowing for future changes in irrigation, the use of fertilisers and the clearance and replanting of forests.

7.4   CEMENT, ALUMINIUM AND COPPER

The prospects for three products, at present of great importance in the world economy, one non-metallic mineral and two metallic, are reviewed in this section. Limestone and bauxite are widely available in the world, but reserves of copper ore are limited in relation to the current level of production. The processing of all three materials requires considerable quantities of energy.

Cement

Although cement does not attract the publicity or cause the concern that many other minerals do, its importance in the development process is crucial in the construction of buildings, transport links and in many other ways. Between 1930 and 1990, the annual production of cement in the world increased 17 times, from 67 million tonnes to 1,140 million. The corresponding world average output per capita increased from 32 kilograms in 1930 to 215 kilograms in 1990 - less than 7 times. Three alternative futures for cement production shown in Figure 7.3 are compared below, and the distribution of production among the countries of the world is then discussed.

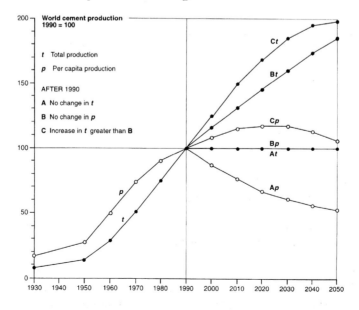

Figure 7.3 World cement production 1930-1950.

- Projection A. It is assumed that there is no change in world cement production between 1990 and 2050 (At). By 2050, per capita production (Ap) would be little more than half what it was in 1990. Even then, twice as much cement would have to be produced in the forty years between 1990 and 2030 as between 1950 and 1990 and three times as much between 1990 and 2050 as between 1950 and 1990.

- Projection B. In this projection world per capita production (Bp) would remain constant after 1990 but production would therefore almost have to double by 2050 to achieve such a target.

- Projection C. While it is reasonable to assume no great increase in per capita cement consumption in the developed countries after 1990 and indeed possibly a decline, the developing countries, with their growing populations and increasing per capita levels of cement consumption, would need much more cement for some decades to come. Projection C hardly does justice to this prospect but shows a modest increase in per capita level. To achieve the growth of cement production indicated in Projection Ct, roughly four times as much cement would have to be produced between 1990 and 2050 as between 1930 and 1990 (see the areas under t to the left of 1990 and under Ct to its right).

The production of cement is a simple process, not greatly affected by economies of scale. There is little international trade in cement, so production and consumption in most countries are roughly equal. In 1990 almost 130 countries produced cement *(UNSYB* 38th edition), most of them developing countries, some very small. In 1970, roughly 450 million tonnes of cement, almost 80 per cent of the world total, were produced in developed countries, only 120 million in developing ones. By 1990 the balance had changed dramatically. Out of a total production in 1990 of twice that in 1970, 575 million tonnes were produced in the developed countries, almost exactly 50 per cent of the world total of 1,140 million tonnes. Since the developed countries had little more than one fifth of the world population by 1990, however, their output per capita was still almost five times as high as that of the developing countries.

During the 1980s there was very little change in the amount of cement produced in the developed countries. On the other hand, in many developing countries production increased rapidly throughout 1970-1990, and per capita levels rose in spite of accompanying population growth. Thus, for example, in India production increased from about 15 to 45 million tonnes, in China from 19 to 210 million. Projection Ct seems well below the production needed in the next few decades if many parts of the developing world are to approach the developed world in consumption of cement and achieve their various development goals.

Aluminium

Like the cement industry, the aluminium industry has expanded enormously between the 1930s and the 1990s. In 1930 only 270,000 tonnes of aluminium were produced in the world compared with 21.8 million in 1990, an increase of about 80 times. In fact, very little aluminium was produced commercially until the 20th century and even in the 1930s its use was limited, for example, in the manufacture of aircraft and cooking utensils. The processing of bauxite is energy intensive and in the early decades of the industry some smelters were located close to 'cheap' hydro-electric power. Three projections are shown in Figure 7.4

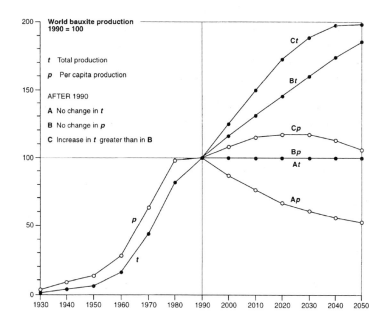

Figure 7.4 World production of aluminium 1930-2050.

- Projection A shows the situation in which world production remains unchanged. After peaking around 1990, per capita production drops sharply to 2050.

- Projection B shows the increase in production (B*t*) needed to keep per capita production (B*p*) at a constant level from 1990 to 2050. In effect it continues the brief trend from 1980 to 1990, during which expansion of aluminium production was much slower than during 1960-1980.

- Projection C allows some increase in per capita production for a time after 1990, then a gradual decline.

The distribution of aluminium production in the world is more concentrated than that of cement. About 80 per cent was accounted for by the developed countries in 1990, their share of cement production in 1970. There is no reason to expect the aluminium industry to follow the widespread growth of cement production. Cement is widely used in the construction of buildings, roads, bridges, dams and other such structures, whereas aluminium is mainly an ingredient in more sophisticated branches of the engineering industry. In the cases of both cement and aluminium there is no restriction before 2050 on the availability of the mineral raw materials used, but rather the possible problem of energy supply. Such does not seem to be the case with copper, the known reserves of which, according to the estimate given in Table 7.1, would last only 30-40 years at present rates of production.

Copper

The expansion of world copper production between 1930 and 1990 has been much less meteoric than that of aluminium but very impressive even so, rising from around 1 million tonnes to 9 million. Copper has been used in small quantities in various parts of the world for several thousand years but the modern large-scale industry dates from the 19th century. The metallic content of copper ores is only a small percentage of the total mineral, a good reason why the initial stages of processing are usually carried out at or near the mines or quarries at the mineral deposits. Copper is one of the most widely used metals in industry. Three projections for the future of copper production are shown in Figure 7.5.

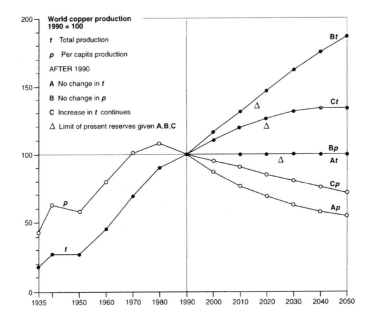

Figure 7.5 World copper production 1935-2050.

- Projection A shows no change in total output (A*t*) between 1990 and 2050 and the consequent reduction in per capita production (A*p*). Such an abrupt change in the trend from 1950 to 1990 seems highly unlikely, but even with no expansion in production, unless further deposits of copper ore are found, reserves would run out around 2025.

- Projection B. Line B*t* shows the amount of copper needed to maintain copper production per capita at the 1990 level (B*p*). Such a level of production would mean the even more rapid exhaustion of reserves, in 25-30 years rather than 35 years in Projection A.

- Projection C. A considerable increase is needed in production (C*t*) to produce a future per capita trend (C*p*) comparable with the trend (*p*) before 1990, which peaked around 1980. Such an outlook is gloomy for the developing countries, even if more reserves are found. If they are not, then the life expectancy of copper would be only about 30 years.

7.5   PIG IRON

In spite of a decline in the relative importance of the iron and steel industry in most developed countries since the 1960s and cutbacks in the absolute amount produced in some, steel has a prominent position in world industry. Pig iron, which is smelted directly from iron ore, is the main ingredient of steel; almost all the pig iron produced in the world is made into steel, although some iron goods are also made.

Between 1930 and 1990 world annual pig iron production increased from 73 million tonnes to 536 million, more than seven times; between 1950 and 1990 the increase was roughly fourfold. Between the mid-1970s and the early 1990s the production of pig iron in the world fluctuated, increasing more slowly than population growth. As a result output per capita was considerably higher around 1975 than in the early 1990s, as can be seen in Figure 7.6. Three projections are made for pig iron production in Figure 7.6.

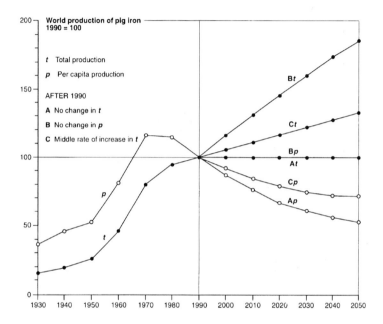

Figure 7.6 World production of pig iron 1930-2050.

- In Projection A, it is assumed that production stays constant after 1990 (A*t*). Per capita production (A*p*) therefore drops to little more than half as the result of an expected 86 per cent increase in the population of the world.

- In projection B, total pig iron production (B*t*) increases at a rate needed to keep per capita production (B*p*) at the 1990 level. Even to achieve such a target, roughly three times as much pig iron would have to be produced between 1990 and 2050 as was produced between 1930 and 1990.

- Projection C shows a more modest rate of increase of pig iron production (C*t*) than that in Projection B, and as a consequence a marked lowering of world per capita production (C*p*). The rate of increase is 5 per cent per decade. Projection C continues the trend of the 1980s, but the continuation of a recent trend is only one of many possible futures for the industry.

Industrial development in Europe, the USA and later in many other countries of the world has depended heavily on the use of iron and steel in the metal-working and engineering sectors and in the construction of buildings and transportation systems. In their First Five-Year Plan (1928-32), Soviet planners stressed the need to expand iron and steel production and to establish new regional production bases. This policy was followed after the Second World War in countries in the Soviet bloc in Central Europe, as well as in China. At the same time the establishment or expansion of integrated iron and steel works took place in several Latin American countries. On the other hand, iron and steel production in Africa is still confined almost exclusively to South Africa, in spite of strong recommendations in the early 1960s by the Economic Commission for Africa of the United Nations (1963) that the industry should be established on the continent.

Since the 1970s iron and steel production has been reduced in most European Union countries. It stagnated in the 1980s in the Soviet bloc and fell sharply there in the early 1990s. In contrast, production has expanded in several developing countries, including China, India and Brazil. The uneven distribution of pig iron production in the world is discussed in Chapter 9.

Between 70 and 75 per cent of the content of steel is pig iron, while scrap steel and ferro-alloys are the other main ingredients. This section concludes with a comparison of steel production in 10 major regions of the world in 1965, 1995 and in a projection by the author to 2025. In this projection, total world production of steel grows between 1995 and 2025 by about 15 per cent, roughly compatible with Projection C*t* in Figure 7.6, the growth of pig iron production between those two years.

Table 7.4 shows the population, and the total and per capita steel production in each of three years, 1965 (Columns (1) to (3)), 1995 ((4) to (6)), and 2025 ((7) to (9)). In this projection, it is assumed that during the 60 years between 1965 and 2025 the population of the world increases by almost 150 per cent; steel production only increases by 94 per cent. A gradual decline in per capita production is expected in the developed regions but per capita production increases in all the developing regions. The per capita gap in steel production between developed and developing regions drops from 23:1 (421 kilograms against 18 kilograms) in 1965 to 7:1 (387 kilograms against 55 kilograms) in 2025.

Although there is a considerable international trade in steel itself and in manufactured goods containing steel, the gap in consumption between the developed and the developing countries does not differ greatly from the gap in the level of production. The outlook for 2025, and even 2050, is that the developed countries will have been able to continue using far more steel than the developing ones and at the same time are better placed to move on, where appropriate, to use new materials in many kinds of manufacturing. The prospect is that only a few developing countries can catch up with the developed countries in per capita steel production or consumption. Most developing countries will have missed out in the steel age, with all the material benefits and accompanying problems that it has brought to the developed countries.

7.6   CONCLUSION

In addition to requiring large quantities of water and energy, modern industry uses a wide variety of plant, animal and non-fuel mineral materials. One feature of the Industrial Revolution has been the shift in emphasis from wood as the main source of fuel in the world to fossil fuels, which are far more abundant. Although there has not been a parallel transformation with raw materials, the use of modern equipment has made it possible to extract far greater quantities of non-fuel minerals in the last two hundred years than previously. Some minerals (e.g. aluminium) have been used extensively for the first time only in the 20th century. In addition, synthetic materials such as plastics have been used extensively only in the second half of the 20th century.

Table 7.4 Steel production by major regions 1965, 1995, 2025

	(1)	(2)	(3)	(4)	(5)	(6)	(7)	(8)	(9)
	1965			1995			2025		
	Population (millions)	Steel (millions of tonnes)	Steel (kgs per capita)	Population (millions)	Steel (millions of tonnes)	Steel (kgs per capita)	Population (millions)	Steel (millions of tonnes)	Steel (kgs per capita)
Western Europe	451	157.6	349	515	180.4	350	520	156	300
Former USSR	184	85.0	462	214	115.5	540	223	112	500
Japan–S. Korea	126	41.4	329	170	127.7	751	177	124	700
North America[1]	232	133.8	577	321	105.4	328	411	123	300
Latin America	245	8.0	33	481	39.3	82	678	68	100
Africa S. of Sahara	250	3.4	14	558	10.1	18	1,190	36	30
N. Africa, S.W. Asia	139	1.8	13	330	21.5	65	600	30	50
S.C. Asia	694	11.3	16	1,355	25.8	19	2,105	63	30
Southeast Asia	248	0.0	0	485	3.3	7	727	22	30
China	725	16.5	23	1,272	92.3	73	1,562	156	100
DEVELOPED	993	417.8	421	1,220	529.0	434	1,331	515	387
DEVELOPING	2,301	41.0	18	4,481	192.3	43	6,862	375	55
WORLD	3,294	458.8	139	5,701	721.3	127	8,193	890	109

[1] Includes Oceania

Whereas the extent of the earth's land surface is finite and the extent of cultivated land can be estimated, it is reasonable to expect that many more fossil fuel and non-fuel minerals will be discovered. Where these are likely to occur depends to a large extent on the already known structural and geological features of the earth's crust. Whatever new discoveries are made in the future it is a fact that at present rates of production, the reserves of some non-fuel minerals would last far longer than those of others.

A feature of recent decades has been the reduction in the per capita production and export of many materials from developing countries. There are several reasons, including: the sharp increase in the population in many developing countries, the exhaustion of many reserves of minerals, the need to grow more food on agricultural land, increasing industrialisation (requiring more materials) and environmental and political constraints on exploration and extraction. The prominence and fortunes of different raw materials can be expected to fluctuate, as, for example, with the reduction in the use of asbestos and lead for certain purposes, but changes in the next few decades are not likely to be characterised by major economic crises, as could occur in the oil industry or food production.

The volume and value (in real terms) of world industrial output has increased several times in the last fifty years, at a faster rate than population. Processed and manufactured products account for an ever increasing share of world trade, itself growing in absolute terms. It has only been possible to give a few examples of the diffusion of modern industrial activities from the areas in which the Industrial Revolution started, to much of the rest of the world. This process has been hastened in recent decades by the search on the part of transnational companies for places with the cheapest labour. In many of the developed industrial countries the number of people engaged in manufacturing has actually declined in the last decade or two thanks partly to automation in some sectors of industry and to many other labour saving devices. The prospect is that by 2050 the net exporters of primary products (food, fuel, raw materials) could be considerably fewer than now. Those very generously endowed with natural resources, especially Canada, Australia and Russia would be in the strongest position in the world economically, at least in this respect.

8

TRANSPORTATION LINKS

'There will probably be a mass market for no more than a thousand motor cars in Europe. There is, after all, a limit to the number of chauffeurs who could be found to drive them.'

Spokesman for Daimler-Benz, *c.* 1900, quoted in Nown (1985)

8.1   INTRODUCTION

In Chapters 5-7 the world output of various products was traced from the 1930s or from 1950 to 1990, as appropriate, and future prospects were considered. Most of the items studied could be measured and compared in a simple way. A tonne of oil or of steel is the same at all times, even if the uses to which it is put and the efficiency of its use change through time and vary spatially (regionally). Modern production depends not only on the continuing introduction of increasingly sophisticated means of production but also on accompanying means of transport and communications, as different places and regions specialise increasingly in what they produce, and market their products over wide areas. It is more difficult to anticipate the scale and growth (or decline) of various modes of transport than to measure the production of most goods, one reason being that systems of transportation nowadays tend to follow other developments, although they still at times lead development by opening up new areas, especially in thinly populated regions.

Several modes of transport and communications have major roles in the movement of passengers, goods and information in the world of the 1990s. Sometimes different modes complement one another, sometimes they compete. Given the complexity of the movement of passengers, goods and information, it is not possible to standardise data to allow exact comparisons, and estimates have to be made to produce a reasonably complete picture of the situation. Before trends since the Second World War are discussed, the changes in transportation in the last two hundred years will be summarised briefly. One lesson for the future is that one means of transport may largely replace another over a relatively short period as the result of a some technological innovation. There is no reason to assume that such changes will no longer occur in the 21st century although 'spotting' them is a matter of luck as well as of reasoning.

The use of steam power, fuelled mainly by coal, but also by wood, was already applied widely in Britain, in nearby parts of the mainland of Europe, and the USA, in the early decades of the 19th century. In due course, the development of machinery for transport, in addition to that already used in factories and mines, allowed the development of railways on land and steamships at sea. Both methods came to be far more powerful, reliable and fast than the animals and wind power hitherto used, although to this day, animals and sailing vessels are still widely used in many parts of the world, especially in remoter areas of developing countries.

By 1900, dense rail networks covered much of North America, Europe and Japan, while many of the countries that are now classed as developing, including parts of Latin America and

India, already had regional networks or single lines. In the absence of motor vehicles, links between stations on the rail system and starting points/destinations of journeys still largely depended on animal transport. Horse-drawn vehicles often figure prominently in photographs of towns and villages taken in Europe and North America around 1900. In the more highly industrialised countries, rail networks were therefore comparatively dense, one reason for the subsequent closure of many lines as motor vehicles came into extensive use, especially in the USA and the UK.

With the development of the internal combustion engine and of rubber tyres (solid then pneumatic) 'rail-less' vehicles came to supplement railways and later to compete with them. The more humble bicycle also came to have a role in local transport and late in the 19th century was one of the first 'consumer' machines to be mass produced. The mass production of passenger cars and commercial vehicles began in the USA around 1910 (by Ford) and in Western Europe after the First World War. In 1930 more than 4 million cars were produced in the world, most of them in the USA; by 1938, about 35 million passenger cars and about 8 million commercial vehicles were in use in the world. Even in the 1930s, however, the railways of the world still carried most of the longer distance passenger traffic and the bulk of the goods traffic (on land).

The development of aircraft, boosted by technology and applications developed during the First World War, began slowly to make an impact on the movement of passengers and mail in the 1920s and 1930s, but even after the Second World War still lagged behind rail, road and shipping services. The movement of goods by air for civilian purposes was negligible in relation to the total movement of goods. Only in the 1960s, with the rapid development and application of jet engines to civil aviation, did planes become large enough and economic enough to compete extensively for passenger traffic with rail and with ships.

During the 20th century rail transport has not changed radically, although innovations have made an impact on the power and efficiency of traction as electric and diesel locomotives have replaced steam in latter decades (the last steam locomotives in India, for example, were phased out in 1997). Special track in Japan, France and other countries has allowed the introduction of fast passenger services. Nevertheless in most parts of the world few new major rail links have been built in the second half of the 20th century, the USSR and China being the main exceptions, although, for example, in Mexico, Colombia and Tanzania, new inter-regional lines have been built. As recently as the 1950s, three provinces in southwestern China, with a combined population of around 100 million at that time, had no railways at all. Here, and in other parts of China, new lines are planned, but it is likely that the ongoing Soviet rail building programme continuing into the 1980s will now be dropped. During the latter part of the 20th century, most new ships, like new rail locomotives, now use diesel fuelled motors rather than steam power.

In addition to the modes of transport that move both passengers and goods, there has been a rapid development of specialised transportation. Thus, in addition to water-carrying pipelines, virtually all of the natural gas and much of the crude oil and its refined products are carried over land by pipeline. Electricity transmission lines also play a major part in the movement of power, 'saving' the transportation of the fuels from which the power is generated, although there is a limit to the distance that electricity can be transmitted commercially.

In the study and comparison of modes of transport, a distinction should be made between the links themselves (railway lines, roads, rivers, pipelines), the conveyances, where relevant (trains, ships), and what is carried. Since some transport links are used much more heavily than others the actual route length in a given region will not necessarily indicate the volume of traffic carried. In order to compile the data sets used below to show the changes in the world's transportation systems between the late 1930s and 1990 the following measures have been used, all obtained from various numbers of the *Statistical Yearbook* of the United Nations.

1. Rail traffic: passenger kilometres and net freight tonne-kilometres.

2. Motor vehicles in use: passenger cars and commercial vehicle units, no indication being given of size and other features. The calculation of passenger-kilometres and tonne-kilometres is not published in the source for all the countries of the world and is presumably an impossible task.

3. Civil aviation: passenger-kilometres and freight tonne-kilometres.

4. Merchant shipping: total fleets in gross registered tonnes.

The quantities of rail and air traffic can be compared, but the measures readily available do not allow direct comparison with road or shipping traffic. The picture is further complicated by the very large numbers that arise when passenger and tonne-kilometres are calculated. Thus for example if one million people are each transported on average 1000 km in a given period, the amount is 1,000 million passenger-km. In 1989 the Soviet rail system carried 4,017 million tonnes of goods on average 959 km each. The astronomical total was 3,851,000 million tonne-km, with on average one tonne moved a distance of 13,400 km for each person in the USSR. Misleadingly, even more goods were carried by road in the USSR, 6,776 million tonnes, but the average length of haul was only 21 km and the total tonne-km a mere 143,000 million! No attempt is made in the next section to produce a comprehensive comparison of the passenger-kilometres and freight tonne-kilometres by different modes of transport. Rather, attention is focused on the rates of change of different modes.

8.2   COMPARING CHANGES IN MODES OF TRANSPORT

Table 8.1 shows the data from which the graphs in Figure 8.1 have been compiled. The basic data are given in columns (1)-(3) and (10)-(13) of the table and the measures used are explained at the foot of the table. The sections of Table 8.1 and of Figure 8.1 will be discussed in turn.

Passenger traffic

Columns (1)-(3). If it is assumed that on average in a year a passenger car travels 10,000 km and carries two passengers, then in 1990, 434 million cars would 'produce' 8,680 thousand million passenger-km, a greater quantity than rail and air combined. The movement of passengers by sea and inland waterway is lower in the European Union and North America than that by road, rail or air, but more locally, in some developing regions (depending on local conditions) is prominent.

Columns (4)-(6) show the total volumes of passenger traffic in columns (1)-(3) in relation to 1990, the absolute value of which is made to equal 100. The upper left graph in Figure 8.1 shows the rate at which the three different modes of transport have changed between 1937/8 and 1990. Rail traffic has experienced the slowest growth, air the fastest. The extent to which the three modes of transport compete for passenger traffic will be discussed later in this section.

Columns (7)-(9) show the effect of population growth during 1937/8-1990 as the population of the world grew from about 2,200 million to 5,300 million, an increase of 140 per cent. In order to take into account the effect of this growth of population on the total movement of

Table 8.1 Traffic carried by selected modes of transport, 1937/8-1990

A. Passengers

	Total amount			Total relative to 1990=100			Per capita relative to 1990=100		
	(1) Rail	*(2)* Road	*(3)* Air	*(4)* Rail	*(5)* Road	*(6)* Air	*(7)* Rail	*(8)* Road	*(9)* Air
1937/8	278	35	–	11	8	–	28	20	–
1950	453	51	29	19	12	2	39	24	4
1960	927	98	108	38	23	6	68	40	11
1970	1,248	191	383	51	44	23	75	63	33
1980	1,688	320	908	69	74	54	83	88	64
1990	2,430	434	1,693	100	100	100	100	100	100

B. Freight

	Total amount				Total relative to 1990=100				Per capita relative to 1990=100			
	(10) Rail	*(11)* Road	*(12)* Air	*(13)* Sea	*(14)* Rail	*(15)* Road	*(16)* Air	*(17)* Sea	*(18)* Rail	*(19)* Road	*(20)* Air	*(21)* Sea
1938	1,107	8	–	66	17	6	–	16	42	14	–	38
1950	2,035	15	0.6	85	32	11	1	20	67	23	2	53
1960	2,844	25	2.2	130	44	18	4	31	79	33	8	55
1970	4,335	50	10.6	230	68	36	21	54	98	53	30	79
1980	5,721	90	26.6	417	89	66	52	98	107	79	63	118
1990	6,406	137	51.0	424	100	100	100	100	100	100	100	100

Notes for Table 8.1

- = 0 or negligible

Columns

(1)   The *Statistical Yearbooks* of the United Nations do not give world totals for the movement by rail of passenger or freight traffic. The author has calculated the total for 14 countries of the world among those with the heaviest amount of rail traffic. Apparently the lack of data for such important countries as South Africa and Australia has apparently precluded the calculation of the world total. Data have been used for the following countries: France, Germany, Italy, Spain, UK, Japan, USA, Canada, former USSR, Argentina, Brazil, Mexico, India, China. Quantities are thousands of millions of passenger-km.

(2)   Passenger cars in circulation in millions.

(3)   Passenger-km in thousands of millions

(10)   Countries as for column (1), tonne-km of freight carried in thousands of millions.

(11)   Commercial vehicles in use in millions

(12)   Tonne-km of freight carried in thousands of millions

(13)   Gross registered tonnes of shipping in millions

passengers, the values in columns (1)-(3) have been recalculated in per capita terms and are shown in columns (7)-(9) in relation to the 1990 level, which is equal to 100. The upper right graph shows the considerable reduction in the rate of growth in this new context. Even so, rail travel has increased about 2½ times per person between 1950 and 1990, road travel about 4 times and air travel about 25 times.

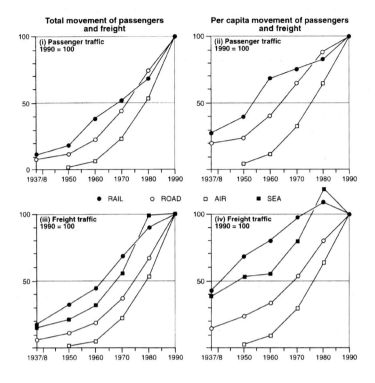

Figure 8.1 The world movement of passengers and freight, 1937/8-1990.

There is no sign in the 1990s of a marked change in the trends in the previous four decades. There are plans in most countries of the world in both the public and private sectors to increase the production and use of passenger cars, to construct new roads, and to allow for greater numbers of passengers to travel by air, with the development of larger aircraft and the expansion of many airports. Although private companies are unlikely to embark on new railway building programmes comparable to those of the 19th century, the explicit policy of many governments, especially those in the developed countries, is to encourage greater use of existing rail routes, to develop urban rail/metro/tramway systems in larger cities, and to construct new high speed track on routes between major centres of population.

Freight traffic

Columns (10)-(13) in Table 8.1 give comparable figures for the transportation of freight, with the addition of data for shipping. The data for the movement of freight by rail are reasonably straightforward. About half of the tonne-km carried in 1990 were accounted for by the Soviet and North American rail systems. The freight-km carried by commercial vehicles are difficult to calculate since commercial vehicles include many taxis, buses and small vans and lorries, only moving people and goods locally and therefore not accumulating large amounts of passenger- or tonne-km, as well as heavy goods vehicles (HGV). The latter number about 10 million worldwide. If each HGV transports on average 10 tonnes a distance of 50,000 km in a year, then they would carry about 5,000 billion tonne-kilometres, compared with 6,400 billion carried by rail. If anything, 5,000 billion is a generous estimate since due to the quality of roads in most parts of the developing world, the distances travelled and the weight carried could be well below the amounts estimated above.

Most of the movement of freight by heavy goods vehicles is accounted for by the USA and Western Europe. In the USA the construction of the interstate highway system beginning in the 1950s (see Jordan (1968)) greatly improved the competitiveness of roads compared with railways. By the 1980s a similar situation was emerging in Western Europe, where the motorway network was still growing, and continuing economic integration in the European Union led to the need for a greater flow of freight between member states, requiring more flexible ways of moving it, provided primarily by the road system. Until the 1990s, the long distance movement of freight by road was very limited in the USSR and virtually non-existent in China.

Column (12) in Table 8.1 shows the enormous growth of air freight services since the 1960s. By comparison with rail traffic alone, however, the freight tonne-km carried by air remains very small, although in general the goods carried are of high value in relation to their weight and volume, or are perishable.

The fivefold growth of the tonnage of the merchant fleets of the world between 1950 and 1990 shown in column (13) is impressive, although less rapid than that of commercial vehicles in use. A rough idea of the tonne-km of freight carried by the merchant fleets can be obtained by calculating that a tanker carrying 120,000 tonnes of oil a distance of 10,000 km would score 1,200 million tonne-km. It would return empty. If eight loads could be carried in one year, then 1 million tonnes would make almost 10,000 million tonne-km. One hundred such tankers at work would account for 1,000 billion tonne-km, about a sixth of the total movement in the world of goods by rail. In practice, about 2,400 billion tonne-km (200 million tonnes × 12,000 km) of crude oil is actually carried from the Middle East to Japan each year.

In 1990 the combined merchant shipping fleets of the world were 424 million tonnes. Only 15 per cent was steam powered, 85 per cent motor powered. Almost one third of the total tonnage was accounted for by oil tankers, almost another third by ore and bulk carriers, with container carriers making up much of the rest of the world's merchant shipping fleet. At present container ships cruise at speeds similar to those of other ships, often with some of their containers perched awkwardly, indeed precariously to the uninitiated, on their decks. Ryan (1997) describes a new design of vessel capable of reaching 45 knots compared with 30 or less, regarded traditionally as the top speed for large vessels. The 770 foot Fast Ship uses water jets instead of propellers to power the vessel.

The days of the passenger liner that also carried mail and some goods on scheduled routes largely passed in the 1960s, leaving airlines to carry most of the passengers. On the other hand the growth of long distance pleasure cruises has been rapid in the 1980s and 1990s. Elliott, H. (1997) refers to problems of safety and of handling very large cruise liners at ports. The *Grand Princess*, launched in 1998, has a displacement of 109,000 tonnes (the QE2 is 'only' 70,000) while the planned *America World City* is to be 250,000 tonnes and to carry 8,600 passengers and crew.

The data in columns (14)-(17) show the different rates at which the carriers of freight have increased their traffic between 1937/8 and 1990. Between 1950 and 1990 rail traffic increased about 3 times, sea traffic 5 times and road 9 times, while air traffic developed in a spectacular way in the jet age. The lower left graph in Figure 8.1 highlights the recent stagnation in the size of the world merchant shipping fleet. The lower right graph in Figure 8.1 puts the movement of goods in the context of traffic in relation to population (columns (18)-(21) Table 8.1) and shows that in per capita terms the amount of goods carried by rail changed little after

1970, while the merchant shipping fleet actually declined, the latter trend related partly at least to stagnation in the production of and international trade in oil.

In North America, the former USSR, the rest of Europe in particular, as well as in the Middle East, a large quantity of oil and most of the natural gas are transported by pipeline. The importance of pipeline transport is illustrated by the 1989 figure for such movement in the USSR, 2,944,000 million tonne-km compared with all goods carried by rail, 3,852,000 million tonne-km.

8.3   IMPLICATIONS OF THE GROWTH OF TRANSPORTATION

Given the great increases noted in chapters 5-7 in the production of many goods, it would be surprising if the tonne-km of goods moved had not increased as it has. For many of the products discussed in these chapters, alternative projections of production, both total and per capita, were made to the year 2050. Clearly, each of the projections depended on changes in other projections. For example, if oil production declines sharply over the next few decades the shipbuilding industry will launch fewer oil tankers than if it grows, with repercussions on other sectors of the economy, which have to be taken into account when making projections. With transport, projections are doubly uncertain since the development or decline of different modes of transport usually follows the needs of other sectors of the economy. For example, a rapid expansion in the generation of electricity in nuclear power stations and a reduction in that generated in coal fired thermal electric stations would reduce the consumption of coal and therefore its movement, thereby reducing the amount of tonne-km overall, since compared with the equivalent amount of coal needed to produce a given amount of electricity, nuclear fuel is minute in weight.

Another feature of transport and communications is that the different modes are potentially in competition for shares of passenger and goods traffic. In this respect, apart from relatively short distance ferry routes and pleasure cruises, the battle for passengers between air and sea transport is virtually over. On land, however, the situation is more complex. Figure 8.2 shows how in relation to the time taken on a journey, road traffic is at an advantage over rail and air for relatively short journeys, while air is at an advantage on relatively long journeys. Rail holds the 'middle ground'. For both passenger and goods traffic, the 'door to door' nature of road journeys means that no time is spent travelling to and from the places (stations, airports) between which the main journey is made in the case of rail or air travel.

Generally, rail travel is faster than road travel, while air travel is much faster than either. The shorter the journey, the larger the proportion of total time travelled is spent getting to and from the station or airport. Since road and air transport are not generally in competition, improvements in each would be at the expense of rail traffic. The use of rail by passengers in the USA in the future can be expected to be confined largely to commuters using profitable lines to inner city destinations. The fast passenger train, pioneered by the Japanese with their Shinkansen 'bullet train' system, and followed by the French in the 1980s, will be expanded, if heavily subsidised, and assuming that air fares remain high. On many main routes in Western Europe the construction of motorways, mainly since the 1950s, has doubled the average speed of passenger travel by car, but (except on a few routes) no comparable increase in average speed has been achieved on the railways. Similarly, the construction of more city centre airports (as in Rio de Janeiro, London City Airport (Docklands)) would cut the average time taken to travel to and from the airport, thereby enabling air traffic to compete with rail on routes at present dominated by rail travel.

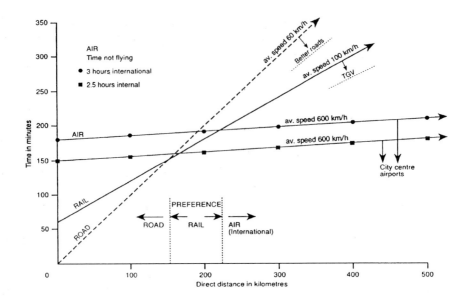

Figure 8.2 The choice of transport for passengers. Direct distance is shown on the horizontal axis, time taken to reach destination on the vertical axis. Road travel is considered for simplicity to be door to door, while for rail and air, travel time is allowed to travel from home to station/airport and to travel from station/airport to destination. The speeds are estimated for journeys in Western Europe. The slope of the line reflects the average speed of travel (the flatter the faster). It is not intended that any particular journey can be calculated exactly from the graph. In developing countries 60 km/h is a far greater speed than can normally be expected on the roads, while railways are thin on the ground or non-existent. The diagram is adapted from Cole and Cole (1997)

As the total amount of traffic in the world's transportation systems increases, three issues have given rise for concern. First, large sections of road transport networks are increasingly prone to experience traffic jams and gridlock. On account of its very high density of population, England is one of the countries in the world facing serious congestion on its motorways. The Department of Transport (see Ramesh (1996)) has identified 18 stretches of motorway on which in 1996 traffic came to a halt on more than half the days in a year. For 2015 the expected number of stretches is over 60. Similarly, air traffic congestion and control problems afflict certain busy air routes and airports. Second, products of the oil (petroleum) industry provide much of the energy used for purposes of modern transport in the world. The general consensus is that the private passenger car, often conveying only the driver in developed countries, is one of the most profligate if not wasteful users of fuel. Third, there is concern over the impact of the burning of fossil fuels on the environment both locally, particularly in larger cities, where health is affected, and globally, because the use of fossil fuels adds carbon dioxide to the atmosphere (see Chapters 6 and 10) and therefore may be contributing to global warming and locally to urban 'heat islands'.

For some time now it has been argued that two apparently cleaner forms of energy should be developed for transport, hydrogen and electric power, the latter already widely used in rail transport. It should not be overlooked, however, that both these forms of energy need electricity, in the case of hydrogen for the process of separating the gas from water. Most of the electricity produced in the world (see Chapter 6) is generated from fossil fuels. The main advantage of motor vehicles run on batteries or with hydrogen would be felt in cities, but unless run by hydro-electric or nuclear power, power stations fuelled by fossil fuels would still be located somewhere, probably polluting a rural area with comparatively few inhabitants, but still emitting carbon dioxide into the atmosphere.

8.4   THE PASSENGER CAR

In the developed countries and in the cities of the developing countries the private car began as a luxury enjoyed by the few, in the early part of the 20th century. Unless subsidised by a company, the ownership of a car was possible only for a few families with an income above a given threshold. Average living standards have risen, if erratically, in all developed countries, and among a considerable proportion of the population in some developing countries. Since most individuals or families aspire to owning at least one car, if they can afford it, more and more cars have been bought as income levels have risen. The thousand motor cars expected by one forecaster in Europe (see quote at the beginning of the Chapter) was quite an underestimate; in the mid-1990s there were more than 150 million cars in the European Union alone.

Ownership of a car allows a change in lifestyle offering greater mobility and flexibility, with travel to work, to retail outlets and for pleasure usually achieved more easily than by public transport. In due course the location of residential areas and places of work, shopping and entertainment have become so dispersed that the ownership of a car becomes a necessity. This situation is unlikely to change globally in the next few decades, although locally car ownership could be reduced by special circumstances. In view of what has been described above, the ownership of private passenger cars differs from all other forms of transport in that *per se* the car leads economic change, rather than following it, as do the other modes. For this reason the production of cars and the number of cars in use are examined in some detail in this section.

The total number of passenger cars produced in the world in 1990 was more than four times as great as in 1950. Per 1000 people, however, the number only doubled. Although car ownership levels are already high in North America and in most countries of Western Europe, production and ownership seem likely to continue to rise well into the 21st century. In the UK, for example, car ownership is expected to rise from 22 million in the mid-1990s to 31 million in 2010. Increases in developing countries are more difficult to forecast. Figure 8.3 shows the production of passenger cars in the world from 1930 to 1990 (t in the graph) and three projections from 1990 to 2050.

- Projection A shows how production in relation to population (Ap) drops in 2050 to little more than half the 1990 level if production itself (At) remains constant at the 1990 level. Such a situation would come about in 2050, for example, if the 1990 car ownership level remained virtually unchanged in the developed countries and a decrease occurred in the developing countries.

- Projection B shows that almost a doubling of total production (Bt) would be needed to maintain per capita production (Bp) at the same level during 1990-2050.

- Projection C shows that almost a fourfold increase would be needed in the level of car production between 1990 and 2050 to allow a doubling of the number of cars in circulation in relation to population, including some increase in the developed regions and a substantial (relative) increase in some developing regions. In such a situation, more than four times as

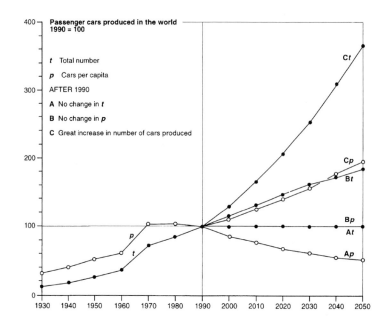

Figure 8.3 Passenger cars produced in the world 1930-2050.

many cars would have to be produced in the world during the 60 years between 1990 and 2050 as between 1930 and 1990.

It is difficult to obtain more than a rough estimate of the ratio of the production of cars in a given year to the number in use in that year. The average 'life expectancy' of a car in years can be inferred from the result of dividing the number in use by the number produced. From 1930 to 1970 the figure was about 8 years but in 1980 it had risen to about 10 years and in 1990 to about 12 years. The latter figure tallies roughly with a sample of the age of cars taken on a British motorway by the author in 1996 in which over 90 per cent were less than 12 years old. The general impression is that cars are kept 'alive' longer in developing countries than in developed ones, in spite of worse road conditions, less careful driving and the generally poor level of servicing.

If the need arises the manufacturers of motor vehicles would have no difficulty in expanding production in the decades to come. For example, Lorenz (1997) notes that Western Europe can build 20 million cars a year but sells only 13 million. The principal producers of motor vehicles in North America, Western Europe and Japan all had excess capacity in the late 1990s. In practice the manufacturers of motor vehicles, like those of many other products, can only look a few years ahead, however attractive it would be to produce models, as earlier this century, that stayed in fashion for 20-30 years or more. Porter and Brierley (1997) ask: 'Has the car reached the end of the road?' an intriguing thought which, however, does not match the hope of manufacturers that demand will rise over the next ten years (especially for their particular products).

In order to give a regional background to speculation about cars in use in the next few decades, the number of cars in use in ten major regions of the world has been calculated for 1965 and 1993 (see Table 8.2). Projections have then been made to 2025 and 2050. An increase

Table 8.2 Passenger cars in use 1965, 1995, 2025, 2050

	1965			1993			2025			2050		
	Population (millions)	Cars (millions)	Cars (per 1000 population)	Population (millions)	Cars (millions)	Cars (per 1000 population)	Population (millions)	Cars (millions)	Cars (per 1000 population)	Population (millions)	Cars (millions)	Cars (per 1000 population)
Europe	451	44.8	99	515	176.7	343	520	234.0	450	460	230.0	500
USSR	184	2.0	11	214	16.3	76	223	33.5	150	230	69.0	300
Japan	126	2.2	17	170	45.0	265	177	62.0	350	160	64.0	400
N.America	232	83.7	361	321	169.3	527	411	246.6	600	470	282.0	600
Latin America	245	4.6	19	481	32.9	68	678	67.8	100	800	120.0	150
Africa S. of Sahara	250	1.6	6	558	5.8	10	1,190	23.8	20	2,190	65.7	30
SW. Asia, N. Africa	139	1.1	8	330	10.7	32	600	48.0	80	810	97.2	120
S.C. Asia	694	0.7	1	1,355	5.6	4	2,105	42.1	20	2,360	70.8	30
S.E. Asia	248	0.8	3	485	6.7	14	727	43.6	60	810	81.0	100
China	725	0.2	0.3	1,272	1.3	1	1,562	15.6	10	1,590	31.8	20
Developed	993	132.7	134	1,220	407.4	334	1,331	576.1	433	1,320	645.0	489
Developing	2,301	8.8	4	4,481	62.9	14	6,862	240.9	35	8,560	466.5	54
World	3,294	141.6	43	5,701	470.3	82	8,193	817.0	100	9,880	1,111.5	113

Cars per 1000 – calculated before rounding of car numbers

of 136 per cent is expected in the total number of cars in use in the world between 1993 and 2050, from about 470 million to 1,110 million. Given the large increase in the population of the world during that period, the number of cars per 1,000 people would only increase from 82 in 1993 to 113 in 2050.

In the above projection, a 'bottom up' approach has been used. A plausible number of cars per 1,000 people has been assumed for each of the ten regions independently. By multiplying this by the expected population of each region in 2025 and 2050, the expected number of cars in use can be calculated. For example, if in 2050 Europe without the USSR has 460 million people and 500 cars per 1,000 people, then there should be 230 million cars in use. With an expected population of 800 million and 150 cars in use per 1,000 people, Latin America would have 120 million cars.

One outstanding prospect emerges from the projections. Assuming they are not too far from what will happen, then the gap between developed and developing regions will widen between 1993 and 2050 in cars per thousand people in absolute terms even though the rate of increase in the developing regions is faster, the tantalising contradiction between absolute and relative. The respective levels of cars in use per 1,000 population in developed and developing regions were 334 and 14 in 1993, a ratio of about 24 to 1, but would be 489 to 54 in 2050, a ratio of only about 9 to 1. The increase in the developed regions (from 334 to 489) would only be 46 per cent, while that in the developing regions (from 24 to 54) would be 125 per cent. However the absolute increase would be 155 (from 334 to 489) cars per 1,000 people in the developed regions compared with a mere 30 (from 24 to 54) in the developing ones. Evidently the expected near doubling of population in the developing regions would be a major factor in keeping the level of cars in use per 1,000 people there comparatively low because it would dilute the number in use in a larger population.

One possible future could be that suddenly enough influential people have persuaded governments and political leaders that a policy of great austerity is needed in the rich countries to help the poor countries and to ensure sustainable development. Given the haphazard, uncoordinated way in which conditions have changed since the Second World War (and before it), more of the same seems more likely. With regard to the motor vehicle industry itself, cars in the 1990s are not vastly different from cars in the 1930s although on average they go faster, break down less often, are safer, more spacious, *and* on average consume more fuel per kilometre (or mile). In the USA and the EU many of the same companies or at least car names operate now as in the 1930s, while some of the big oil companies, including Esso and Shell, which struck rich oil deposits in Venezuela in the 1920s, are still in business.

It is quite possible that there will be twice as many cars in the world in 2050 as in the 1990s but they may be slower, smaller, cleaner, and travel only half as far on average as in the 1990s. Such a trend would be a reversal of the trend in Europe towards larger cars since the Second World War but not in the USA, where there has not been a great change in car size in the last fifty years. Such would be a compromise between banning private cars entirely, a situation experienced in China until the 1990s, and having even more lavish vehicles, travelling greater distances than ever, and using the last reserves of oil.

8.5 INNOVATIONS IN MODES OF TRANSPORT

As noted at the beginning of the chapter, major innovations in modes of transportation have often come over short periods of time. Before 1800 propulsion largely depended on animal and wind power. With the development of the steam engine, early in the 19th century, steam power was used for transport, the first steam vessel of note being the *Clermont*, developed by R. Fulton (1765-1815), plying the Hudson River, USA, in 1807. Steam locomotives were developed in the 1820s, when the world's first public railway, between Stockton and Darlington, England, was opened in 1821. The 19th century was dominated by coal and steam power, but earlier forms of transport were still used extensively. The internal combustion engine and diesel motor have become the principal forms of propulsion for most modes of transport by the end of the 20th century.

It is not implied that big shifts in emphasis can be expected yet again at the turn of the century, but the use of electric power to propel motor vehicles is now of considerable interest to the world's major manufacturers. Electric traction from overhead lines (or in a few cases, a third rail) has been developed successfully in the 20th century. It has been less successful with other modes of transport without direct access to the supply of current. Electric batteries, although cumbersome, have been used successfully in otherwise conventional motor vehicles since the 1930s and indeed were invented at about the same time as the internal combustion engine. At present it is difficult to see how they could be used for ships or aircraft, the mind-boggling prospect for the latter being of a terse call to the passengers in an aircraft in the air that the batteries had lost power. Some tentative prospects for the next fifty years are noted for consideration.

Rail

In spite of various proposals it seems unlikely many new long distance rail links will be built. The recent negative experience of one of the most ambitious, the BAM (Baykal-Amur Magistral) in Russia, should raise doubts in the minds of prospective rail builders, as also should the experience of the Channel Tunnel. Some new lines may be built in China, where according to Zhou Xin (1997) the completion of the new direct Beijing-Kowloon (Hong Kong) line has brought life to many remote parts of the near interior of the country. The EU has a very ambitious programme for the construction of new high speed rail links and the upgrading of existing lines. As and when further countries join the EU they will need to make improvements to their rail systems, like those being carried out in the former East Germany since Germany became unified in 1990.

In addition to new rail construction and improvements on longer routes, interest is growing or being revived in the use of suburban railways, and of tramways in urban centres, not exclusively very large ones. For example, Jabez (1997) describes a new type of overhead railway, Futrex, being developed in the USA (Charleston, South Carolina), which consists of a steel beam alongside which the trains travel. Such a beam, on concrete piers, would be about five metres above the ground and would not generally interfere with existing structures or street traffic except in very heavily built-up city centres. Its cost would be between an eighth and a tenth of the cost of conventional urban transit systems. Meanwhile the number of metro/subway/underground systems has proliferated in the last fifty years not only in cities in the industrial countries but also in large cities in many developing countries (e.g. Mexico City, Rio de Janeiro, Beijing, Hong Kong).

Road

The development of road transport in the next fifty years is more complex and difficult to anticipate than the future of rail transport. Issues include the question of whether enough roads can be built to accommodate growing traffic demands, to what extent the movement of passengers can be transferred to railways, whether public or private, and to what extent electric cars can be made attractive enough to current and future car owners. According to Sperling (1996): 'new technological developments have put practical electric cars within reach, but politics may slow the shift away from internal-combustion engines.' Attempts to get habitual car users to use bicycles for short journeys have been made in Western Europe (e.g. in Freiberg, Germany) but the mix of cars and bicycles on conventional roads is not a happy one. A further possibility is to adopt the Taiwanese model. Here there are 10 million motorcycles, one for every two people, and they vastly outnumber cars and commercial vehicles (see Zich (1993)). Car-pooling, with special lanes only for cars with more than one (or two) passengers are a further possibility, but they cause new problems themselves (see Figure 8.6, p. 190).

In the second half of the 20th century, existing road networks in the developed countries have been greatly improved in North America, Western Europe and Japan, and motorways have been built. In most developing countries there were few good roads before the 1950s, but since then it has been the aim of many more remote communities to be linked to the regional or national road network. In Brazil, roads combining strategic and economic goals were built in the 1970s to integrate the 'other half', the 'empty' forests of Amazonia. China now has an ambitious medium-term plan to build an inter-province motorway network not unlike the US interstate highway system.

There is increasing pressure to get motor vehicles that are fuelled by petrol or diesel out of city centres in the developed countries or to substitute them as soon as possible by electric cars. The following view is however expressed in *The Economist* (1992b): 'Electric cars and vehicles powered by alternative fuels will make traffic jams easier on the lungs, but do little to shorten queues or calm tempers. More radical ideas are needed. Carlo Ripa di Meana, a former EC environment commissioner, says he is prepared to give up his Alfa Romeo in order to live in a car-free city. He says it would cost between 50 and 80 per cent less (sic) to live and work in a city where no cars are allowed by not having to buy, park, insure and maintain a vehicle.' For most car-owning families the cost of buying and running their car or cars is considerable, but not as much as 50 per cent.

Some large cities have, however, grown in such a way that public transport cannot replace the car, yet there is no room for still more roads. Los Angeles is probably the most extreme case of a large city with this problem. Between 1991 and 2010 its population is expected to rise from 13 million to 19 million and the vehicles in use from 8 million to 10 million. As people live progressively further from their place of work, average journey lengths increase. Vehicle kilometres travelled are expected to rise from 385 million a day to 620 million, but the average speed is expected to drop from 56 km/h to 30 km/h.

Air

It is estimated that world airlines will need 16,000 new aircraft between the mid-1990s and 2020. In the early 1990s, over 1,600 billion passenger-km were flown by world airlines, just over half of them international. Almost half of the total air traffic in the world and about a quarter of all international air traffic were accounted for by the USA. The USA is three times as large in area as the EU, but has only two thirds as many inhabitants. That may be one reason why it does not have such serious problems of air traffic congestion (except at a few airports) in spite of the great amount of air traffic. According to French (1997) it is expected that: 'on typical high growth levels and assuming that all feasible improvements were carried out, all but four of Europe's 27 leading airports would be congested in terms of runway capacity by 2010.'

Congestion at many of the world's busiest airports can be relieved in various ways, one being to make greater use of less busy secondary airports. Another partial solution is to carry more passengers per aircraft. Designs already exist for a 'single-wing' giant aircraft in the USA and France. Windle (1995) describes a new 'super jumbo' plane capable of carrying up to 800 passengers, proposed by McDonnell Douglas (now merged with Boeing). Windle (1996) also describes a plane planned by France's Aérospatiale, capable of carrying 1,000 passengers and expected to be in service by 2020. The great increase in the amount of freight carried by air is shown in Table 8.1. Glaskin (1998) describes Hydro 2000, a cargo plane three times the size of a Boeing 747, which could accelerate the growth of freight movement by air. Probably its main limitation is that it has to take off and land on water.

The relative importance of road, rail and air in the movement of passengers in the decades to come depends on how innovations affect the present relationships, shown earlier diagrammatically in Figure 8.2. In the model shown it is evident that road and rail compete over shorter distances (represented by time taken to travel), rail and air over longer distances. Improvements in both road and air times tend to reduce the range of journey times over which railways are currently well placed to compete.

8.6   GLOBAL LINKS

As already noted, globalisation is not a new idea. Figure 2.1 in Chapter 2 shows the trade routes already used by Spain and Portugal less than a century after the establishment of trading posts and the conquest of territory, mainly in the tropics. During 1580-1640, when the crowns of Spain and Portugal were united, Iberian influence truly encircled the globe. In the 19th century the steamship, railway and telegraph linked most parts of the world. Capital flowed in numerous directions. The global system used by the UK to integrate its empire, including countries to which virtual sovereignty had been granted, was by 1900 not unlike that organised by Spain and Portugal three centuries earlier. The opening of the Suez Canal in 1869 shortened the sea journey between Europe and Australia and particularly the Far East. The opening of the Panama Canal mainly benefited US traffic.

At the end of the 20th century, most international passenger traffic of more than a few hundred kilometres goes by air. The range of long distance aircraft can be extended sufficiently to have non-stop flights on most of the busiest intercontinental routes between large centres of population. Developments in passenger transport by air are now likely to focus mainly on increasing the size of 'conventional' jets and on developing commercially viable smaller aircraft capable of travelling at several times the speed of the fastest aircraft of today. An increase in the volume of freight carried by air may also be expected, but only of goods of a high value in relation to their weight, usually needing urgent delivery. Now that flights passing over the former USSR and China are possible, the great detours on flights between Europe and the Far East are no longer necessary.

It is impossible to represent the whole of the earth's surface on a flat map. When more than about half is put on a single map, serious distortions of shape and scale begin to appear. Figures 8.4 and 8.5 show the northern hemisphere without great distortion of shape and scale. The North Pole is at the centre, and distances along the lines (meridians) radiating from it are correct. With increasing distance from the Pole, however, distances other than those along the meridians increase on the map. Places south of the Equator in Latin America, Africa and Australia are shown, but the distances between them are greatly exaggerated.

In Figure 8.4 great circle distances between all 15 possible pairs of six nodes are shown, as are the three principal parts of the developed world, Europe, the USA and East Asia. The latter area has been extended beyond Japan to include the coastal provinces of China and the cities of Southeast Asia, in which rapid industrialisation is occurring. Frankfurt, Chicago and Shanghai have been chosen as the centres of these regions for the purpose of measuring distances between them. Three cities represent the much smaller regions of the 'southern' continents in which industrialisation is occurring. The measurement of sea distances has been made where appropriate from seaports reasonably close to the big centres (e.g. Rotterdam for Frankfurt).

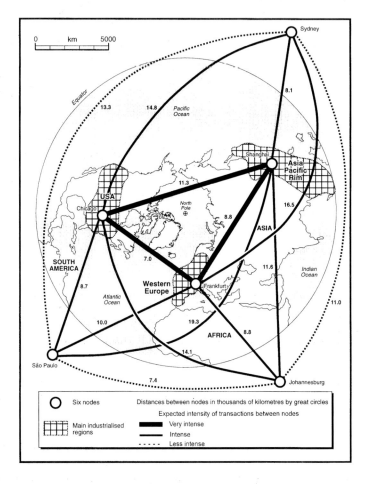

Figure 8.4 The diagram is based on a polar zenithal projection of the northern hemisphere and part of the southern hemisphere. Distances are correct outwards from the North Pole. Six places are shown, the central three being roughly at the centre of the three largest industrial regions of the world, the other three representing southern continents. The great circle distance (the shortest distance on the spherical surface of the globe) is shown between each pair of the six places.

Much of the movement of goods between the six regions in Figure 8.5 and the general areas that they represent must go by sea. A comparison of the shortest distance (great circle) and the distance by sea shows that in only two of the 15 journeys does distance by sea greatly

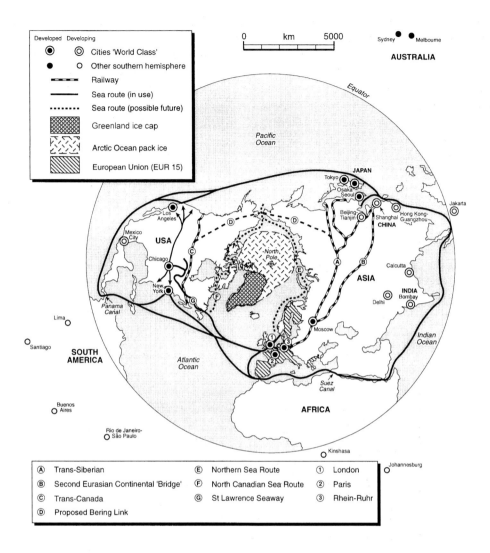

Figure 8.5 The three main concentrations of industry in the world in relation to the northern hemisphere and each other. Land and sea links between the regions are shown. World Class cities have at least 8 million inhabitants.

exceed direct distance. The journey from Europe to South Africa (Rotterdam to Durban) by sea is 'bent' outwards by the shape of western Africa and is almost 50 per cent longer than the direct distance. There is no way that this detour can be avoided or reduced. The greatest excess of sea distance over direct distance is between Europe and the Far East, Rotterdam and Shanghai, 127 per cent more. A large and increasing amount of goods traffic is carried on this route. The sea distance from Rotterdam to Shanghai is about 20,000 km, and to Tokyo about 22,000 km.

Now that the former USSR has been opened up to through traffic, the Trans-Siberian Railway offers a shorter and faster route for carrying container traffic between Europe and East Asia than the long sea route via Suez and Singapore. Even more recently, with the completion of the missing link between Kazakhstan (a former Soviet Socialist Republic) and Xinjiang (China), a

Table 8.3 Great circle and sea distances between selected places in the world in thousands of kilometres

(1)	(2) Places measured for great circle distances	(3) Expected amount of traffic	(4) Distance in thousands of km Great circle	(5) By sea	(6) Sea compared with great circle (excess per cent)	(7) Places measured for sea distances	(8) Sea route taken
1-2	Frankfurt-Chicago	VL	7.0	7.7	10	Rotterdam-Chicago	Via St Lawrence Seaway
1-3	Frankfurt-Shanghai	L	8.8	20.0	127	Rotterdam-Shanghai	Via Suez, Singapore
1-4	Frankfurt-São Paulo	M	10.0	10.5	5	Rotterdam-São Paulo	Atlantic Ocean
1-5	Frankfurt-Johannesburg	M	8.8	13.0	48	Rotterdam-Durban	Atlantic Ocean
1-6	Frankfurt-Sydney	M	16.5	20.0	21	Rotterdam-Sydney	Via Suez
2-3	Chicago-Shanghai	L	11.3	9.9	Small[2]	San Francisco-Shanghai	Pacific Ocean
2-4	Chicago-São Paulo	M	8.7	9.2	Small[2]	New York-São Paulo	Atlantic Ocean
2-5	Chicago-Johannesburg	S	14.1	14.3	Small[2]	New York-Durban	Atlantic Ocean
2-6	Chicago-Sydney	S	14.8	12.0	Small[2]	San Francisco-Sydney	Pacific Ocean
3-4	Shanghai-São Paulo	S	19.3	20.5[1]	6	Shanghai-São Paulo	Indian, Atlantic Oceans
3-5	Shanghai-Johannesburg	S	11.6	13.0	12	Shanghai-Durban	Indian Ocean
3-6	Shanghai-Sydney	M	8.1	8.9	10	Shanghai-Sydney	Pacific Ocean
4-5	São Paulo-Johannesburg	VS	7.4	7.7	4	São Paulo-Durban	Indian Ocean
4-6	São Paulo-Sydney	VS	13.3	13.3	0	São Paulo-Sydney	Pacific Ocean
5-6	Johannesburg-Sydney	VS	11.0	11.3	3	Durban-Sydney	Indian Ocean

VL = Very large; L = Large; M = Medium; S = Small; VS = Very small

Notes

[1] 24.0 via Panama

[2] For Chicago Great circle distances may exceed sea distances because the latter are measured from sea ports on the coasts of the Pacific (San Francisco) or Atlantic (New York)

transcontinental railway between Europe and China, crossing Russia and Kazakhstan, now provides another route, referred to by Li Wen (1996) as the new Eurasian Continental Bridge. This route is 11,000 km in length compared with 13,000 km by the Trans-Siberian Railway.

There remain two links in the world's shipping system that may possibly be made into regular shipping routes by 2050. From Rotterdam it is about 20,000 km by sea to Shanghai. The Northern Sea Route, used briefly in the late summer by Russian shipping when the ice melts, gives a short cut from Europe to the Pacific along the northern coast of Russia and through the Bering Strait. The distance from Rotterdam to Shanghai is about 15,000 km by this route and to Tokyo about 13,000 km. Whether or not it is feasible technically and realistic financially to keep this route open for much or all of the year is a challenge for the shipping industry in the 21st century. Keeping the route on the other side of the Arctic Ocean along the northern coast of Canada and Alaska open at all for regular shipping services is an even greater challenge. The journey from New York to Shanghai would be reduced from 20,000 km via the Panama Canal to 15,000 km on the Arctic route.

Arguably the most ambitious project is the proposal to link the Canadian and Russian rail systems by a line passing under the Bering Strait through a tunnel and crossing through Alaska. It would provide a rail link between East Asia and North America, similar to the Eurasian Continental Bridges already referred to. It would however pass through very thinly populated areas, at present producing little that could usefully be taken on the new rail link, the main purpose of which would therefore be to transport containers between North America and East Asia more quickly if not more cheaply than by sea across the Pacific Ocean.

There has been much publicity about the development of communications between all parts of the globe and about the ease with which financial transactions can be handled as transnational companies extend their influence. In this section attention has focused on a less familiar aspect of globalisation. In spite of the emphasis on the service sector and on the post-industrial era, the amount of goods carried internationally around the world has grown throughout the 20th century and can be expected to continue to grow in the next century, quite possibly doubling between the 1990s and 2050.

In 1895, *Scientific American* (see Gibbs (1997)): '... devoted almost an entire issue to innovations in bicycles, ships and the new steam-, electric- and gas-powered automobiles. "If there are faults" with cars, the editors [in 1895] concluded, "only time is wanted to make them disappear ... There is no mechanism more inoffensive, no means of transport more sure and safe."' This simplistic appraisal of the future of transport as seen a century ago is a reminder that to forecast prospects in the next 50 years is extremely difficult.

An outstanding feature of the development of transport in the world in the last fifty years has been the success in developing and introducing ever faster modes, whether on the land, over the water or in the air. One result has been a rapid increase in the use of energy, particularly of petroleum products. Three of many features and problems associated with the development of present means of transport have been the following:

- Medium-term concern over oil supplies.

- Environmental pollution, especially in urban areas.

- The availability of different modes of transport varies enormously around the world.

To elaborate on the third point, while many citizens of the developed countries and some in developing countries have access to ever more sophisticated means of transport for themselves

Figure 8.6 Keeping cars off the road or using them more efficiently: two advertisements prominently displayed at the side of motorways in Belgium in the mid-1990s. The story is that they caused accidents by distracting drivers and were duly removed. The woman driver in the lower picture may have upset macho Belgian men drivers.

and for their products, billions of people in developing countries still carry loads on their backs, pull carts or push bicycles, or depend on draught animals. As with the development and diffusion of healthcare facilities and advances in medicine and pharmacy, most developments in transport largely reach only a minority of the world's population, whereas a modest expenditure on appropriate research and development could ease the lot of many people in poor countries.

In the next fifty years a priority in the area of transport is to develop, produce and persuade people to use or buy vehicles that consume far less fuel, even at the expense of speed and comfort, and to persuade them to travel less. Mercedes have developed a very economical 'smart' car, the Swatch, with room (it is said) for two people and two crates of beer (see Porter and Brierley (1997)). Wouk (1997) describes the advantages of hybrid electric vehicles (HEVs), which carry a small internal-combustion engine and an electric generator as well as batteries. 'Will the HEV finally unite consumer acceptance, high fuel economy and reduced emissions?' he asks.

In *The Past and Future of Global Mobility,* Schafer and Victor (1997) make a forecast of the absolute increase in world passenger travel between 1960 and 2050 and the share of the total accounted for by each main mode of travel. In trillion passenger-km, the observed and expected amounts have been/could be as shown in Table 8.4.

Table 8.4 World passenger travel

	1960	*1990*	*2020*	*2050*
Total in year (trillion passenger-km)	5.5	23.4	53	103
Percentage shares				
Railways	20	9	6	4
Automobiles	54	53	43	35
Buses	23	29	26	20
High-speed transport	3	9	25	41

Characteristically there is no explicit reference to the humble modes used by the world's poor, but their total passenger-km scores are so small that there is apparently no need to consider them.

9

THE DEVELOPMENT GAP

'Today, the net worth of the 358 richest people [in the world], the dollar billionaires, is equal to the combined income of the poorest 45 per cent of the world's population - 2.3 billion people.'

UNDP *Human Development Report 1996*

9.1 INTRODUCTION

Before the Second World War little attention was given to the existing gap in per capita production or income between the rich and poor regions of the world. Almost all of Africa and much of Asia were still colonies of the industrial countries of Europe, or of Japan. Information about colonies in statistical publications of the League of Nations was provided at the discretion of the colonial powers. The colonies were still seen basically as exporters of primary products to the industrial countries, although some development of industry had taken place in the larger Latin American countries, independent politically from Spain and Portugal since early in the 19th century, in India, still part of the British Empire, and in coastal areas of China and especially in Manchuria (China), occupied in the 1930s by Japan.

The attitude of the immediate post-Second World War years are nicely expressed by Davies (1948): 'Outside Europe and North America most of the world's peoples do not share the life of the great industrial areas. Man still lives largely by hunting, tilling and herding. The benefits we associate with modern progress - well-planned dwellings, good plumbing and sanitation, fast train services and streamlined entertainment - are not known to all those who live in the West. They are almost unknown, except to minorities, in Central and South America, Africa and Asia.' Fifty years later the statement is still broadly true, especially if 'train' is replaced by 'car'. Davies describes the lifestyle of the hunting peoples, the 'world's children', as a struggle against nature.

After the Second World War concern grew over the economic and technological backwardness of the poorer countries of the world. In addition to its role in keeping peace in the world, the newly founded United Nations quickly began to gather information about the world economy, to make recommendations about the need to assist poor countries and, through various institutions, to provide assistance for economic and social improvements. The 'development gap' was thus recognised, and the general consensus about it, at least as expressed in public, was that the poorer countries would in due course catch up with the rich ones. Such a view seems to have been based on the assumption that the countries of the world were all advancing along a race track to a finishing line. There is not, however, a specific point at which the rich countries will stop their economic growth. Nevertheless, hope was given to some developing countries by the pronouncements of the Soviet Communist Party on the faults of the capitalist system in preventing equal development. Encouragement also came in the form of the stages of economic growth, postulated by the US economic historian W. W. Rostow in 1960, whereby, eventually, any or every country could arrive at a stage of mass consumption.

While the development gap was recognised around 1950, the assessment of its nature and magnitude depended on what single criterion or combination of criteria was used to measure it and, with more than one, what weight should be given to each of the measures. The development gap still exists in the 1990s, and indeed according to some assessments is actually wider than it was in the 1950s. Two issues will form the main theme of this chapter: has the development gap widened, remained about the same or narrowed between 1950 and the 1990s, and what are the prospects that it can be narrowed between the years 2000 and 2050?

Before attention is focused on disparities between individual rich and poor countries and between developed and developing groups in general it must be noted that marked regional disparities also exist within countries, especially the largest. In the USA, the relative gap between the richest and poorest states is actually narrower now than in the 1930s. On the other hand, Thurow (1987) notes a surge in inequality among different segments of the US population, as opposed to states. Since the Second World War the policy in most countries of Western Europe (e.g. Italy, France, the UK, Spain) has been to reduce regional disparities, a policy also of the European Commission with regard to lagging regions of the European Union as a whole (e.g. Portugal, Greece, southern Italy). On the other hand, in large developing countries (e.g. China, India, Brazil, Mexico, Indonesia) marked differences exist in per capita income between regions, and as particular parts of each country industrialise, leaving other parts heavily dependent on agriculture, the gap seems likely to widen in the next few decades.

In India there are marked differences in per capita income between states and also between income groups. Thomas, C. (1997) notes: 'The Indian economic miracle predicted when reforms began six years ago has not even begun to materialise, for all the ostentatious new wealth held by tight circles of a well-connected, English-speaking minority! The rich-poor divide carries echoes of neighbouring Pakistan, one of the last feudal cultures, where the middle class barely exists. Most Pakistanis are very rich or very poor, a trend increasingly evident in India.'

Jiang Wandi (1995) explains why income disparities in China occur and have indeed been increasing: 'Generally speaking, the income disparity now exists primarily in three spheres - between people living in different areas, between people living and working in urban and rural areas, and between people working in units of different ownerships... Unequal development of China's southeast and northwest regions has been an enduring headache for the Chinese government. More investment and labour has poured into the southeast and, in particular, the fast booming coastal areas since the reform began... Take farmers for example. The proportion of the per capita income of farmers in southeast and northwest was 1.6:1 in 1983, increasing to 2.8:1 by 1992.' In anticipation of the theme of the world development gap, to be discussed below, it is worth noting that even *within* countries, as modernisation and development takes place, it is difficult to reduce regional disparities. How much more difficult it must be, then, at global level.

Table 9.1 shows the approximate population in 1950, 1970 and 1990 of four major developed regions, and projections to 2010 and 2050. The share of the world's population in these regions is given as a percentage, which can be compared with the percentage for all the developing regions combined. Small adjustments have been made in the membership of the first three developed regions after 1990. In the 1990s, some countries classed as developing, all small in population, had real GDP per capita levels well above some of the countries in the developed regions (e.g. Hong Kong, Singapore and United Arab Emirates all had levels above those of most EU countries) but conventionally they remain part of the developing world.

Table 9.1 shows that according to the 'preferred' projection of the author (see Chapter 4), between 1950 and 2050 the total population of the world can be expected to increase about four

Table 9.1 Actual and projected population percentages of the world total in individual developed regions and in all developing regions 1950 - 2050

	(1) 1950	(2) 1970	(3) 1990	(4) 2010	(5) 2050
Western Europe	11.8	9.3	6.8	5.8[2]	3.5
C. Europe and USSR	12.3	10.1	8.1	5.9[2]	3.4
Japan	3.4	2.8	2.3	2.6[3]	1.6
N. America etc[1]	7.8	7.2	6.4	5.9	5.5
All developed	35.3	29.4	23.6	20.2	14.0
All developing	64.7	70.6	76.4	79.8	86.0
World	100.0	100.0	100.0	100.0	100.0
Population in millions	2,250	3,650	5,300	6,980	9,880

[1] USA, Canada, Australia, New Zealand, South Africa

[2] After 1990, E. Germany and the Baltic Republics are transferred to Western Europe

[3] S. Korea is included with Japan

Sources: *WPDS 1996* and earlier, *UNSYB* various years. 2010 and 2050 are estimates by the author

times, from 2.5 to 10 billion. The combined population of the developed regions, as defined in Table 9.1, is likely to continue to increase at least in the first two or three decades of the 21st century, mainly due to growth in North America. The share of world population in the present developed regions can however be expected to drop from 35 per cent in 1950 to only about 14 per cent in 2050.

If the forecasts are correct, two prospects stand out immediately. First, the present countries with high per capita consumption of energy, raw materials and, to a lesser extent agricultural produce, will hardly increase in population. Second, however, since these 'rich' countries will account for a much smaller proportion of total world population by 2050, the development assistance they can provide (if any) for the developing countries will have to be spread even more thinly than now if they provide it at the same rate as at present.

Further prospects that arise from the situation described above must also be noted. Whether by agreement or by pressure that cannot be contained, there could be a considerable migration of people from poor to rich regions in the next few decades (e.g. from Mexico to the USA, Northwest Africa to the European Union, see Chapters 4 and 12). Such a movement could slightly alter the percentages in Table 9.1. Furthermore, the effect of rapid economic growth in some of the newly industrialising countries could elevate them to the realm of the present developed countries. Symbolic of such a trend has been the transfer by the author of South Korea from its previous developing status to a place alongside Japan after 1990. On the other hand, in the mid-1990s some parts of Central Europe (e.g. Romania, Bulgaria) and much of the former USSR could equally realistically be demoted to the developing world, if only temporarily. In whatever way Central Europe and the USSR are defined, for a decade or two, if not permanently, they are likely to be net recipients of development assistance, some at least from the more affluent European Union. They will no longer be net donors of assistance, as most of them still were in the early 1980s, focusing, for example, on Cuba and North Korea.

The regions as used in Table 9.1 will for simplicity serve as the basis for projections of various sectors of production and consumption, with comparisons of past and possible future shares between the developed and developing worlds. Five aspects are considered: GDP/GNP, agriculture and food, energy and pig iron production, mineral raw materials, and cars. These relate back to various sections and diagrams in Chapters 5-8.

9.2 THE GAP ACCORDING TO GDP

One problem of measuring the development gap relates to the way in which data for income and wealth are collected and grouped. To make the handling of information on the subject feasible it is necessary to aggregate individuals into income classes or by countries. An example of the former method is the comparison of the richest and poorest people in the world given at the head of this chapter. The numbers cited reveal an enormous difference in wealth between the world's very rich people and the mass of poor people. To obtain a more comprehensive but still very basic comparison of the rich and poor countries of the world it is common practice to create two categories of country. In the example that follows, these are 'industrial' (equivalent to developed as used elsewhere in this book) and 'developing', for which average per capita levels are compared. A common refinement is to subdivide the developing countries into three or four sub-groups according to their level of development.

According to *HDR 1996*: 'The largest share of global production is in the industrial countries. Of the 23 trillion dollars of GDP in 1993, 18 trillion is in the industrial countries - only 5 trillion in the developing countries, even though they have nearly 80 per cent of the world's population.' The disparity is considerably less marked, although still very great, if real GDP (in which parity purchasing power is applied), is used instead of GNP or GDP as calculated from exchange rates of the time between national currencies and the US dollar. Until the 1990s prominence was given to GDP (or GNP) as the 'ultimate' measure of development, but in the United Nations Development Programme additional measures are used, notably life expectancy and educational levels, and real GDP is preferred to conventional GDP. Some limitations of GDP as a measure of development were discussed in Chapter 2.

The answer to the question 'has the gap widened in recent decades?' is given in *HDR 1996* in very general terms: 'Over the past thirty years the global growth in income has been spread very unequally - and the inequality is increasing. Consider the relative income shares of the richest and poorest 20 per cent of the world's people. Between 1960 and 1991 the share of the richest 20 per cent rose from 70 per cent of global income to 85 per cent - while that of the poorest declined from 2.3 per cent to 1.4 per cent. So, the ratio of the shares of the richest and the poorest increased from 30:1 to 61:1.'

For at least several thousand years there have been marked differences in the organisation, technological levels and living conditions between different regions of the world and also within countries and regions. In some fictitious ideal communities people have been roughly equal in what they consume. Such a situation can still be found in very small communities of pastoralists and cultivators today, although even here men might get better cuts of meat than women and children. It would be naive and simplistic to expect that between now and 2050 poverty in the world could suddenly be eradicated and a reasonable approximation of equality achieved.

One of the most serious problems of comparing the developed and developing groups of countries is that the gap is much wider in some sectors of production and consumption than in others (see Table 9.2). For example, the average daily calorie supply in all developing countries in 1993 was about 65 per cent of that in all developed countries, while average life expectancy was 68 per cent. Common sense indicates that the range between the lower and upper limits of food intake and of average life expectancy cannot be very great. Between the extremes of food

Table 9.2 The quality of life gaps beween developed and developing countries

Human Development	Life expectancy at birth		Adult literacy		Daily calorie supply		Access to safe water		Under-five mortality	
	1960	1993	1960	1993	1960	1993	1960	1993	1960	1993
High[1]	83	95	86	96	83	91	–	–	36	74
Medium[2]	69	90	–	–	71	87	–	–	21	37
Low[3]	60	75	34	52	72	72	–	–	17	13
Least developed	56	68	32	50	72	65	–	–	15	12
Sub-Saharan Africa	58	68	30	57	75	67	–	–	17	12
Industrial	100	100	100	100	100	100	100	100	100	100
29 Rep. of Korea	78	96	95	100+	77	100+	66	96	33	100+
48 Mexico	83	95	80	93	90	100+	–	–	28	56
58 Brazil	79	89	71	86	81	91	62	90	23	30
102 Indonesia	60	85	58	87	65	88	11	64	19	16
108 China	68	92	–	–	69	88	–	–	20	42
135 India	64	81	37	53	72	77	–	–	17	15
137 Nigeria	57	68	27	57	77	68	–	–	20	9
168 Ethiopia	52	64	–	–	62	52	8	26	14	9

Source of data: United Nations Development Programme (UNDP) (1996), *Human Development Report 1996*, Oxford: University Press

- means data not available.

Notes[1-3] 'Non industrial' countries classed according to human development level [1] (26 countries), [2] (53 countries), [3] (48 countries). Related to 100 for the average for all industrial countries.
29-168 Human development rank according to UNDP assessment, representative countries out of a total of 174.

intake at national or regional level it is not much more than about 2:1 in favour of the developed countries. Similarly, at national level there is almost exactly a 2:1 ratio in average life expectancy between the extremes of Japan at 80 years and Sierra Leone at 40 years.

When GDP is used as a measure, much greater disparities occur. According to *HDR 1996*, the average gap in real GDP per capita between countries of 'High human development' and the rest (Medium and Low) is about 7 to 1, between 14,900 dollars and about 2,100. The ratio is therefore much greater than the 2 to 1 for food intake and life expectancy. An even more marked gap exists (*WPDS 1996*) in average GNP per capita between 18,130 for the 'more developed' countries and 1,090 for the 'less developed' ones, a gap of more than 17 to 1. Table 9.3 shows the different results in a comparison between GNP and real GDP for the 12 largest countries in the world in population. In the early 1990s the exchange rates between the US dollar and both the Japanese and German currencies overstated for GNP the scale of production per capita, as is evident when it is compared with real GDP per capita. Similarly, but in the reverse direction, GNP understated the scale of production per capita in Latin American countries and Russia by half and for Asian and African countries by about four fifths.

When GNP and GDP total and per capita production are compared through time, the change in the real value of the US dollar also has to be taken into account. Thus, for example, if the average purchasing power of the US dollar as measured by producer prices was 1 unit in

Table 9.3 GNP and real GDP per capita in the twelve largest countries of the world

		(1) GNP per capita (US dollars)	*(2)* Real GDP per capita in 1993 (US dollars)	*(3)*	*(4)* *(1) and (2)* *(USA=100)*
1	Japan	34,630	20,660	134	84
2	USA	25,860	24,680	100	100
3	Germany	25,580	18,840	99	76
4	Mexico	4,010	7,010	16	28
5	Brazil	3,370	5,500	13	22
6	Russia	2,650	4,760	10	19
7	Indonesia	880	3,270	3	13
8	China	530	2,330	2	9
9	Pakistan	440	2,160	2	9
10	India	310	1,240	1	5
11	Nigeria	280	1,540	1	6
12	Bangladesh	230	1,290	1	5
	World	4,470	5,430	18	22

Sources of data   (1) *World Bank* (1996)
                   (2) *HDR 1996* (1996)

1982, it was 3.55 units in 1950 but only 0.76 in 1995, due to inflation. The continuous fluctuations in exchange rates must also be taken into account, as well as the different rates of growth of population in each region. In view of the above technical problems and the fact that GNP and GDP in theory cover a complete range of products and services (see Chapter 2), provided non-commercial activities are also allowed for, other measures will be used in addition to GNP to trace changes in the relative levels of developed and developing countries through reference to specific sectors of the economy.

The reader should appreciate that in this chapter emphasis is placed on the gap between developed and developing countries. In most comparisons, per capita quantities are used. Although the world average remains at 100 through time in the comparisons, it will represent different absolute quantities at different points in time.

9.3   THE GAP IN BIOCLIMATIC RESOURCES AND PRODUCTS

Four aspects of food and agricultural production will be considered in this section: cropland (covering arable and permanent crops), cereal production, forest and woodland, and fish catches (see Chapter 5, sections 3 and 4). Table 9.4 shows the method used to make the calculations needed to compare the developed and developing parts of the world for 1950, 1970 and 1990 with regard to availability of cropland. The percentage of the total cropland of the world in each region is divided by the region's share of the total population of the world and then multiplied by 100 (to remove the decimal point). Thus, for example, for Western Europe in 1950, 7.3 divided by 11.8 gives 0.62 which when multiplied by 100 gives 62, compared with the world level of 100.

Between 1950 and 1990, the ratio of cropland per capita in developed regions to cropland per capita in developing ones increased from 1.7:1 to 3.0:1. During 1950-1990 the cropland

Table 9.4 The distribution of cropland, 1950–2050

	% of world population			% of world cropland			Index of concentration (world average = 100)				
	(1) 1950	(2) 1970	(3) 1990	(4) 1950	(5) 1970	(6) 1990	(7) 1950	(8) 1970	(9) 1990	(10) 2010	(11) 2050
Western Europe	11.8	9.3	6.8	7.3	6.4	6.4	62	69	94	110	183
E. Europe[1]	12.3	10.1	8.1	21.5	19.7	21.1	175	195	260	358	621
Japan	3.4	2.8	2.3	0.4	0.4	0.3	12	14	13	15	25
N. America +[2]	7.8	7.2	6.4	19.2	19.4	22.3	246	269	348	378	405
All developed	35.3	29.4	23.6	48.4	45.9	50.1	137	156	212	248	358
All developing	64.7	70.6	76.4	51.6	54.1	49.9	80	77	71	63	58
Developed to developing ratio							1.7:1	2.0:1	3.0:1	3.9:1	6.2:1
World	100.0	100.0	100.0	100.0	100.0	100.0					

[1] Central Europe plus former USSR
[2] USA, Canada, Australia, New Zealand, S. Africa

increased in some developed regions (notably the USSR, Canada and Australia) but diminished in others (notably the EU and Japan). Similarly, there was some increase in the cropland area in parts of Latin America, Africa and Southeast Asia. The sharp deterioration of the developing regions in relation to the developed ones was largely due to differences in the rate of growth of population because, as seen in Chapter 5, the area of cropland in the world has not increased much since the 1940s.

Figure 5.1 in Chapter 5 shows three possible futures for the area of cropland in the world. In projection A*t* there is virtually no change in the area of the world's cropland between 1990 and 2050. Table 9.4 shows the possible new scores and ratios of cropland per capita between regions in 2010 and 2050. It is expected that losses of cultivated land in some regions (e.g. in Kazakhstan, Japan, China), will be compensated for by gains in others (e.g. in tropical South America).

The projections for 2010 and 2050 are calculated on the assumption that the share of cropland in 1990 (column (6) of Table 9.4) stays the same while the share of population changes as in Table 9.1, columns (4) and (5). The developed to developing ratio of cropland per capita would rise from about 3:1 in 1990 to almost 4:1 in 2010 and over 6:1 in 2050. The effective gap will be even greater if crop yields in the USA, Europe and Japan remain above the world average, as they have done for some decades up to 1990, while those in most parts of the developing world remain well below.

The reader might not agree with the prospect for the distribution of the per capita availability of cropland around 2050 and indeed might argue that the area under cultivation could be extended. Even then, there is no reason to expect greater expansion in developing countries than in developed ones. Indeed in general the developed countries have superior means and resources to reclaim, improve, and irrigate new areas of cultivation than do most of the developing countries. The growth in yields in some developing countries, especially those of Asia, could continue, but there is also considerable scope for increasing yields in Canada, Australia and much of Russia. All in all it may be expected that around 2050 the developed countries will have about six times as much land per capita under arable and permanent crops on average as the developing countries, a feature discussed in some length in Chapter 5.

About half of the world's cropland is used to grow cereals. It is not surprising, therefore, that a broadly similar situation to that for all cropland is found with cereal production. In 1950 the ratio of developed to developing countries in per capita cereal production was 2.1:1 but by 1990 it was 2.8:1. Assuming production is distributed worldwide in 2010 and 2050 broadly in the way it was in 1990, then the ratios would be 3.4:1 in 2010 and 5.4:1 in 2050. The major difference between developed and developing countries in the sector of cereal production is that much of the total produced in the developed countries is fed to livestock, comparatively little in the developing countries.

The changing balance in the availability of cropland and, representing agricultural production, of cereal production in particular, have serious implications for world agriculture. Table 9.5 shows the value of the imports and exports of agricultural, forestry and fisheries products by major regions of the world and of selected countries in 1994. It is important to appreciate that only products entering international trade are recorded here and that in most regions such trade only accounts for a small part of total agricultural production. The data show that in the mid-1990s the presence of surpluses and of deficits was not related to developed and developing regions. As population grows in the developing regions it seems likely that Latin America and particularly Asia will join the regions that are already net importers, while Europe achieves a surplus.

Table 9.5 Trade in agriculture, forestry and fisheries products in 1994 in billions of US dollars

		Imports	*Exports*	*Balance*	*Ratio of Exports to Imports (×100)*
1	Oceania[1]	6	22	+16	367
2	South America	13	38	+25	292
3	Canada	12	33	+21	275
4	USA	55	69	+14	125
5	Rest of Asia[2]	80	87	+7	109
6	Europe[3]	260	237	-23	91
7	Central America[4]	14	12	-2	86
8	Africa	20	17	-3	85
9	Japan, S. Korea	83	7	-76	8
	World total	555	525		

Source: Food and Agriculture Organisation *Trade Yearbook 1994*, Vol. 48, FAO Rome 1995

Notes:
[1]   Mainly Australia and New Zealand
[2]   Excludes former USSR, Japan, S. Korea
[3]   Includes former USSR
[4]   Mexico, C. America and the Caribbean

What has been said about cropland and its main product, cereals, can be applied to the future of the world's forests and woodlands. Figure 5.3 in Chapter 5 shows possible futures for the world's forests. Even assuming that the preservation of as much as possible of the world's existing forests is considered desirable and a strict policy of conservation is effectively implemented, the gloomy forecasts make the prospect of maintaining the same area of forest over the next sixty years very unlikely. Projection C*t* in Figure 5.2 is used here to examine the differences between developed and developing countries in terms of the share of the world's forests. A 15 per cent reduction is assumed in the total area of forest in the world, two thirds of it in the developing countries. Currently reforestation is generally taken more seriously in the developed countries than in the developing countries and in some respects is actually more easy to apply, given the nature of the ecological conditions outside the tropics.

In 1990, out of about 4,310 million hectares of forest in the world, the developed countries had 48.5 per cent, developing ones 51.5 per cent. Under these circumstances the developed regions scored 206 in 1990 against the world average of forest per capita of 100, the developing countries only 67, giving a ratio of forest per capita of 3.1:1 in favour of the developed countries. If it is assumed that there is a reduction by 2050 of about 10 per cent in the area of forest in developed countries and a reduction of about 20 per cent of the area in developing ones, the shares would change to 51.5 per cent and 48.5 per cent respectively in a diminished forest area of only 3,655 million hectares. By 2050 the scores per capita would be 368 against 56, a ratio of 6.6:1, in relation to a considerably smaller total area of forest and as a result of the large increase of population in the developing countries.

The situation with regard to fish landings is more difficult to appraise than for forests (see Chapter 5). The dominance of the developed countries around 1950 is shown by the 12.4:1 per capita fish catch ratio in their favour, but this ratio was reduced to 2.3:1 by 1970 as a result of increased fishing by many developing countries, including China, Peru and Chile. By 1990 it was still at a 2.3:1 ratio. Given that some fish stocks are dwindling and total world production is not expected to rise greatly in the next few decades, there is little room for manoeuvre and expansion unless some developed countries reduce the present level of catches or stop fishing altogether. Given the increase in population in the developing countries and the continuation of the present situation, by 2050 the ratio might rise again to about 4:1 in favour of the developed fishing countries.

9.4   ENERGY, AND IRON AND STEEL

Energy

The growth of per capita energy production and consumption is of particular importance in the present world economy. It reflects both the growth of modern industry and transportation, and the great gap between developed and developing regions. As noted above, the extremes in per capita food consumption and in life expectancy between developed and developing countries are about 2:1 while for real GDP the rate is about 50:1. In contrast, the annual consumption of commercial energy per capita in coal equivalent ranges between about 10,000 kilograms (10 tonnes) in the USA and 25 kilograms in Ethiopia, roughly a 400:1 ratio.

Table 9.6 shows the arithmetic of the calculations of the energy gap between developed and developing countries; only one of many possible projections is shown. In Projection B*t* in Figures 6.1-6.3 (Chapter 6) the production of the three main fossil fuels increases between 1990 and 2050 in such a way that world consumption per capita remains the same throughout. An increase of over 85 per cent in energy consumption (and therefore production) is needed to offset the expected 86 per cent increase in population from 5.3 billion to 9.9 billion. If it is assumed that less energy is consumed per capita in the developed countries as time passes, such that in 2050 their consumption is about 20 per cent less than in 1990, then a modest amount could be 'transferred' to the developing countries, the population of which is, however, expected roughly to double between 1990 and 2050.

The per capita energy gap between developed and developing countries narrowed between 1950 and 1990 from 24:1 to 9.3:1. If total world energy consumption rises from almost 11 billion t.c.e. (tonnes of coal equivalent) in 1990 to 14 billion in 2010 and the per capita consumption level in the developed countries falls by 10 per cent then the developed to developing ratio of 9.3:1 in 1990 would drop to 5.7:1 in 2010. If 20 billion t.c.e. are consumed in 2050 (85 per cent more than in 1990) and per capita consumption falls by another 10 per cent in the developed countries, then the ratio at 3.5:1 would still be considerable. The possible energy future described above has different assumptions about the situation in 2050 from that discussed in Chapter 6 and shown in Table 6.11. That in Chapter 6 assumes substantial increases in per capita consumption in developing regions between 1995 and 2050. Some reservations and conclusions about the projections follow:

*   To reach an annual consumption of about 20 billion tonnes of coal equivalent of energy in 2050 after a steady rise from 11.5 billion in 1995, about 900 billion t.c.e. would be consumed in the 55 years from 1995 to 2050 compared with about 400 billion t.c.e. in the 55 years from 1940 to 1995, and only about 150 billion in the 55 years up to 1940. The world

Table 9.6 Energy consumption

	1950	1970	1990	2010	2050
			Population (percentage)		
All developed	35.3	29.4	23.6	20.2	14.0
All developing	64.7	70.6	74.6	79.8	86.0
World	100.0	100.0	100.0	100.0	100.0
	1950	1970	1990	2010	2050
			Energy consumed (percentage)		
All developed	93.0	84.3	74.3	57.6	36.3
All developing	7.0	15.7	25.7	43.4	63.7
World	100.0	100.0	100.0	100.0	100.0
	1950	1970	1990	2010	2050
		Consumption related to world = 100 and ratio of developed to developing			
All developed	263	287	315	285	259
All developing	11	22	34	50	74
World	24:1	13:1	9.3:1	5.7:1	3.5:1

economy in 2050 would then be needing around 20 billion a year thereafter. Consumption could not suddenly stop or even decrease very sharply.

- The environmental impact would be devastating if fossil fuels continue to form the basis of the energy supply.

- Even if the level of consumption achieved by 2050 reached a world average of about 2,000 kilograms per inhabitant, consumption in many parts of the developing world would still fall far short of that at present in Japan and the lower level consumers of the EU, let alone the USA.

Iron and steel

Like the use of energy, the use of steel is crucial to the modern world economy. The dominance of iron and steel as a material in modern industry and construction has been reduced relatively in the 20th century with the rapid growth of consumption of other metals such as aluminium and of non-metallic materials such as plastics. Nevertheless, for the purposes of this section the production of pig iron is taken to represent broadly the development gap in metallurgical industries. Pig iron is the main ingredient in the manufacture of steel, but production is 70-75 per cent of that of steel in weight because ferro-alloys and scrap steel are added to pig iron in the steel-making process.

In 1950 world pig iron production was about 133 million tonnes, in 1970 it was 440 million tonnes, and in 1990, 543 million. As recently as 1950, developing countries only accounted for about 2 per cent of world pig iron production, the main producers of this small amount being

India, China and Brazil. In 1950 the USA (48 per cent) and Western Europe (29 per cent) dominated the industry. By 1970, however, great increases in production in Japan, the former USSR and Central Europe reduced the dominance of the USA and Western Europe among the developed regions. Production meanwhile was also growing quickly in some developing regions, which by 1970 accounted for almost 10 per cent of world pig iron production and by 1990 for over a quarter. Thus during 1950-1990 the per capita 'pig iron gap' between developed and developing countries dropped as follows: 1950, 92:1; 1970, 22:1; 1990, 9:1.

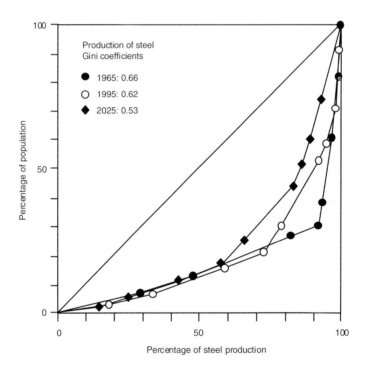

Figure 9.1 The distribution of steel production among 10 major regions of the world in 1965, 1995 and (projected) 2025. The gini coefficients show a gradual shift towards a more even distribution in the world during 60 years. See Figure 6.9 for other applications of the Lorenz curve technique.

In the 1980s and early 1990s the iron and steel industry in the developed countries stagnated. The USA has been a net importer of steel while in the EU the capacity has been trimmed and since the late 1980s production has dropped in the former USSR. If it is assumed that the level of pig iron production remains roughly the same in the developed countries from now until 2050, while it increases three times in the developing countries by that year, then world pig iron production should increase from about 540 million tonnes in 1990 to 830 million in 2050. The output of the developed countries would remain at about 400 million tonnes, while that of the developing countries would rise from 140 million in 1990 to 240 million (out of 640) in 2010 and 430 (out of 830) million in 2050. The percentage of world production in the developing countries would thus rise to 38 per cent in 2010 and 52 per cent in 2050. The developed to developing ratios per capita would consequently drop from 9:1 in 1990 to 6.8:1 in 2010 and 5.7:1 in 2050. Therefore, even if the level of production in the developed regions stays the same to 2050 and all the increase is achieved in developing regions, there will still be a very large gap in 2050.

9.5   OTHER SELECTED PRODUCTS

In this section the 'development gap' is assessed for three other products, two mineral products, aluminium and cement (see Chapter 7), and one industrial product, cars (see Chapter 8). Differences between the three products must first be noted. Much of the world's bauxite is extracted in developing countries, but until the 1980s almost all was converted to aluminium in developed countries. Limestone, the main ingredient of cement, is much more widely distributed around the world than bauxite and there is little international trade either in limestone or in cement. The data used to illustrate the motor vehicles industry relate to passenger cars in use, not to production. A few developed countries are net exporters of finished vehicles, commercial and passenger, both to other developed countries and to developing ones, and in the 1990s South Korea and Malaysia also started to export.

Aluminium

As shown in Chapter 7 (see Figure 7.4), the world production of aluminium has grown rapidly since the Second World War from less than 2 million tonnes in 1950 to almost 10 million in 1970 and about 22 million in 1990. In 1950 the USA and Canada accounted for about 60 per cent of total production, Western Europe and the USSR for most of the rest. In spite of the beginnings of aluminium production in some of the developing countries that exported bauxite (e.g. Suriname, Ghana) and also in India and China, the developing countries produced less than 7 per cent of the world total. By 1990 their share of production had risen to 18.5 per cent, with Brazil, China and India producing the largest amounts. Even then, the USA and Canada together still accounted for almost a third of the much larger output. The per capita 'aluminium gap' between developed and developing regions was as follows: 1950, 282:1; 1970, 35:1; 1990, 14.4:1. In 1990 about 22 million tonnes were produced.

If it is assumed that between 1990 and 2010 there is an increase of 11 million tonnes (50 per cent), shared equally among developed and developing regions, then the ratio would be about 10:1 in the latter year. If a further increase in production of 11 million tonnes is assumed between 2010 and 2050, the result of a much slower rate of expansion of the industry, but again with half of the expansion taking place in developed and half in developing regions, then the ratio would rise again in favour of the developed countries, to about 12:1.

Cement

Like energy and steel, cement is one of the major ingredients of development. Since there is little international movement of cement, the amounts produced and consumed in most countries are similar. The per capita consumption of cement at any given time is therefore a rough indicator of the capacity of a country to construct buildings, transportation links, dams and other such works. World cement production rose from 116 million tonnes in 1950 to 567 million in 1970 and to 1,152 million in 1990. During those 40 years, per capita production rose almost four times. As with most other industries, in 1950 and even in 1970 cement production was heavily concentrated in the developed countries (86 and 81 per cent of production respectively). Thanks to the recent rapid expansion of cement production in many developing countries, by 1990 they were producing about half of the world's cement. The ratio per capita of cement production in developed to developing countries was therefore as follows: 1950, 11.1:1; 1970, 10.2:1; 1990, 3.2:1.

Figure 7.3 in Chapter 7 shows projections for cement production. Here it is assumed that Projection C*t* is the future for cement production. The total produced is 50 per cent higher in 2010 than in 1990, but expansion is much slower after 2010. Production of cement is assumed to stay the same in the developed regions after 1990 and the increase therefore occurs exclusively in the developing regions. In round numbers, production in the developed countries remains at 570 million tonnes in 2010 and 2050 but in the developing regions it rises from 580 million in 1990 to 1,160 in 2010 and 1,730 in 2050. Under the above conditions, the per capita cement production ratio would be roughly 2:1 in favour of the developed regions in both 2010 and 2050. Even with this comparatively narrow gap, during the 100 years from 1950 to 2050 the developed regions would have produced (and used) about four times as much cement per capita as the developing regions. Since most of the cement used during that time would still be in place in some form or other, even the 'generous' assumption used in the cement projection leaves a huge disparity in the availability of cement between the developed and developing countries.

Passenger cars

Over recent decades there have been between four and five times as many passenger cars in use in the world as commercial vehicles, but the ratio of cars to commercial vehicles tends to be higher in developed countries than in developing ones. As commercial vehicles are on average larger than passenger cars and in general are used more intensively, the two categories consume roughly similar amounts of fuel altogether. For simplicity, only the passenger car gap is considered here. The number of passenger cars in the world has increased more than eight times between 1950 and 1990 and the regional distribution has also changed markedly.

In view of the importance in the world economy of road transport, the regional distribution of cars in use was examined in Chapter 8.4 with regard to 10 major regions of the world. From Table 8.2, in which assumptions are made about the future level of car ownership in developed and developing regions, the following profile of ratios of developed to developing country levels may be expected: 1950, 30:1; 1970, 32:1 (Western Europe follows North America); 1990, 23:1; 2010, 18:1; 2050, 12:1. By 2010 saturation should almost have been reached in North America, Japan and Western Europe, and by 2050 in Central Europe and the former USSR as well. The changes according to the assumptions made above about car ownership in the world give, in 2050, a ratio of more than 10:1 against the developing regions as a whole and around 20:1 between North America on the one hand and Africa, South Asia and China in particular, the three latter regions containing over 60 per cent of the population of the world in 2050.

Only a few of many possible comparisons of per capita production have been made in this chapter; the results are summarised in Table 9.7. The picture is a complicated one. It is certain, however, that if current demographic trends continue, the per capita amount of cropland, forest and permanent pasture will diminish in the next 50 years in the developing countries, whereas in the developed ones it will not change markedly. On the other hand, some parts of the developing world will become more highly industrialised than at present, rivalling the present developed countries in more basic, less sophisticated branches of industrial production, although still lagging well behind in more sophisticated sectors of industry. The matter of how much the developed countries are likely to contribute to help to narrow the development gap will be discussed in the next section.

Table 9.7 Summary of the development gap in selected years

	Ratio of per capita between developing and developed countries				
	1950	1970	1990	2010	2050
Cropland	1.7:1	2.0:1	3.0:1	3.9:1	6.2:1
Cereal production	2.1:1		2.8:1	3.4:1	5.4:1
Forest and woodland			3.1:1	4.5:1	6.6:1
Fish landings	12.4:1	2.3:1	2.3:1	3.0:1	4.0:1
Energy consumption	24:1	13:1	9:1	5.7:1	4.0:1
Pig iron production	92:1	22:1	9:1	6.8:1	5.7:1
Aluminium production	282:1	35:1	14.4:1	9.8:1	11.8:1
Cement production	11:1	10:1	3.2:1	2.1:1	2.1:1
Cars in use	30:1	31.5:1	23.3:1	18:1	12:1

Developing countries = 1

9.6 OFFICIAL DEVELOPMENT ASSISTANCE

It has been widely accepted since the Second World War that the rich countries should assist the poor ones with development projects through grants and through loans on favourable terms. Such assistance is referred to in United Nations publications as Official Development Assistance (ODA). A smaller amount of assistance is provided by Non-Government Organisations (NGOs). Private investment in transnational companies, which exceeds ODA, is also regarded as a contribution to development, but will not be considered in this section since its principal aim is to obtain returns on such investment rather than to bring benefits to host countries, although these may occur.

In the 1970s the western industrial countries agreed in principle that they should make available 0.7 per cent of their respective Gross National Products (GNP) for development assistance to the developing world. This proportion was reconfirmed at the Rio Earth Summit in 1992 but in the mid-1990s the average provided was only 0.27 per cent of GNP. Table 9.8 shows the sixteen countries that made the largest absolute contributions in 1994, the total in US dollars being 59,160 million, of which the European Union provided over half (30,420 million dollars), 0.42 of its GNP. That total was minute compared with the total Third World debt of 2.2 trillion dollars. It should be noted that ODA is not explicitly provided to pay off the debt.

The situation was very similar in the late 1970s, with Iceland and South Africa in addition to the 16 countries referred to above contributing then, but not Spain (see e.g. Cole (1983)). In addition to the total amount of 14,470 million dollars disbursed in 1977 by the western industrial countries, the Soviet bloc and China then contributed 3,740 million dollars, of which 2,920 million came from the USSR. In the 1980s a third group of countries were also net donors of assistance, Saudi Arabia, Kuwait and other oil producing states of Southwest Asia. During the 1980s assistance from the Soviet bloc was reduced and in the 1990s the countries of Central Europe and the former USSR have become recipients of assistance. After the Iraqi invasion of Kuwait in 1990, assistance from the countries of Southwest Asia also virtually dried up.

Among the western industrial countries some have been more forthcoming with ODA than others in the last two decades. The 'generosity' or sacrifice of a donor can be measured in various ways. In Table 9.8, column (2) shows the percentage of total GNP of each country devoted to ODA. Over the last two decades the three Scandinavian countries and the

Table 9.8 Official development assistance (ODA) from developed countries, 1994

		(1) Net official development assistance disbursed (millions of dollars)	(2) (as % of GNP)	(3) ODA per capita of donor country (dollars)			(1) Net official development assistance disbursed (millions of dollars)	(2) (as % of GNP)	(3) ODA per capita of donor country (dollars)
1	Norway	1,137	1.05	247	9	Germany	6,818	0.34	166
2	Denmark	1,446	1.03	260	10	Austria	655	0.33	73
3	Sweden	1,819	0.96	201	11	Belgium	728	0.32	75
4	Netherlands	2,517	0.76	162	12	UK	3,197	0.31	52
5	France	8,466	0.64	279	13	Japan	13,239	0.29	94
6	Canada	2,250	0.43	86	14	Spain	1,305	0.28	33
7	Switzerland	982	0.36	121	15	Italy	2,705	0.27	50
8	Australia	1,088	0.35	55	16	USA	9,927	0.15	38

Netherlands have been the most forthcoming, whereas the UK, Japan, Italy and the USA have made much lower contributions. If every donor country contributed 0.7 per cent of its GNP to ODA, an annual total of about 130 billion dollars would be available rather than the 59 billion actually disbursed in the mid-1990s.

It is much more difficult to generalise about the recipients of ODA. In 1994, only 21 western industrial countries gave ODA, whereas almost 150 countries, including those of Central Europe and the former USSR, received assistance. South Korea and the United Arab Emirates were apparently the only developing countries still providing assistance. In principle it might be expected that official development assistance should be directed mainly to the poorest, least developed countries of the developing world. In practice, where assistance has been bilateral, most of the donor countries have had political and strategic reasons as well as altruistic ones for choosing recipients. Assistance channelled through multilateral institutions has been more impartial.

In 1994 the equivalent of 60,930 million US dollars of net official development assistance, was received by developing countries. Part (a) of Table 9.9 shows several classes of recipient countries. All developing countries fall into High, Medium or Low Human Development according to the Human Development Index of *HDR 1996*. Subsets from these three classes have been allocated to two further classes, least developed and Sub-Saharan Africa (Africa south of the Sahara). It can be seen in column (1) that the first three classes of country differ greatly in real GDP per capita.

The principle of concentrating ODA on the poorest countries is clearly being broadly adhered to. For example, both Mexico and Malaysia are in the class of High Human Development. In each country the ODA received in 1993 amounted to a mere 0.1 per cent of their GNPs. Among the countries in the Medium Human Development class there are great variations. In terms of dollars per inhabitant, Brazil only received 1.5 and China 2.7 whereas Sri Lanka received 31, Egypt 37, Guyana 104, Suriname 198 and Cape Verde 314. Among the countries in the Low Human Development class, the dollars per capita received also vary widely, but in many countries the total accounts for a substantial percentage of GNP, as much as 90 per cent in Mozambique and 64 per cent in Somalia. On account of its great size, India, like China, lost out, receiving only 1.7 dollars per capita, while Nigeria, also large, received 2.0.

Although difficult to quantify precisely, it is clear that in the disbursement of ODA, countries with a small population get much more per capita than countries with a large population. Many islands with populations well below one million in the Caribbean, the southern Pacific and elsewhere get very large amounts per capita: Seychelles (in the Indian Ocean) 139 dollars, Dominica (in the Caribbean) 141. Martinique and Guadaloupe (also in the Caribbean) are part of France and they have received massive assistance from France itself and from the budget of the European Union. Their GDP per capita is about 45 per cent of the EU average (*Profils Régionaux* (1995)), evidence that with intensive assistance, initially poor places, if small enough, can be raised a long way on the development scale. Part (b) of Table 9.9 contains data for eight large developing countries. They are ranked from high to low according to real GDP per inhabitant, the reverse of the order in which in theory they should be assisted. Only the two poorest, Bangladesh and Ethiopia, are convincingly above the rest in assistance received per capita.

Table 9.9 Recipients of Official Development Assistance

	(1) *Real GDP* *per capita* *(US dollars)*	*(2)* *Amount received* *(millions of* *dollars)*	*(3)* *GNP* *(percentage)*	*(4)* *Amount received* *per capita* *(dollars)*
a) Groups of countries				
High Human Development	8,050	2,370	0.3	6.7
Medium Human Development	2,950	19,340	1.0	8.2
Low Human Development	1,270	23,630	4.7	13.4
Least developed	890	16,240	13.4	28.3
Sub-Saharan Africa	1,390	18,890	10.5	31.5
All developing	2,700	60,930	1.4	10.6
b) Selected large countries				
Mexico	7,010	431	0.1	4.4
Brazil	5,500	336	0.1	1.5
Indonesia	3,270	1,642	1.2	10.6
China	2,330	3,232	0.6	2.7
India	1,240	2,324	0.9	1.7
Nigeria	1,540	190	0.6	2.0
Bangladesh	1,290	1,757	6.8	11.8
Ethiopia	420	1,070	17.2	23.3

Source: *HDR 1996*

While the Scandinavian countries explicitly give assistance with few or no conditions attached, some other countries are using assistance for political purposes. According to *Statistical Abstract of the United States 1996* (1996) US Government Foreign Grants and Credits were as follows (in billions of dollars): 1992, 17.0; 1993, 16.6; 1994, 16.0. In 1994, more than a third of the total (33.6 per cent) went to two countries, Israel (3.1 billion) and Egypt (2.2 billion), the former developed, the latter developing, but much better off than most countries of Africa south of the Sahara. In 1993 Russia received 1.9 billion from the USA, in 1994 1.1 billion. Turkey and

Thailand, both allies of the USA, neither particularly poor, also did well. On the other hand, in 1994 India received only 32 million dollars from the USA yet it is very poor even by standards of the developing world and is a distinguished model of democracy; this disbursement by the USA amounted to 3 cents per inhabitant of India.

9.7   THE FUTURE OF DEVELOPMENT ASSISTANCE

The prospects for the future of ODA do not seem bright. New recipients of ODA have emerged from the Soviet bloc. In the end, even within the European Union, Spain, Portugal, Ireland and Greece are net recipients of assistance (in their case from fellow member states via the EU Structural Funds, even if they themselves contribute to the assistance given to the developing countries). The remaining net donors of assistance have mostly gradually been reducing their contributions. Meanwhile the population of the developing world is growing by about 80 million people a year, so the diminishing contribution from the rich countries is compounded by the presence of more people in the countries needing it.

If development assistance is to continue, virtually all of that provided in the next decade or two will have to come from the developed countries. There are however developing countries in the class of High Human Development, with an average real GDP per capita of over 8,000 dollars. Some of these countries are in line to become 'developed' if their economies continue to grow. *HDR 1996* includes 26 countries in this class with a combined population of 340 million in 1993. Most of them (e.g. Kuwait, Barbados, Fiji) are very small, but the following countries all have more than 20 million inhabitants (population in millions): Mexico (102), Thailand (62), South Korea (47), Colombia (38), Argentina (24), Malaysia (22). Could these countries in due course begin to assist the poorest countries in the world? McNulty (1997) reports the formation of Yayasan Salam Malaysia, a Malaysian version of the US Peace Corps: 'Yayasan Salam is the most ambitious group of its type in Asia. It's also a clear sign that Malaysia now feels wealthy enough for do-goodism.' Small beginnings.

A reverse trend to some extent offsets the possible elevation of some developing countries to developed status. Apart from Russia and Latvia, which come lowest in the High Human Development class in *HDR 1996*, all the remaining 13 former Soviet Socialist Republics have ended up in the Medium Human Development class. How long will it take for the countries of Central Europe and the former USSR to return to a level in which they once again give development assistance? Not for some time, it seems. In May 1997 a new 'Marshall Plan' was proposed by President Clinton to help Central Europe and the former USSR. It would be a repeat of the US Marshall Plan of 1947, which assisted the non-communist countries of Western Europe, devastated by the Second World War, to rebuild industries, cities and transportation systems. The difference is that the new 'Marshall Plan' for Central Europe and the former USSR would mainly be funded by the European Union, rather than by the USA. According to EP News (1997), it has been proposed by the Commission of the EU that 75 billion Ecu (about 82 billion US dollars) should be available to enable countries of Eastern Europe to improve their economies and prepare some of them for membership of the EU in the near future. As to be expected, however, this allocation would mean a cutback in EU financial aid going to poorer existing member states.

While it is known how much ODA has been transferred from the developed countries to each developing country it is difficult to assess what difference the assistance has made to their development. According to many criteria, the gap between rich and poor countries has widened in the last 50 years, although it may be argued that without ODA it would have become wider still. One can only speculate about the amount of assistance needed to transform the developing world to the present level of the developed world. Something nearer to 7 per cent of the GNP of the rich countries, rather than the 0.7 per cent considered desirable, might make differences at least in some parts of the developing world, but over decades rather than years. A tax explicitly earmarked for ODA would have to be levied in the developed countries. The disbursements would have to be used effectively, instead of some being spent on wasteful projects or being syphoned off into the pockets of conveniently placed individuals, as now happens. In this respect, NGOs are more likely to ensure that their limited contributions are used in the right places and reach the poorest people.

In the campaign for the UK 1997 General Election virtually no reference was made by any political party to ODA. Making a pledge to raise more tax to help the developing world is not a vote winner in the developed countries and does not seem likely to become one in the decades to come. Influencing the consciences of most people in the rich countries seems a lost cause. An oblique approach has to be taken, assuring voters that assistance is necessary to help poor countries because in the longer term the outlay will pay off by creating larger markets and more trade. Another argument may soon gain strength: for example, the USA must help Mexico, and the European Union must help Northwest Africa, in order to keep potential migrants at home. In both cases the donor countries may however feel it reasonable to request widespread birth control in the beneficiary country, just to keep the population from doubling again as it has done in the last three decades, otherwise the transfer of such aid would not achieve its goal. In the last fifty years world affairs were greatly influenced by an ideological capitalist-communist, West-East confrontation. In the next fifty years this could be replaced by an economic rich-poor or North-South confrontation.

While it can be expected that the rich countries will continue to assist the poor countries in the next fifty years as they have in the last, the amount will be negligible in relation to the growing scale of the gap. In theory the assistance should be used in poor countries to increase agricultural production, to improve infrastructure and to encourage the development of appropriate sectors of industry. Much of the assistance seems likely in practice to end up in the form of food, medical supplies and other emergency items to cope with the increasing impact of natural hazards and military conflicts. Some countries are already 'kept afloat' by ODA and NGO contributions as, for example, Ethiopia, the plight of which is described as follows by Green (1995): 'Between 1988 and 1992, gross national product grew by two per cent per annum. In the same period, however, its population was growing at a rate of more than three per cent. Aid now comprises over three quarters of all foreign imports in Ethiopia and as much food is being shipped into the country as it was during the height of the famine in 1984 to 1985.'

In their book *The Year 2000*, researched and written more than 30 years ago, Kahn and Wiener (1967) gave an impressionistic, but not wholly unreasonable, economic rating of the world in the year 2000. Influenced by W. W. Rostow's *The Stages of Economic Growth*, they identified five levels of income and industrial development in the year 2000, when there would be a total world population of about 6.4 billion. The five groups of countries (population in millions) are shown in Table 9.10.

Kahn and Wiener list the larger member countries of each of their five groups (for example, Group 2 includes India, China, Brazil, Nigeria). Their expected populations in 2000 are reasonably accurately distributed but the expected total of about 6.4 billion (only 6.33 in their Table) exceeds the 6.1 billion now expected in 2000. Their expectations of the size of the 'development gap' (column (2)) are also reasonably close to the situation in 1995 when countries are compared

Table 9.10 Kahn and Wiener on the economic situation in the year 2000

	(1) Expected population (millions)	*(2)* GNP per capita (US dollars) Kahn and Wiener 2000	*(3)* Actual in 1995
1 Pre-industrial	850	50–200	100–500
2 Partially industrialised	3,180	200–600	300–5,000
3 Mature industrial	700	600–1,500	1,000–5,000
4 Mass consumption	400	1,500–4,000	2,000–10,000
5 Post-industrial	1,200	4,000–20,000	10,000–30,000

(column (3)) but it is not possible to compare the real value of their dollars with the actual dollars for 1995. There is no doubt, however, that the gap between the extremes of Pre-industrial and Post-industrial is much greater both according to the expected values of Kahn and Wiener and the observed values of 1995, than it was in the mid-1960s, if only because conditions have hardly changed in the poorest countries, while great advances in the production of both goods and services have occurred in the richest countries during that time. There are no obvious initiatives in the world around 2000 to change the trend in the next 2-3 decades. Why should the past trend continue? That depends on governments, popular initiatives and views, and individuals in the developed countries.

Developed countries

• Do-gooders will argue that the rich countries should help the poor ones, without appreciating the great upheavals and logistical problems such a procedure would cause.

• The poor should help themselves, helping beggars is a bad policy, their state is not our fault (or is it?)

• Governments of rich countries have higher priorities than to help poor countries with more than the present token amounts of assistance.

Developing countries

• 5-20 per cent of the population of the developing countries is doing quite well or very well, including big landowners, manufacturers, professionals, and many people in commerce. It is not in their interest (apparently) to help the poor in their own countries. They turn up at conferences, UN meetings, social occasions, impeccably dressed in Western-style suits and dresses or in dazzling national costume.

• In many developing countries political leaders have achieved a great amount of power and have acquired considerable shares of total national wealth. Before his death in 1974, the Emperor of Ethiopia, Haile Selassie, was credited with the ownership of half of the country. In (very poor) Zaire, Mobutu owned great wealth, as did the Duvaliers in Haiti. In Cuba, Fidel Castro, and in Iraq, Saddam Hussein have each managed to amass fortunes of several billion dollars, while the Sultan of Brunei (the small oil state on the island of Kalimantan) has a fortune worth 38 billion dollars (see Rhodes (1997)).

- It would be naive to argue that there is a conspiracy among the rich, whether whole countries or individuals, to keep the world situation as it is. Perhaps there is a kind of inertia that inhibits change. In theory (although not much in practice) international socialism, now in decline in many parts of the world, should have reduced global, regional and individual inequalities. The Western market economy system tends to increase inequalities. Will it predominate in the next 50 years?

10

ENVIRONMENTAL CONCERN

'She
But ye have craft to shoot a shaft
And slay the forest deer;
And who would sup from better cup
Than river-water clear?'

The Nut-Brown Maid,
a fifteenth century English ballad
(New version by FB Money-Coutts, London: John Lane, 1901)

10.1   INTRODUCTION

The word 'environment' has come to be used very widely, covering not only the natural world and the tangible man-made world but also more abstract ideas such as social and political ones. In this chapter 'environment' refers to the material features of the world: what is left of the natural environment, plus rural ones, affected by cultivation, grazing, forestry and the extraction of minerals, as well as urban environments, with their exceptional concentrations of people in small areas.

The production of goods and services, the material side of development, is generally regarded as positive, desirable and beneficial. The downside of development, the cost of material progress, is the emission of harmful gases into the atmosphere, the release of toxic industrial liquids and solids into waterways and seas, and of domestic waste, to be disposed of with the minimum of cost and inconvenience. Military conflicts can be added to the negative side of human activity when the 'insurance' of defence is activated to cause damage. After almost 30 years, land is still blighted from Agent Orange defoliant used in the Viet Nam War, the infrastructure of Afghanistan has largely been destroyed following its internal conflicts, and after the Gulf War in 1991, Kuwait's oil wells burned for the best part of a year before the fires were extinguished. In *Aftermath*, Webster (1997) describes the remnants of war, focusing not only on the results of actual conflicts but also on peacetime damage from testing weapons, as at the US atomic test site in Nevada where, over 12 years, 126 atomic weapons were atmospherically tested.

Concern over the environment is now widespread not only among those who put its conservation first among human problems but also by scientists (considered to take an impartial view of nature), by politicians (at least those thinking beyond the next election) and by the media. But disquiet over the environment is not new. Runnels (1995) describes how archaeological and geological evidence confirm concern expressed in Greece two thousand years ago: 'the ancient Greeks were responsible for the deforestation and erosion that have reduced much of Greece to a barren, stony - if picturesque - wasteland.' In the 18th and 19th centuries, European colonial powers were concerned about vegetation and animal preservation in their colonies in the tropics, although for the value of the resources rather than for its own sake (see Grove (1992)). For example, the Dutch established mandates to protect forests in South Africa, the British created forest reserves in Tobago, and the French passed conservation laws in Mauritius. With droughts and famines in India in the 19th century the British administration became concerned about deforestation there. One example of idealistic concern over the future of the natural environment was the establishment of a National Park system in the USA in the 1870s. It later became a model for similar systems in the UK, Canada, Australia and Kenya. In the urban environments of the early industrial cities, smoke pollution was a problem, while the widespread use of horses for the movement of goods and passengers required constant street cleaning and contributed to the introduction of 'underground' railways and electric trams (the earliest of the former being overhead or 'cut and cover', not tunnels).

Although disquiet about environmental problems is not new, the scale of the problems has grown enormously in the 20th century. World population has increased almost four times and the consumption of energy and materials has increased even more quickly in the industrial countries and in parts of the developing world. The earth's surface and its natural resources are finite, even if new technology allows a wider range of materials to be used as time passes. For how long can how many people be supported at what level of material consumption before natural resources run out, become inadequate, or pollution becomes unacceptably widespread?

Awareness of pollution and other urban problems is not new. The French Gustave Doré artist portrayed the above scene in 1871 in 'Over London by Rail'.

Concern for the future of humans on the planet has been expressed on numerous occasions since the 1960s, often in books or articles with dramatic titles, usually serious but sometimes flippant. For example, the ecologist R. F. Dasmann (1972), working in Switzerland for the International Union for the Conservation of Nature wrote *Planet in Peril? Man and the Biosphere Today.* R. Allen (1980) based his book *How to Save the World,* on the World Conservation Strategy prepared by the International Union for Conservation of Nature and Natural Resources (IUCN). In 1987, L. Timberlake used the title *Only One Earth, Living for the Future.* The 'amusing' side of environmental change is caught in R. Girling's (1997) article entitled 'Paddling down the A1 in the rush hour?' Some commentators on the state of the environment simply describe the problems and prospects, others offer solutions, while some question whether there are simple answers at all.

Does the consensus of a large number of, presumably, influential people make greater impact than a book by an individual, supported or not by a well-known name providing a foreword? If so, the Union of Concerned Scientists (1993), based in Cambridge, Massachusetts, should be taken seriously. No less than 1,680 prominent scientists from 70 countries signed *World Scientists' Warning Briefing Book*, a collection of papers, including some from prestigious journals and institutes such as *Scientific American* and the World Resources Institute, on the atmosphere, water resources, oceans, soil, forests, living species and population. Stanners and Bourdeau (1995), working for the European Environment Agency Task Force, edited a volume almost 700 pages in length: *Europe's Environment, the Dobris Assessment*. Preliminaries and conclusions apart, the book covers no less than 35 aspects of the environment. Policy options are offered, but the brief was to provide information to the environment ministers for the whole of Europe, not to propose solutions.

Publications on the environment come and go, politicians support resolutions about the need to do something, but in practice little has been done by the late 1990s, in spite of two world summits on the subject, in Rio Janeiro in 1992 (the Rio Summit) and Rio 2 in 1997. At best, proposals are made by politicians to stabilise or phase out the use and consumption of products that are considered exceptionally harmful to the environment. 'Buying time' is often the result. Prevention may be better than cure, but effective measures to tackle environmental problems at their sources are difficult to introduce and to implement. Guidelines, regulations, laws may be fine in theory but controlling environmental pollution, patrolling protected areas, enforcing proposed measures are all difficult, whether at international or national level. Large private companies may prefer to pay (often derisory) fines rather than give up damaging practices, although attitudes are now changing. For example, in ICI's Report *Progress 92* (1993), environmental expenditure is shown to have increased greatly between 1988 and 1992 while the number of fines and prosecutions dropped from 36 in 1990 to 21 in 1992, the amount paid not being specified. Imposing fines on public sector enterprises, virtually the whole economy in the case of the former USSR, are circular because in effect the state is fining itself.

In the end, investment in anti-pollution and other measures to protect the environment does not produce returns, let alone a profit except for the manufacturers of the various appliances needed. Even if the international community does become more involved in environmental issues, the contribution of measures to improve the situation will be small in the next few decades. More of the same is the prospect, as will be argued in the rest of the chapter.

10.2   CAUSES OF ENVIRONMENTAL PROBLEMS

Long before human beings began to alter the natural world with the advent of cultivation, irrigation and the herding of domesticated animals, various forces caused changes in the natural world, among them a few enterprising species of animal, including beavers and ants. In comparison with the timescales of change in human activities in the last few centuries, many changes, such as climatic variations (including onsets of glaciation and resulting sea-level change, and the movement of tectonic plates on the earth's surface), usually take place very gradually (see Chapter 2). For example, depending on the local vegetation, climate and underlying rock, it takes about 100 years for an inch of soil to form naturally, whereas when disturbed by ploughing or deforestation, the effects of water and wind erosion can remove that depth of soil in a very much shorter time. On the other hand, fires caused by lightning, floods, earthquakes, outpourings of volcanic materials and the occasional meteorites could cause serious local damage to other natural features, and in some cases even cause global changes. Nature has its own way of coping: for example, areas of tropical forest destroyed by exceptionally extensive floods recover quickly (see Colinvaux (1989)).

Such natural processes, some unpredictable, have taken their toll of human lives, structures and farmlands. Among others, the large rivers of the USA, China, India and Bangladesh have caused great damage in the 1990s. Cyclones, hurricanes and tornadoes affect many areas in both the tropics and mid-latitude locations, including Southeast Asia, the Caribbean islands and coastlands, and southeast and interior USA. Although it is not possible to make more than rough comparisons through time and impossible to quantify the results meaningfully, it can be argued that particularly during the last few centuries human activities have made a much greater impact on the natural environment than natural forces have. The following have produced environmental change, often detrimental and sometimes irreversible.

- Agriculture: tilling (by hand, with animals or mechanisation), the widespread use of inorganic fertilisers, clearance of forest, loss of biodiversity, overgrazing of natural pastures.

- Extractive and energy industries: opencast mining (usually without replacement of topsoil), deep mining, subsidence, slag-heaps, dams and reservoirs for hydro-electric power. Such activities and structures are limited in the area they affect compared with agricultural activities, but their impact can be devastating locally.

- Industrial: burning of fossil fuels for power, smelting ores, refining oil, emission of waste materials (some toxic), from processes such as dyeing.

- Transport: use of fossil fuels, clearance of swathes of land for road building, breaking up areas of natural vegetation.

- Residential: often occupying land suitable for agriculture, using energy for domestic heating or air conditioning.

- Warfare: often resulting in damage not only to man-made structures but also to natural environments.

The above activities and land uses have an immediate impact on the places in which they are located, but some of the 'products' disperse in the atmosphere or are carried over great distances by waterways.

Gases and particles enter the atmosphere where, according to their composition and to atmospheric conditions of the time, they may disperse widely. Thus carbon dioxide remains in the atmosphere whereas sulphur dioxide disappears eventually, the atmosphere being capable of flushing some of its impurities out. Lead from the combustion of petrol mostly ends up locally, close to the traffic that emits it.

Waste materials are transported in rivers or more locally are piped into the sea, making many coastal areas particularly highly polluted. In many places one would be less enthusiastic about drinking river water now than 500 years ago, as the lines at the head of the chapter imply. Some materials are transported out to sea and dumped; the fuel tanks of ships may be emptied into the sea, and occasionally aircraft jettison fuel. While the world's oceans are still largely 'clean', many inland waterways and lakes as well as certain seas, including the Mediterranean,

Black and Baltic Seas, and those close to the coasts of Japan and China, are heavily polluted. The European seas referred to above are virtually closed off from any interchange of water with the oceans, but have many centres of population and industry on their shores or on rivers draining into them.

On the land itself liquid waste may seep into the ground, contaminating groundwater, as with nitrates from fertilisers in areas under which there are sedimentary rocks. Solid waste, including toxic materials or materials that may later emit gases, are used as landfill. The problem of permanently disposing of nuclear waste has hardly been confronted yet (see Chapter 6) since only a few nuclear power stations have as yet been decommissioned, while the dismantling of large numbers of nuclear warheads and the decommissioning of nuclear powered naval vessels has largely become a problem only recently. In 1998, for example, widespread concern was expressed in Britain about the transfer of nuclear waste from Georgia (formerly part of the USSR) to Dounreay in Scotland. In Belgium in a referendum in 1998, 94 per cent of the citizens of Beauring voted against the use of the former base at Baronville as a site for nuclear waste (*Le Soir*, Brussels, 29 June 1998). Nuclear power is not only a matter of general concern globally, but also of very strong feeling locally.

A taste of things to come for the nuclear industry is described by Mundzeck (1997). In 1957 an underground waste tank at the Mayak nuclear centre in the Ural region of the USSR exploded. A cloud of radioactive material was released into the atmosphere and over a quarter of a million people were exposed to radiation. Ten years later a heavy storm lifted and dispersed lethal dust from a dried-up lake bed in the same area. Even in 1997 the River Techa, into which nuclear waste was earlier dumped, continues to be a health hazard. Also in 1957, the UK's worst nuclear accident occurred when a nuclear reactor caught fire at Windscale. Contaminated smoke affected milk supplies over 500 sq. km. The seriousness of the accident was not fully appreciated and its implications were played down. Forty years later the damaged structure has still not been dismantled.

10.3   SOURCES OF POLLUTION

The developed regions of the world consume almost ten times as much commercial energy per capita as the developing regions. They also process more materials, consume more fertilisers and use various other sources of pollution in much larger per capita quantities . Nevertheless, according to one source (see Table 10.3) the share of total world carbon dioxide emissions produced by the developed countries has dropped from 84 per cent in 1960 to 69 per cent in 1991. The change is accounted for by the combination of faster population growth in the developing countries during that period and faster per capita growth of consumption, although from a very small base level in 1960 in most.

Table 10.1 shows the consumption of commercial sources of energy, not exclusively fossil fuels, while Tables 10.2 and 10.3 show two different versions of carbon dioxide emissions. The fact that the United Nations Development Programme states the world total of greenhouse gas emissions (CO_2) to be 21,826 million tons (sic) in 1993 while the UN *Statistical Yearbook 1990/1* gives the total as 5,859 million tonnes in 1991, points to two completely different methods of 'weighing' carbon dioxide, plus a lack of consultation. The total amount of energy consumed is itself known, so the differing sets of figures can each be considered regionally on a relative basis. Tables 10.1-10.3 will now be referred to in turn.

If it is assumed that the consumption per capita of polluting sources of energy decreases appreciably in the industrial countries in the next few decades, thanks to the greater use of clean sources of energy, combined with taxes and other deterrents on energy use, then in spite of an expected modest increase in population between 2000 and 2050, the industrial regions might consume between 4 and 5 billion tonnes of oil equivalent in 2050. In contrast, if the expected doubling of population of the developing countries takes place and per capita energy consumption rises from 540 kgs to about 1,600, then 5-6 times as much energy would be used by them, an increase from 2.3 billion tonnes of oil equivalent in 1993 to between 11.5 and almost 14 billion in 2050.

Expanding on the columns in Table 10.1:

(1)   The population of the world in millions in 1993

(2)   Total energy consumption by regions in billions of tonnes of oil equivalent, in 1993. The 'Industrial' regions consumed 71 per cent of the total. In addition to North America, the European Union and Japan they include the rest of Europe and the whole of the former USSR, as well as Oceania.

(3)   The per capita consumption of energy, in kilograms of oil equivalent, in 1993 was 8.5 times higher in the industrial regions than in the developing regions.

(4)   The per capita consumption in kilograms of oil equivalent; only as recently as 1971, however, the per capita gap between developed and developing was 16 times.

(5)   Change in per capita consumption 1971-93 (1971=100); during 1971-93 the per capita level of consumption has more than doubled in the developing regions whereas in the industrial regions it has increased only by 9 per cent.

Table 10.1   Consumption of energy

Level of human development	(1) Population (millions)	(2) Energy total 1993	(3) Energy per capita 1993	(4) Change per capita 1971	(5) Change 1971– 1993
High	1,030	5.06	4,910	4,310	114
Medium	180	0.49	2,730	n.a.	n.a.
All industrial	1,210	5.55	4,590	4,210	109
High	340	0.54	1,590	710	224
Medium[1]	2,190	1.42	650	300	217
Low[2]	1,770	0.31	180	90	200
All developing	4,300	2.30	540	260	208
North America	290	2.29	7,910	7,500	105
European Union	370	1.33	3,590	3,040	118
Japan	127	0.44	3,640	2,550	143
World	5,510	7.83	1,420	n.a.	n.a.

n.a. not available

Source of data: United Nations Development Programme (UNDP), *Human Development Report 1996*, Oxford: OUP

Notes: [1] includes China
                   [2] includes India

Table 10.2 shows the level of consumption in the group of seven industrial countries. With about 12 per cent of the total population of the world in 1993 they accounted for over 40 per cent of greenhouse gas emissions, much more than could be accounted for (or justified) by their generally colder climatic conditions and consequent need for domestic and other heating. The lifestyle in North America requires the consumption of twice as much energy per capita as that in Western Europe and Japan. In terms of GDP output per kilogram of energy used, Japan is almost four times as 'efficient' as Canada (see Chapter 6, Figure 6.10). While it could be argued that present lifestyles could be maintained in some industrial countries even with a reduction in energy consumption, and therefore in greenhouse gas emissions, the likely saving is very small compared with the increase expected in the developing countries, already discussed above.

Table 10.2 Greenhouse gas emissions (GGE) by the 'Big 7' countries in 1993

	(1)	*(2)*	*(3)*	*(4)*	*(5)*	*(6)*
	Population (millions)	*GGE (millions of tonnes)*	*Population (percentage of world)*	*GGE*	*Times world average*	*GDP output (per kg US dollars)*
USA	257.9	5,129	4.7	23.5	5.0	3.1
Japan	124.5	1,146	2.3	5.3	2.3	9.3
Germany	80.9	922	1.5	4.2	2.8	5.7
UK	57.9	564	1.1	2.6	2.4	4.4
Canada	28.8	459	0.5	2.1	4.2	2.4
Italy	57.1	435	1.0	2.0	2.0	6.4
France	57.5	416	1.0	1.9	1.9	5.4
Big 7 total	664.6	9,071	12.1	41.6	3.4	–
World	5,510.0	21,826	100.0	100.0	1.0	–

Source: United Nations Development Programme, *Human Development Report 1996*, Oxford: OUP

Table 10.3: Given the great importance for the environment of future levels of greenhouse gas and other potentially harmful emissions it is worth including a second view of the same picture. Columns (1)-(3) show the rate of increase of annual emissions of carbon dioxide during 1960-91. The fastest rates of growth of consumption of energy have mostly been in countries in Asia and Africa, including Japan, although in many cases from very modest levels in 1960. A possible future based on 1960-91 experience could be as follows. The increase of 2.35 times between 1960 and 1991 is repeated between 1991 and 2020 and again between 2020 and 2050 for the developing regions. The level stays unchanged in the developed regions. Carbon dioxide emissions would therefore stay at about 4 billion tonnes in the developed regions, but in the developing regions would rise from 1.8 to 4.2 billion per year between 1991 and 2020 and reach almost to 10 billion in 2050. The combined emissions would be about 14 billion tonnes per year, an increase of 2.4 times for the world as a whole compared with 5.86 billion in 1991.

Even if the more subdued rates of economic growth during 1975-95 continue, rather than the generally fast rates during 1955-75, it may be expected that the consumption of energy and raw materials, together with the accompanying processing and manufacturing, would result in at least a doubling of the amount of pollution produced annually in the world by 2050. The prospect could be altered fundamentally only through drastic cuts in levels of production and

Table 10.3 Emissions of carbon dioxide, CFCs and halons by world regions and selected countries

	(1)	(2)	(3)	(4)	(5)
	Carbon dioxide emissions millions of tonnes		Change 1960–91 (1960=100)	Consumption of CFCs and halons 1990	
	1960	1991		Total (1000s of tonnes)	World (percentage)
North America[1]	881	1,582	180	177	17.2
USA	800	1,346	168	146	14.2
Canada	53	112	211	15	1.5
Oceania	28	80	286	8	0.8
Europe	732	1,127	154	315[2]	30.7
Former USSR	396	977	247	134	13.6
Japan	64	298	466	120	11.7
South America	55	163	296	15	1.5
Africa	40	184	460	9	0.9
South Africa	27	76	281	7	0.7
Asia	366	1,747	477	193	18.8
India	33	192	582	n.a.	n.a.
China	215	694	323	53	5.2
World	2,498	5,859	235	1,028	100.0

Source: United Nations *Statistical Yearbook 1992* (39th edition), New York: United Nations, 1994

n.a. = not available

Note: [1] includes northern part of Latin America
[2] of which 208 (20.3 per cent of world total) by EU

consumption and a moratorium on further economic growth in developing countries. Alternatively it could be influenced to some extent by the highly improbable cessation of population growth in the developing countries in a decade or two. On the other hand, more of the same could result in a threefold increase in annual pollution emissions by 2050. Moreover, even the maintenance of present world levels over the next five decades would merely be living on borrowed time.

One of the big issues in the media in the 1990s is the environment. So many problems are under consideration that it is not possible to cover more than a few in the rest of this chapter. Some of those most under scrutiny in the world at present have been chosen, with an emphasis on issues that are relevant to a timescale of half a century. In section 10.4 the tropical rain forest is discussed, in section 10.5 the atmosphere and global warming. Pollution in general is considered in section 10.6 and several other issues briefly in the final section.

Many of the statements about the future of the environment came from academic researchers, generally freer than researchers engaged by governments or large private companies to focus on the environmental impact of particular practices or products. In recent years one of the outstanding expressions of uncertainty about the environment has come from the Union of Concerned Scientists, already referred to. The enthusiasm with which different scientists of the world have embraced the environmental issues of the late 20th century can be broadly gauged by the strength of participation of scientists from different branches. The following are the subjects represented, ranked from least to most concerned: mathematicians (whose subject is in some respects very abstract), physicists and chemists, many of whose research topics, findings and laws are not directly concerned with the environment, medics and biologists, who are genuinely concerned about the relationship between the environment and mortality, and finally at the forefront, agricultural scientists and scientists in mining and geology.

Among those deemed unworthy of inclusion in the scientific establishment are economists, greatly interested in economic growth but less concerned about the natural environment. Ehrlich and Ehrlich (1972), ecologists of some distinction, noted that in arguably the earliest and most influential book on the future by the 'professional' generation of the 1960s and 1970s, *The Year 2000* by Kahn and Wiener (1967) and associates, there is no reference to the environment or to ecology in its index. Geographers have long regarded the relationship between humans and the environment as one of the themes or traditions of their subject.

10.4   TROPICAL RAIN FORESTS

Almost all of the world's tropical rain forest is in developing countries. Very few of the inhabitants of the developed countries have ever set foot in this kind of forest except in botanical gardens in their own countries or, remotely, via television documentaries. There is increasing concern on the part of people in developed countries, however, that tropical rain forest is being cleared and cannot be replaced, and that to some extent they are responsible. The title of a recent book, *The Last Rain Forests* edited by Collins (1990) is a poignant reminder that in a few decades time there could be only token patches of the tropical rain forest left in the world.

Without going into the problems of defining tropical rain forest and the misgivings about the accuracy with which its area is estimated, there is much evidence to show that in the last fifty years much larger areas (relatively) have been cleared in, for example, Central America, the Caribbean islands, India, the extreme south of China, and West Africa, than in South America or Central Africa. Roughly a quarter of the world's 40 million square kilometres of forest are described as 'tropical rain'. All forests need some rain, but the high temperatures and heavy rain all or most of the year provide the conditions for the growth of an evergreen forest characterised by a very large number of tree and other plant species as well as of fauna. Tropical rain forest extends mainly over lowland areas, but is found on mountain ranges and also along the flood plains of rivers, where it may actually be partly submerged during flood periods. Paradoxically, except where, for example, the forest is or was on volcanic soil (as in Java, Indonesia), or on alluvial lands, the soil is usually poor in nutrients and only supports the growth of field crops for a few years before losing its fertility. The forest lives largely on its own dead remains.

One estimate of the rate at which the tropical rain forest is being cleared puts the area lost annually at about equal to that of England, which does not reveal much unless it is appreciated that England is about 130,000 sq km in area (13,000,000 hectares). If clearance continues at that rate, over half the world's tropical rain forest will disappear by 2050 and all of it by 2100. Throughout the last five centuries forests have been cleared for fuelwood and for timber for construction in many parts of the world. As noted in Chapter 6, however, in parts of Europe wood for smelting, heating, cooking and building houses and ships was already becoming scarce in the 17th century.

The tropical rain forest in many countries has already been extensively cleared, whether to provide land for field or tree crops, or by logging enterprises. In the past, and in places even now, the indigenous forest dwellers have generally existed in a sustainable situation, practising slash and burn cultivation, shifting their patches of cropland every few years, and leaving the forest to re-establish itself. These original forest dwellers combined cultivation with fishing, hunting and gathering. Gradually they are being squeezed out by new settlers with various aims and activities.

The newcomers establish their own farms to grow crops mainly for their own use, work on commercial cattle ranches, extract minerals (either with their own limited means of production or with large mineral companies) cut trees for timber, often only selecting certain species (e.g. teak, mahogany) or extract the by-products (e.g. Brazil nuts, wild rubber).

Often only a few species of tree are sought out of hundreds present in the forest and in quite small areas. Even the cutting of a single tree may disturb the vegetation around it. One example is the *pau roa* (Aniba duckei) from which an essential oil is extracted for the production of Chanel No. 5 perfume (see Bell (1997)). French conservationists argue that this tree will disappear because its extraction is ecologically unsound. In many areas of former tropical rain forest, especially in West Africa and Southeast Asia, large areas have been planted with such trees as the oil palm and the rubber tree, the latter a native of South America, but not amenable to plantation conditions there. In addition, there is a large hydro-electric potential on the rivers of the tropical rain forest of South America (the Amazon basin) and Central Africa (the Congo basin).

The survival of the remaining rain forests of the 1990s depends on a number of influences. The policy of national governments can to some extent determine the future of the remaining forests, a positive future requiring strict regulations and sanctions with regard to clearance, settlement and commercial activities. The size and location of the forests can also be crucial. The tropical rain forests of the Amazon basin and adjoining areas forms a large critical mass which was hardly explored, let alone settled by outsiders, until the 1880s, when the rivers determined the direction of penetration. Subsequently, airfields allowed other limited areas to be opened up. Since the Second World War, roads with both economic and strategic goals have been built into the forest of Amazonia from six of the nine countries that share it.

In 1990, Brazil had about 500 million hectares of the tropical rain forest of Amazonia out of a total of 750 million. The less extensive tropical rain forest of Brazil's eastern coastlands has already almost all been cut, as also have the pine forests of Paraná further south. The sheer size and remote location of the Amazon forest and the comparatively low density of population in Brazil have helped to save most of it from destruction so far. As it is, large areas in the eastern and southeastern sides of the forest have now been cleared, almost 70 per cent, for example, in the state of Maranhão in the east, compared with only about 2 per cent of the state of Amazonas in the west.

Arguably, the prospects for the tropical rain forest of Brazil depend on the decisions and actions of a number of 'players' with different degrees of influence. The fate of other tropical rain forests is broadly similar, but on account of their much more limited extent they are even more vulnerable. The national government of Brazil, representing the whole population of the country, sees the tropical rain forest as 'the other half' (*a outra metade*) of the country, making only a minute contribution to the national economy. Each of the nine states of Brazil with tropical rain forest has a governor, whose job it is to oversee and facilitate the economic development of his territory, if necessary accepting the need to clear forest. The influence of the world outside Brazil on the future of the forest is considerable but indirect. Forest products and minerals from Amazonia contribute to the exports of Brazil and to the repayment of foreign debts. On the other hand there has been increasing pressure especially from concerned people in the USA and EU to halt the clearance of forest in Brazil and in other developing countries on environmental and ecological grounds.

Yet another set of players in the Amazon forest game are the indigenous American Indian tribes, most now affected, often adversely, by contact with the outsiders, and unable to afford more than token legal representation. Their best future is to be 'preserved' in reservations, a second prospect is to be assimilated by mixing with the increasing number of migrants into the forest, a third to die out through diseases or even by deliberate extermination. Gamini (1997) reports that in the mid-1990s several thousand armed gold diggers and diamond hunters have illegally invaded the rainforest reserve of the Yanomani Indians, causing the spread of diseases and pollution. The Brazilian government has done little to protect the Indians and the process of elimination continues. There remain two 'ghost' players, neither with any say at all and no explicit advocates to put their cases: the plants and animals of the forest, and future generations of Brazilians and indeed of citizens of the world as a whole.

In the end, the fate of the tropical rain forests of the developing world is in the hands of the governments and people of the countries in which they are located. Forests have been cleared for centuries in Europe and North America and no one in the rest of the world has interfered with the process. Why should some people in the industrial countries now expect to influence policy in developing countries? Since, however, many of the products of the natural environment have been purchased by companies in industrial countries, could it be possible for such companies or international institutions to buy large tracts to preserve them for posterity? Foreign ownership of natural resources is an accepted condition of many countries, although not popular politically.

In Chapters 5 and 12 it is argued that there is not much scope for changing the extent of the world's cropland in the next 50 years, only a small increase being possible. In contrast, the extent of the tropical rain forests of the world around 2050 is far more difficult to forecast and as will be shown below, again with the key case of Amazonia, could be unchanged or could be reduced almost to nothing. The alternative prospects by the year 2050 for the tropical rain forest of Amazonia, only about 10 per cent of which has been cleared in the last fifty years, are as follows:

- An instant moratorium is put on all further clearance of the forest by the year 2000, a very unlikely prospect.

- Controlled clearance and/or sustainable development is permitted in certain areas, especially along rivers and existing routes, leaving large areas intact. Patrolling such areas could be difficult, but the use of satellite images to monitor clearance and other interference could be a help.

- The forest is fragmented into a large number of patches, with about half of the original area left. In these conditions, much of the wildlife, especially the fauna, could be disturbed. This seems nevertheless a reasonable, pragmatic compromise.

- Uncontrolled development, leading to the elimination of 80 - 90 per cent of the forest by the end of the 21st century. The Brazilian economy might actually benefit in the short term, but in addition to the undesirable contribution to the carbon dioxide in the atmosphere, huge numbers of species would disappear because the forest cannot return to its original state if seriously interfered with over a very large area.

It remains to note a few of the numerous references on the controversial issue of the future of the world's tropical rain forests, partly as a reminder of the difficulty of making forecasts. Writing early in the 1970s, Richards (1973) stated: 'One of the oldest ecosystems and a reservoir of genetic diversity, the wet evergreen tropical forest, is threatened by the activities of man and may virtually disappear by the end of the 20th century.' This has obviously turned out to be wrong. In the late 1980s, a paper by Colinvaux (1989) is introduced as follows: 'The climatic history of the Amazon rain forest indicates that the ecosystem is well adapted to certain natural disturbances. Does it have the resilience to tolerate human exploitation?' Rice *et al.* (1997) discuss the problem of the sustainable management of the tropical forests of the world and describe some possible approaches, but conclude that: 'the management of tropical forests for sustainable timber production is unlikely to become a widespread phenomenon, at least in the near future. Contrary economic incentives, limited government control and a lack of local political support will constantly thwart the best efforts in that direction, particularly in developing countries.'

Policy towards the clearance of tropical rain forest has varied greatly from country to country. Catton (1992) describes the virtual elimination of the forest on the island of Hainan in the extreme south of China in the last forty years due to a large influx of settlers from the mainland and the establishment of a Special Economic Zone there. In Central America, much of the forest in Costa Rica has been cleared in the second half of this century. Almost all has been cleared in Nigeria, which now imports timber, and the forests of the Philippines have been reduced to fragments. Concerned over the depletion of its teak trees, Thailand has restricted their cutting, but many people depend on the timber for the production of high quality furniture and other wood products; teak is imported from neighbouring Myanmar, where there is less concern at present over environmental issues. In Malaysia, however, there is growing awareness of the need to manage the forests; according to North (1997 p. 18): 'strict government rules ensure that levels of tree cover and biodiversity are maintained or improved on.' Tilling *et al.* (1997) have described the situation in Malaysia in great detail. Hirsch (1990) gives the annual forest loss (percentage) in eight countries of Southeast Asia, the highest being 2.6 per cent in Thailand and 1.2 per cent in Laos and Malaysia, the lowest in Cambodia and Myanmar at 0.3 per cent. Only in the Philippines and Viet Nam is reforestation equal to more than half the rate of deforestation.

10.5 GLOBAL WARMING AND ASSOCIATED ISSUES

As noted earlier, it is unlikely that there will be much change in the cultivated area of the world in the next 50 years, whereas the prospect for the area of tropical rain forest is much more open, in spite of the fact that its present extent and its attributes are known. The state of the atmosphere in the next few decades is still more problematic since natural forces (e.g. a massive volcanic eruption pouring dust into the air) or human activities (especially the burning of fossil fuels) could affect it profoundly, but the possible effects of, for example, global warming (the 'greenhouse effect') or global cooling are difficult to assess. The relative 'fragility' of the atmosphere compared with the hydrosphere and lithosphere is illustrated by the fact that if the air in it was compressed to the density of water it would only be about 10 metres thick: not much space to hold all the pollutants being emitted into it.

After the Second World War, 'strange' weather conditions were blamed on the atmospheric nuclear tests. In the 1970s, desertification was a much discussed issue. In the 1980s the realisation that industrial products, such as chlorofluorocarbons (more commonly referred to as CFCs), were thinning the high ozone layer, became public knowledge. Well before the 1990s, global warming was anticipated by various scientists, and in the volatile perception of the atmosphere by the public, it has become the flavour of recent years, often referred to as an irrefutable fact.

The subject of global warming is of interest to many different sets of people. Environmentalists and ecologists want to be proved right in the argument that unless there is greater concern over the impact of human activities on the natural environment, disasters will occur. Governments and industries in countries depending heavily on the extraction, export, or consumption of fossil fuels do not want a reduction in the amount used. Numerous scientists in various disciplines are keen to obtain support and funding for their research on the subject. It would be surprising if behind the scenes there is no lobbying of people of influence about the 'greenhouse effect', a process investigated and documented in a BBC 2 programme (Scifile, March 1997).

Over varying lengths of time, some quite short even by the timescale of modern humans, the average temperature of the atmosphere has changed markedly. About 20,000 years ago, under colder conditions, far more of the water of the world than now was held in ice caps and ice sheets on northern parts of Asia and North America as well as in Greenland and Antarctica, where (see Chapter 5) large amounts still remain.

The impact, if any, of global warming in the first half of the 21st century depends initially on the speed at which physical changes can take place. Stock (1995) refers to a change 120,000 years ago in world sea-level during no more than a single century. Imprints on limestone in the Bahamas show that as a result, presumably, of 'climatic havoc' at the end of an ice age, sea-level first rose 20 feet above that of today, then fell 30 feet below it. The evidence is that world sea-level *can* change markedly over a few decades, which does not mean that it *will* happen in the near future.

Changes have taken place in the temperature of the atmosphere in historical times, causing brief onsets of unusually cold conditions, as in Europe about 300 years ago. One thing is certain, until the 19th century human activities could only have made a slight impact, if any at all, on temperature change. A number of problems and issues complicate the assessment of global warming that at least part of the 'greenhouse effect' is caused by an increase in carbon dioxide and other gases that influence the temperature of the atmosphere.

- It has not been established to everyone's satisfaction that the slight rise in global temperature in about the last 100 years is more than part of 'normal' fluctuation of temperature. If a significant increase is occurring, then it is not easy to establish how much, if any, is due to human activities, for example, the burning of fossil fuels, and how much is due to natural causes and random fluctuations. Nevertheless it is asserted as a fact by Mundzeck (1995) that: 'New research offers proof that global warming, also known as the greenhouse effect, is a consequence of man's activity on earth, not a result of some as yet unidentified phenomenon.'

- Even if global warming is occurring, whatever the cause, it is not known what the effect will be on various other elements of the environment. In particular two effects are not clearly known:

(i) if temperature increases, will some of the existing ice in the ice sheets and glaciers melt (causing sea-level to rise) or will the higher temperatures cause more moisture to be moved around in the atmosphere and some of it to be duly deposited as ice on existing ice sheets (or elsewhere) leading to a small fall in sea-level? McWilliam (1995) refers to the work of Prof. D. Sugden: 'Sugden has studied relict landforms on exposed mountains in Antarctica which, he claims, show that the ice was actually thicker when climate was warmer, both during the Pliocene and more recent interglacial periods.' It is now accepted that the main ice cap of Antarctica has been in place about 15 million years and presumably a massive change in temperature would be needed to shift it. There is not complete agreement however as to the amount sea-level would rise if all the ice in the world did melt. Estimates are between about 40 and 60 metres.

(ii) if temperature increases, what effect will that have on the weather conditions and climate in various parts of the world, of special interest being those areas of cultivation where precipitation and/or temperature are low and/or unreliable. It might be expected that climatic belts would move away from the equator, possibly bringing hotter, drier conditions to the interior of North America, the Mediterranean region and parts of Russia, with corresponding, if smaller changes in the southern continents.

- The whole question of global warming is complicated by evidence that global cooling in the next few decades is a distinct possibility, including that caused by some human activities. One possible cause of global cooling in the decades to come could be fluctuations in the sun's 11-year sunspot cycle. If sunspot activity ceases altogether for several decades (as it did in the 17th century, causing a sharp drop in temperature and the 'little ice age' in Europe), the global warming now anticipated by many researchers could be counterbalanced by a reduction in temperature. In theory, global warming and cooling could cancel each other out, leaving the temperature of the atmosphere virtually unchanged.

The effects of a rise in sea-level are clearer than the effects of climatic change. Depending on how great the rise or fall is, places on and near the coast, not located on high ground, would be at risk. Many of the large cities in the world are seaports, and their harbour works would be affected, together with any other kinds of built-up areas near sea-level. Among the largest urban agglomerations in the world, some (e.g. Chicago, Paris, Mexico City, São Paulo) are well out of reach of a rise in sea-level but others (e.g. New York, Tokyo, Los Angeles, London, Bombay) are on the coast. The Netherlands and Bangladesh are among countries with large reclaimed areas barely above present sea-level, or actually below it and appropriately protected. Relative to the territorial and population sizes of many small island states, however, the impact of a marked rise in sea-level could be even more serious than in the Netherlands or Bangladesh. Many such islands were colonies of France, the UK or the USA and it is not a surprise, therefore, that the European Parliament (1996) has held a public hearing on the effect of climatic change on small island states. The Minister of the Environment in Barbados, representing 42 island states in the Alliance of Small Island States (AOSIS) described these small countries as the canaries in the coalmine, an oblique reference to the use of canaries as a warning system to detect dangerous gas in underground coal mine tunnels.

The effects of a fall in sea-level, no less inconvenient and indeed devastating locally, have been shown in the case of the two inland seas in the former Soviet Union – the Caspian Sea and the Aral Sea – neither of which is joined to the continuous seas and oceans. In the case of the Caspian, dams and irrigation works on its main source of water, the Volga, reduced the flow for some decades, but sea-level is now rising. The experience of the Aral Sea in former Soviet Uzbekistan and Kazakhstan has been far more negative, because much of the sea has now disappeared. A rise or fall in the level of the world's oceans would affect far more people than the changes in that of the two more 'local' former Soviet water bodies. Space does not allow a thorough examination of the state of the global warming debate at the time of writing but some facts and references are noted briefly.

One estimate of the relative importance of different causes of the greenhouse effect is as follows: carbon dioxide 49 per cent (mainly from burning fossil fuels), methane 18 per cent (from animal dung and also potentially from permafrost bogs in Canada and Siberia), CFCs 14 per cent (from aerosols, fridges), nitrous oxide 6 per cent (from fertilisers, car exhausts and power stations). Thus the causes of possible global warming from human activities are known, but what to do about them is another matter. Schneider (1995) recommends that in spite of widespread hot, dry conditions in the 1980s one should keep an open mind on global warming: 'but the past few summers have been neither particularly hot nor dry, and some researchers suspect the scorching 1980s may have been the result of natural variability. The scientific community has simply not reached a consensus on whether greenhouse warming has yet been demonstrated.' Hargrave (1997) notes the fact that global warming has not been as fast in the 1990s as would be expected, a possible cause of this situation being the eruption of Mount Pinatubo in the Philippines in 1991. This released very large quantities of sulphur particles into the atmosphere and, according to one theory, these reflect solar radiation, reducing the effect of the more prevalent carbon particles.

Whatever the prospects for global warming, the possibility is serious enough for official reports to appear on the extent to which conditions could change. In HMSO (1996) the potential effects of global warming on Britain are examined. If 2050 is 1.6 °C warmer than the average for 1961-90, sea-level would have risen by 30-40 cm, enough to threaten low-lying areas such as the Fens, Humberside and the Somerset Levels. Climatic conditions could change, making about a 200 km south-north difference in warmth, with the southeast of England hotter and drier but the northwest wetter. Global warming has, however, also been seen as the cause of an increase in the quantity of icebergs carried southwards from glaciers originating in the north of Greenland, released by increased precipitation on the ice-sheet. In due course the temperature of the sea would be lowered and the Gulf Stream, which keeps temperatures in the Northwest Europe anomalously high for the latitude, might be weakened, with resulting lower temperatures in Britain rather than higher ones.

In the Netherlands, preparing the sea defences for a rise in sea-level is of greater concern than in England (see Schneider (1997)). Should there be a catastrophic collapse of part of the Antarctic ice cap, notably the west Antarctic Ice Sheet, which is a thick slab of ice resting on bedrock well *below* the surface of the ocean, world sea-level could rise several metres. In 1953 a deadly combination of winds and tides raised the sea-level to the top of the protective dikes of the Netherlands and in a very short time 2,000 people died, 200,000 hectares of farmland were flooded, and a sixth of the Netherlands was covered with sea water. Other comparable low-lying areas in the world that are at risk of flooding, with a five metre rise in sea-level, include southern Florida, southern Viet Nam, including Ho Chi Minh City (formerly Saigon), and the area around Bangkok in Thailand.

Karl *et al.* (1997) focus on climate change in the decades to come rather than a rise in sea-level. On the basis of precipitation changes in the 20th century, high latitudes have mostly become wetter. Such a trend seems likely to continue: 'most models predict an increase in precipitation in winter at high latitudes because of greater poleward transport of moisture derived from increased evaporation at low latitudes... But for tropical and subtropical land areas, precipitation has actually decreased over the past few decades. This is especially apparent over the Sahel (northern Africa) and eastward to Indonesia.'

A striking instance of the potential global effect of a local change is the phenomenon of El Niño, an ocean current (see Nash (1997)). Shifting ocean currents in the Pacific Ocean at times bring abnormally warm water and moist air eastwards to the Pacific coasts of South, Central and North America, giving heavy rain, strong winds and storms. Warmer conditions occur in the Americas and eastern Asia, but rainfall is lower in eastern Brazil, southern Africa and southeast Asia. Nash notes: 'Until recently El Niños came more or less periodically every two to seven years. But in the early 1990s several El Niños appeared in a row... Are the frequent El Niños a signal of global warming caused by human tampering with the atmosphere?' The El Niño phenomenon has been blamed for below normal rainfall in Indonesia, facilitating the spread of fires in Sumatra in 1997 and making it difficult to extinguish them. Hardly any marked change in physical conditions escapes scrutiny by scientists as awareness of the impact of humans on the environment is appreciated.

10.6   WASTE AND POLLUTION

Almost four decades ago Vance Packard (1963) published his book *The Waste Makers*. Most of the themes in this chapter that are relevant to the USA were addressed by Packard, who quoted another American author (details not given) as follows: 'We Americans have used more of the world's resources in the past forty years than all the people in the world had used in the 4,000 years of recorded history up to 1914... Man is becoming aware of the limits of the earth.' The point is made, even if the arithmetic is difficult to verify.

Since the early 1960s awareness of the subject of materials, their depletion, processing and eventual fate as waste has grown greatly, as has the quantity generated in the world. In this section a few examples show what is involved, what happens to waste, and what is being done to reduce waste and pollution. From projections already made in earlier chapters of the production and consumption of various things it may be expected that the yearly output of waste and pollution will continue to increase in the next 50 years, in spite of efforts to curb it, if only because there will be about 4 billion more people in 2050 than in the 1990s.

Tables 10.4 and 10.5 give details of a selection of accidents involving hazardous substances and accidental oil spills. Since 1970, as far as is recorded in the source of Table 10.4, the number of direct deaths from a given accident exceeded 1,000 only in the case of the explosion at the Union Carbide works in Bhopal, India. Injuries (e.g. Mexico City, 1984) and serious after effects (e.g. Chernobyl, 1986) have been large only in a few cases. Accidents have occurred in both the production and transportation of toxic materials.

Table 10.4 Selected accidents involving hazardous substances

Year	Country and location	Origin of accident	Products involved	Number of Deaths	Injured	Evacuated
1974	UK, Flixborough	Explosion	Cyclohexane	28	104	3,000
1976	Italy, Seveso	Air release	TCCD (Dioxine)	–	>200	730
1979	USA, Three Mile Island	Reactor failure	Nuclear material	–	–	200,000
1984	Mexico, St J. Ixhuatepec	Explosion (storage tank)	Gas (LPG)	>500	2,500	>200,000
1984	India, Bhopal	Leakage	Methyl isocyanate	2,800	50,000	200,000
1986	USSR, Chernobyl	Reactor explosion	Nuclear material	31[1]	299	135,000
1988	UK, North Sea	Explosion, fire (platform)	Oil, gas	167	–	–
1989	USSR, Acha Ufa	Explosion, pipeline	Gas	575	623	–

Source: OECD (1991), pp. 200-203

– = none

[1] but see Chapter 6 for details of subsequent deaths

Table 10.5 The seven largest accidental oil spills 1967–1989

Year	*Name of ship*	*Flag*	*Country affected*	*Quantity spilled (thousand tonnes)*
1967	Torrey Canyon	Liberia	UK, France	121
1972	Sea Star	South Korea	Gulf of Oman	120
1976	Urquiola	Spain	Spain	101
1978	Amoco Cadiz	Liberia	France	228
1979	Atlantic Express	Greece	Tobago (Caribbean)	276
1980	Irenes Serenade	Greece	Greece	102
1983	Castello de Belver	Spain	South Africa	256
1989	Exxon Valdez	USA	Alaska	35[1]

Source: OECD (1991)

Exxon Valdez included for comparison
[1]   Many tankers fly flags of convenience which are in no way connected with their owners or their cargoes.

Oil spills at sea have not usually caused loss of life or injury but, depending where they have occurred, have caused great environmental damage in some cases. According to OECD (1991), somewhere between 0.1 and 0.2 per cent of the total annual production of crude oil in the world actually causes pollution, about 3.5 million tonnes, half of marine origin, half of continental origin. Accidental oil spills account for only about 12 per cent of all pollution, compared with more than 25 per cent from non-accidental maritime transport and about 40 per cent from urban and industrial sources. Some of the more spectacular accidental oil spills (see Table 10.5) have however caused the greatest damage to plant and animal life when ships have run aground, since their escaping cargo can be moved quickly by currents over considerable distances.

The full list of serious accidents from hazardous substances and oil spills shows that although the developed countries still account for most of the processing of fuel and raw materials they do not cause all the damage. Some of the worst industrial accidents have occurred in cities in developing countries, where residential and industrial zones are often in close proximity, also a feature of Soviet industrial planning.

There have been many cases of situations in which developed countries have continued to 'export' their waste and pollution. In 1997, for example, Taiwan shipped some of its nuclear waste to North Korea, which presumably needed the money (or the materials) and has suitable sites for its storage. In 1988, Italy shipped drums of toxic waste to Beirut in the Lebanon (*Sunday Times Magazine*, 26 February 1989) but was forced to take them back. In the end, arguably, the ocean floor may be the most realistic place to dispose of waste, especially hazardous materials. Nuttall (1996 a) reports on a United States Defence Department project to develop an oceanic site at 6,000 metres below sea-level where deep-sea disposal at the right depth and the right place will, it is claimed, safely lock away the pollution permanently. A site in the Atlantic has been proposed; complicated equipment would be needed to ensure that properly protected cargoes of waste reach the right location. Local landfill and other sites near to the places that generate waste are cheaper and more convenient to reach, especially if the 'producers' of the waste are not close to a port, and it could be some decades before the ideal conditions are widely available for waste disposal.

Some processes may cause pollution where materials are produced rather than where they are consumed, a case of the 'export' of pollution. In the 19th century many of the metallic ores destined for the manufacturing sector in the USA and Europe were smelted and refined there. In the 20th century much of the most polluting part of the work, the refining of metallic ores, is carried out predominantly where they are extracted, often, in developing countries. Such a procedure has the advantage for the producing country of creating employment and adding value to the metals, while reducing the cost of transport to the industrial countries. Most of the international trade in oil, on the other hand, involves the movement of crude oil, since it is cheaper to transport by sea or pipeline one item rather than several different refined products that have to be kept separate. Oil refineries and petrochemical plants are therefore mostly located in industrial countries and are the source of much pollution there.

The extraction and movement of oil can themselves cause environmental problems and actual damage in areas of production rather than consumption. The hitherto largely unspoilt landscape and economy of Alaska, for example, has been affected by the development since the 1960s of what are now the largest producing oilfields in the USA. Mitchell (1997) describes the dilemma between the economic benefits of the North Slope oilfields and the environmental disruption. Oil is extracted at/near Prudhoe Bay, and conveyed by the Trans-Alaska Pipeline (800 miles in length) to the south coast of Alaska for shipment to various destinations. The land on which the oilfields and pipeline are located is claimed by the native peoples and the oil companies (and depending on one's view of the natural world) also belongs to the caribou. The northern coastal plain of Alaska is one of the last undisturbed tundra ecosystems. Here, it is hoped, is the best chance of finding large new oil deposits in the whole of the USA. For example, Brodie (1997) reports the discovery of oil very close to the boundary of the Arctic National Wildlife Refuge, under which the deposits probably extend, but in which the US Government would oppose oil drilling.

The south coast of Alaska was the scene of one of the world's most serious ecological disasters of recent decades. The quantity of oil spilt from the tanker *Exxon Valdez* was relatively small compared with that from the largest spills, but an area of coast several hundred miles in length was ecologically damaged. The Alaskan oil situation is similar to numerous other parallel situations: in order to obtain a product, especially a fossil fuel or non-fuel mineral, much environmental damage and disruption to local activities can be caused far from where the product is to be consumed.

Although, globally, pollution is on the increase as various countries continue to industrialise, road transport expands and forests are burned, there are many cases of successful efforts to reverse pollution levels. One such case is the River Rhine (see Malle, (1996)), in the drainage area of which (with tributaries) parts of six countries are situated: Germany, France, Switzerland, the Netherlands, Luxembourg and Belgium. Before the 1950s industrial waste and urban sewage were released untreated into the river. The first five of the six countries listed above formed the International Commission for the Protection for the Rhine against Pollution to coordinate multinational efforts and to monitor the level of contaminants in the river. In the early 1970s many fish species had been wiped out or greatly reduced, the river became unsuitable for swimming or bathing, and the supply of drinking water was threatened. By the 1990s great progress had been made in cleaning the waters of the Rhine.

10.7   OTHER SELECTED ENVIRONMENTAL ISSUES

Wildlife

The threat to wildlife is not a new one, but in the 20th century the growth of population and the even faster growth of production have led to a great increase in the clearance of forests, the reclamation of marshes, fishing and whaling activities, and encroachment on areas of wilderness, by extractive industries, grazing and settlements. In the process, numerous plant and animal species have disappeared altogether and others are threatened. According to Doyle (1997): 'For some time, many naturalists have felt that the world is entering a period of major species extinction, rivalling five other periods in the past half billion years.' According to a study by the World Conservation Unit (IUCN): 'an astonishing 25 per cent of mammal species – and comparable proportions of reptile, amphibians and fish species – are threatened.' Particularly at risk are those in geographically isolated areas. For example, in the Philippines and Madagascar, both islands, 32 and 44 per cent respectively of all mammal species are threatened.

The prospect that in 50 or 100 years time the number of species in the world may be greatly reduced, with many present wilderness areas taken over by an increasing population, is of little obvious direct concern to most people. One reason for the concern on the part of environmentalists is the erosion of the world's biodiversity, although it has not been easy to justify the worry. Another matter for the concern over the depletion of the tropical rainforest has been the potential loss of many plants of medicinal value. Schneider (1996) reports that ecologists have now demonstrated an additional advantage of biodiversity: a multiplicity of species makes some lands more productive. In a world dominated by the human species, the natural world seems to have no right, *per se,* to stand in the way of human progress and increasing needs, so an economic justification for protecting wildlife has to be given.

One of the most promising attempts to save species of mammals from extinction has been worldwide bans on whaling. Ryan (1995) reports that several species that were drastically reduced earlier this century are now recovering. Norway and Japan are the only two countries to continue killing smaller minke whales despite a 1986 moratorium. Whales are still at risk indirectly from human activities, by becoming entangled in fishing nets, absorbing toxic compounds in their food and colliding with ships.

The Everglades of southern Florida is an example of a unique ecosystem extending over 33,000 sq km, with strings of lakes and streams that are the home of wading birds. The Everglades have been drying up and now receive only a fifth as much water as they did a hundred years ago. Holloway (1994) describes the state of the Everglades at present: 'Four great gates at the northern end of the Everglades National Park and 1,400 miles of canals and levees determine the quantity of water that can enter the area. Sugar plantations and vegetable farms to the north and east use fertilisers and pesticides that determine the quality of that same water. Demands from agriculture, urban living and flood control have made the Everglades too wet in the wet season, too dry in the dry season, too rich in nutrient phosphorus and therefore too close to extinction.'

It is proposed to apply in the Everglades the largest and most expensive attempt at ecological restoration ever undertaken in the USA. There will be many problems, the most basic being that the exact 'natural' state of the original environment is not known, so there is a problem as to how to achieve a reasonable reconstruction, and whether it should be self-sustaining or managed. The Everglades case has been described in some detail here because it involves an attempt to remove non-indigenous plants, to reintroduce endangered fauna and to transform canals that replaced rivers back into rivers, a process to which the term 'wilding' is now sometimes applied.

In China the reservoir of the three Gorges Dam on the Chang Jiang river will flood the present homes of over a million people. In western democracies the general policy is to avoid disturbing people to make way for projects of public interest. The proposal of Popper and Popper (1987) to return a large area of the Great Plains of the USA to buffalo pasture (the 'Buffalo Commons'), and virtually remove all human presence, is therefore surprising. DeBres and Buizlo (1992) point to many problems and inconsistencies relating to such a project.

Most attempts to preserve wildlife in areas of special interest and importance have been confined to protecting them rather than changing them back to their natural state. One such case is the area of Lake Baykal in Siberia (Russia). Lake Baykal contains the largest volume of water of any inland water body in the world. In the Soviet period many industries were established in the area that drains into the lake and in the 1960s concern was expressed by scientists and many other people about the growing pollution, particularly from pulp and paper mills actually on the shores of the lake. Serious attempts are now being made to protect the lake from pollution. Gibbs (1994) notes: 'For Baykal, protection arrives none too soon. More than a mile deep and flush with oxygen, the lake is home to some 1,800 species found nowhere else ... the rain over Baykal has turned acidic, contaminated by smokestacks to the west.' Attempts are being made to zone the use of land in the Baykal drainage basin, setting aside areas for national parks, scientific reserves, landscapes, scenic rivers, greenbelts and landmarks. Russian and US ecologists have followed the experience of the New York State Adirondack Park, in which the first US regional land-use plan was applied.

It is now widely appreciated that sustainable development is the only way in which humans can continue for more than a century or two without destroying their means of existence. Part of the concept of sustainability is based on the view that humans are part of nature and that some of the world should be left undisturbed, with its wildlife protected, although how much cannot be calculated at the moment. The Wildlife Fund for Nature now has 200 sites, identified by scientists, which if properly protected could conserve 95 per cent of the world's wildlife. Nuttall (1996b) lists a sample of 16 key wildlife sites (see Table 10.6). The success of the plan depends on the cooperation of the government, companies, and local people because the charity could not alone obtain the resources needed.

Table 10.6 World wildlife key sites

Location	What conserved
Northern Rockies, Canada	coniferous forests
Everglades, USA	wetlands
Galapagos Islands, Ecuador	mainly animal species
Pantanal, Brazil, Bolivia, Paraguay	wetlands
Forests, Brazil	tropical rain forest
Taiga, Russia	coniferous forests
Taimyr tundra, Russia	cold (Arctic) desert
Mediterranean, Southern Europe	shrublands and marine ecosystems
Cross River, Nigeria	river ecology
Fynbos, South Africa	shrublands
Marine ecosystems, Mozambique, Tanzania	marine life includes coral reefs
Forests, Madagascar	forests unique to the island
Himalayas, Nepal, India, Pakistan	mountain ecosystems
Nansei Shoto, Japan	marine ecosystems
Sichuan, China	interior forests
Forests, Indonesia, Malaysia	tropical rain forest

Source: Nuttall (1996b)

Volcanoes (see Burroughs, (1996))

The precise time and place of serious volcanic eruptions cannot be forecast, but some areas are more prone to volcanic activity than others, while most parts of the world are outside the zone on the earth's surface where activity can occur. Any powerful volcanic eruption is a potential hazard for settlements and agricultural land within a limited radius, but usually direct loss of life is small. On a global scale, a very large volcanic eruption can emit dust that causes the whole atmosphere to cool. In particular, when sulphur dioxide is emitted into the atmosphere, it converts into sulphuric acid particles, forming a veil of dust at altitudes from 15 to 30 km, absorbing sunlight and cooling places near to and at ground level.

The study of past volcanic eruptions shows what can happen. For example, the volcano Tambora, in what is now Indonesia, erupted in 1815. It is estimated that of 92,000 people who died, 80,000 starved to death on account of the damage to their harvests due to cool conditions resulting from the dust in the atmosphere. Today it is more easy to transport emergency food to such disaster areas. Nevertheless, a series of recent volcanic eruptions has given the subject a high profile. Mount St Helens in Washington State, USA, erupted in 1980, but did not emit a large quantity of sulphur compounds. El Chichón in Mexico erupted in 1982 producing a greater effect on climate conditions. It was however the eruption of Mount Pinatubo in the Philippines in 1991 that made it possible to gauge the impact of an eruption. Twenty million tonnes of sulphur compounds were emitted into the stratosphere, duly reducing global temperature by half a degree before returning to normal after about three years. Another volcanic eruption on the scale of that of Tambora in 1812 would emit 5-10 times more material into the atmosphere than the Mount Pinatubo eruption, with correspondingly serious results.

While measures can be taken to alleviate the damage and reduce the loss of life locally from volcanic eruptions, as in the case of Montserrat in the Caribbean in 1997, nothing can be done either to anticipate the next 'big one' or to modify its impact, let alone prevent it. Here, indeed, is one of the unknowns of the next few decades, a good situation for informed speculation.

Desertification

According to Thomas (1993) about 7.5 per cent of the world's land area is defined as hyper-arid and almost another 40 per cent as drylands, of which 12 per cent is classed as arid, 17.7 per cent as semi-arid and 9.9 per cent as dry sub-humid. It is therefore not surprising that there has been widespread concern about both the short term occurrence of droughts and subsequent famines, and the long term loss of cropland through desertification. Thomas notes that in the popular mind desertification and famine have become synonymous. The UNEP stated in 1987 that 27 million hectares of productive land were being lost through desertification each year. Thomas (1993) argues that: 'natural fluctuations in dryland vegetation communities caused by inherent environmental instability need to be distinguished from degradation of the soil system caused by human activities.'

Even if, as according to Thomas, improved satellite-based monitoring allows better assessment of environmental changes and it is now accepted that previous statements of the scale of desertification have over-estimated the worldwide extent of the phenomenon by a factor of three, there still remains a threat to some of the existing cropland of the world. The most extensive drylands are in northern Africa, the Arabian Peninsula and the interior of Asia. Much of the western part of North America, parts of South America and almost all of Australia are also classed as drylands.

Urban pollution

The difficulty of achieving a standard measure of the population size of large cities and a consistent basis for comparisons was discussed in Chapter 4. Nevertheless, by comparison with the experience of previous centuries, the 20th century has seen the emergence of some very large urban agglomerations in developing and developed countries alike. In Chapter 12 further reference will be made to the question of very big urban populations. Almost 20 years ago the United Nations produced projections of the populations of the largest cities in the world to the year 2034 (UN, 1982) - see Table 10.7. Other projections will be discussed in Chapter 12. By 2034 nine of the ten largest cities are expected to be in developing countries.

Table 10.7 The world's ten largest urban agglomerations in 2034

Mexico City	39	Dacca (now Dhaka) (Bangladesh)	29
Shanghai	39	Calcutta	29
Beijing	37	Jakarta	27
Sâo Paulo	32	Madras	23
Greater Bombay (now Mumbai)	31	Greater Tokyo	19

Source: UN (1982)

Los Angeles has the reputation of having the most polluted air of any large city in the USA and its experience in recent decades may be an indication of what could happen in the next century to the fast growing cities of the developing world. Lents and Kelly (1993) describe Los Angeles in the early 1990s: 'On some hot, sunny days, the 14 million residents of the Los Angeles area inhale a thick brownish-gray haze and none can ignore its effect. The smog obscures the San Bernadino Mountains and the warm California sun; it irritates the eyes and nose; it restricts the activities of athletes and people who have breathing disorders; it injures the lungs of the young and old.' In spite of the negative image of Los Angeles and its current problems, and in the context of a threefold increase in population and more than a fourfold increase in the number of motor vehicles in use since the 1950s, improvements have been made in air quality. Los Angeles has the resources to carry out research on local pollution, to experiment with improvements, and to implement measures to reduce pollution.

Greater Mexico City is even larger than Los Angeles and the financial resources of the government are much smaller. A description of the pollution in Mexico City by Cohen (1999) points to a dismal future: 'The lingering smell of sulphur - pumped out by 60,000 factories, four million cars, 200,000 buses and 35,000 taxis - hits you the moment you set foot in the city. Some days the yellow haze which hugs the skyline is so dense it can feel like you are sucking the air through a narrow straw. Even on normal days, the air is so bad it is common to see mothers covering their children's mouths in an attempt to protect them from the vile pollution.' There are schemes to limit the number of cars in use in the city and to cut back activity in factories when smog emergencies are declared.

Many large cities in the developing world already have problems of air quality similar to those of Los Angeles and Mexico City, but they also have more basic problems in the human environment, while lacking the resources of cities in developed countries to combat pollution. Falkenmark and Widstrand (1992) summarise the situation as follows: 'The lack of adequate safe drinking water and sanitation is one of the major health and economic consequences of surging world urbanization. Increasing population concentration has contributed to the depletion and contamination of fresh water... In Manila [Philippines], a recent assessment showed that the most important sources of urban pollution were the uncollected solid waste, flooding, and river bank erosion around the squatter settlements that contain some 38 per cent of the metropolitan population.'

In its broadest sense the environment directly covers the whole of the natural world plus the impact on it of many human activities. Behind these is the 'mental environment' in which various countries, groups and individuals make decisions about how to use the environment and speculate about how to cope with environmental issues and problems. In comparison with longer periods in the past, changes in the natural environment have not been all that marked in the last fifty years. Can the same be said for the next fifty years? Arguably, National Geographic Society's *Restless Earth* (1997) is the best readily available background to the subject 'under one roof'.

For thirty years now constant improvements in the quality (resolution), quantity and coverage of images from artificial satellites have allowed a far greater appreciation of many environmental features and processes than was possible even as recently as the 1950s. Many natural hazards can be anticipated much more accurately than previously and the risks from them reduced. The prospect remains, however, that if world population continues to grow to the year 2050 and increasing numbers of people are concentrated in urban centres, insurance and re-insurance companies will find to their cost that risks increase as well. Most natural hazards cannot be controlled, but with appropriate knowledge and resources their effects can at least be reduced.

This chapter ends with a checklist of environmental problems, some already discussed earlier, others introduced here for the first time.

1. Mainly **water** related aspects. Apart from many relatively small and a few large fresh water lakes, and a few saline inland seas, the oceans are interconnected, which means that in time currents can transfer water over great distances.

    - Coastal flooding, mainly caused by winds and, in places, high tides, but a global threat if sea-level rises.

    - Tsunamis, waves caused by earthquakes (see Glossary).

    - Changing currents: most notable recently, the change in direction of the Pacific current El Niño, especially in 1982-83 and 1997, the latter bringing unusually severe storms and high temperatures to the Pacific coast of the Americas while causing droughts in southern Africa and Southeast Asia.

    - Caspian and Aral Seas, 'case studies' of the effects of marked changes in sea-level, threatening the total disappearance of the latter.

    - Droughts and desertification.

    - River flooding: frequent in Bangladesh, in effect the delta of the Ganges and Brahmaputra rivers. Mississippi basin in 1993. Oder (Poland and Germany) in 1997.

    - Polar regions. Antarctica is a large continent (surrounded by sea) with mountain ranges of considerable altitude and mostly covered with thick ice. In contrast, the Arctic is a deep ocean (surrounded by land), covered by polar sea ice. If the Arctic ice melts it will not affect sea-level whereas if part of the Antarctic ice sheet melts (the most vulnerable being the West Antarctic ice sheet which rests on the sea floor) global sea-level could rise about 6 metres, with devastating effect on human settlements and activities.

2.   The **atmosphere** extends several hundred kilometres above the earth's surface (unlike the sea it does not have a distinct surface). Its pressure is about ten times as high at sea-level as at 20 km and much of it is below 10 km. Humans on the earth's surface in relation to the atmosphere resemble life on the sea floor in relation to the oceans.

-   Winds: hurricanes, tornadoes, blizzards, thunderstorms. In 1987 an unusually strong hurricane over southern England destroyed or damaged among other things 150 million trees, 12 per cent of all the trees in Britain. In 1991, 139,000 people lost their lives in a hurricane in Bangladesh.

-   Dust storms, dust bowls.

-   Combustion of fossil fuels: sending various impurities and carbon dioxide into the atmosphere, causing 'acid rain' to fall, regarded as a cause of damage to forests (see Hedins and Likens (1996)).

-   Ozone 'hole', identified over Antarctica in the 1970s, would allow more biologically destructive ultraviolet radiation to reach the earth's surface. Some countries voluntarily banned the use of chlorofluorocarbons (CFCs), a major cause of ozone depletion, while others (e.g. India, China), continue to use them in manufacturing, but there is an illegal international trade in the products.

3.   The **earth's crust**

-   Volcanoes: distributed in well defined zones, mainly mountain ranges, but difficult to forecast eruptions.

-   Earthquakes: it is known where in the world there are risks of serious earthquakes, but not when they will occur. In 1923 143,000 people died in Tokyo and in 1976 there were 655,000 deaths in the coal-mining city of Tangshan in China. The 1985 earthquake in Michoacán, Mexico, caused about 10,000 deaths, mostly in Mexico City, and destroyed or seriously damaged many tall buildings in and around the centre, picking out very clearly those that were built with an inadequately reinforced concrete structure.

4.   The **biosphere**

-   There are numerous projects underway to protect various species of plant and animal and to repopulate areas from which they have disappeared. Canada, for example, can ensure that wild animals are protected over vast areas, whereas the case of the Milu deer in China shows that population pressure leaves little 'wild' land at all. This deer, the Milu, was wiped out in China a century ago but some animals were taken to England and a herd was established. A decade ago some were taken back to China and a herd was established in captivity near Beijing. Great difficulty was anticipated however in finding any suitable wild wetland area in China for the deer to be sent to, given the intensive use of every possible piece of potential agricultural land. Once most of the world's land area was virtually wild or semi-wild and very thinly populated or unpopulated. Human activities were confined to 'civilised islands' of settlement. The prospect in the next 50 to 100 years is that most of the land will be 'humanised' and areas of genuine wildlife, plant and animal, will fragment into 'islands' a few of them quite large, as in Amazonia, northern Canada and Siberia.

11

THE PLAYERS IN WORLD AFFAIRS

'There are, at the present time, two great nations in the world which seem to tend towards the same end, although they started from different points; I allude to the Russians and the Americans ... while the attention of mankind was directed elsewhere, they have suddenly assumed a most prominent place among the nations.'

Alexis de Tocqueville (1835)

11.1   THE SIZE OF COUNTRIES

Between the late 1940s and the late 1980s world affairs were greatly influenced by the ideological West-East conflict between two 'superpowers', the USA and the USSR. In spite of the growing influence of the 'Third World' during the second half of the 20th century, it is a fact that the USA and its allies in Western Europe and Japan, together with the Soviet bloc, controlled most of the world economy and virtually all the sophisticated military technology and equipment. The dominance of the industrial or developed world has, however, been reduced since the 1960s in various ways: the impact of the Organisation of Petroleum Exporting Countries (OPEC) on oil prices, the emergence of newly industrialising countries, and in particular the rapid growth and opening up of the Chinese economy since the late 1970s. The biggest changes in the political map of the world have been the granting of independence to numerous colonies of European powers in Africa and Asia since the Second World War, as well as the break-up of the Council for Mutual Economic Assistance (CMEA) and then of the USSR itself. The passing of the era of the two superpowers has left a completely new situation, the starting point from which the balance of power and influence in the world can be expected to change in the first half of the 21st century.

It is not possible to quantify objectively or precisely the weight or amount of influence on world affairs of each country in the world. This may be one reason why few people have tried. An attempt by German (1960) (in which 25 criteria were used) rated 18 other countries in relation to the USA (=100): 2nd, the USSR at 98, 3rd, the UK at 19, 4th, China at 15 and so on to the 19th, Belgium at 2. The initial total scores of the USA, the USSR and the UK, the only credible nuclear powers of the time, were doubled on top of the total of 'civil factors.' In 1963 Cole (1963) made a similar assessment using more limited criteria to compare the weightings of world powers from 1910 to 1959. For the purposes of this chapter a similar type of assessment has been made for the mid-1990s. Table 11.1 shows, in order of absolute size as opposed to per capita amount, the 'top' twenty countries according to five criteria (numbers as in columns in Table 11.1). In Figure 11.1 the disparities and irregularities in the size of the countries according to the same criteria are highlighted graphically.

Table 11.1 The most powerful countries of the world according to five criteria (percentage)

	(1) Population (per cent)		(2) Area (per cent)		(3) Natural resources (per cent)		(4) Energy consumption per cent		(5) Real GDP (per cent)	
1	China	21.1	Russia	12.8	Russia	13.6	USA	25.4	USA	20.9
2	India	16.5	Canada	7.5	USA	8.1	China	10.2	China	9.1
3	USA	4.6	China	7.2	Brazil	6.4	Russia	7.7	Japan	8.3
4	Indonesia	3.5	USA	7.0	China	6.2	Japan	6.0	Germany	4.9
5	Brazil	2.8	Brazil	6.3	Canada	4.8	Germany	4.1	India	3.8
6	Russia	2.6	Australia	5.7	Australia	4.1	France	2.9	France	3.5
7	Pakistan	2.3	India	2.2	India	3.7	India	2.8	Italy	3.3
8	Japan	2.2	Argentina	2.2	Indonesia	2.1	Canada	2.8	UK	3.2
9	Bangladesh	2.1	Kazakhstan	2.1	Iran	2.1	UK	2.7	Brazil	2.8
10	Nigeria	1.8	Sudan	1.9	Zaire	1.7	Italy	1.9	Mexico	2.1
Percentage in top 10		59.5		54.7		52.8		66.5		61.9
11	Mexico	1.6	Algeria	1.8	Mexico	1.6	South Korea	1.8	Canada	2.0
12	Germany	1.4	Zaire	1.7	South Africa	1.6	Ukraine	1.8	Russia	1.9
13	Viet Nam	1.3	Saudi Arabia	1.6	Argentina	1.6	Mexico	1.3	Spain	1.7
14	Philippines	1.2	Mexico	1.5	Algeria	1.1	Brazil	1.3	Indonesia	1.5
15	Turkey	1.1	Libya	1.3	Chile	1.1	South Africa	1.3	S. Korea	1.4
16	Egypt	1.1	Iran	1.2	Nigeria	0.9	Spain	1.2	Thailand	1.2
17	Iran	1.1	Mongolia	1.1	Iraq	0.9	Australia	1.2	Australia	1.1
18	Thailand	1.1	Indonesia	1.1	Peru	0.9	Poland	1.2	Iran	1.1
19	UK	1.0	Peru	1.0	Morocco	0.8	Iran	1.1	Argentina	0.9
20	France	1.0	Chad	1.0	Venezuela	0.8	Saudi Arabia	1.1	Pakistan	0.9
Percentage in top 20		71.4		68.0		64.2		79.8		75.6
World¹		5,771		134.0		100.0		8,136		31,320

Notes: ¹ World totals

(1) Population in millions
(2) Area in millions of sq km.
(3) Notional scores – percentages
(4) Energy consumption in millions of tonnes of oil equivalent
(5) Real GDP in millions of US dollars

(1) Population size. Almost 60 per cent of the population of the world is to be found in the 20 largest countries in population. Figure 11.1 illustrates the situation and some of the problems, including the long 'tail' of smaller countries with little or virtually no influence on world affairs. Indeed China and South Asia (India, Pakistan, Bangladesh) each contain over 20 per cent of the total population of the world. China and India are much larger than the third in size, the USA, but after that there is a fairly smooth decline in population size, continuing beyond the 20th country, France, to include 154 countries with over 1 million inhabitants in the mid-1990s, of which 47 in Africa, 25 in the Americas, 47 in Asia and Oceania, 35 in Europe, and about 100 more with under 1 million. In time it may be more realistic to consider the European Union as a single country for some purposes, in which case, with 374 million people in 15 existing sovereign countries, it would come third in ranking.

Throughout the half-century since the end of the Second World War, developed countries have dropped in the world ranking of countries according to population size. The year 2025 is not far off, but projections of population for that year (*WPDS 1996*) show considerable further changes in ranking even by then, assuming no further break-up of countries, or mergers between them. China's share could drop from 21.1 to 18.2 per cent and those of India (16.5 to 16.9) and the USA (4.6 to 4.1) also change. The UK and France could drop out of the top 20, replaced by Zaire and Ethiopia, while Nigeria's share could rise from 1.8 to 3.0 per cent. The combined population of the 15 member states of the European Union of the late 1990s would drop from 6.4 per cent of total world population in 1996 to 4.6 in 2025. The 20 expected largest countries in 2025 are shown in Table 11.2.

Table 11.2 The expected population of the 20 largest countries in the world in 2025[1] in millions

1	China	1,570	11	Japan	121
2	India	1,385	12	Philippines	114
3	USA	335	13	Ethiopia	112
4	Indonesia	276	14	Iran	112
5	Pakistan	233	15	Viet Nam	104
6	Nigeria	232	16	Zaire	104
7	Brazil	213	17	Egypt	98
8	Bangladesh	180	18	Turkey	90
9	Mexico	141	19	Germany	76
10	Russia	131	20	Thailand	71

Source: *1997 WPDS*

[1] The total population of the world is expected to be about 8,036 million in that year

Since industrialisation is proceeding rapidly in several of the developing countries among the top 20, although from a limited base in the 1990s, and population is growing rapidly in some, their need to import primary products is likely to grow. The prospect is that the situation a century ago, when a few industrial countries imported primary products from a large number of other countries, many of them colonies, will continue to change, leaving relatively few countries by 2050, if not by 2025, still able to produce a large surplus of primary products for export.

(i)

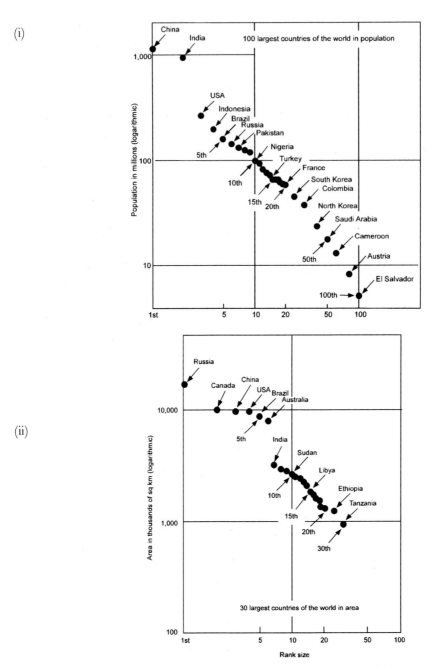

(ii)

Figure 11.1 Graphical comparisons of the size of selected countries of the world according to various criteria. All the graphs have logarithmic scales (base 10) on both axes. Many sets of entities such as countries, companies, differ in size in such a way that if they are ranked according to size and plotted on the double logarithmic graph they fall on or near a diagonal straight line from upper left to lower right. There is no strict law, but a widespread tendency. The five graphs in this Figure bring out the following features of the distributions (i) The 'anomalously' very large population sizes of China and India; (ii) The cluster of five large countries with roughly similar areas; (iii) and (iv) The outstanding position of the USA with regard to total GDP and to general influence in the world; (v) The enormous and administratively inconvenient variations in the population sizes of the present 15 member states of the European Union and of the 'next six' to apply for membership.

Note: From the 1st to the 20th in size, every country is shown, but after that, only selected countries.

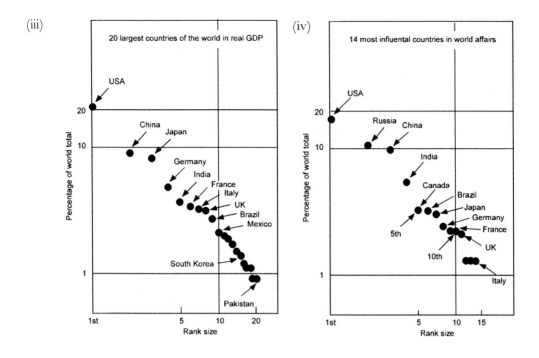

(iii) 20 largest countries of the world in real GDP

USA
China
Japan
Germany
India
France
Italy
UK
Brazil
Mexico
South Korea
Pakistan

Percentage of world total

Rank size
1st   5   10   20

(iv) 14 most influental countries in world affairs

USA
Russia
China
India
Canada
Brazil
Japan
Germany
France
UK
5th
10th
Italy

Percentage of world total

Rank size
1st   5   10   15

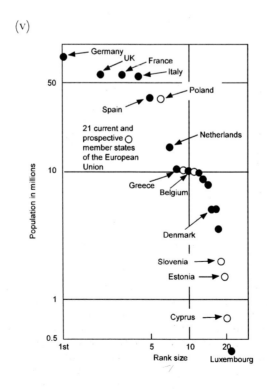

(v)

Germany
UK
France
Italy
Poland
Spain

21 current and
prospective ○
member states
of the European
Union

Netherlands

Greece
Belgium

Denmark

Slovenia ⟶ ○
Estonia ⟶ ○

Cyprus ⟶ ○

Luxembourg

Population in millions

Rank size
1st   5   10   20

(2) Area. Conventional world maps draw attention to the territorial rather than the demographic size of countries. In most maps of the world using projections that are not equal area, the area of countries nearest to the poles is exaggerated, especially of Canada and Russia. The territorial size of a country, measured against population size, has both positive and negative aspects. Other things being equal, the larger the area, the greater the natural resource endowment to be expected, except where it is inaccessible, notably in Greenland and Antarctica. Until the era of long range bombers and intercontinental missiles, a large country was less easy to invade and occupy. On the other hand, the larger the territory, the more difficult it may be to integrate it.

(3) Natural resources. The present total amount of natural resources in the world is difficult to estimate. While the water and bioclimatic resources are broadly known, it is probable that many new reserves of fossil fuels and non-fuel minerals will be discovered, since many land and most offshore areas of the world have as yet hardly been explored and assessed. The natural resource scores in column (3) are therefore only very approximate. They consist of water, bioclimatic resources, fossil fuels and non-fuel minerals, together with an extra weighting for large area. The five elements are arbitrarily given equal weight (see Cole (1996)).

Since the scores in column (3) of Table 11.1 are percentages of an absolute total, they should be considered against the population percentages of the countries. Thus, with 37.6 per cent of the total population of the world, India and China together have only 9.9 per cent of the natural resources according to the estimate given here. In contrast, Canada and Australia together have only 0.8 per cent of the population of the world but 8.9 per cent of the natural resources. For what the estimates are worth, therefore, Canada and Australia have over 40 times more natural resources per capita than China and India. Japan, and Europe excluding the former USSR, are also very poorly endowed with natural resources in relation to population whereas the USA is better placed in terms of bioclimatic resources and coal reserves, although for much of the 20th century it has been using up its large (exhaustible) reserves of oil, natural gas and non-fuel minerals at a fast rate.

In terms of natural resource endowment, among the largest countries of the world in terms of natural resource availability per capita, Australia, Canada, Russia and Brazil appear to have the best futures. The Middle East countries, with their large oil and natural gas reserves, also score highly on the resources to population ratio, but their profiles are very uneven, with poor water, bioclimatic and non-fuel mineral resources.

(4) Energy consumption. This variable is ambiguous in what it shows about the size of countries. In the first place, all the main industrial countries except Russia and the UK are net importers of sources of energy and, while that is not necessarily a weakness, it does imply vulnerability in relation to security of supplies and predictability of prices. Again, the consumption of fossil fuels and indeed of nuclear energy, has a potentially negative impact on the environment at various levels of geographical scale (see Chapter 10). On the other hand, per capita consumption of energy correlates broadly with GDP per capita and material standards of living. The USA and Canada consume much more energy per capita than any other large countries, while among the industrial countries Italy and Japan are more sparing users. In 1995 the eight largest industrial economies consumed over half of the world's energy, and, as already noted in Chapter 10, 'produced' about half of the various forms of pollution in the world.

(5) Real GDP. Since GDP includes all forms of production in an economy it is the most comprehensive measure of economic strength. In the case of Europe (excluding Russia), Japan, and to a lesser extent the USA, much of the GDP is produced by adding value to primary products, especially raw materials, imported from elsewhere. A number of developing countries in South and Southeast Asia, together with China, although less dependent on imports of primary products, are also beginning to do the same as the older industrial countries and some are already net exporters of manufactured goods.

The size and influence of countries can be measured in a number of other ways as well as those discussed above. In the 20th century military strength has been a priority with countries of both world and regional significance. Before the First World War seven countries in Europe had formidable military establishments: Germany, France, the UK, Italy, Austria-Hungary, Russia and Turkey. In the 1930s huge forces were built up in Germany and Italy under the dictatorships of Hitler and Mussolini. By this time Japan had also become a major military power. Arguably the American Civil War (1861-65) was the first large-scale war in which use was made of modern transport, the railway, and sophisticated weaponry, but until the Second World War there was less emphasis in the USA on keeping a large military establishment.

In the 1990s, thanks to their vast armouries of nuclear weapons, the USA and Russia remain military superpowers, although the USA now appears to have a much more sophisticated military establishment than Russia for policing the world when required. To attribute precise percentages of total military power in the world to individual countries would be difficult, but it is reasonable to allocate some of the remaining countries of the world to two lower levels of military capacity. China, India, the UK, France and Pakistan have nuclear weapons and enough conventional forces to do more than defend their own territories if required. A considerable number of other countries have military establishments of some size, including Turkey, Iran, Iraq and Israel in the sensitive area of the Middle East, as well as Canada and Australia. North Korea, Iran, Iraq, South Africa, Algeria, Libya and Israel also have a nuclear capacity or are 'going nuclear'. The following notional scores, percentages of the total world military capability, have been given to the most powerful countries: USA 35, Russia 25, China 5, UK 5, France 5, India 3, Germany 3, various other countries 1-2 (see *The Economist* (1992a), 'Defence in the 21st century').

11.2 POLITICAL AND MILITARY INFLUENCES

In section 11.1 an attempt was made to quantify various attributes of the largest 20 countries in the world in the 1990s according to five criteria and to take into account military strength. The membership of the top 20 varies from attribute to attribute, with several countries, through sheer size, appearing in all the lists, others present only in some. In order to obtain a broad, very crude, index of potential influence in the world for the larger countries, the percentages achieved by each country in columns (1)-(5) in Table 11.1 have been summed and the military scores given at the end of the previous section have been added. The totals have then been divided by 6 to give a new overall percentage share of the world total. The countries listed in Table 11.3 all have a score of more than 1 per cent of the world total. The decimal place has been left although the apparent precision is spurious, given the very approximate and in some cases subjective nature of the information on which the scores are based. The 14 countries in Table

11.3 fall into five classes according to the way in which they achieve their scores. Smaller countries can mostly also be allocated to these classes.

Table 11.3 Percentage share of potential influence in world affairs

1	USA	16.8	8	Germany	2.4
2	Russia	10.6	9	Australia	2.2
3	China	9.8	10	France	2.2
4	India	5.4	11	UK	2.1
5	Canada	3.3	12	Indonesia	1.3
6	Brazil	3.2	13	Mexico	1.3
7	Japan	3.0	14	Italy	1.3

1. Exceptionally well endowed with per capita natural resources, developed, but with small populations: Canada, Australia.

2. Reasonably well endowed with per capita natural resources, developed, with large populations: USA, Russia.

3. Poorly endowed with natural resources, developed, with sizeable populations: Japan, Germany, France, UK, Italy.

4. Reasonably well endowed with natural resources, developing, but with increasing industrialisation, with large/sizeable populations: Brazil, Indonesia, Mexico.

5. Poorly endowed with natural resources (in relation to population size), developing, but with increasing industrialisation, with very large populations: China, India.

In an article entitled 'Back to the future' in *The Economist* (1994) a new world order, 'the next arrival on the conveyor belt of history', is described: 'The four powers fairly certain to take part in the new pattern are the United States, China, Russia and Europe, in that order of probability. Then come two merely possible contenders: one is Japan, the other a hypothetical centre of power in the Muslim world (which, if it did come into being, could prove the most explosive of the lot).'

Another feature of the countries of the world should also be taken into account when their potential influence is being considered: their location on the earth's surface in relation to other countries. A rough index of potential involvement in regional, if not global, affairs can be calculated by counting the number of other countries with which each country shares its boundaries. Alternatively, the number of other countries within a particular radius of a country could be counted. The number of neighbours was used in various publications on war early in the 20th century by a physicist, L. F. Richardson, to assess the probability of conflict of a country with its neighbour or neighbours in the days when aerial warfare hardly existed. A paper was published on the subject in 1961 (see Richardson (1961)). Both the USA and the USSR have had missiles capable of reaching virtually all parts of the earth's surface for four decades. Assuming these will not be used in the next few decades, then shorter distances may again be of military interest in the future. For example, Adams (1997a) refers to the development of missiles in Libya, Syria and Iran capable of reaching areas in Southern Europe, including parts of the former USSR. Evans (1997) notes the concern in some NATO countries about the threat: 'Plans are being discussed between the United States and Germany to form a combined anti-missile brigade that would protect NATO bases and forces from the so-called "Club Mad" group of regimes - Iran, Iraq and Libya.'

There are several hundred distinct stretches of international boundary in the world, of greatly varying length. Among the seven largest countries in the world, in area, the number of different neighbours varies greatly: China and Russia each with 14 and Brazil has 10, contrasting with the USA with 2, Canada with 1 and Australia with none. Among smaller countries in area there are also marked contrasts: Germany (9), France (6), Israel (5 plus 5 more within 500 km), Spain (2), the UK (1), New Zealand (0).

Most countries are still likely to be involved largely with their own internal affairs in the decades to come, but in foreign trade and other international transactions they will interact with other countries. During the second half of the 20th century there have also been many instances in which one country has attacked another militarily rather than competing with it economically. In his *The State of War and Peace Atlas,* Smith, D. (1997), lists more than seventy countries that have been engaged in a war at some time during 1990-95 alone, whether interstate or civil (or both). For someone in the late 1940s speculating about the future it would have been very difficult to anticipate exactly where conflicts would take place. Indeed, immediately after the end of the Second World War the general hope was that there would be no further military conflicts at all. With the experience of the last five decades it is reasonable to assume that there will be many more in the first half of the 21st century, although not directly between the major world powers, in whose interest it would usually be to smother more local disputes before they spread. Again, most smaller countries are likely to engage in conflict only with immediate neighbours; Bolivia would not launch an attack on Bangladesh or Burundi (or vice versa).

Can the type of government of a country be a guide to its inclination to enter into a conflict with one or more other countries (formally declaring war is not fashionable nowadays)? Conflicts in the 20th century have in many cases been related to the type of government of a country. By definition, colonies of the industrial powers were not in a position to start a conflict. Of the sovereign states, some have had democratically elected governments while others have been totalitarian. The totalitarian (or authoritarian) countries are mainly one of three types according to how they are or have been governed:

1. By a single party of professional politicians, but with the support of the military (the USSR, China, Poland). In the late 1990s, China was the only major world power in the list of 14 in Table 11.3 in which a single political party is still firmly entrenched.

2. Directly by the military, with at least some ministers from the armed forces (common in Latin America until recently, in Africa).

3. By hereditary emperors or monarchs, but not constitutional (in contrast to the UK, Sweden), with support from the military and industry (Japan 1941, Saudi Arabia).

If it is assumed that countries in which the constitution stipulates the need for opposition parties are less prone to start military conflicts, then on the whole the prospect is better for peace than it was in the period 1950-1990. In the late 1930s the situation was particularly unfavourable because four of the six largest countries of Europe, the USSR, Germany, Italy and Spain, all had dictatorships, and Germany was armed to the teeth with the most sophisticated weaponry of the time. Japan was already busy occupying increasingly large areas of China.

Although China is the only major world power with, in effect, a dictatorship, its geographical situation is such that there is no obvious incentive for it to attempt to occupy any neighbouring country apart perhaps from Taiwan, which Chinese leaders regard as part of China anyway. There remain, however, a number of smaller countries of regional importance in which the taste for military conflict remains strong in the minds of the leaders, with the occupation of new territory (preferably with big oil reserves) a common goal: Iraq, Iran, Syria and Libya come to mind. In Africa south of the Sahara, also, some countries are capable of trying to make territorial gains, and even in Latin America, territorial claims are public knowledge, but it is likely that here the USA would manage to discourage if not suffocate military action once border skirmishes occur. North Korea's threats to invade South Korea and its attempts to develop nuclear weapons have alarmed the USA, which apparently contemplated an attack in 1994.

Political leaders and the military establishment tend to fight past battles, or rather to recall past battles when it suits them, either to instil a feeling of emergency or to obtain greater funding. Chinese leaders have predicted a war between their country and the USA, although where it would be fought is difficult to imagine. They may recall the conflict in Korea in 1950-53, when the USA was representing the United Nations in South Korea, while China supported North Korea. Some German politicians have argued that if their country is not committed to strong integration with other countries of Western Europe, most recently through a common currency, there could be another war in Europe. One British commentator has argued that if there is such a currency there could be a war. While it can be expected that there will be numerous military conflicts around the world in the first half of the 21st century it will be assumed that they will be local or regional, not global. The fiercest competition is likely to be economic rather than military.

Thanks partly, perhaps, to their position as victors in two world wars, France and the UK have enjoyed considerable influence in the 20th century, 'punching above their weight'. Between 1965 and 1995 their share of world population has lessened considerably and between 1995 and 2050 it can be expected to diminish even more. More than three decades after most of France's African colonies were given independence, France still had a considerable military and cultural influence in the continent, but in the mid-1990s, after a number of setbacks, its military presence is to be cut and unilateral intervention in African countries is to cease (Mather (1997)).

In discussion with leaders in southeastern Asia in July 1997, the British Foreign Secretary Robin Cook found that political leaders in this part of the world are not prepared to be told what to do by the UK, the EU or the West in general. Myanmar is unlikely to stop growing opium poppies to please its former colonial ruler, while the Association of South East Asian Nations (ASEAN), of which Indonesia is the most powerful member, is not prepared to reject the applications of Myanmar and Cambodia to join, in spite of their undesirable (in Western eyes) political systems. Nor can the UK dictate what arms countries of the region should buy (or not buy) or how they should use them; since it is the second largest exporter of arms in the world, pragmatism will usually win over principles, economic considerations over moral ones.

11.3 NEW COUNTRIES FOR OLD?

The nature of world affairs in the first half of the 21st century will to some extent depend on whether or not there are marked changes in the composition of the countries of the world. Between 1945 and 1996 the number of members of the United Nations increased from 51 founder members at the end of the Second World War to 185 in 1996; almost all the new members were colonies of European powers before they gained independence. A further 'round' of the birth of new states has taken place in Europe in the 1990s, the emergence from three existing countries, the USSR, Czechoslovakia and Yugoslavia, of 22 new sovereign states. By 1996-7 Europe had 49 countries, some minute ones, competing for places in the finals of the 1998 World Football Cup. In the opposite direction there are trends towards the formation of free trade areas between various countries. In the European Union, however, in which the ultimate goal of political union of a federal kind between the 15 member states is seriously considered, progress towards integration is likely to be slow.

In this section attention focuses only on the most influential countries of the world, as defined in Table 11.3, because a complete break-up on Soviet lines of some larger countries could reduce the present dominance in world affairs of a few countries or groups of countries. Whether or not Belgium breaks up into new Flemish and Walloon states would have very little impact on world affairs whereas the break-up of China or even Canada could have. The most influential countries will be discussed roughly in order of appearance in Table 11.3. Figures 11.2a-e show weaknesses in the cohesion of five of the largest countries of the world.

1. The USA. The indigenous population of the USA is small in number, now to a considerable extent mixed with the European settlers, but is allowed some autonomy in reservations. The victory of the North over the South in the Civil War (1861-65) did not entirely remove a cultural divide over slavery that had formed in the early decades of US history. The three Pacific states and also Alaska and Hawaii are remote from the main concentration of population in the USA but economically closely integrated with the rest. Hawaii appears to be the only state in which some degree of autonomy may be sought. As Mexicans and other Latin Americans migrate in large numbers into the southern and southwestern states of the USA, as well as into New York, the Spanish language is becoming widely used.

It is not expected that the USA will break up along Soviet lines, one reason being that there has been a 'melting pot' policy that has developed awareness among immigrants from many parts of the world of an American (US) 'nation', in contrast to the Soviet system, in which cultural differences were tolerated, even encouraged on the assumption that economic forces were dominant. Nevertheless it is interesting to note the nine regions recognised by Garreau (1981) in North America, which includes Canada, Mexico, Central America and the Caribbean Islands, in addition to the USA itself (see Figure 11.2a). They consist of New England, the Foundry (industrial northeast), Dixie (southeast USA), the Islands (plus the southern tip of Florida), Mexamerica (much of southwest USA), Ecotopia (the Pacific coastlands), the Empty Quarter, the Breadbasket, and Quebec. In this regional scheme the US borders with Canada and Mexico largely disappear.

Although the USA is still expected to be a single sovereign state in 2050, its present strong influence in world affairs, briefly boosted by the demise of the USSR, seems likely to decline gradually. Possible reasons for this relative decline include the prospect that its share of total world population and production are diminishing, its national cohesion and sense of purpose are being diluted by continuing immigration, and its own natural resource base is being eroded, making it more dependent on foreign trade.

The final paragraph of Paul Kennedy (1987) in his book *The Rise and Fall of Great Powers* is as follows; the reader may disagree with the content-: 'Viewed from one perspective, it can hardly be said that the dilemmas facing the United States are unique. Which country in the world, one is tempted to ask is *not* encountering problems in evolving a viable military policy, or in choosing between guns and butter and investment? From another perspective, however, the American position is a very special one. For all its economic and perhaps military decline, it remains, in Pierre Hassner's words, "the decisive actor in every type of balance and issue." Because it has so much power for good or evil, because it is the linchpin of the western alliance system and the centre of the existing global economy, what it does, *or does not do*, is so much more important than what any of the other Powers decide to do.'

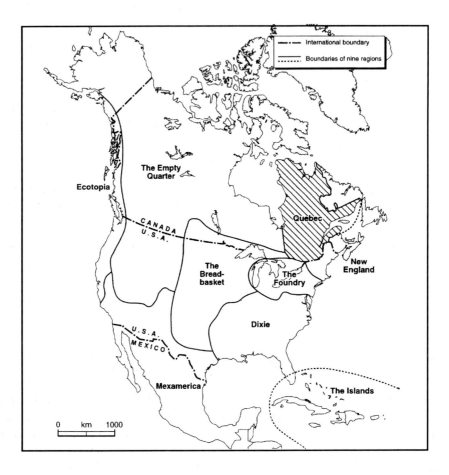

Figure 11.2a The USA and Canada, Central America and the Caribbean as nine distinct 'cultural' regions after Garreau (1981). Maddox (1997b) goes further, highlighting the devolutionary tide sweeping away Washington's power.

2. The Russian Federation has lost 14 other non-Russian Soviet Socialist Republics, even if it still has considerable influence in many of them thanks to economic interdependence, and the presence of many Russian expatriates in some. Russia itself however still contains many non-Russian ethnic groups concentrated in former Autonomous Soviet Socialist Republics (ASSRs), some numbering several million, many much smaller. Figure 11.2b shows the location of these predominantly non-Russian peoples. Up to the late 1990s there was little evidence that the areas in which Russians are in the majority are showing signs of breaking apart. West Siberia, East Siberia and the Far East have been major planning regions of the Soviet Union since the 1920s. The Far East region is very roughly the

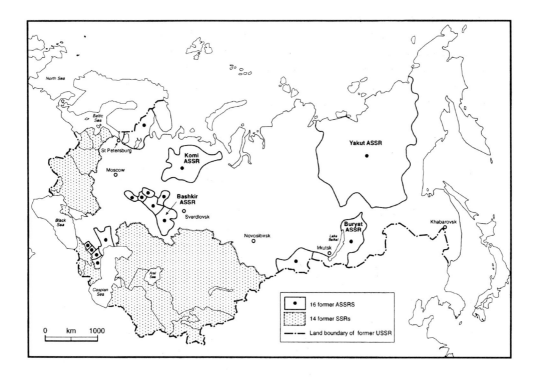

Figure 11.2b The former USSR. The shaded areas are the 14 non-Russian Soviet Socialist Republics.

counterpart of California in the USA or British Columbia in Canada. Its small population (for its area size) appears increasingly to manage its own affairs.

Russia has already been greatly weakened strategically, if not financially, by the break-up of the Soviet Union, and its leaders are not likely to tolerate, let alone encourage, movements for greater regional autonomy. Certainly they would not relish complete independence for any national minority group, as the struggle in Chechnya has shown. In July 1997 the Prime Minister of Russia stated that the ultimate aim of Russia's reforms is to qualify eventually for membership of the European Union (see Bremner (1997)).

3. China has the ingredients for some degree of regional disquiet in the next few decades; there are two main ways in which the country could become fragmented. First, the 9 per cent of the population that is non-Han is mostly found in five so-called Autonomous Regions (see Figure 11.2c). Three of these are landlocked, Xinjiang (Sinkiang), Tibet and Nei Mongol (Inner Mongolia), very extensive territorially, but very thinly populated. The other two are smaller in area and are closer to the main area with a high density of population in China, the southeastern two-fifths. Second, the generally richer coastal provinces (see also Chapter 9) could resent having to support the rest of China. Three areas in which rapid industrialisation is taking place and to which foreign investment is attracted stand out: the Bohai Bay area, which includes the capital, Beijing, the Lower Chang Jiang valley, which includes Shanghai, and in the south Guangdong province with Hong Kong.

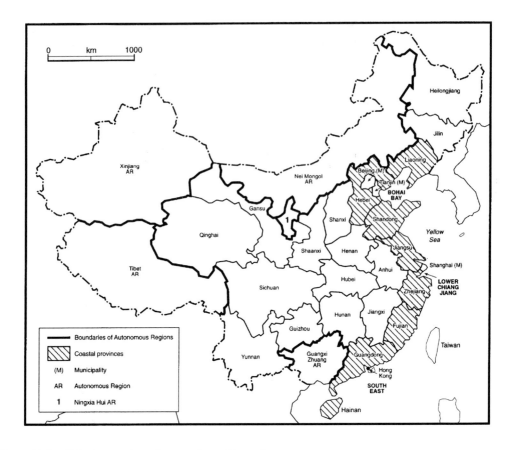

Figure 11.2c China's coastal provinces and non-Han regions

4. British India was subdivided following its independence from British rule in 1947, in that case on a religious basis (see Figure 11.2d). Many different languages are spoken in modern India, but the whole country is predominantly Hindu in religion. The five most southerly states have Dravidian languages, distinct from the Indo-European languages spoken to the north, but there is no obvious reason why India should split along a linguistic divide. As with China, some states are richer than others and people in Mumbai, in particular, could argue that their region should not be expected to support poorer states. A complete break-up of India seems very unlikely in the next few decades.

5. Canada ranks among the potentially most influential countries of the world, mainly on account of its extensive natural resources, although politically it tends to exist under the shadow of the USA, keeping a low profile in world affairs. Of all the major world powers it is the one most likely to break up, assuming that in due course a majority of the inhabitants of French-speaking Quebec (see Figure 11.2a) vote for independence, which almost happened in 1995.

6. In Brazil (see Figure 11.2e) there are two main concentrations of population, those of the Northeast and the Southeast. The Portuguese developed the Northeast first and large numbers of African slaves were taken there. Today it lags far behind the Southeast in both

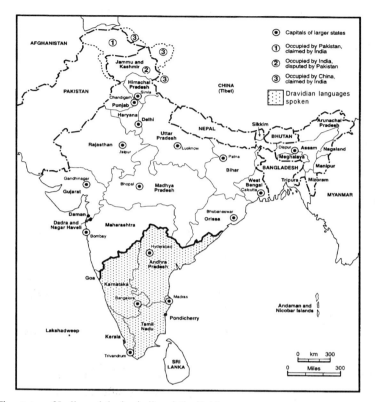

Figure 11.2d The states of India and the basic linguistic divide.

Figure 11.2e The five major regions of Brazil.

agricultural and industrial strength and has been supported financially by the Southeast for some decades. In some respects the Northeast is a liability to the Southeast, but that does not seem to be a reason for the break-up of Brazil.

7, 8 and 9 Japan, Australia and Germany all have limited ethnic and cultural problems, with small minority groups, but there is little to indicate the prospect of break-up in the next few decades. Australia usually keeps a low profile in world affairs, but Binyon (1997) reports how concern has now surfaced over the way Aboriginal children were taken away from their tribes earlier this century, to be transformed and assimilated into white Australian culture.

10, 11 and 14 France, the UK and Italy all in different ways have situations that could lead to an increase in autonomy for some regions. Before the Second World War, France and Italy were highly centralised unitary states but since the war moves have been made to allow some recognition of regional aspirations. After the First World War the Irish Free State (Eire, now the Republic of Ireland) started the break-up of the UK, synonymous at the time with the British Isles. Devolution of some political power to Scotland and Wales in 1999 may further weaken the power of England, but in the context of the European Union, the UK in general and England in particular are gradually losing their sovereignty to the emerging supranational entity.

12, 13 Indonesia and Mexico are both very extensive territorially, Mexico greatly elongated, Indonesia a farflung archipelago. Modern Mexico has its origins as a Spanish colony in the 16th century and it became independent early in the 19th century, making it one of the 'senior' non-European modern sovereign states; it seems unlikely to break up in the next few decades. Indonesia's independence from the Netherlands came only after the Second World War, but it is unlikely to break up in the next few decades if only because it is dominated by one of the more central islands, Java, where much of the population lives.

In conclusion to this review of possible break-ups of the more influential countries of the world, the prospect is that there will be few large-scale changes. China and Canada appear to be most at risk. In the case of China, as long as the Communist Party remains in control, the country can be expected to remain unified. In a speech, the General Secretary of the Chinese Communist Party (CPC), Jiang Zemin (see *Beijing Review*, Vol. 40, No. 34, Aug. 25-31 1997) confirmed the continuity of socialist policy in his country, referring to a new stage in the development of Marxism in China: 'Deng's theory on building socialism with Chinese characteristics, a synthesis combining Marxism with China's practice and characteristics of the epoch has inherited and developed Mao Zedong thought under new historical conditions.' With such flexibility and ideological pragmatism the Chinese Communist Party could escape the fate of its older Soviet counterpart.

There do not appear to be many more parts of the world in which new sovereign states are likely to emerge through the break-up of existing ones. Those that currently have independence are likely to wish to keep it and its accompanying trappings: a national flag, currency and postage stamps, a seat in the United Nations, athletic and football teams competing internationally. Since the Second World War there have however been several attempts to form trading blocs and even new federal entities (e.g. the United Arab Republic of Egypt and Syria). One of the most ambitious has been the European Union (EU), formerly the European Economic Community (EEC), then just the European Community (EC). Even after 40 years of its existence, however, the member states of the EU have only lost a small part of their sovereignty, as measured, for example, in a comparison of the size of national budgets and of contributions by each country to the EU budget, at about 3 per cent of combined national budgets, and less than 1.3 per cent of the total GDP of the EU. The EU has taken a long time to integrate to its present level in spite of the fact that all the member states are located in a relatively small area (in a world context) and have a broadly similar cultural history going back hundreds of years. It therefore seems unlikely that much progress will be made towards the formation of comparable economic unions elsewhere in the world in the next few decades.

The North American Free Trade Agreement (NAFTA), signed in 1994 by the USA, Canada and Mexico, is now under criticism in the USA, especially on the issue of whether it has helped the US economy, or has cost it jobs in manufacturing to the benefit of Mexico. Maddox (1997a) reports that there has been controversy over whether or not increased trade with Mexico both before and since the signing of NAFTA has created jobs in the USA. It seems unlikely that many Central or South American countries will want to join NAFTA in the near future or would be accepted if they applied. Political integration between the present NAFTA three is a distant prospect, the Quebec question in Canada being an added complication.

Other trading blocs in the 1990s include Mercosur in South America, ASEAN in Southeast Asia and the Economic Community of West African States (ECOWAS), none of which as yet has gone far towards EU style integration. A partial resurrection of the USSR is a possibility and indeed the Commonwealth of Independent States (CIS) is a shadow of most of the former USSR, but it is unlikely that any of the former Soviet Socialist Republics would give up their independence, in most of them easily won in 1991, for political re-integration. A grouping more on the lines of the British Commonwealth seems the maximum integration that Russia can expect.

The author's expectation is that the basic political map of the world will not change markedly by 2050 from its form in the late 1990s. Trade agreements and military alliances may come and go, and organisations on the lines of the Organisation of Petroleum Exporting Countries (OPEC) may come into being as and when particular primary products of special importance to the industrial countries are concentrated in a few developing countries (although nothing on the scale of the world oil trade is on the horizon at present).

Some outlandish changes in international relations in the next few decades cannot, however, be ruled out. The implications of a reduction in inspection by customs services at borders are discussed by Snape (1997): 'The reforms - being undertaken jointly by the World Customs Organisation (WCO), the World Trade Organisation (WTO) and the United Nations Conference on Trade and Development (UNCTAD) - are to make customs clearance a formality, so eliminating delays at borders that can in some countries run into weeks.' Many developing countries obtain much of their government revenue from import and export duties, and could lose out if their control on these is weakened.

The economist W. Rees-Mogg (1995) argues that in the next 30 years, the cyber-economy will overtake conventional states. He foresees three outstanding changes: 'the second stage of the revolution in electronic communications, the rise of Asia and the weakening of the nation-state relative to the citizen.' In his view, other nations likely to repeat the pattern of disintegration of the Soviet Union include the European Union, Canada, China, India and even the USA. A major reason according to Rees-Mogg is that in spite of the expectation commonly held up to the 1980s that computers would strengthen centralised power: 'small nations with good natural protection against their neighbours, are most likely to adjust successfully to this new world.' England, New Zealand, Switzerland, Catalonia, British Columbia could all have bright futures.

11.4 CHANGING ECONOMIC AND IDEOLOGICAL INFLUENCES

So far in this chapter the world political situation has been the focus of attention. Now that most of the world's colonies have become independent and most sovereign states are broadly organised as market economies, world affairs in the next few decades seem likely to become more simple, allowing issues such as natural resource availability, the environment, and the development gap to receive more attention.

Since the Second World War, until the 1980s, the world economy was influenced by an ideological divide between centrally planned and market economy countries. Each type included developed and developing countries. In general, the countries with a centrally planned system aimed to achieve a higher degree of economic self-sufficiency than those with a market economy. The USSR and China were able to do this on account of their large size and wide range of natural resources and products. Smaller countries with similar command economies, including the Council for Mutual Economic Assistance (CMEA) partners of the USSR such as Poland and Romania, as well as Cuba and North Korea, were relatively more dependent on foreign trade, but traded mostly with the USSR or among themselves. Thanks to its size and its great variety of natural resources the USA has also been less dependent on foreign trade than the countries of Western Europe, with its imports valued at roughly 10 per cent of total GNP in the 1990s. The industrial countries have mostly imported primary products from the developing countries and exported manufactured goods to them, although the 'pattern' has been changing recently.

In the 1990s the former USSR and its CMEA partners have moved from centrally planned, command economies towards market economy systems. In so doing, ownership of the means of production has shifted from the state to private enterprises. In China the dominant role of the state in the economy is also being reduced, although as noted above there has been little parallel relaxation of the political control of the Communist Party.

In the traditional market economies, however, the state has a large and in some cases increasing influence. Various measures can be used to calculate the direct influence of the state in the economy. In the UK in the 1990s, for example, according to Bassett (1996) about a quarter of the employed population worked in the public sector, while according to Duncan and Hobson (1995) public spending accounts for about half of total GDP. In most other member states of the EU the public sector is even more influential, whereas in the USA, Japan and Switzerland it is less influential. There is now a spontaneous move towards convergence among the industrial countries (including the former USSR), contrasting with the polarisation into centrally planned and market economies after the Second World War.

International relations are, however, still likely to be influenced by ideological considerations. In the broadest sense, any set of beliefs about how human society and behaviour works (or fails to work), and how society should be run, can affect the policy of governments. Christian beliefs greatly influenced life in Europe and the Americas long before the 20th century. It is common for Americans to refer to the USA as 'God's country', but in Brazil 'Deus e brasileiro.' Future historians may be able to assess the extent to which the Roman Catholic Church helped to break the influence of the USSR in parts of Eastern Europe. Its policy regarding family planning has apparently been much less effective, since Italy and Spain have the lowest fertility rates of any major countries in the world. Whether by choice or by chance, many of the Islamic countries now have much higher fertility rates than most Roman Catholic countries.

The days of eye to eye confrontation between ideologies seem to be less marked than in the 1940s and 1950s, when with reference to crucial Italian elections in 1948 Stalin allegedly asked how many divisions the Pope had, while the Pope pointed out to Italian voters that God could see them cast their votes into the ballot box but Stalin could not. If Christian and Islamic leaders alike were opposed to atheist Marxism as practised in the Soviet bloc and in China, it could have been because their own influence and clientele were greatly reduced there and were often persecuted. The unacceptable face of capitalism, with its marked economic and social irregularities and inequalities, may now become a target for religious criticism.

At global level, the movement of people, goods and information between the countries of the world has never been easier for two main reasons. First, there has been considerable relaxation in some major world powers with regard to the entry and exit of passengers and of goods. Second, transport and communications are generally faster and relatively cheaper than ever before. Some countries still attempt to maintain a reclusive role in world affairs, trading as little as possible in order to keep their own identity or to shut out ideas that might breed dissidents: Myanmar (Burma), North Korea and until the late 1990s Albania. In general, however, as foreign trade becomes less restricted through recent GATT and subsequently WTO agreements, the value of world trade has grown faster than population or GDP. The break-up of the USSR overnight turned internal trade into foreign trade between the 15 newly independent states. On the other hand, trade between the member states of the EU, while still officially regarded as foreign or international, increasingly looks like internal trade. At the same time, 'unwanted' products and diseases, such as drugs and the Human Immuno-deficiency Virus (HIV), can circulate with ever greater ease between countries thanks particularly to air travel. The Chinese government hoped that AIDS could be prevented from entering the country. Its occurrence in Japan is very low, thanks to the traditional practice of making the introduction of anything foreign difficult. Japan was said to have accepted four Vietnamese boat people in the 1980s.

International trade, and the movement of capital for investment, mainly by transnational companies into countries often far from their home bases, have been features of increasing globalisation. On the other hand, restrictions on immigration have if anything been tightened in many of the countries that hitherto have accepted, if not welcomed migrants. Illegal immigration is now seen as a major problem throughout the developed world. Since the Second World War the main flows of international migration have been from poorer to richer countries. There has been speculation that the North-South divide between developed and developing regions of the world will become a new zone of conflict, which more and more people from poorer regions will attempt to cross, legally or otherwise. This already happens between Mexico and the USA, and to a lesser extent across the Mediterranean between Northwest Africa and the European Union, principally via Spain (see also Chapters 4 and 12).

One of the most difficult subjects to speculate about is the possible future role of international organisations. Even after five decades the influence of the United Nations is very restricted; its mandate usually does not allow it to interfere in internal problems of member states. Given the magnitude of the problems it is supposed to confront its budget is very small. Its success in keeping peace between many pairs of countries previously in conflict has not been given much publicity. More of the same seems to be the prospect for the next few decades, with the USA at times using its position in the Security Council to veto proposals, in the way that the USSR frequently did as recently as the 1980s. Since the USA is expected to provide 25 per cent of the UN budget it is in a position to use its financial contribution to influence the running of the organisation.

No doubt there is still scope for a psychopath to take over a country, as Hitler did with Germany, and Saddam Hussein with Iraq and, regardless of the suffering of his or her own citizens and of the economy, to send people to their deaths. Technically, the term psychopath refers to a person with a dissocial personality disorder. Such people (not all described as psychopaths) must be ruthless, with no qualms about issuing or endorsing the order to send their forces into battle, whether they be Winston Churchill in the Second World War, various US presidents during the Viet Nam War, Brezhnev and other Russian leaders in the war in Afghanistan. In the distant past the leaders accompanied and even led their forces into the conflict; now they remain at a good distance, ready if necessary to slip into nuclear-proof bunkers.

It is not easy in the 1990s to spot possible future aggressors on the lines of Hitler, but one candidate might be the Russian politician Vladimir Zhirinovsky. Frazer and Lancelle (1994) have produced an anthology of his pronouncements about what he would do if elected to the presidency of Russia. He would reconstitute and extend the Soviet Union and drastically modify the map of Central Europe - if allowed to do so. In their book on Zhirinovsky, Solovyov and Klepikova (1995) recount a story about him, an appropriately light note to conclude this grim subject: 'There is a joke about two psychotics screaming at each other in the middle of Deribasovskaya Street, Odessa's main pedestrian boulevard. "I'm Napoleon! I'm Napoleon!" one kept yelling. "I'm Zhirinovsky. I'm Zhirinovsky!" the other screamed back. Soon the police arrived and took Napoleon to a psychiatric hospital. The other, more disoriented man was released. After all, you can't arrest a man for shouting his own name.'

11.5 CHANGES IN ATTITUDE TO THE STATE OF THE WORLD

Two of the most active, prominent and in terms of publications on the future, prolific, teams of experts are Kahn and associates, and Meadows and associates. They appear to be in agreement that human activity as practised in the 20th century cannot continue much longer without dire consequences. New attitudes and approaches are urgently needed. Kahn and associates (1977) describe the prospects as follows: 'Indeed, a consensus is emerging among many scholars and journalists that a turning point has been reached in world history, one that portends either a much more disciplined and austere - even bleak - future for mankind, or a dramatic and revolutionary change in domestic and international society, or perhaps both.' Kahn and associates are only bluffing, because the above passage is followed by one in which they assure their readers that all is not lost, and that they have the answers.

At the end of a very cold, clinical, technical examination of past trends and future prospects for human activity, Meadows and associates (1992) themselves turn human to state: 'The deepest difference between optimists and pessimists is their position in the debate about whether human beings are able to operate collectively from a basis of love. In a society that systematically develops in people their individualism, their competitiveness, and their cynicism, the pessimists are in the vast majority ... The sustainability revolution will have to be, above all, a societal transformation that permits the best of human nature rather than the worst to be expressed and nurtured.' Meadows and associates are in deadly earnest. What they do not appear to consider is the possibility that the vast majority of the population of the world are neither optimists or pessimists in the above sense. They carry on with their lives with no interest in or concern about whether or not people (in general) can operate collectively from a basis of love.

The state of the world in 2050 will depend on the extent (if any) to which new attitudes replace current ones. A number of major issues and problems will be introduced in the rest of this section and are then discussed more fully in turn in sections 11.6 and 11.7. The resourceful earth has been exploited intensively in the 19th and 20th centuries and particularly in the second half of the 20th century. Resourceful *people* are needed to ensure that the even more intensive use of the earth's resources expected in the next 50 years does not destroy for good the planet on which we depend. A letter to *The Times* (Feb 18, 1989) admirably summarises the situation:

From Mr Roy Boulting

Sir, There are few in Britain, I imagine, who will not be sharing Mr Nikolai Uspensky's hopes (February 15) for the coming visit of the Soviet leader, Mr Gorbachov, to this country. I would venture to suggest, however, that the fundamental problem to be faced is not one of building "a safer and more predictable world ... worthy of the human race," but rather our need of a safer and more predictable human race worthy of the world it threatens.

If there are to be new attitudes, then they must materialise in the developed countries, where leading a full life and ensuring a high level of material consumption (the limit to what an individual or a family can have is apparently enormous) have been accepted as the norm. The eight issues discussed in the following sections are now noted. They are all interrelated, but for simplicity they are discussed separately.

In virtually all the countries of the world some kind of *economic growth* is government policy. On account of population growth, some is necessary in most countries simply to keep per capita levels the same. Only some kinds of economic growth require a large increase in the use of materials, but in general it requires the use of *natural resources*, some of which are exhaustible. The lavish use of natural resources and the development of industry have led to a view that *nature has to be conquered* and harnessed. A consequence has been the degradation of the *natural environment*, and pollution affecting human existence in many areas. The situation has been aggravated by unprecedented *population growth* in most parts of the world in the 20th century.

The wider use of technology and the growth of modern industry, mainly concentrated in certain regions of the world, have led to an increasingly unequal division of the 'cake' of production, a *development gap* of massive proportions. At the end of the 20th century the credibility of all major *ideologies* can be questioned with regard to their contribution to the above problems, even if some have claimed to provide the solution to world problems. In the last resort, views of the prospect for the world depend on *how far ahead* one looks.

The human world is unlikely to collapse in the next year or even ten years, and if it does in a hundred years time then, unless we are concerned about our descendants, why care? Arguably only a concerted effort on the part of some international institutions, with appropriate power and information, can alter the state of the world. When an undergraduate in the late 1940s, the author supported a movement for world government. The prospect of one with unlimited powers to plan the world economy and society, a latter-day Union of the World's Republics, is one unlikely to be seriously considered in view of the general reluctance of political leaders and ordinary citizens alike to renounce any of their sovereignty, or relished by those aware of the negative side of governments with too much power.

11.6   CONVENTIONAL AND ALTERNATIVE ATTITUDES TO DEVELOPMENT

Unlimited economic growth

In the developed Western market economy countries the business of achieving economic growth has proceeded during the last fifty years largely without regard for limits to growth. In the former Communist bloc a similar process occurred, encouraged by the attitude that concern over natural resource limits was a capitalist problem. In both Western Europe and Japan, however, there was awareness of their vulnerability due to dependence on other regions of the world for primary products, especially oil (crises occurred in 1956, 1967, 1973 and 1990). Even so, the general consensus in the developed regions has been that abundant natural resources are available somewhere in the world, whether in the form of new areas to be cultivated, mineral deposits at great depths, to be reached in due course, or even on other bodies in the solar system. In spite of isolated misgivings of such people as Thomas Malthus, only in the 1960s did concern about the limits to growth begin to receive wide publicity.

During the Second World War the citizens of Europe and Japan experienced varying cuts in consumption that were required for war efforts, ensured in some cases by rationing; the difference between needs and wants became evident. In the UK private motoring was greatly reduced, and such non-essential items as bananas, and films for private photography, were not available. Austerity was tolerated because conditions were expected to improve rapidly after the war. Today the majority of the population of the rich countries is unlikely to accept austerity voluntarily, either to help poor countries with more than token contributions, or to save natural resources, the environment or wildlife. No universal or even widespread changes of attitude to economic growth seems likely to occur suddenly. The economy has to be bigger each year.

Natural resources

On account of the drive for economic growth in the second half of the 20th century, natural resources have been exploited at an unprecedented rate. The 'non-renewable' natural resources, meaning mainly minerals, have formed over very long periods of time, in particular the fossil fuels. They have been extracted with no concern over the more distant future. Similarly, the land resources (arable land, forests, pastures) are being used ever more intensively. Natural resources have been used wastefully, although efficiency has increased in recent decades.

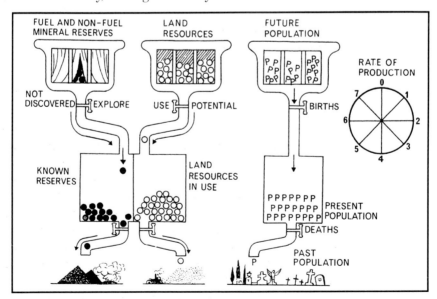

The use of exhaustible natural resources is related to the size of world population and the amount of production and consumption by its members. The clock on the right, GNP, is a meter that measures this process.

Two concepts have received much thought and publicity in recent decades: zero population growth, and sustainability. A state of zero population growth, already discussed in Chapter 4, gives the impression that once population stops growing, then the problem of limits to growth goes away. But so long as there are any people at all, consumption of goods (and services) will continue, and materials from non-renewable minerals or from the land will be needed.

Sustainability (see Meadows *et al.*, (1992)) is a more difficult concept to tie down and even more so, to apply. The implication is that humans should arrive at a type of economy that can go on indefinitely. Bioclimatic resources should not be depleted or overworked. Energy from non-renewable resources should be replaced by energy from renewable ones. As far as possible, materials should be recycled, a process not difficult to apply to newspapers and old cars, but difficult if not impossible to apply to reinforced concrete structures and chemical fertilisers. Elliott, J.A. (1994) quotes a number of different definitions of sustainable development, none of which is honest enough to admit that the two words are contradictory.

Some progress could be made towards sustainability if attention focuses more clearly on the intensity of material use of different products. For example, public passenger transport vehicles use less fuel per passenger-kilometre travelled than private cars, provided the public vehicles are reasonably full and the cars they replace only carry one or two passengers. More relevant, perhaps, is the question constantly asked in Britain in the Second World War: 'Is your journey really necessary?' Newspapers use more materials than news presented on television screens or information on personal computers. Pharmaceutical products and photography are less materially intensive than motor racing or air travel. A vegetarian diet uses less agricultural produce than one based heavily on meat and dairy products. A small dwelling uses less materials to build and less energy to run than a large one. A small car covers twice as many miles as a large one for the same amount of fuel. As long as people are consuming goods, complete sustainability is impossible, although 'virtual sustainability' might be achieved ('virtual' here meaning 'close to' rather than 'imaginary').

Arguably, only the simplest of economies and societies are completely sustainable, if only because they would die out if they overuse the resources that provide products from hunting, fishing and gathering fruits, roots and nuts. The relics of such societies are still found in a few parts of the world, beleaguered by modern progress.

The conquest of nature

This has been a popular theme over the centuries. The establishment of irrigation systems thousands of years ago already illustrates the capability of growing crops in places where rain (or lack of rain) itself would not permit. In the 19th century, much publicity was given in North America, and on a smaller scale in Australia, to the pioneers who pushed forward the frontiers of settlement, albeit at the expense of the sparse indigenous population. In the Soviet Union a similar attitude was encouraged as industry, hydro-electric stations and new agricultural lands were established in Siberia. Under socialism, it was claimed, climate itself could be changed favourably by the planting of trees in dry areas. For Christians there appear to be mandates in certain parts of the Bible and Apocrypha (e.g. Genesis, Esdras) given to humans to use as they wish the resources of the land and its flora and fauna.

In the 20th century, encroachment on the natural environment has proceeded fast, with the increasing destruction of natural vegetation and the elimination of some wild animal species. Dams, quarries, and transport links destroy or break up areas in which the natural environment has largely remained intact. People continue the conquest of nature without considering that as predators they violate the principle that they should not destroy their life support, as has happened with over-fishing in some areas. The question as to whether humans are apart from nature or a part of nature deserves more thought. But achieving harmony with the natural world in the next century would require changes of attitude, policy and lifestyle, far beyond any sacrifices most people seemed prepared to contemplate in the 1990s. If humans cannot live in harmony with each other, how can they be expected to live in harmony with nature and the environment? The idea that other species of plants and animals have an equal 'right' to a place in the world usually causes amusement, embarrassment or hostility.

The natural environment

There is much evidence to show how in various ways humans are destroying or modifying the natural environment. Some changes have not been proved conclusively; these include: the damage to forests attributed to acid rain, mainly from the burning of fossil fuels, and the extent, if any, to which global warming might change local climates and world sea level. Environmental damage and pollution that can be seen, such as forest being burned or trees felled with chain saws, and smoke from burning low grade coal, seem more likely to attract public attention and the implementation of measures to prevent such practices than invisible pollutants such as nuclear fallout. Nevertheless, quick action to reduce or prevent further growth of the holes in the ozone layer, and the successful eradication of smallpox, are examples of what can be done.

The general attitude to the degradation of the environment in the second half of the 20th century has been either to ignore problems completely or to recommend measures that may be commendable, but are limited in their impact. 'Drops in the ocean' seems an appropriate description of many attempts to save resources and limit pollution. For example, in the mid-1990s it was proposed that emissions of carbon dioxide in the European Union should be cut by 10 per cent within a decade. Over the next 50 years, such a cut would 'buy' five years of time. In some hotels in the USA guests staying more than one night are asked if they are willing to use towels and sheets again rather than having them replaced each night. Probably 90 per cent of the rural population in developing countries do not even own towels or sheets at all. In a chain of retail outlets in the UK, shoppers were asked if, to save the environment, they would mind forgoing plastic bags for their purchases. A notice in the bathroom of a hotel in Greece reminded clients that 'Greece is going dry' and urged them to use water sparingly. Small beginnings? Or do such well intended sacrifices, while helping to soothe the consciences of concerned environmentalists, simply emphasise the lack of appreciation of the scale of natural resource and environmental problems? By comparison, against the nightmare of where to dispose of nuclear waste from military and civilian sources alike, the positive achievement of saving minute quantities of energy, water and raw materials pales into insignificance.

Population growth

For at least several decades now there have been two opposing views with regard to the size of the world's population: it is *not* a problem and it *is* a problem. Those who assert that it is *not* a problem do not usually attempt to put an upper limit to the world population, although in theory a population could grow to such an extent that there would only be room for people to stand (see Figure 11.3).

Figure 11.3 'You see. Already in 1966 a writer had predicted that our generation was not going to have more than one square metre for every ten persons.' Source: *El Correo*, UNESCO, February 1967 (Año XX) p. 11. Drawn by H. Martin in *Saturday Review*

Those who consider that population growth *is* a problem are more concerned about achieving zero growth than about how many people, at what levels of consumption, the earth could support sustainably. What in short is the carrying capacity? World population in the 1990s can be likened to an area of livestock farming in which some farms have relatively few animals in relation to the fodder available, others obtain some fodder from other farms, and still others are carrying far more animals than they can realistically support (see Figure 11.4). Without taking the analogy too far, it can be shown, for example, that if the natural resource to population balance of Australia was considered desirable worldwide, the population of the world would have to be around 500 million rather than 6 billion. How such a total could be achieved defies the imagination. On the other hand, with the present natural resource to population balance of India or China the world population would be around 20 billion rather than 6 billion. These estimates illustrate the difficulty of determining a satisfactory population size for the world, let alone an optimum one. Overpopulation is a difficult term to define objectively.

In the 20th century the attitude to population size has varied from country to country and ideology to ideology. The idea that population growth is not a problem or indeed that it is an advantage has been expressed at various times in the 20th century, as in interwar (Nazi) Germany, (Fascist) Italy, and the Soviet Union. It is claimed that one president of Mexico, himself the father of (at least) eight children, advocated large families in his country so that it could in due course overtake the neighbouring USA in population size. In the first two decades of Communist rule in China, population growth was regarded as desirable and even in the 1970s the official view was that overpopulation was a 'capitalist' problem. Officially the Roman Catholic Church does not permit its members to practice birth control with the help of contraceptives, while Islamic countries of North Africa and Southwest Asia have some of the fastest rates of population growth in the world. One thing is certain, overpopulation at local and even regional level has little to do with density of population.

The opposite view has also been widely expressed in the 20th century. For example, early in the 20th century the US agronomist Showalter expressed concern about the world food supply for a population little more that a quarter what it is now (see Chapter 5). Numerous publications of the United Nations, the Food and Agriculture Organisation, and the Population Reference Bureau, have underlined the need to keep population size and food supply in balance. Attempts have been made in India to encourage people to have smaller families while in China the initial pro-natalist policy of the Communists was reversed in the 1970s. In many other developing countries some family planning measures have reached rural as well as urban areas.

The population of the world will probably reach about 10 billion in the year 2050 if little or nothing more is done in the developing world to encourage family planning, or about 9 billion if coercion, incentives and the growing proportion of the population living in cities reduce total fertility rates. A population of 10 billion will be assumed as the basis for the picture of the world in 2050 to be outlined in Chapter 12. The last United Nations projections of world population, published in 1998, give, for 2050, a High one of 10.7 billion, a Medium one of 8.9 billion and a Low one of 7.3 billion (see Gelbard *et al.* (1999))

11.7   FURTHER CHANGES IN ATTITUDE

The development gap

Whatever economic and social criteria are chosen, a large gap is evident between the extremes of rich and poor countries (see Chapter 9). It is more difficult to demonstrate whether or not happiness correlates with wealth. Indeed in a thought-provoking if semi-spoof article, Norman (1975) found that in spite of their very low GDP per inhabitant compared with that of Britain, on appropriate criteria there was little to choose between Botswana and Britain with regard to satisfaction with life. The attitude that the poor are just as happy as the rich and that the citizens of poor countries should not have to go through the experience of industrialising and living in a stressful environment can easily be misinterpreted. It could appear that the rich fear that if everyone had their lifestyle, with its high consumption of material things, there would be less available for the rich themselves, which indeed could be the case.

Ideologies

Whether or not the poor should be helped is not entirely an academic question. If the present dire poverty of somewhere between a tenth and a fifth of the population of the world is to be reduced, at least to provide a basic minimum lifestyle, a much larger amount of development assistance will have to be provided by the rich countries than is provided at present. The opposing views each have supporters. The view that one *should not* encourage beggars by giving anything to them is in tune with the idea that people should help themselves; two centuries ago Samuel Smiles wrote *Self-Help*. Much more recently, in the 1980s US politicians cut development assistance to poor countries; in the early 1990s much of the USA's modest overseas development assistance went to Egypt and Israel, neither desperately poor countries. Only a few small developed countries still devote around 1 per cent of their GNP to development assistance, notably the Netherlands and the countries of Scandinavia (see Chapter 9).

The opposing view, that the rich *should* help the poor, is frequently expressed by individuals, institutions, or ideologies that are not in a position to provide much funding themselves. Helping the poor is regarded as a positive action in most Christian sects; Socialist and Communist parties have also expressed such a view. In developed market economy countries, in addition to or even instead of the altruistic, moral, view that the poor should be helped, it has been argued that it is in the longer term interest of the rich countries themselves to help to expand the economy and the market in developing countries, thereby increasing trade to their own advantage while also discouraging people from trying to emigrate to developed regions.

In the view of the author the one-way flow of resources to poor countries from rich ones, as opposed to actual trade between such countries, will if anything be relatively less than it was two or three decades ago. People will continue to be reluctant to give money away to help the poor, while the rich countries will account for a much smaller part of total world population in the next century than in the decades after the Second World War. The naval expression 'I'm alright Jack' seems to sum up the future attitude of the rich countries, at least until they are demographically or militarily threatened to such an extent that they will have to act.

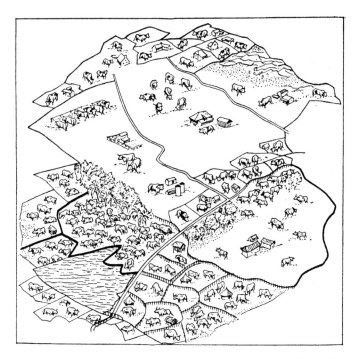

Figure 11.4 The farms pictured above are like the world. Population is very badly allocated according to the natural resources and fodder available.

How far ahead should we look?

If problems are to be avoided in the next century it is crucial that national economies are not run on a day-to-day basis, but that a longer term view should be taken. The world after 2050 will be considered in Chapter 12. Here it may be noted that in most countries with democratically elected governments and more than one political party, minds are concentrated on what to do to be re-elected at the next election. On the other hand, in the second half of the 20th century, in countries with centrally planned economies, while five-year plans usually formed the basis of policy implementation, longer term goals were set, such as catching up in some respect with a capitalist/market economy country. In some other countries still longer term goals have been set, as for example in Malaysia, to become developed by 2020, and China by 2050. Such goals are made on the assumption that there will not be a change of government that would itself change policy with regard to such distant goals.

There is not a mechanism in the world as a whole for overseeing all aspirations and assessing if long-term goals are compatible. In attempting to create a picture of the world in 2050 it is assumed that there will be more of the same. Globalisation may continue and indeed transactions and interactions between places anywhere in the world (except in a few reclusive countries) may grow, but there will not be an institution at which states will renounce much of their sovereignty. Like large companies in market economy countries, which get taken over in mergers, demerge, collapse and absorb small companies, there will be further changes in the political map, for example, the transfer of Hong Kong to China in 1997 and the proposed expansion of the European Union early in the 21st century. No other group of countries seem likely to integrate to such an extent, but associations of countries in the Americas, Africa and Southeast Asia, will also develop. For different reasons, as noted earlier in this Chapter, China and Canada seem to be the countries most likely to lose cohesion.

The similarity of world affairs to an informal, but very complex game, with loose rules and numerous players, has often been noted. Two distinct sets of players may distinguished:

1. Governments and institutions that manage *territorially* defined areas, whether sovereign states (the most influential at present), subdivisions of these (major administrative divisions), or groups of states at supranational level (e.g. the European Union) or global level (e.g. the United Nations). The direct influence and role of the state on the lives of citizens varies considerably among the countries of the world.

2. *Non-territorial* enterprises and institutions, including transnational companies and religions operating in many countries, usually with the headquarters in one country.

What changes can be expected in the next fifty years in territorially based entities?

- The number and relative size of the more influential countries in world affairs seems more likely to change gradually than abruptly, as the share of the world's population and industrial output shifts potential power from the present developed countries to the developing ones.

- There is no obvious reason why any of the most influential countries should break up on the lines of the former USSR (but ten years ago few would have predicted its break-up). China seems most at risk.

- Democracy as understood in the USA and the EU is new and is not fully established in many countries of the world.

- The market economy seems likely to prevail in most countries, whether or not democracy is effectively practised and human rights respected.

How are non-territorial entities likely to perform in the next fifty years?

- The influence of transnational companies has grown in absolute terms in the last fifty years, with the emergence of some with a turnover equivalent to that of small countries. Such companies 'behave' as predators (not unlike states in time of war), taking other companies over, merging, demerging, collapsing. Many of the present companies are likely to be around in 2050.

• In spite of a relative reduction in the influence of religious institutions in some countries, and the virtual absence of formal religion in secular China, religions have maintained considerable influence in the 1990s, their survival and possible expansion depending to some extent on a readiness to change with the times. Christianity and Islam are the dominant religions in the largest number of countries, Buddhism is more localised, while Hinduism is almost entirely confined to India. More of the same seems to be the most likely prospect.

Are military conflicts likely to continue on the level experienced in the decades following the Second World War? Regional conflicts yes, as long as enough ruthless national leaders with enough followers can coerce their citizens into combat, or enough such people within countries can run campaigns against their own governments or adversaries. Whether the bullies of the world behave as they do through their genes or the environment in which they have grown up is of little relevance to their victims. A century ago it was hoped by some that humans were evolving into more considerate, caring creatures and the good guys would prevail. That idea was shattered in the two World Wars and the disillusionment perpetuated by events in numerous countries, not least Korea, Viet Nam, Iraq, Iran, Angola, Afghanistan, Burundi and Rwanda, Yugoslavia and Algeria. Where will the next serious conflict take place?

One zone of global proportions seems likely to experience various diplomatic if not military conflicts over the years. Figure 12.10 shows a discontinuous interface between the developed ('north') and developing ('south') regions and countries of the world. South–North migration, already considerable in some places, whether successful or not, is likely to increase in the next few decades. The impact of such a confrontation might be reduced if the developed regions adopted adjoining or nearby developing ones to provide assistance: North America to Latin America, Europe to Africa, Russia to India, Japan to Southeast Asia.

12

TO 2050 AND BEYOND

'Mephistophilis: Now, Faustus, what wouldst thou have me do?
Faustus: I charge thee wait upon me whilst I live,
To do whatever Faustus shall command,
Be it to make the moon drop from her sphere
Or the ocean to overwhelm the world'

Christopher Marlowe, about 1592

12.1   1950-2000-2050: PERFORMANCE AND PROSPECTS

In his book *Der Untergang des Abendlandes* (*The Decline of the West*), published in 1918, Oswald Spengler (1880-1936) referred to the soul of Western culture as Faustian. The state of the world at the end of the 20th century has been likened to the predicament of Dr Faustus. In the play *The Tragical History of Dr Faustus* (about 1592) by Christopher Marlowe (1564-1593), the hero sells his soul to Mephistophilis in exchange for unlimited powers for twenty-four years. His last fling is to ask for the beautiful Helen of Troy. Analogies are only useful within limits, and it is not implied that the remarkable scientific discoveries and technological applications of the last three centuries in Europe and North America have been achieved with the help of the devil. Nevertheless, humans consider themselves capable of all kinds of further achievements, assuming the availability of unlimited resources well into the future, not concerned that their deal with the natural world may run out one day. Could it be that the western attitude towards nature has been influenced by the apparent mandate in Genesis 1: 28 given to humans: 'And God blessed them, and God said unto them, Be fruitful, and multiply, and replenish the earth, and subdue it: and have dominion over the fish of the sea, and over the fowl of the air, and over every living thing that moveth upon the earth.'?

The aspirations of Marlowe's Dr Faustus expressed in the quotation at the head of the chapter and again below were fantasy four hundred years ago. It is not intended to argue that Marlowe was being prophetic in anticipating rising sea level or aircraft, but to draw a parallel with the present.

'Had I as many souls as there be stars,
I'd give them all for Mephistophilis.
By him I'll be great emperor of the world,
And make a bridge through the moving air,
To pass the ocean with a band of men ...'

What would Westerners ask of Mephistophilis now? Enough food to feed the population of the world? An end to all forms of conflict? Doubtful. Give us the means to take us to the nearest habitable planet outside our own solar system? Time travel? Immortality? The last is a possible request, but read first in *Gulliver's Travels* about the distressed state of the *Struldbruggs* or *Immortals* who were unable to depart from this life.

In looking ahead, whether over a few days, a few weeks or, more pertinently here, several decades, the forecaster is likely to be influenced by what she or he wants to happen. It may be in the hope of being right, of winning a prize, or because some future situation would be desirable. It is very difficult to weigh up impartially all the various possible prospects and alternative futures. Under these circumstances the author disclaims any pretence that his picture of the world in 2050, sketched in sections 12.3-12.7, is anything more than a reasonably possible future, one of many, but worth examining by the reader in relation to his or her own hopes and expectations. This picture of the world in 2050 is the result of a combination of approaches: a consideration of what has happened (and not happened) during 1945-2000, an appraisal of attitudes to the future prevalent during that period, and the effect of possible changes in attitude during 2000-2050, already discussed in Chapter 11.

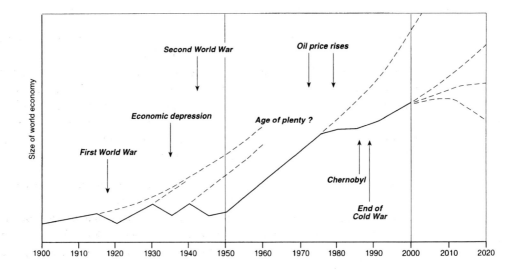

Figure 12.1 A bumpy ride through the 20th century for the world economy. Broken lines show projections that might have been made on the eve of the World Wars, the Depression and the oil price rises. Where, then, will it go after the year 2000?

Figure 12.1 shows a very general picture of economic growth and development in the 20th century (see also the graph of Italian steel production in this century in Figure 3.8). At world level, four events have dented the otherwise comparatively smooth growth curve of production of goods and services: the First World War, the Wall Street Crash and ensuing depression, the Second World War, and the oil price rises of the 1970s. In 2000 one can look back at what actually happened and compare it with other possible paths through the last decades of the 20th century. Four of a number of mutually exclusive prospects are:

- Seen in the 1960s, the curve could have been expected to continue smoothly, riding over the subsequent irregularities, continuing to grow at a regular rate.

- It could have begun to level out after picking up after 1975.

- It could continue the post–1970s trend.

- A third world war could devastate much of the world economy, with subsequent recovery as after the previous world wars or an ongoing downward trend.

With hindsight it is interesting to compare what the author felt about the prospects for the world in the late 1940s. At the age of 16 in 1945, when the Second World War ended, even as near ahead as 1955 seemed to him a long way off. What he expected or hoped for in his lifetime (say to the year 2000) was based on the popular expectations of the time in the industrial countries. These included the following prospects:

- The age of plenty lay ahead. It would only be a matter of time before the inevitable development process would enable the poor regions of the world to catch up with the rich ones. But would the rich ones be standing still during the catching up? The general view, supported by a mass of evidence, some given in Chapter 9, is that the gap between rich and poor regions of the world has in many respects widened between 1945 and 1995.

- There would be peace. The United Nations and the victorious great powers could ensure that no rogue dictatorship could again threaten world peace. This turned out to be wrong. The United Nations has been unable to stop regional conflicts. Perhaps the development of nuclear weapons could be given some of the credit for deterring the outbreak of a war between the superpowers. Smaller countries, mainly of the developing world, served as battlegrounds for the ongoing struggle between the USA and USSR, places where among other things new weapons (non-nuclear) could be tested. Mass destruction occurred in several, notably Korea, Viet Nam and Cambodia, Angola, Afghanistan.

- An all-out nuclear war was a distinct prospect. Despite the Cold War, this also turned out to be wrong. It never occurred, although the weaponry is still available for use and an accident or a dramatic change in attitude *could* set the USA and Russia against each other. Alternatively, secondary powers such as Iran, Iraq or one of the former Soviet Republics in Central Asia could acquire nuclear weapons with limited range and damage capability and the means to fire them some distance.

- There would never be a shortage of energy. In August 1945, after the dropping of nuclear bombs on Japan, scientists in their thousands speculated about a superabundance of energy from nuclear power. A liner the size of the Queen Mary could, it was said, cross the Atlantic on an amount of nuclear material that would fit into a matchbox. Things were not that simple. In the 1990s the nuclear power industry in the world was in disarray, while the discovery of new oil reserves has only kept up with production in the 1990s. Extraction at present rates of production would last less than 50 years if no new oil is discovered (see Chapter 6); it is possible that some will be, but how much? The burning of all kinds of fossil fuel is however a threat to the environment.

The above examples show how incorrect many of the expectations of the future held in the late 1940s have turned out to be. There were, nevertheless, worse prospects for the future, at least from the point of view of the actual victors of the Second World War. For example, if during the Second World War Germany had developed an effective atom bomb before the USA did, the Nazis would have had no qualms about dropping one or two to help their war effort, London being one of the prime targets, Moscow another; they could not have got near enough to the

USA to target it except from a submarine. Germany could then have imposed a *modus vivendi* in which it controlled Europe and Africa, leaving Japan to retain its existing conquests in Southeast Asia and to add India and Australia. The USA could have been neutered and left to itself, prevented under threat of nuclear attack from developing nuclear weapons itself, and Russia would have developed Siberia for the use of Germany and Japan.

What has happened between 1945 and 2000 is not a sudden catastrophe and the sinking of the human 'ship' with all on board, the prospect following an all out nuclear war and the subsequent 'nuclear winter,' or the impact of a large meteorite. What is happening is more like the plight of the *Titanic*, into which water is leaking from a proliferation of holes and cracks on one side of the hull. The evidence discussed in Chapters 5-9 shows that in many of the sectors used to illustrate economic growth in the second half of the 20th century, the per capita output or availability was passed before 1990 (see upper part of Table 12.1). Other sectors were still increasing in per capita output up to the last year considered, 1990: these are shown in the second part of Table 12.1. Here are proposed dates at which the per capita peak may be reached in the future in those for which the highest level per capita so far was reached in 1990. The sectors and products listed in Table 12.1 all represent material production. In the late decades of the 20th century, GDP has grown mainly thanks to the growth of the service sector, especially in the developed countries. People cannot eat, be clothed or drive their cars with the products of the service sector.

Table 12.1 Summary of per capita change 1950-1990, 1990 in relation to 1950

	Total in 1990	*Per capita in 1990*	*Per capita peak year*
		1950=100	
Peaked before 1990			
Arable area	111	52	1950
Forest area	103	49	1950
Pasture area	142	67	1950
Cereals area	117	55	1950
Livestock units	184	87	1950
Roundwood	232	110	1975
Copper	365	174	1975
Pig iron	409	194	1975
Cars produced	418	199	1975
Oil	607	268	1975
Cereals	287	127	1985
Tractors in use	431	204	1985
	Total in 1990	*Per capita in 1990*	*Future possible per capita peak year*
		1950=100	
Highest level in 1990			
Cotton	237	113	2000
Fish catch	456	216	2000
Fertilisers	1,171	559	2000
HEP	636	303	2010
Coal	240	114	2020
Total electricity	1,218	579	2020
Aluminium	1,584	749	2020
Cement	810	384	2030

The results of the survey of major sectors of production are disappointing, quite apart from the very uneven way in which the production and consumption of goods (rather than services) are distributed globally. Even assuming that there is little change in the next few decades in the level of material consumption in the present developed countries, the population of the developing areas seems likely to double between 1990 and 2050, with, therefore, a doubling of consumption of material products needed just to maintain the current level. The aspirations of the leaders of some developing countries to catch up with the developed ones would require great changes. For example, a goal set by the leaders of Malaysia is for their country to become 'modern developed' by 2020. According to Dong Yuguo (1991) the goal of Chinese leaders is to make their country 'moderately developed' by 2030-2050, which would have a much greater impact on the world economy than the graduation of a few smaller developing countries such as Malaysia and South Korea to developed status. To reach the level achieved by Spain in the 1990s, China's expected population of around 1.6 billion in 2050 would have to consume about seven times as much then as was consumed in the 1990s, some on account of the increase in population, most to raise the real GDP per capita six times. To achieve, in 2050, the level of cars in use (in relation to population) to one similar to that in Spain in the early 1990s (330 cars per thousand people), China would have to have over 500 million cars in use, almost three times the present US total.

12.2   THE ELEMENTS OF MODERN DEVELOPMENT

In Chapters 5-8 alternative futures were mapped out for a number of the elements that are basic to human activities; those major elements form the centre of *clusters* of interrelated variables (see Figure 12.2). The production of food, for example, is related to bioclimatic resources, including pastures and forests (soil, climate), means of production (fertilisers and agricultural machinery), labour and management. Energy supply is related at present mainly to the production and distribution of fossil fuels, and to the generation of electricity from these and from nuclear and hydro-electric power. Energy is associated with the bioclimatic resources cluster since fuelwood is a source of mainly non-commercial energy. In this section clusters of variables are examined in turn and prospects for 2050 are noted. A number of initial assumptions must be discussed before the clusters are considered.

It is assumed that the population of the world will be around 10 billion in 2050. Very probably it will not be less than 9 billion unless drastic measures are applied globally to curtail population growth, and not more than 11 billion unless the almost worldwide gradual reduction of fertility rates observed in the last 2-3 decades is reversed in many developing countries.

It is assumed that there will not have been any major catastrophes, natural or man-made, before 2050. In particular, there will be no radical changes in the effect of the sun on the earth and the internal forces that cause the movement of tectonic plates and the occurrence of volcanoes and earthquakes. It is also assumed that there will not be a 'Third World War' ending in a nuclear conflagration and ensuing 'nuclear winter'. Psychopaths on the lines of Hitler, prepared to attack other countries, may come to power in smaller countries, but not in any of the major world powers.

Finally (see Chapter 11), it is assumed that the world political map will be broadly the same in 2050 as in 2000. By 2050, however, there will be many more people in most developing countries than in the 1990s but little change of population size in most of the developed countries of today.

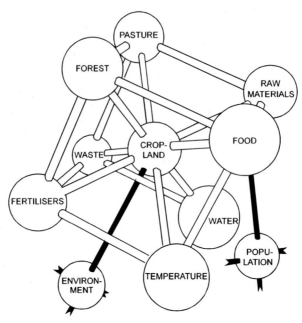

Figure 12.2a A cluster of closely related elements. Cropland is placed in the centre here in view of its importance for the production of food and raw materials. It is related to all the other aspects shown in the diagram. Links to two other clusters are also shown (darker).

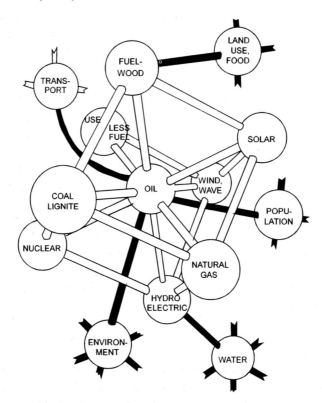

Figure 12.2b Oil is placed at the centre of the cluster of energy elements in view of its present prominent position in world energy. Each of the nine elements can be linked, although not all the links have been drawn on the diagram. As in Figure 12.2a, links (darker) are shown with other clusters, themselves all potentially linked.

Water (see Chapter 5, Section 2 and Figure 12.2a).

Fresh water itself is finite in quantity but is a renewable resource. Two basic problems affect water supply. First, the location of some of the main sources of fresh water in the world does not now coincide conveniently with the location of large concentrations of population, notwithstanding the fact that two centuries ago population was mainly agricultural, and the location of agricultural land was closely related to the availability of water, among other factors. By 2050 much larger concentrations of urban population can be expected in developing countries than exist now. Second, while water is a renewable natural resource, water transfers that are not carried out through gravity (mainly in rivers) require energy for pumping, much of it supplied directly or indirectly (as electricity) from fossil fuels, themselves non-renewable.

As with other infrastructure projects, the poorer countries of the world are not as well provided as the industrial countries to increase transfers of water. In 2050 the greatest water supply problems are likely to be in northern Africa, Southwest Asia, India and China. In contrast to famines and food supply, water shortages cannot easily be dealt with by emergency transfers, given the high cost of moving enough water to make an impact. Hutchings (1997) refers to a description of water scarcity as the 'sleeping tiger' of the world's environmental problems.

Cropland (see Figure 12.2a)

Only about 11 per cent of the world's land area is currently under field or permanent (tree and bush) crops. Some reduction in the existing area of cropland can be expected as the built-up area encroaches on it or as soil is eroded or affected by salinisation. On the other hand, some existing areas of forest and permanent pasture could be turned into cropland, depending on improvements through irrigation, drainage and other reclamation measures. Most of such land would not be naturally as highly productive as, for example, existing cultivated areas of blackearth, volcanic, alluvial and other naturally fertile soils in various parts of the world. It would be unreasonable to expect more than 12-13 per cent of the world's land to be under cultivation in 2050. By then there would be several times as much cropland per capita in developed as in developing countries (see Chapter 5).

It is frequently pointed out that world grain production in particular, and food supply in general, have increased more quickly since the Second World War than population. Smil (1997) attributes this achievement above all to the great increase in the use of nitrogenous fertilisers. In recent decades it has often been possible to assist people in areas afflicted by famine on account of droughts or conflicts, but not to maintain a constant supply of food to large populations with problems of malnutrition through insufficient food and poor diets. One estimate of the total number of malnourished people in the world in 1990-1992 (see Bender and Smith (1997a)) is 840 million, about 20 per cent of the total population of the developing regions, including 180 million underweight children.

Whether or not famines could be overcome through appropriate political action or agreements, they have still occurred in the 1990s, notably in North Korea, Sudan and the eastern part of the Congo (formerly Zaire). Adams (1997b) reports that there is evidence from satellite images and Chinese visitors of mass starvation in North Korea, reminiscent of famines in, for example, North China in 1877-1878 and in Morocco in 1878: 'Chinese traders have told stories that are impossible to confirm about women selling their children for food; of soldiers shooting farmers for a potato; and of men even killing their own families to eat their flesh.' In North

Korea the troubles started when rice crops failed through heavy flooding. In the Congo they have been caused by tribal conflicts (see e.g. Swain (1997)). Since the 1960s various regions in Ethiopia have been afflicted as a result of the combination of droughts and civil war. In 1973 the author visited villages in Ethiopia not on the road network: the only way food aid could be delivered to such places is by aircraft or helicopter, but at great cost.

In 2050 there will probably be almost twice as many people in developing countries as in the 1990s. Even if there are fewer conflicts, there are more people to feed, probably on roughly the same amount of land, so there is scope for further famines over the next few decades. The reader may think of reasons why the next 50 years should be different from the last 50. When you are starving to death it hardly matters whether the cause is natural or man-made. However, what about cropland *after* 2050? In Figure 12.3a projections in Figure 5.1 have been extended to 2100.

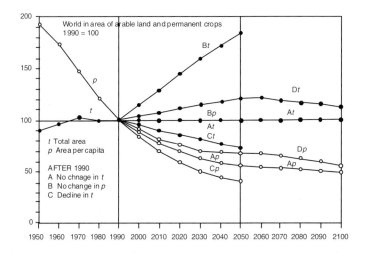

Figure 12.3a Projections for world cropland to 2050 in Figure 5.1 are extended to 2100. The total population of the world may increase from 9-10 billion in 2050 to 11-12 billion in 2100. Projection D*t* shows a plausible future, in which between 1990 and 2050 there is an increase in the area of cropland (mainly at the expense of forest), which cannot however be sustained after 2050. The area of cropland per inhabitant declines inexorably (see D*p*).

Energy (see Figure 12.2b)

In the 1990s oil was the largest single source of energy in the world, providing 40 per cent of all commercial energy consumed, compared with 27 per cent from coal and 23 per cent from natural gas. It is the largest single item in international trade. Oil is cheaper to transport than coal and more versatile in its applications than coal or natural gas. In view of its key position in world energy consumption the fact that new discoveries in the 1990s have only kept pace with consumption (see Chapter 6) is cause for concern, particularly on account of the expected growth of motor vehicles in use in many developing countries. In public there seems to be little concern over the prospects for the oil industry, but behind the scenes oil companies, whether state or private, cannot ignore the implications. Examples were given in Chapters 1 and 6 of forecasts for the oil industry. In Figure 12.3b the projections in Figure 6.2 have been continued to 2100.

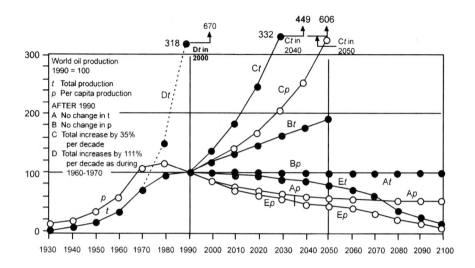

Figure 12.3b Projections for world oil production to 2050 in Figure 6.2 are extended to 2100. Projection A*t* shows what happens if the total 1990 production remains unchanged, a highly unlikely future since it would require about four times as much oil to be extracted between 2000 and 2100 as was extracted between 1930 and 1990. Even then, per capita production (A*p*) would gradually decline. E*t* is a more plausible future, characterised by a slow, dignified exit around 2100. Oil can be extracted from tar sands, shales and coal, but the cost seems likely to be high and pollution a problem.

There is a basic difference between the consumption of food and the use of energy. Although some people in the world consume more food than they actually need and many do not get enough, everyone needs broadly the same amount. In contrast, the basic needs of cooking, domestic heating, industrial processes, travel and other uses of energy vary greatly around the world, and much slack could be taken up by reducing consumption without life-threatening results. The energy situation in 2050 is therefore much more difficult to anticipate than the food situation, but on account of the limited scale of oil and natural gas reserves and the now widely assumed threat to the natural environment of burning fossil fuels, alternative sources will have to be developed quickly if the per capital level of consumption of energy in the world in the 1990s is to be maintained in the next few decades, let alone increased.

Figure 12.4 shows the growth of consumption of nuclear energy from 1970 to 1995. In spite of the setback of Chernobyl in 1986, the growth of capacity has continued into the mid-1990s, but after the first thirty years of the life of the industry almost all of the generating capacity is still located in the industrial regions, the respective shares of which in 1995 were as follows: Europe 38, North America 35, Japan 12, former USSR 8, leaving a mere 7 per cent in the rest of the world, over half of it in South Korea and Taiwan, themselves highly industrialised (and energy deficient) countries.

Alternative sources of energy were described in Chapter 6. Their contributions are minute at present, and on the earlier experience of the development of current sources of energy, could need several decades of development before they make a major contribution. There remains the prospect of reducing energy consumption, especially in the industrial countries, and of continuing the development of technology to use energy more efficiently.

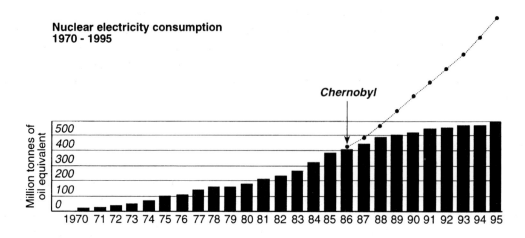

Nuclear electricity consumption 1970 - 1995

Figure 12.4 A future for nuclear power? The broken line shows how the consumption trend from 1970 to 1985 might have been projected just before the Chernobyl disaster. New nuclear power stations are going into production in the late 1990s but in a decade or two, the loss of capacity through de-commissioning could mean a net loss of capacity. Another disaster on the lines of Chernobyl, whether through human error, equipment failure or a natural hazard such as an earthquake could persuade more countries to give up nuclear power.

Materials

In comparison with food and energy, there is a much greater variety of products and uses of materials, derived from plants, animals and minerals. There is some existing 'competition' with food and forestry production for agricultural products and timber, and with energy for fossil fuels. The production to reserves ratio of a number of key minerals was given in Chapter 7. The short life expectancy of some minerals has already received the attention of various researchers, including Meadows *et al.* (1972), as they debated the limits to growth theme in the 1970s.

In the 1990s concern over water supply, food, energy and the environment appears to be more widespread than concern over non-fuel minerals. Many parts of the world's land surface have only been explored superficially for minerals, while the oceans and sea bed remain to be prospected systematically. One obstacle to future mineral exploration in some parts of the world, as for example in Australia and Canada, is the presence of protected areas, whether on account of indigenous populations or of nature reserves, or both (see e.g. Manners (1981)). The future for materials in the next few decades is more difficult to anticipate than that for food production. Some minerals may be nearing exhaustion by 2050 but there is great scope for substitution, more flexibility than in energy production, good prospects for recycling many materials, and continuing prospects for greater efficiency, as noted in Chapter 7.

Manufacturing

Many branches of manufacturing have expanded enormously between 1945 and the mid-1990s, production techniques have changed, with labour saving devices, automation and greater flexibility in the range of finished products. Trends such as these seem likely to continue, with great emphasis on using energy and materials as sparingly as possible. If, however, in the next half century the developing countries are to move towards present levels of industrial production in the developed countries they will have to expand greatly the production of metals, cement (see Chapter 7) and other items of heavy industry before achieving the level of sophistication of production in Japan, the USA and the EU.

Social issues

In the developed countries, many of the features that improve the quality of life and sustain it at a high level do not reach the comparatively few poor. The situation is reversed in developing countries, where many of the products and services taken for granted in the developed countries are available only to the few. Whether adequate water supply, healthcare facilities or domestic appliances are considered, most of the population of developing countries is inadequately provided for. For example, heart surgery, organ transplants and high powered medicines, the latest results of medical research and technology, cost far too much to be applied widely.

The annual publication (since 1990) of the *Human Development Report* of the United Nations has focused attention on the quality of life throughout the world. Basic features of education and healthcare, the position of women in society, the rights of children, marriage and divorce, are among themes given prominence. Issues such as the loosening of the traditional heterosexual, patriarchal structure of society in Western Europe and the USA are now openly discussed. There are, however, strikingly different priorities between the issues and problems included in the *Human Development Report* for developed and developing countries. Unemployment, road accidents, smoking, the consumption of alcohol, drug crimes, homicides, prison population, suicides are issues reviewed and quantified in developed countries. In developing countries such problems also exist, but data for some are not available, while more pressing issues are addressed: safe water, sanitation, daily calorie supply per capita, adult literacy rate, children not in primary school, malnourished children under five, maternal mortality rate, malaria cases, population doubling date.

Two of numerous possible examples of situations in developing countries not experienced in the present developed countries in the 20th century are taken from Haiti and India. In Haiti it is estimated that the level of unemployment is 70 per cent. In such circumstances it is possible for foreign companies to pay only two or three dollars a day to employees in clothing and other factories, far less than they would have to pay workers at home, but still enough to attract local workers. In India, China and other countries of southern and eastern Asia, traditionally females have been treated less favourably than males in virtually all aspects of life. Popham (1997) reports that in India the government is introducing measures to prevent or at least discourage parents from aborting female foetuses, killing baby girls at birth and neglecting young girls. How recent the social values of the present developed countries are is illustrated by the fact that in Britain, France and elsewhere in Europe, in the 19th century, infanticide was widely practised (see Langer (1972)).

As stressed earlier, there is not a clear cut division of the countries of the world into developed and developing. The Human Development Index for 1993 (see *HDR 1996*), with a possible maximum of 1000 'points', extended from 951 points, the highest score, for Canada, to 204 for Niger (Africa). Within a year, the 1994 leader was still Canada, but with 960 points, while Sierra Leone achieved only 176. In 1993 144 countries with over 1 million inhabitants were included. These have been divided into quartiles and their locations in the world are shown in Figure 12.5. Comparable data are not available for the 1940s, but the distribution by quartiles was roughly similar then. Is this a broad indication, then, of the situation around 2050? A thought-provoking piece of speculation would be to consider which countries might change positions.

The environment

For simplicity this can be subdivided into five types:

- Cultivated land is no longer part of the natural environment. In many areas it has been subjected to intensive ploughing and fertilisation, with resulting soil erosion and pollution.

- Forests. It might appear that because most of the cold and temperate latitude forests are located in developed countries and are increasingly being managed in a sustainable way their future is not threatened. In contrast, there have been many estimates of the amount of tropical rain forest cut and not replaced in the last few decades and forecasts that virtually all will disappear in a few decades time. The developed regions of the world may have reason to be complacent about supplies of forest products, as indeed of basic foodstuffs, up to 2050, but the situation could arise in which in one way or another they have to supply developing countries with timber and food products.

- The permanent pastures of the world range from very productive meadows to very low yielding mixes of plants, often available for grazing only for part of the year. A small part of the world's permanent pastures could be afforested or improved for cultivation in the next few decades.

- Land of no productive value at present is low on the agenda with regard to improving it for agriculture or forest uses and is unlikely to be markedly different in 2050.

- The built-up areas of the world, particularly the largest urban centres in developing countries, seem likely to experience increasing problems of pollution, congestion, stress, crime and terrorism in the first half of the 21st century as well as drawing on other places at increasing distances to supply water, food, power and materials.

12.3   THE WORLD MAP

What will the world be like in 2050? Some parts of the earth's surface, large and small alike, will be virtually unchanged: for example Antarctica, the Sahara Desert, northern Siberia and the Himalayas. Some places will have similar features to now but more of everything: for example, Mexico City and Calcutta. Some places will be entirely transformed through new uses of the land. For example, much of the present tropical rain forest will disappear, extensive areas of the world will be covered with solar panels or wind farms. Exactly where and when the changes will occur cannot usually be forecast. Some of the greatest changes expected by the author between now and 2050 are outlined in the rest of this section and in sections 12.4 -12.7.

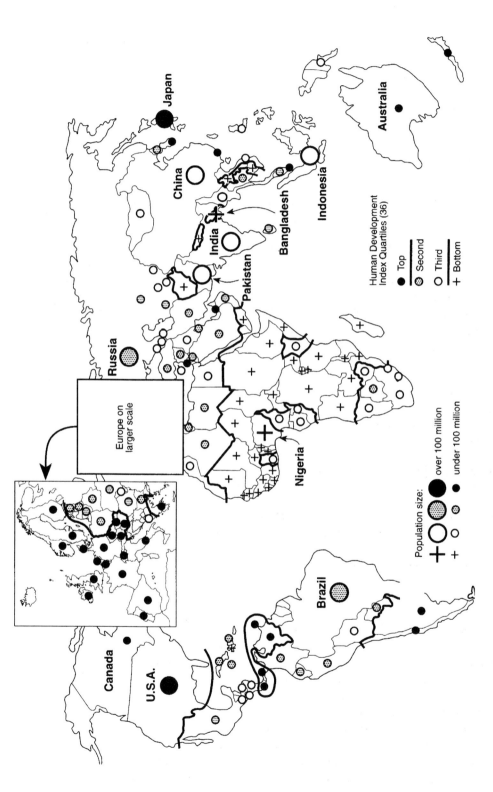

Figure 12.5 The haves and have nots in the mid-1990s according to the Human Development Index of the United Nations Development Programme. 144 countries with a population of over 1 million are shown on the map. Larger symbols are used for countries with over 100 million inhabitants. No data are available in the source for the former Yugoslavia or for Taiwan, the latter not recognised by the UN as a sovereign country.

At the end of Chapter 8, the tendency towards globalisation started by Spanish and Portuguese traders in the 16th century was described (see Figure 2.1). What will the world map be like around 2050? On the polar zenithal map projection used in Figure 8.4 three developed regions in the northern hemisphere were located at three corners of a 'triangle,' roughly centred at the North Pole. These regions will continue to be at the centre of further modernisation, including industrial development along new lines, the development of services, and the maintenance of present living standards, well into the next century.

Europe

In Figure 12.6 the European Union is shown to have a fairly central core area in which most of the highest income regions are located (Eastern France, the Benelux countries, West Germany, North Italy and Southeast England). One of the initial policy goals of the EU was to raise standards in its various backward areas (see map) but little further convergence has been achieved since the early 1970s. In the early decades of the 21st century, much of the EU budget, set at or below 1.27 per cent of total EU GDP, is expected to be spent on raising living standards in Central Europe, as and when countries in this much poorer part of the continent join the EU. Negotiations over membership started in 1997 with six countries: Poland, the Czech Republic, Hungary, Slovenia, Estonia and Cyprus. Several more countries, including Romania, Bulgaria, Slovakia, Lithuania and Latvia could follow the first six candidates in the 2010s. By 2050 a larger, but more closely integrated Europe could be in existence, but with a considerably diminished share of total world population compared with now, and less influence worldwide.

The main reasons for the slow progress towards integration of the EU since it was founded in the 1950s have included the presence of regional feelings in 'suppressed' nations in several of the present EU countries, and a desire not to lose too much sovereignty by some member states. A dubious prize to the east for the EU is the integration of Russia, with its vast (by European standards) natural gas and coal reserves, non-fuel minerals, forests, water resources and cropland. Such a move would notionally stretch Europe across what has traditionally been referred to as northern Asia, all the way to the Pacific coast and to within a short distance across the Bering Strait from North America (Alaska). Northwest Africa and Turkey seem likely to have some kind of association with the EU well before 2050, without obtaining full membership.

North America

Some of the essential features of North America (excluding Mexico) are shown in Figure 12.7. The oil and natural gas deposits of the region have a high production to reserves rate and many older fields are nearing exhaustion. There are however abundant reserves of coal about which Atwood (1975) already asked the question in 1975: 'If the US is to become self-sufficient in energy terms, it will have to take large amounts of coal from the thick shallow deposits of the western states. Can it be done without despoiling the land?' Arguably the greatest resource asset of North America, is its very extensive area of cropland, only the main part of which is shown in Figure 12.7.

The 'white' population of North America is haunted by one particular spectre, about which little can be done: the prospect of ever increasing immigration, no longer from its traditional

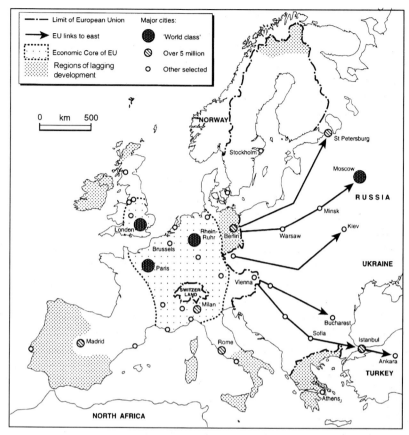

Figure 12.6 Salient features of Europe on the eve of the eastward expansion of the European Union.

source, Europe, but from Latin America, East Asia and other developing regions. Otherwise, apart from more natural disasters (earthquakes, hurricanes, floods) and increasing ethnic tension in some states, leading to a 'white flight' migration from some areas including California, in which Hispanics are numerous, it is difficult to foresee great changes, apart from the probable secession of Quebec from Canada. Monmonier (1997) has published an atlas of the USA showing areas in which the risk of being the victim of various natural and man-made hazards is highest.

East and Southeast Asia

The third industrialised region of the world, that of East and Southeast Asia (see Figure 12.8), differs from the other two in that most of its population is in so-called developing countries and only Japan is at present a *bona fide* developed country, although statistically South Korea, Taiwan, Hong Kong (to 1997) and Singapore are also developed. Many of the world's newly industrialising countries are in East and Southeast Asia. The picture is however more complicated than it appears on the map. In China much of both internal and foreign investment in industries and services in the last 20 years has been in coastal provinces, with much of it concentrated in the larger cities (e.g. Guangzhou and Shenzen, Shanghai, Beijing). In the Philippines, Thailand, Malaysia,

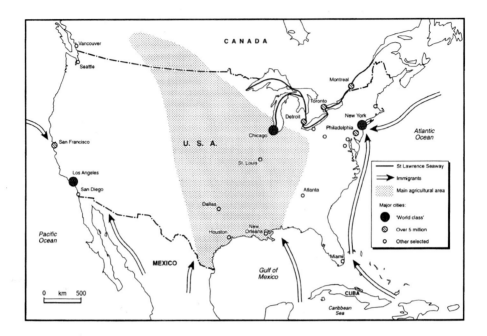

Figure 12.7 The USA and southern Canada, exposed to migration from many parts of the world. Not all the land in the main agricultural area (dotted) is cultivated, while many other smaller areas are cultivated. Only 20-21 per cent of the land area of the USA is classed as arable or under permanent crops in any one year, while the proportion in Canada is only around 5 per cent. The main industrial area of the USA dating from the 19th century extends between New York and Chicago and has been referred to as the 'rust belt', on account of its concentration of heavy industry in decline for some decades.

Indonesia and Viet Nam much of the recent industrial development has been in the capital cities and a few other centres. China and the other countries referred to all have a very large part of their population in the agricultural sector, made up mostly of people with virtually no wealth other than the land they cultivate (if they actually own it) and very low living standards. Further massive migration from rural areas to the larger cities can be expected in all the countries except Japan in the next few decades (Chapter 4).

Other regions

In the rest of the world, outside the industrial triangle described above, there is much diversity. Several large individual cities or clusters of cities are highly sophisticated and industrialised in comparison with other regions in their vicinity. They include Mexico City (capital of Mexico), São Paulo and Rio de Janeiro (Brazil), Buenos Aires (Argentina), Johannesburg (South Africa), Mumbai, Calcutta, Madras, Delhi (India) as well as the largest cities of Australia (these latter by definition are actually part of the developed world). In contrast, large areas of Russia (east of the Urals), Canada, Australia and Brazil are very thinly populated. Although mostly unsuitable for cultivation, they contain large reserves of forest and minerals as well as abundant water and vast areas of wilderness, an asset that is increasingly becoming appreciated. Finally, a very large proportion of the population of the world lives in relatively densely populated rural areas, including many people in India, eastern China, West Africa, Central America and the Caribbean.

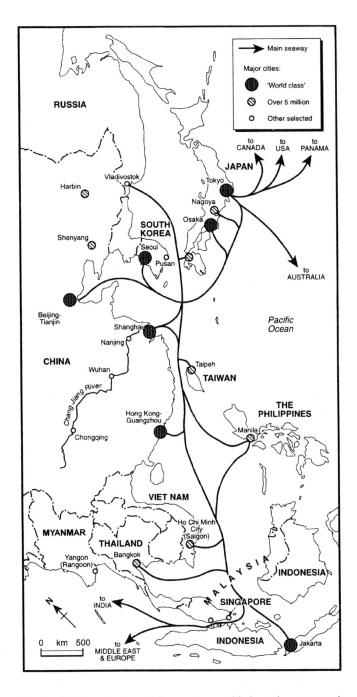

Figure 12.8 The Asian Pacific Rim. In the 1980s much was said about the prospect that the countries of the Pacific Rim would be the main focus of world development and economic power in the 21st century. A glance at a globe shows how enormous the Pacific Ocean is and how far apart and diversified countries are on this Rim. This map shows parts of East and Southeast Asia between mid-latitude Japan and equatorial Indonesia. Until the 1980s Japan was seen as the most influential power in the region both industrially and financially, although South Korea, Taiwan, Hong Kong and Singapore were beginning to make an impression on the world economy. On account of its sheer size, China is likely to become a major economic power in the next century, while several countries in the southern part of this region are also becoming more industrialised. At present the impact of Russia's Far East outpost is negligible.

12.4   MIGRATION AND URBANISATION

Two related trends are likely to continue and intensify up to the year 2050: internal migration within developing countries is set to continue, and international migration from developing to developed countries is likely to grow. The continuing growth of population in agricultural areas in developing countries is likely to produce massive migration from the countryside to urban centres, often in stages through smaller ones to larger ones. The effect will be to swell the already considerable numbers of unemployed and underemployed poor in urban areas, many of them living in squatter settlements. The author has followed one instance closely, the case of Lima, Peru. In 1955 Greater Lima had a population of about 1,250,000. To a mixed reception of disbelief and scorn, publicised in the Lima press, he forecast that the population of Greater Lima would exceed 5,000,000 in the year 2000. That total was reached in the mid-1980s. The concrete evidence of migration from elsewhere in Peru is the fact that in recent decades up to half of Lima's population has been born elsewhere in the country.

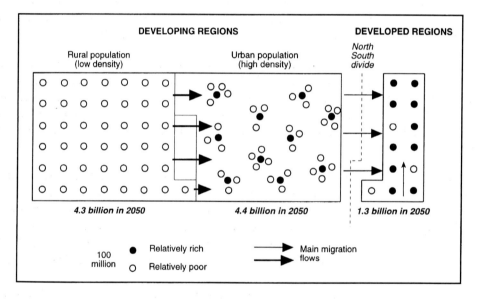

Figure 12.9 The demographic status of the present developing and developed regions of the world around 2050. By then some of the developing regions may officially graduate to developed status. In the centre of the developing regions is a small empty space, representing areas that are thinly populated and have the potential for receiving migrants from traditional rural areas. Most such migrants are attracted to cities in their own countries or even to developed countries rather than to thinly populated areas.

The diagram in Figure 12.9 summarises the spatial aspect of the two trends referred to above. Of the total population of the world in 2050, only 12-13 per cent will be in the present developed countries of the world. Five types of population and two main directions of migration are indicated. The five types of population are:

• The comfortably off and the very affluent population of the present developed countries as so defined in the 1990s.

• The relatively poor of the present developed countries, deprived, unemployed, many in Central Europe, many immigrants from developing countries, fewer in Japan, the USA or the EU. Apart from a tiny minority who choose dire poverty or cannot escape from it, and 'sleep on the streets', even the poor in the developed countries of 2050 should still be protected by various forms of welfare safety nets.

•   The affluent and reasonably well-off in the present developing countries. Almost all live in urban centres. Many of them own various household appliances that are standard in developed countries, can afford domestic servants, have access to good healthcare and education facilities and own a car. In Figure 12.9 a billion of such people are shown by the black dots. They consist of owners of land, manufacturing establishments or services and of professional people such as doctors, engineers, architects and accountants. While in principle they may lament the widespread grinding poverty in their own countries they are understandably reluctant to renounce some of their wealth, for example through high taxes, to assist their poor compatriots.

•   The affluent billion in the developing countries in 2050 will be encircled in their often protected suburban areas by 3-4 billion urban poor, including the domestic servants of the rich, many people in retailing, construction work, small scale manufacturing, menial work with the urban government, as well as numerous underemployed and unemployed.

•   Around 4 billion rural poor in the developing countries in 2050. On account of a number of negative conditions in rural areas in developing countries, increasing numbers of people are leaving the countryside. There will be little change in the amount of cropland available. Some mechanisation will contribute to a reduction in the workforce needed to farm it, while the total fertility rate of the population is likely to remain above replacement level for some decades.

Figure 12.9 shows the result of the growth of population in developing countries and the consequent rural to urban migration. Below the main containers of rural and urban population in developing countries in 2050 is a notional space with a low density of population into which some of the population from the other two areas might migrate. Outstanding recent examples have been migration into the Amazon rain forest of South America from Brazil and other countries, and from Java and other densely populated areas of Indonesia into West Irian and other relatively sparsely settled areas.

In terms of problems of the quality of life, arguably the worst prospect for 2050 will be the existence of many very large cities in the developing world. For millennia the rural population of the world has coped with adversity of all kinds. Similarly, the largest cities in the present developed countries, those with well above 10 million inhabitants in their 'Greater' areas, notably New York, Los Angeles, Tokyo and Osaka-Kobe, continue to function (see Table 12.2a). The vulnerability of all these cities has been tested and revealed, as by a lengthy power cut in New York (where 9 months later three times as many babies were born as normal) and by earthquakes in Tokyo (1923), Los Angeles (1994) and Osaka-Kobe (1996). It has been suggested that if a very serious earthquake destroyed the central part of Tokyo there would be chaos in the world financial institutions.

Many cities in developing countries also have well over 10 million inhabitants. Some (e.g. Mexico City in 1985) have been hit by earthquakes or hurricanes, but as yet there have not been any major disasters, whether natural or man-made. Table 12.2b contains data for 18 developing world urban agglomerations expected to have at least 10 million inhabitants in the year 2000 according to one or more estimates. Thirteen more that are likely to reach 10 million early in the 21st century are also listed at the foot of the Table.

Table 12.2a The ten largest urban agglomerations in the developed countries, mid-1990s

	City	Country	Population (millions)	'Great' city areas
1	Tokyo	Japan	25.7	Prefectures of Tokyo, Chiba, Kanagawa
2	New York	USA	19.8	N.Y.-north N.J.-Long Island
3	Los Angeles	USA	15.3	L.A.-Anaheim-Riverside
4	Osaka	Japan	14.2	Prefectures of Osaka and Hyogo (Kobe)
5	Paris	France	10.7	Ile de France
6	London	UK	10.3	Greater London and adjoining areas
7	Rhein-Ruhr	Germany	9.2	Regierungsbezirke of Dusseldorf and Koln
8	Moscow	Russia	8.8	Greater Moscow area
9	Chicago	USA	8.1	Chicago-Gary-Laek County
10	Nagoya	Japan	6.8	Prefecture of Aichi

Sources: numerous sources have been consulted, with wide margins of disagreement, due partly to the use of different definitions of actual areal extent.

There has been much speculation about the future of very large urban agglomerations in developed countries. For example, Conway (1993) speculates about 500-storey office buildings and cities floating on the sea: 'with the world population constantly growing and putting ever more pressures on urban areas, the creativity of city planners will become extremely important during the next several decades.' Nuttall (1990b) describes a design for an underground world of offices and shops to ease overcrowding in large cities. Cornish (1986) visualises 'Billion City', which could provide a very desirable place for people to live and not even seem crowded.

The above visions assume much further growth of the existing very large cities of the present developed countries. Demographic trends make such growth unlikely in most. In the view of the author, the biggest urban problem around 2050 will be how to cope with the expected huge populations in developing countries. Quite apart from the sheer lack of financial means even now to provide adequate water supply, transport and housing conditions for the majority of the population in such cities, the problem of organisation seems unsurmountable, as the following words of Beier show (1976): 'The planning going into ameliorating urban problems [in developing countries] is negligible. It is not unusual, for example, to find at most a dozen trained professionals in the planning office of a city of 5 million inhabitants which is adding to its population at a rate of 300,000 persons per year. In contrast, the British new towns, designed to accommodate 200,000 people over 15 years, have staffs of over 400.'

From the diagram in Figure 12.9, consistent with the various projections made and 'justified' in the book so far, and discounting the poor in the developed regions, there will be about 2.3 billion reasonably well-off people or very affluent people in the world in 2050 (or 2060 or 2070) and 7.7 billion poor. Even if only half the 'poor' are genuinely below some hypothetical poverty line, there would be as many poor people in the world in 2050 as people in the world altogether in 1970. It is not within the scope of this book to make precise estimates of the number of poor people in developing countries, but various estimates have been made including the following: in *Population Today* (1984) according to an FAO estimate 1.34 billion people lived in the rural areas of the 68 developing countries studied, with just over half of them (700 million) in absolute poverty. This number does not include the poor in China or other Communist developing countries.

Table 12.2b The possible 2050 population of 18 of the largest urban agglomerations of the developing world

City	Country	(1) 1995 population (millions)	(2) 2000 Cornish	(3) 2000 Beier	(4) % urban	(5) TFR	(6) National doubling	(7) increase to 2050	(8) Expected 2050 population (millions)	(9) Adjusted 2050
São Paulo	Brazil	20	24	26	76	2.5	48	2.25	45	40–45
Mexico City	Mexico	18	26	32	71	3.5	32	2.72	49	45–50
Mumbai	India	15	16	19	26	3.5	36	2.53	38	35–40
Shanghai	China	14	14	19	29	1.8	67	1.81	25	25–30
Cairo	Egypt	13	13	16	44	3.6	34	2.62	34	30–35
Delhi	India	13	13	n.a.	26	3.5	36	2.53	33	30–35
Beijing	China	13	n.a.	19	29	1.8	67	1.81	24	25–30
Seoul	S. Korea	12	14	19	74	1.7	75	1.74	21	20
Calcutta	India	12	17	20	26	3.5	36	2.53	30	30–35
Rio de Janeiro	Brazil	12	13	19	76	2.5	48	2.25	27	25–30
Buenos Aires	Argentina	12	13	14	87	2.8	56	1.98	24	20
Dhaka	Bangladesh	11	11	n.a.	26	3.6	35	2.57	28	25–30
Manila	Philippines	11	11	13	47	4.1	30	2.83	31	30–35
Jakarta	Indonesia	11	13	17	31	2.9	40	2.14	24	25–30
Karachi	Pakistan	10	12	16	28	5.6	25	3.20	32	30–35
Teheran	Iran	10	13	n.a.	58	4.7	26	3.21	32	30–35
Tianjin	China	9	n.a.	n.a.	29	1.8	67	1.81	16	15–20
Istanbul	Turkey	9	12	n.a.	63	2.7	43	2.28	21	20–25

n.a. not available

Other developing world cities likely to have over 10 million inhabitants early in the 21st century

Baghdad	Iraq	Guadalajara	Mexico	Lagos	Nigeria
Bangalore	India	Guangzhou	China	Lima	Peru
Bangkok	Thailand	Shenzhen	China	Madras	India
Bogotá	Colombia	Hyderabad	India	Wuhan	China
Chongqing	China	Kinshasa	Congo		

The columns of data in Table 12.2b are now discussed:

(1) contains 'best estimate' populations in millions for 1995 made by the author for each agglomeration.

(2) and (3) two estimates for the year 2000 by Cornish (1986) and Beier (1976) respectively.

(4) The lower the percentage of population currently defined as urban in a country, the greater the rate at which in the next 50 years city population can be expected to grow.

(5) and (6) The higher the national total fertility rate and the shorter the doubling time of the total population of the country, the faster the expected growth of the cities.

(7) and (8) The expected population in 2050 assuming the rate of growth from 1995 to 2050 to be equal to the rate of doubling (e.g. 2.25 means multiply the initial population by that much).

(9) An adjusted expected population range for 2050. If anything, the expectation is a conservative one, since it allows very little extra for the attraction that very large cities currently tend to have in developing countries, as they did in the developed countries in the 19th century and earlier decades of the 20th century.

An example of evidence at a more down-to-earth national level rather than at global level is given in a Peruvian publication, INEI (1995). Out of 4,763,000 households (*hogares*) in the country, 2,196,000 (46.1 per cent) had satisfactory basic necessities, but 2,567,000 (53.9 per cent) did not have satisfactory basic necessities and 1,108,000 (23.3 per cent of the total population) of the latter lived in misery (*miseria*). Peru is well in the top half of all developing countries according to its Human Development Index (see *HDR 1996*) and the GDP per capita. A larger proportion of people in dire poverty than Peru's 23 per cent might be expected in most developing countries.

The situation in the developing world during 2000-2050 will be something like that in the UK between 1800 and 1850. An ongoing flow of migrants from the countryside to the industrial towns was swollen in the 1840s by people escaping the famine in Ireland. Then and later in the 19th century the rural poor in Europe had the possibility not only of moving into their own cities but of emigrating to other continents. Now and well into the 21st century the prospect is that some of the well-off in developing countries with professional qualifications and skills and/or transferable financial resources will be able to settle in developed countries, creating a limited 'brain drain'. On the other hand, with considerable to high levels of unemployment in EU countries and other 'plausible reasons' for not wanting unskilled immigrants, the developed countries will close their borders to most aspiring immigrants.

In spite of efforts to discourage migration there will be attempts to enter the developed countries. Figure 12.10 shows a number of interfaces that have been emerging in the last decades of the 20th century and are likely to figure prominently in world affairs in the 21st century, causing incidents and from time to time even conflicts. The US-Mexican border is the most vulnerable. The interface between the EU and countries directly across the Mediterranean (especially Northwest Africa) is also frequently penetrated. Turkey (in NATO), the countries of Central Europe (some applying for EU membership), and the former USSR have a different relationship with the EU and strictly do not qualify as developing (Turkey is a member of OECD and for some purposes is considered part of Europe).

Unlike the USA and the EU, Japan does not face the prospect of receiving many unwanted immigrants on account of its isolated position in relation to developing countries of East Asia and its consequent ability to exercise tight control at its ports and airports. Another interface is that between Indonesia and the northern, almost uninhabited coastlands of Australia. A recent bizarre 'problem' has been connected with Hong Kong, which when a colony attracted immigrants from the much poorer population of adjoining parts of China. As part of China it now has to be protected from its own fellow Chinese. South Africa has attracted many temporary and some permanent migrants from adjoining countries to its north.

What might be called the North-South economic 'divide' has replaced the West-East ideological divide. There is less ideology in the North-South divide, but in addition to the prospective demographic confrontation described above there is likely to be much resentment in the developing countries over foreign debts, terms of trade, development assistance (or lack of it), and preaching by leaders of developed countries as to how developing countries should conduct their affairs, particularly with reference to protection of the natural environment. In the next three sections some of the prospects and issues discussed in this and the preceding section (12.3) are related to what could happen in 10 major regions of the world up to 2050.

12.5   PROSPECTS FOR THE MAJOR REGIONS OF THE WORLD

On the assumption that the world political map will not change drastically and that economic growth will remain the goal of most governments, the major regions will drift along in the next

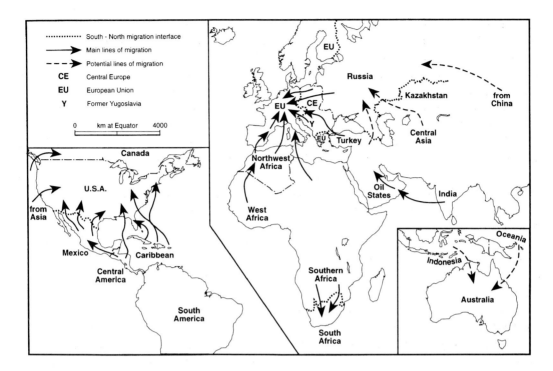

Figure 12.10 'North-South' interfaces, areas in which rich and poor countries share land boundaries or are in close proximity across seas such as the Gulf of Mexico and the Mediterranean.

fifty years. The greatest changes will probably include the increase in the number of people in the world and at least a twofold increase in the quantity of energy and raw materials used each year. Evidence of the extent of the gap between rich and poor countries in the 1990s was shown in Chapter 9 and it was argued that in the next few decades the gap could not even be narrowed, let alone closed.

It is difficult to compare regions objectively since there is no absolute basis against which various aspects of major regions can be assessed and, where appropriate, quantified. The performance and prospects of regions depend on a large number and variety of features and factors. Some are related to the availability of natural resources, others to material production, yet others to human satisfaction about non-material matters. In Table 12.3 scores have been given to each of the ten regions according to a number of arbitrarily chosen features. Equal weight has been given to all the attributes except one, population change, which is given double weight. The range is between 5 for 'best' and 0 for 'worst' (10-0 for population change).

The direction of the scoring in Table 12.3 is somewhat subjective and in the view of other people some scores could be reversed. For example, in column (13) fast population growth is regarded as 'bad' or unfavourable insofar as it is widely blamed for slowing down per capita economic growth in developing countries. Economic growth, the aim of most governments, is itself deplored by environmentalists. Indeed GDP can be regarded as a meter measuring roughly the rate at which natural resources are being used up and the environment negatively affected. In column (10) democratic elections and freedom of expression are regarded by the author and in general by Westerners as desirable. In contrast Chinese leaders have their own views about freedom and human rights as we understand them and, in theory at least, prefer for example to regard full employment as a more important human right than freedom of expression. Although India is regarded in the West as the world's largest democratic country in the sense that it has free elections and a multi-party system, there remain many 'non-democratic' features there such as the caste system (in theory abolished), and a disregard in some states for women's rights and their very existence in extreme cases.

Table 12.3 serves as a starting point for comparing the prospects of ten major regions of the world. The first four, the so-called developed regions, will be considered first. The emphasis will be on issues and problems that may cause their high position to deteriorate. When the six developing regions are considered, the opposite view will be taken: what changes could improve their positions in relation to the developed countries and among themselves? There follow notes on the data in Table 12.3. The scores are relative, not absolute and, where appropriate, are related to population size. The attributes are of three main types: (1)-(4) natural resources per capita; (5)-(9) production of goods and services per capita; (10)-(13) organisational aspects, issues and problems.

(1) Fresh water resources. A score of zero does not mean a complete absence of present or possible future water supplies, while a high score does not mean an abundance of water everywhere in a region. It is assumed that in the next few decades greater movement of water by pipelines will be possible and some may be transported by sea.

(2) Bioclimatic resources include all sources of plant and animal products: cultivated land, forest, natural pasture, fresh and salt water.

(3),(4) Energy and non-fuel mineral resources. In view of the large international trade in fuels and raw materials, mainly from developing to developed regions, consumption levels do not necessarily coincide closely with reserves or quantity extracted.

(5)-(8) Self-explanatory.

(9) The Human Development Index (HDI) is calculated by the United Nations Development Programme on the basis of health, education, and real GDP per capita up to a ceiling of about 6,000 US dollars, above which the excess makes only a minute addition. It summarises the attributes (6)-(8) but has been included to give extra weight to living standards.

(10) Political freedom is a subjective concept and moreover the score for each region may be an average covering a variety of political situations among the member countries of a major region.

(11) Ethnic stability reflects the presence or lack within individual countries of ethnic diversity and dissatisfied minorities.

(12) Regional stability, the presence of neighbouring unstable regions and/or of the possible political break-up of countries within the region.

(13) The scale of population change is from a maximum of 10 for a state of near stability to 0 for the fastest growth. This attribute is given double weight in view of its influence on economic growth and consumption levels. In Table 12.4 comparison of the final scores on the criteria used in Table 12.3 shows that the regions fall 'naturally' into five categories.:

Table 12.3 Performance and prospects for 10 major regions

	(1) Fresh water	(2) Bio-climatic resources	(3) Energy resources	(4) Non-fuel minerals	(5) Industry	(6) Education	(7) Health care	(8) Real GDP per head	(9) HDI	(10) Political freedom	(11) Ethnic stability	(12) Regional stability	(13) Population change	(14) Total maximum 70	(15) % maximum 100
Europe[1]	3	3	2	1	4	4	4	4	4	4	3	4	10	50	71
Former USSR	4	4	5	5	3	3	3	2	3	4	2	2	8	50	71
Japan/S. Korea	2	0	0	0	4	4	5	4	5	4	5	4	9	46	66
North America[2]	4	5	4	5	5	5	4	5	5	5	4	5	6	62	89
Latin America	5	3	2	3	2	2	2	2	2	3	3	3	4	36	51
Africa[3]	2	2	1	3	0	0	0	0	0	1	0	0	0	9	13
NA/SWA[4]	0	0	5	1	1	1	1	2	2	1	3	2	1	20	29
South Asia	3	2	1	1	1	1	1	0	1	4	3	3	2	23	33
Southeast Asia	4	3	1	1	1	1	1	1	2	1	3	3	3	25	36
China[5]	2	1	2	1	2	1	1	1	2	0	2	3	4	22	31

Notes

1   Excludes former USSR in Europe apart from Baltic states
2   Includes Oceania
3   Excludes five northernmost countries
4   North Africa and Southwest Asia
5   Includes some small neighbours

- North America
- Rest of the developed countries
- Latin America
- Rest of the developing countries except
- Africa south of the Sahara

Table 12.4 Regional scores from Table 12.3

		Score out of 100 maximum
1	North America and Oceania	89
2	Europe	71
	Former USSR	71
	Japan and South Korea	66
3	Latin America	51
4	Southeast Asia	36
	South Asia	33
	China	31
	Southwest Asia and North Africa	29
5	Africa	13

In this book attention has focused on futures that are possible and plausible. Space does not allow more than a brief reference to a completely different approach. To what extent do the developed and developing regions depend on each other? Is one exploiting the other? How would each develop or decline in the next half century if the other disappeared completely under the sea?

Without the developing countries, the developed ones would quickly have an energy problem since almost 90 per cent of the world's oil reserves are in developing countries, although there would be less of a problem with natural gas, and none with coal or nuclear power. Tropical agricultural products would be almost unknown. On the other hand, with Russia, Canada and Australia in the developed world, only a few non-fuel minerals would be in very short supply (e.g. phosphates, tin and possibly copper).

Without the developed countries, the developing countries would above all miss out on a wide range of manufactured goods as well as access to some services. They would no longer have the benefit (or at times the negative impact) of the results of scientific research and innovations in technology in areas such as agriculture, medicine and military equipment. Presumably a few countries would pick up the threads of industry, probably Brazil, India, China and its neighbours, South Africa, and they would restore a low key industrial world.

12.6   PROSPECTS FOR THE FOUR MAJOR DEVELOPED REGIONS

In this and the following section the future of 10 major world regions is sketched out. In section 11.3 of Chapter 11 the prospects of the most influential countries in the world were outlined with special reference to the possibility that they might break up, as the USSR did in 1991. There is therefore some overlap of material between section 11.3 and sections 12.6 and 12.7

1. In the present context Europe includes everywhere traditionally in the continent except the European part of the former USSR; the exception is the inclusion of the three Baltic states (Estonia, Latvia and Lithuania). In the early 1980s, Western Europe was still easily distinguished from Eastern Europe by the 'Iron Curtain', but in the 1990s the revived term Central Europe gave recognition to the group of countries no longer in the Soviet orbit. Western and Central Europe have many features in common. Everywhere population has virtually stopped growing. Water supply and agricultural land are reasonably plentiful in relation to population, and coal reserves are abundant. Oil and natural gas reserves are, however, very limited in relation to energy consumption, and most non-fuel mineral reserves are very small. There is a high level of industrialisation in most countries, and health and educational levels are high by world standards. In the 1990s, however, there was a great gap in real GDP per capita between the average of the European Union and the average of the countries of Central Europe.

    Europe faces both internal and external concerns. Internally, future problems could include the impact of greater integration of the present EU and its enlargement, with the need to assist new members from Central Europe economically, together with ethnic issues, with attempts to achieve greater autonomy by 'suppressed' national groups such as the Catalans, Basques and Scots, embedded within member states. Externally, concern is likely to continue and indeed grow over energy and raw material supplies from elsewhere in the world, whether through political problems (especially affecting oil) or because former traditional exporters of primary products will need these themselves as their populations grow and industrialisation proceeds. By 2050, the share of the world's total population in Europe will only be about half what it was in the 1980s.

2. The former Soviet Union was broken up in 1991 into 15 separate states, three of which, the Baltic states, have dissociated themselves completely, while the rest remain to varying degrees associated economically with the largest, Russia, through the Commonwealth of Independent States (CIS). The former USSR is generously endowed with natural resources, but most of these are in the territorially very large Russian Federation and in Kazakhstan. Emphasis in the Soviet Five-Year Plans (the first was 1928-32) was on industrialisation, especially the growth of heavy industry. By the 1950s the former USSR was counted as part of the developed world, and before its break-up in 1991 it had achieved reasonably high levels of education, healthcare and other services, although the quantity, quality and range of consumer goods left much to be desired.

    In terms of real GDP per inhabitant, the former USSR now has a very low rating compared with the USA, the EU and Japan. Several decades could be needed for Russia to 'catch up' the Western market economy countries in areas in which it lags behind at present, for example, financial stability, road transport and consumer goods. Following the break-up of the USSR, Russian responsibility towards the former predominantly non-Russian Soviet Socialist Republics, some with local population 'explosions' and poor natural resources, has diminished sharply, but (see Chapter 11 and Figure 11.2b) there is still concern over the loyalty of some 20 sizeable non-Russian minorities still within the Russian Federation itself (e.g. Chechnya). A break-up of the Russian Federation itself on ethnic lines is a possibility, but a compromise seems more likely, with autonomy given to some of the larger or more vociferous former Autonomous Soviet Socialist Republics (ASSRs) such as the Tatar and Bashkir Republics.

3. Japan and South Korea are very poorly endowed with natural resources in relation to population size. To sustain their high levels of industrialisation they need to import almost all of the fuel and raw materials they use, while a very limited area of agricultural land in relation to population means they also have to import most of the food consumed. Population is not likely to grow much in the next few decades and immigration (or emigration) is unlikely. Like Europe, therefore, Japan and South Korea depend heavily on other parts of the world for essential imports, and in world affairs it may suit them to continue keeping a low profile politically, avoiding a major role in world affairs that might upset, for example, the government of China or of countries of the Middle East. The strengthening of economic contacts worldwide seems a strategy likely to continue, with investment in many developing countries, particularly China, as well as in the USA and the EU. It is too soon at the time of writing to assess the seriousness and possible long-term effects of the financial crises that have beset several countries of Southeast Asia in 1998 or of the ongoing paralysis of the Japanese economy.

4. North America and Oceania have the highest overall score on the criteria used in Table 12.3 to measure favourability of prospects. Among the larger countries of the world, Canada and Australia are by a long way the most generously endowed with natural resources per inhabitant, while the USA is also reasonably well endowed. Due to the high levels of industrialisation and material consumption, however, the exhaustible natural resources have been intensively used in the 20th century and the future of energy supplies, notably oil and natural gas, is a matter of concern. Like the EU and Japan, the USA is a large importer of oil from the Middle East and also from Latin America.

    As the decades pass, North Americans may find it necessary to lower their standard of living somewhat in, for example, the lavish use of passenger cars and, by world standards, the high level of consumption of meat. Arguably the greatest problem in both the USA and Canada is related to their populations. Growth and immigration, ageing, and ethnic issues related to minorities of African Americans, Hispanics and Asians in the USA and French Canadians in Canada are all matters of concern. While Canadians already worry over the large number of Asian immigrants in some cities, the Asians in the USA are considered to be a model minority, easily assimilated. The growing influence on the economy and on political decisions of the indigenous populations of North America, Australia and New Zealand could also cause problems in the future.

12.7   THE PROSPECTS FOR THE SIX MAJOR DEVELOPING REGIONS

1. Latin America is a major region of great contrasts in physical conditions but it has considerable cultural homogeneity on account of the influence of Spain and Portugal for almost three centuries, with linguistic, religious (Roman Catholic) and other Iberian features imposed on the indigenous population. By 1820 almost all of Latin America had become independent from Spain or Portugal (Brazil), but the whole region soon became a source of primary products for West European countries and the USA. Some decades ago Latin American countries were mostly regarded as very unstable politically, with frequent revolutions and with military dictatorships and democratic governments alternating. Many of the old boundary disputes have now been settled, and democratically elected governments now predominate. Population growth has been rapid in most countries of Latin America in the

20th century but is now slowing down. There has been much migration from rural areas to cities, especially the large ones.

Only Argentina has a large extent of good agricultural land in relation to population size, while most of the oil and gas resources are concentrated in Venezuela and Mexico. Non-fuel minerals are abundant in some countries. Of all the six major developing regions, Latin America has the best prospects for the next few decades, but its social problems, including ethnic and economic inequalities, will not go away easily, while environmental problems, especially the conservation of the world's largest area of tropical rain forest in Amazonia, seem likely to escalate.

2. Africa south of the Sahara resembles Latin America in that almost every part of the continent has been in the colonial empire of some European power. The colonial period has been much shorter and much more recent, roughly from 1880 to 1960 in many countries. Nevertheless the impact of European colonisation has had a profound effect on the way the continent is divided into about 50 sovereign states and the way in which investment has been placed in many areas to grow agricultural products or to extract minerals for export to the industrial countries. At the same time, enough improvements have been made in healthcare to lower mortality rates of infants and young children without there being a corresponding reduction in total fertility rate.

A large proportion of the total population of Africa south of the Sahara is engaged in agriculture, but the area under cultivation, much of it in regions that suffer frequently from droughts or have poor soil, has not been extended to keep up with population growth. There is little modern industry in Africa except in South Africa. One of several reasons for ethnic tension within countries and conflict between them is the fact that the boundaries of the present countries, based almost exactly on European colonial boundaries, largely ignore tribal territories and therefore cut through old tribal areas. The prospect that the population of Africa south of the Sahara could increase at least three times by 2050 leaves one wondering how so many people can be adequately fed unless drastic changes take place in the economy of the region.

3. North Africa and Southwest Asia extend from Morocco on the shores of the Atlantic Ocean in the west to Afghanistan in the heart of Asia. Most of the region is desert or semi-desert and even the main agricultural areas are mostly characterised by low rainfall. The small extent of irrigated land forms the most productive part of the region's cropland. Oil and natural gas deposits arguably provide the most important natural resources of the region. Five countries together have about 60 per cent of the world's oil reserves: Saudi Arabia, Iraq, Iran, Kuwait and the United Arab Emirates. At the rate of extraction of the 1990s the proved oil reserves of these countries would last for over 100 years.

In virtually all of North Africa and Southwest Asia the religion is Islam, which in some countries exerts a strong influence on political and even economic activities as well as on lifestyles. The status and rights of women are regarded as at risk in some Muslim countries, at least according to Western criteria. As long as countries in other parts of the world import oil, there is a large source of revenue for the governments of the oil rich countries. Nevertheless, with a rapidly growing population, the need to import food and manufactured goods, a shortage of water for development, and religious opposition to many of the ways of the Western type of market economy thinking and practice, it may be expected that the governments of the region will not always conform with the wishes and expectations of the developed countries in the next few decades.

4.   South Asia coincides broadly with the former British India, subdivided in 1947 into India, West and East Pakistan (later Pakistan and Bangladesh). Sri Lanka and Nepal also belong. The whole region has about 20 per cent of the population of the world, 1.2 billion people, on about 3 per cent of the world's land area. To be sure, about half of the total area is cultivated and much land is double-cropped, but yields of the main crops are well below the world average. In relation to population size, apart from coal deposits in India, energy and non-fuel mineral reserves are very modest in quantity. An indication of the scarcity of primary products in the countries of the region is the fact that in the exports of India, Pakistan and Bangladesh, manufactured goods are of greater value than primary products. The prospect that the population of the region could be well in excess of 2 billion by 2050 does nothing to inspire confidence in the expectation that India is about to 'take off' economically, as China, or at least some provinces of China, appear to have done in the 1980s. Given the great cultural diversity of India, it could break up as the USSR has done. Whether or not the 'sub-continent' subsides into religious conflict between Hindus and Muslims depends on the restraint or aggressiveness of religious leaders. The testing of nuclear weapons in both India and Pakistan in 1998 and the long-standing dispute over Kashmir underline the tension between the two countries.

5.   Southeast Asia is even more diverse and certainly more 'far-flung' than South Asia. The UK, France, the Netherlands and the USA (Philippines) held much of the region in their colonial empires until their control was challenged by Japan in the Second World War. The countries of Southeast Asia contain particular mixes of population, with very simple economies surviving from an earlier age in remote parts, mostly in mountain areas or in the remaining areas of tropical rain forest, alongside dense agricultural populations, depending heavily on rice cultivation. The region has a few oil and non-fuel mineral deposits of world significance, and some very large cities, including the capitals, in which industrialisation has been rapid since the 1960s through foreign investments, using cheap labour as well as local initiatives. In spite of the creation of the Association of South East Asian Nations (ASEAN), each country in the region goes very much its own way, as, for example, in the enormous contrast in modernisation levels between neighbours Thailand and Myanmar. More of the same for some decades seems to be the prospect for Southeast Asia.

6   For simplicity, here China also includes a number of close and closely associated countries, Taiwan, North Korea and Mongolia, as well as its new acquisition, Hong Kong, still separate from China politically when the data for this book were collected. Throughout the 20th century most of the modernisation and development of China has taken place in cities and surrounding areas on or near the coast. In the early part of the Communist period (from 1949) the policy was to decentralise industry from the coast to the interior. Reasons were both economic and strategic, to open up new areas to industry and to place factories in safer areas with regard to the coast, from which an invasion was anticipated.

The introduction of private ownership of means of production since the 1970s, the acceptance of 'foreign' investment, much actually from Hong Kong and Taiwan, and the incentive under market socialism to optimise returns on investment, have meant that the coastal provinces have attracted more than their 'fair share' of development. Densely populated and still predominantly agricultural provinces are characteristic of the poor 'inner interior'. Beyond that, the 'outer interior', the west and north of the country, was originally the home of non-Chinese populations, but now has many Han Chinese settlers. Pressure of population on land and on water and mineral resources in China is very great, but could be even greater if the effects of the policy to reduce the total fertility rate had not slowed down the rate of population growth.

Of all the large countries in the world China now appears to be the one at greatest risk of breaking up, whether for ethnic reasons or economic ones. In the first instance the cause would be the unlikely acceptance by the Han Chinese that independence should be given to Tibet, Xinjiang (Sinkiang), Inner Mongolia and smaller areas of non-Chinese population. The economic cause of fragmentation would be the reluctance of comparatively developed prosperous provinces to share their good fortune with poorer provinces, in which case Guangzhou (with Hong Kong), Shanghai and the lower Chang Jiang valley, and northeast China could be likely candidates for claims to greater autonomy. More altruistically, the more industrialised and prosperous coastal regions could be persuaded or coerced into channelling assistance into the interior.

12.8 BEYOND 2050 IN TIME AND SPACE

The expectation of conditions in 2050, which the author hopes his grandchildren will be able to compare with the actual situation, is the result largely of a continuation of trends observed between 1950 and 2000. But 2050 is only a pause for reflection on the journey further into the future. Things will not suddenly stop then and people will still be there even if their numbers do not increase greatly after 2050. Even if there is no increase in per capita production between 2050 and 2100, about 25 per cent more of everything will be needed because the *average* number of people alive each year during 2050-2100 will be about 10-11 billion compared with only 8 billion during 2000-2050. In this section some examples are given of forecasts and timescales explicitly extending beyond 2050.

- A projection of the population of the USA from the 1980s shows the ageing of the baby boom and no stabilisation of the population structure until well into the second half of the 21st century. The youngest cohorts in a population 'pyramid' show roughly how many people alive now could be alive still in 2050 (see Figure 4.2).

- The Chinese demographer Liu Zheng (1981) proposed the goal of a population of about 700 million for China in 2080 as the optimum, given the quantity and distribution of fresh water in the country and the prospects for food production. It is already difficult to see how the above population goal in China could be achieved without a drastic reduction in fertility rates and rationing of babies in a kind of lottery (see Figure 3.1). The elimination of part of the population would be unacceptable even by the Chinese Communist Party's harsh standards of treating its citizens, and emigration to foreign destinations in any useful numbers is out of the question.

- Kahn and associates (1977) writing in 1976 sketch out what they expect to happen in the world up to the year 2176. While they allow plenty of leeway in their forecast for 2176, they assume a massive increase in production per capita but a continuation of the wide gap between rich and poor countries: 'The earth-centred perspective assumes that the world population flattens out at least for a while at 15 billion people, give or take a factor of two (that is, a range of 7.5 to 30 billion); the per capita product at 20,000 dollars, give or take a factor of three; and the GWP (Gross World Product) at about 300 trillion US dollars (10 times the level of the 1990s), give or take a factor of five. The possible ranges of variability are, of course, larger than those given, but we find the above quite plausible.' After 2176 Kahn (1977) expects 'Full development of post industrial institutions and cultures almost everywhere on earth. People turn their attention to the creation of such societies everywhere in the solar system and - eventually - perhaps to the stars as well.'

- The Chinese see events in their history hundreds and even thousands of years ago as just a little way back down the road. There is a feeling of continuity lacking in Europe, although in Western Europe there is a strong feeling of affinity with the civilisations of Greece and Rome. It is not surprising, therefore, that a Chinese geomorphologist has estimated that by the year 2500 there will be no soil left on the loess plateau, home of China's first civilisations, an area composed of a fine material, easy to cultivate but easily washed away into the nearby Huanghe River. Cultivators living there around the year 2000 are unlikely to be concerned about the prospect (see Chapter 3, Figure 3.12).

- In a rare piece of speculation linking the past to the future, Naudin (1997) compares the achievements of Leonardo da Vinci (1452-1519) with those of Bill Gates, American multi-billionaire. He goes on: 'If we remember Johann Gutenberg (*c.* 1400-1468), a 15th century craftsman from Mainz in Germany, as the originator of a method of printing from movable type that was used almost unchanged until the 20th century, we can bet that Bill Gates, head of Microsoft, will be remembered five centuries from now.' Perhaps Naudin should have compared Gates, a leader in the development of information technology, with Gutenberg rather than with Leonardo da Vinci. A nice thought, anyway.

- There is controversy in New Mexico over the plan to bury permanently large quantities of nuclear waste from military and civilian sources. Such waste must be placed where it is safe for 10,000 years. The plutonium will still be radioactive in 160,000 years' time.

- In 5 billion years the planet earth should be absorbed by the sun.

We are clearly ill-prepared to contemplate possibilities for human beings more than a few decades ahead. In *The Time Machine* of H.G. Wells, the time traveller went ahead a long way in time and found himself on a beach, with no sign of life. In his science fiction story *The Last and the First Men*, Olaf Stapledon recorded the end of humans in the distant future. The way some of the pessimists have written, one might expect the end to come in a century or so.

12.9   EXPANDING TIME AND SPACE

Since the launching of the earliest earth satellite in 1957, the first manned satellite in 1961 and the first moon landing less than a decade later, people have started to take seriously the prospect of establishing a permanent base on the moon and of a manned space flight to Mars. Following the successful landing of an unmanned vehicle on Mars in 1997, the proposal of the US Space Agency NASA to send astronauts to Mars in about 2020 seems credible (see Whittell (1997a)), but the prospect of a permanent settlement on Mars other than for research work seems unlikely before 2050. Problems include the 'journey' of several months' duration in a very confined space, with exposure to high doses of radiation from cosmic rays, which could cause cancer, cataracts, sterility, and brain damage, and the nail-biting moment of launching back to earth. The remaining planets of the solar system are too hot or are unsuitable in other ways for manned landings in the present state of technology.

Ideas about space travel have led to the belief that minerals might be obtained from the moon or from the planets. The next leap in the imagination of both scientists and the general public is to consider the exploration and possibly the settlement on the planets of other solar systems. A problem with the last idea is that stars are very conspicuous since they emit light, whereas their planets, if they have any, cannot be detected easily unless in early stages of formation because they are generally much smaller anyway and only *reflect* light. Nevertheless, in 1999 planets were detected in a system about 44 light years away from our solar system (see Hawkes (1999)). Three giant planets orbit the star Upsilon Andromedae, which is ten times as far away as Alpha Centauri, our nearest star.

While the idea of exploring space beyond our solar system seems an admirable one if scientific curiosity is the only reason, the colonisation of the planets of other stars is so far off that it need not be taken seriously as a solution for such problems as overpopulation or natural resource depletion on our own planet for the next few centuries, let alone the next 50-100 years. One reason is the sheer distance of even the nearest stars to the earth (which may not have planets anyway), and therefore the time needed to reach them, even if, as has been asserted (see e.g. Leake (1995)), *in theory* it is possible to travel faster than the speed of light, approximately 300,000 kilometres per second (186,000 miles).

Before speculating about the prospects of space travel and the establishment of permanent settlements other than on our own planet the reader should get distances and travel times in perspective. The logistics then of setting up bases, taking supplies there and moving settlers is itself daunting, apart from the cost. Even to maintain permanent bases in Antarctica is costly and is beset with many problems. The temperature may be around -20°C in midsummer. According to Jenkins (1996), a population of 3,000 lives and works on the national stations scattered widely across Antarctica.

Even in somewhat less harsh conditions than those in Antarctica, the Russians had to evacuate thousands of people from settlements along their northern coastlands bordering the Arctic Ocean in the autumn of 1996 because they had been inadequately provided with fuel and food and could have starved or frozen to death (Beeston (1996)). The cost of producing and transporting materials even from the most northerly parts of Canada and Russia is very great and is only economically viable in exceptional circumstances, as with the oil fields of Alaska, the non-ferrous metals mined and smelted in Norilsk (almost 70° North) and the diamonds extracted at Mirnyy, both in Siberia.

According to *National Geographic* (1997), in the mining settlement of Polaris (Little Cornwallis Island), in Canada, more than 75° North, the 240 residents have a median income of 70,000 US dollars, several times the average level for the rest of Canada. Given the high cost of maintaining settlements in the coldest areas of our planet, whether mines in northern latitudes or research stations in Antarctica, it is questionable whether it is economically realistic to contemplate 'importing' minerals even from the moon. According to Newbery (1997), by 2050 tours in spacecraft in orbit round the earth may be available, at a price, but getting further than that, even in a tour, let alone as an emigrant from the earth, is unlikely in 2050 or even 2100.

Table 12.5 shows the distances to a selection of bodies in space beyond the earth. Time and space begin to merge: distances can be measured either in space distance or in the time it

Table 12.5 Distances between the earth and some other heavenly bodies

	Kilometres	Light travel time	Astronomic units
Moon	384,000	1.24 seconds	0.0025
Sun	149.5 million	8 minutes	1
Mercury	58 million	about 3 minutes	0.39
Venus	108 million	about 6 minutes	0.72
Mars	228 million	about 12 minutes	1.53
Main asteroid belt			
Jupiter	779 million	about 42 minutes	5.21
Saturn	1,432 million	about 77 minutes	9.58
Uranus	2,884 million	about 154 minutes	19.29
Neptune	4,509 million	about 4 hours	30.16
Pioneer 10 in 1997			67
Cloud of comets enveloping solar system			50,000
Alpha Centauri (nearest star)	36,375,000 million	about 4 years	250,000

takes light to travel. Spacecraft travel far more slowly than the speed of light. Some idea of how long it could take to travel to the nearest star to our own sun, Alpha Centauri (also referred to as Proxima Centauri), is given by the progress of *Pioneer 10*, the spacecraft launched in March 1972 first to explore Jupiter and then to go on a trajectory to escape from the solar system altogether. In 25 years it has travelled about 10 billion (10,000,000,000) kilometres, impressively far, one might agree, since that is about 250,000 times round the earth's equator. However, this distance is only about 7 light hours away.

Alpha Centauri is about 4 light-years away form our sun, a distance of some 36 trillion (36,375,000,000,000) km away. To reach the distance of Alpha Centauri at the speed *Pioneer 10* travels it would take about 4,000 times 25 years or 100,000 years (see Hawkes (1997a)). With a spacecraft that could travel at 1 million kilometres per hour it would take a mere 4,660 years to reach Alpha Centauri. Even travelling at the speed of light a round trip to our *nearest* star would take almost a decade.

The problems of landing just a probe on a moon of Saturn are stressed by Ahuja (1997). The Cassini-Huygens mission was launched in October 1997: it is expected to arrive at Saturn in July 2004. Saturn is less than 10 astronomic units from Earth. Alpha Centauri is therefore about 25,000 times as far away. Even deducting two years from the seven needed by the Saturn mission to get clear of Venus and Earth, following its flybys, it would take 5 × 25,000 years, or 125,000 years, to reach Alpha Centauri, a timescale broadly compatible with that calculated from the speed of *Pioneer 10*. There is no guarantee that Alpha Centauri has planets at all, let alone ones with conditions suitable for a landing to be made. Indeed, Alpha Centauri is a multiple system with three stars locked by gravity in orbit around each other. Single stars seem more likely to have planetary systems like our own. The next nearest to our sun is Barnard's star, six light-years away.

The impressive development of science and technology in the last two centuries in particular has led many people to think that nothing is impossible. In forecasting it is unwise to say that something could never happen, a mistake made by the British Astronomer Royal, Sir Harold Spencer Jones, who stated in 1957: 'Man will never set his foot on the moon ...' (Nown (1985)).

It is almost certainly impossible that humans will ever set foot on a planet in another solar system, if only on account of the sheer distance, the problems and hazards a manned spacecraft travelling there could encounter (collision with debris in space, absence of solar power once in interstellar space), and the physiological and psychological stress on the traveller(s), imprisoned in a situation that would make solitary confinement in a Soviet labour camp in the Arctic seem like a Five Star Hotel.

The prospects for space exploration and travel, whether by unmanned spacecraft or manned ones, with scientists or with tourists (or both), have been quantified in terms of distance in Table 12.5 and discussed in the accompanying text. In the mid-to late 1990s much publicity has been given to future space travel, with reference to technology, fuel, short cuts through the Universe in the form of 'worm holes' (see e.g. Grimston (1999)), tourism (see e.g. Prigg (1999)) and many other aspects. A tourist round trip into space for an hour could cost around £50-60 thousand (see Nelson (1999)). Table 12.6 shows the prices (in US dollars of 1999) likely to be quoted for space trips some time before 2050, insurance not included. Assumptions made about tourism in space include the continuing readiness of the American taxpayer, or private companies, to fund space research and exploration, and the continuing concentration of great wealth in the hands of a minute proportion of the world's population. In one British newspaper published in April 1999, two articles ended up side by side (by chance?). Space travel for tourists was the subject of one, a search in Indonesia for a tribe of cannibalistic women the other. Is 'worlds apart' a big enough gap to describe the extremes of human existence?

Table 12.6 Tourism outside the earth's atmosphere

Possible cost in US dollars per round trip per person	
1 Up and down (one hour)	80,000
2 Up, orbit briefly, down	200,000
3 Orbit moon	2,000,000
4 Moon landing	4,000,000
5 Mars landing (a bit pointless to orbit only)	400,000,000
One way in Concorde (for comparison)	5,000

Many have questioned the feasibility of using extra-terrestrial resources to tackle global problems. Ehrlich and Ehrlich (1972) point out: 'Many Americans, who see science fiction dramas on television and movie screens, in addition to being tax-paying participants in the real-life performances of our astronauts, think it entirely reasonable to regard space as the next frontier. Actually the obstacles to interstellar or even interplanetary migration are stupendous and far beyond present or foreseeable technological capabilities.'

No doubt enough research funds will be forthcoming in the USA (but nowhere else) to allow scientists and manufacturers of equipment to continue with the exploration of space, and it is not argued here that the limited amount of money they are likely to get would be enough, if diverted elsewhere, to solve other major problems on our planet. The discussion in this section has however highlighted another aspect of the way we perceive the universe outside our solar system. The possibility that there is life outside our own planet has been a subject of speculation in many quarters, particularly in the 20th century. Assuming such life does exist in a material form, probably very different from the usually anthropomorphic aliens populating the works of science fiction and allegedly encountered in many parts of the world in recent decades, would they not face the same physical and technical problems posed by sheer distance in interstellar space in travelling to *our* solar system?

12.10 WHAT THEY SAID ABOUT THE FUTURE

If, in addition to filling a whole book, you were asked to summarise in one paragraph what you think about the future of the planet earth and its inhabitants, you would probably put the paragraph near, if not precisely, at the end. In scouring a large number of books and other publications explicitly or implicitly about the future for that critical paragraph, subtle variations on a number of themes have been found . In principle it is not fair to quote a few lines out of context, but in practice it is fun and can be illuminating. For convenience the handful of quotations (out of probably hundreds eligible) that follows has been arranged chronologically; in places comments have been added.

- 1972 Back and Sullivan (1972) questioned the ideology of growth: 'Thus, the ideological struggles of the last two hundred years have been fought within the general framework of a philosophy of growth. The fact that growth was possible and desirable was not doubted. Instead, the question was whether the people who owned capital or those who provided labour should profit most from growth... Concern for the environment and for the effects of rapid population growth has led to some questioning of the ideology that growth is a necessary and beneficial component of modern industrial life.'

- 1972 In *Population, Resources, Environment*, Ehrlich and Ehrlich argued for a change in attitude towards development and economic growth: 'There is no technological panacea for the complex of problems comprising the population - food - environment crisis, although technology, properly applied in such areas as pollution abatement, communications, and fertility control can provide massive assistance. The basic solutions involve dramatic and rapid changes in human *attitudes*, especially those related to reproductive behaviour, economic growth, technology, the environment and conflict resolution.' But who is going to initiate and lead the revolution in attitudes?

- 1972 Dasmann wrote: 'In 1972, it is difficult to be hopeful about the prospects for man and the biosphere he now controls... How long will it take to gather the facts on which our actions to save man and his biosphere must be based? ... The answer seems to be related to the old question "How much do you want to pay?" For the cost of perhaps ten space rockets we might take meaningful steps to save the colour of our blue planet, to save the life-sustaining layer of the biosphere. Can we afford it?' Twenty five years later this 'solution', reminiscent of the peace dividend, seems inadequate and greatly oversimplified.

- 1976 In *The next 200 years* H. Kahn and associates referred to economic growth: 'We believe that the prospects are good and getting better for the coping nations, and that these are the developing countries that will help drive the world's economic growth in the 21st century ... We further believe that the key to accelerating this process is not primarily exploitable natural resources or economic aid or population-control assistance but instead training, education, innovation, savings and investment, institutional change and what Joseph Schumpeter called "creative destruction".' Organisation and management are stressed rather than natural resources and the environment.

- 1978 One of the first people in the second half of the 20th century to emphasise the importance of natural resources was S. R. Eyre in *The Real Wealth of Nations*. Eyre refers nostalgically to two pleasant rural scenes, one in the English Lake District, one in Kenya. Aware of the difficulty of returning 'back to the past', he nevertheless seeks utopia for some time in the future: 'The adoption of a utopia which makes modest demands on the resources of the earth will permit our little earthly paradises to survive and grow in number, though life within them will be different from now. Petrol, plastics, stripey toothpaste, snap, crackle and pop are not essentials for fulfilment, and there is no reason why, if science and an ordered way of life can be preserved, all those who can then live in quiet places should not be able to produce a little bit of metal and the tools with which to fashion most of their necessities.'

- 1978 According to C. H. Waddington in *The Man-Made Futures*: 'It seems that both the components necessary for dealing with the world's crisis are at least in existence and probably growing: on the one hand, social pressures with some political and economic power behind them, and, on the other, individuals who are willing to strive after goals of fulfilment of a kind different to those which have motivated historical changes of the last century or so. The real question for the young generation of today is, I think, whether these two forces can be brought together to co-operate quickly enough to save the world before some mischance pushes it irretrievably into a disastrous breakdown.'

- 1984 *Population Today* (1996) quoting J. Simon and H. Kahn's (eds.) *Resourceful Earth*: 'If present trends continue, the world in 2000 will be less crowded (though more populated), less polluted, more stable ecologically, and less vulnerable to resource-supply disruption than the world we live in now. Stresses involving population, resources and environment will be less in the future than now ... The world's people will be richer in most ways than they are today ... The outlook for food and other necessities will be better ... Life for most people on earth will be less precarious economically.' According to Simon (1981) there is no meaningful limit to our capacity to go on for ever.

- 1987 In *The Causes of Progress*, Emmanuel Todd argued that cultural change, particularly the diffusion of literacy, is crucial for future development: 'To illuminate the primary of cultural changes and the illusory, even harmful, nature of some of the economic policies currently in force in no way requires us to be pessimistic about the future of the world ... literacy rates are everywhere rising. Today's statistical graphs make it possible to foresee a not-too-distant future when the whole world will be literate - that is to say, freed from ignorance ... For mankind it will bring to a happy conclusion what has been a lengthy childhood.'

- 1992 Meadows and associates have already been quoted in section 11.5, but their theme is put slightly differently here with reference to their various models projecting basic elements into the future. The point they make here is that the world faces not a preordained future, but a choice: 'It is difficult to speak of or practice love, friendship, generosity, understanding or solidarity within a system whose rules, goals and information streams are geared for lesser human qualities. But we try and we urge you to try. Be patient with yourself and others as you and they confront the difficulty of a changing world. Understand and empathize with inevitable resistance; there is some resistance, some clinging to the ways of unsustainability, within each of us.'

- 1996 In *Caring for the Future* the Independent Commission on Population and Quality of Life stresses: 'All these schemes and proposals notwithstanding [new funding mechanisms], official development assistance (ODA) is bound to remain the backbone of the international development effort. To preserve the viability of the present multilateral arrangements - no matter how unsatisfactory they might be - the commission urges once again that a determined international effort be made as a minimum to arrest the downward spiral in ODA; and to induce industrial countries to realize their 0.7 per cent commitment as quickly as possible.' So narrowing the gap between rich and poor regions is still the solution?

12.11 SUMMARY OF PROSPECTS FOR 2050

The end of the 15th century was a crucial time for Europe and for the world as a whole. The exploration and conquest of much of the rest of the world by Europeans had just started. New technologies and instruments such as printing and telescopes were introduced and applied in the 15th and 16th centuries. In the 18th and 19th centuries wood, water, wind and animal sources of fuel and power were supplemented and subsequently largely replaced by steam power and other types of energy, mainly from fossil fuels. Although it was suspected by some before the 16th century, the circumnavigation of the globe by Magellan-Elcano (1519-22), showed conclusively to most that the earth's *surface* is finite but unbounded. The existence of the New World and an appreciation that there were other land areas to be explored and communities to be colonised extended the horizons of the Europeans beyond their own continent. The end of the 20th century is again a crucial time for the whole world, the end of Mackinder's Columbian epoch and the virtual end of the colonial empires of European powers. Few areas and communities now remain untouched by the impact of the global economy. Speculation has now turned towards space, the possibility of travel to and the colonisation of other heavenly bodies, and the prospect that there is some form of life elsewhere in the universe. Nearer home, however, the finite nature of the natural resources on the earth's surface and immediately below it has been increasingly appreciated as the world population has grown almost four times in the 20th century.

A number of reasonable goals for the future, to be approached if not reached by around 2050, include the achievement of a virtually sustainable economy, arguably contradicted however by the goal of continuing economic growth, and a reduction of the gap between rich and poor major regions, countries and divisions within them as well as between individuals.

Much of the rural population of developing countries uses only limited quantities of natural resources. In a notional checklist of the numerous types of material consumed by the world's relatively rich people, it is possible to distinguish between products and activities that consume large and small quantities of exhaustible materials, especially non-fuel minerals. In Britain during the Second World War, in addition to rationing, pleas were put out to the public to take their holidays at home (is your journey really necessary?), to grow their own vegetables, share the bathwater. Iron railings, aluminium pans, and newspapers were called in for recycling. Today a European or American might choose between a holiday near home or in another continent. Communication by telephone or computer uses less energy than a journey by car or plane. Any level of consumption of a non-renewable natural resource that involves its destruction or disappearance threatens sustainability.

The general public of the world has been encouraged by politicians to expect improvements in living standards, whether in the consumption of material goods or in the provision of services. Many economists question the need for concern over the depletion of non-renewable resources or the rise in pollution levels. In *Population Today* (1996) the view of economists is summarised as follows: 'Some economists have argued that with technical ingenuity and properly functioning markets, there are no limits to the number of people the planet can sustain. When markets function well, they argue, resource scarcity will trigger warning signals in the form of higher prices, which will set in motion adaptive behaviors - substitution, recycling, technological innovation, conservation - that will prevent resource depletion.' In theory, economic mechanisms can sort out problems of resource use and environmental degradation and widespread poverty. In theory, according to some scientists (see e.g. Leake (1995)) it will be possible to travel faster than the speed of light. Which theory is more plausible?

Expectations of the fruits of further economic growth are widespread in the developed countries and, if something goes wrong - shortages of particular household goods, shortcomings in health services, traffic congestion - indignation surfaces quickly. Among the masses of the poor in developing countries, concerns are more down-to-earth and hopes rather than expectations prevail: access to a reasonable supply of water not too far from home, sufficient food to survive, fuel to cook with, clothing and shelter, some materials such as old cans to carry water, old tyres to make into footwear, and metal implements for cultivation, not forgetting the ultimate, a sewing machine and a radio that work.

What, then, are the prospects for the next fifty years? Throughout the book, it has been stressed that speculation about the future should be made on a scale ranging from near (or virtual) certainty, to remote possibility. There follows an assessment of the odds and prospects for selected changes in the next 50 years. Another way of looking at the prospects would indeed be to consider the amount of change likely (see Chapter 2).

- *Virtually certain.* Many *non-renewable* (i.e. exhaustible) *natural resources* are being used up on far, far shorter timescales (a few decades, a couple of centuries) than they took to form naturally (millions of years): fossil fuels, non-fuel minerals, plant and animal species (the Dodo or Humpty Dumpty effect), in some circumstances, soil. Even water under the ground in aquifers in some places is being used up more quickly than it accumulates, but the timescales of extraction and natural accumulation are much closer than those for the formation of mineral deposits.

- *Very near certain.* The influence of the *sun* and of the forces in the *earth's interior* will change very little, as also the total quantity of *water* in the world (although its form and location may change), the *atmosphere* (although its content may change slightly), the area of *land* and *sea*, the movement of tectonic plates. Change in *sea level* will only be at most a few tens of centimetres by 2050, no big meteorite (or asteroid or comet) will strike the earth, there will not be drastic changes of *climate*. A devastating *Third World War* will not occur.

- *Near certain.* No journey will be started by a *manned spacecraft* to a destination beyond our own solar system (for example to Alpha Centauri). No *life* will be conclusively proved to exist outside our own planet (other than our own astronauts/cosmonauts out there in space). It follows, therefore, that no aliens will arrive on our own planet. This issue, which is a matter of great curiosity for many people, but of scepticism among many scientists, is dicussed for example by Connor (1996b), Clarke, A.C. (1997), Roger *et al.* (1996). In a paper entitled '*Homo monstruosus*' de Waal Malefijt (1968) gave numerous examples of the credulity of people who accepted over the centuries the reality of monstrous people (not only in the sense of size). She concluded: 'Curiously, however, *Homo monstruosus* is not quite dead. Reports of an "abominable snowman" living in hidden fastnesses of the Himalayas are still (even in the late 1990s) in circulation. Speculation about life on other planets gives rise to new monsters with pointed heads and strange appendages ... When man can conceive of some remote place where other men or manlike creatures might exist, he is profoundly motivated to populate the unknown with creatures of his imagination.' Is gullibility an appropriate description of this tendency or is it just a craving for something unusual or different?

- *Quite near certain.* In 2050 the total *population* of the world will be somewhere between 9 and 10 billion. It will grow much more quickly in some major regions than in others and a larger proportion will live in urban areas than now. In the longer term, population growth is on a knife edge. Small differences in the global fertility in the next few decades could lead to vastly different numbers (see Haub (1992)) by 2150. If, for example, each woman has an average of 2.5 children from 1985 to 2150, the total population of the world will grow from about 5 billion in 1985 to about 28 billion by 2150. In contrast, 2.06 would give about 11 billion, and at 1.70 (above that observed in some European countries now and in Japan recently) it would decline to 4 billion.

  The area of the earth's land used for *arable and permanent crops* will be somewhere between 10 and 13 per cent (11 per cent now). The area of *tropical rain forest* in the world will diminish considerably, to around half what it is now.

  The extraction of *oil* will be less than half what it is now (3.36 billion tonnes in 1996). Some further oil products will be obtained from tar sands and shales.

- *Good probability.* *Coal* and *natural gas* extraction will diminish more gradually than oil production. *Nuclear* power output will increase 2-3 times. Production from *alternative*, clean sources of energy will increase quickly (relatively) but will still account for only 10-20 per cent of electricity generated in 2050.

- *More difficult to say.* The *'development gap'* may be narrower relatively than it is in the 1990s but may be greater absolutely. Official development assistance and other assistance may increase, but would be diluted by the presence of far more people in poor countries than in 2000. Even a fundamental change in attitude towards development and the present gap between rich and poor countries (not much sign of it at present), coupled with the existence of a very powerful global central planning authority, would still not be able to change the situation.

  The Development Gap (Cole (1981)), gives evidence and examples to show that even the maximum feasible international redistribution of population and/or means of production from countries poor in natural resources to countries rich in these, or from predominantly agricultural to predominantly industrial ones, could not be on a scale large enough to change the situation radically in the next 50 years. Figure 12.11 shows the abyss as illustrated by the author in 1981 and Figure 12.12 the greater abyss in the late 1990s.

- *Difficult to anticipate.* Any expectation of a boring post-historical age following the demise of the USSR and the end of the Cold War seems, like rumours of the death of Mark Twain, greatly exaggerated. Like population change, democracy as understood in North America, Western Europe, Australia, New Zealand and a few other countries is a fragile state of affairs, on a knife edge. Of the estimated 106 billion people who have ever lived in the world, only a few billion, almost all in the 20th century, have lived (and voted) in a country with universal adult franchise, one of the attributes of a democratic system. Even around

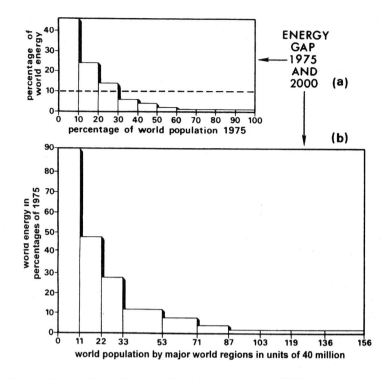

Figure 12.11 The global abyss. Shows the scale of the global energy gap in 1975 and as expected in 2000, (see Cole (1981)). The population of the world is subdivided into 10 groups, each with 10 per cent of the total population of the world (about 4 billion in 1975) and the 10 groups are ranked according to the amount of energy used. In 1975(a) to achieve a hypothetical even shareout of energy use, the three highest columns would have to be truncated at the broken line and transferred to the other seven. By 2000(b) the total world population will be more than 50 per cent above the 1975 level and more energy will be used per capita. The relative gap will not have changed much so the absolute amount of transfers needed to level out energy use will be much greater.

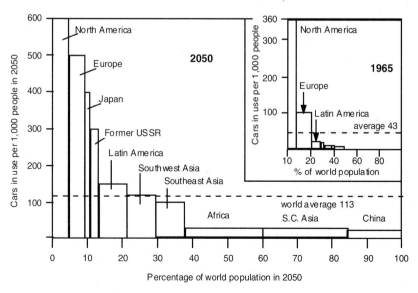

Figure 12.12 A similar comparison on a much longer timescale has been made for cars in use. Between 1965 and 2050 the population of the world will have grown three times while the number of cars in use could increase about eight times. As shown in Table 8.2, the distribution of cars in use would be somewhat more equable, but the absolute magnitude of the 'car gap' would be far greater.

1920, after women had won the vote in the UK and the USA, one person one vote was still not established because in the UK university graduates had two votes while in Southeast USA non-whites were effectively excluded. Even in those countries of the world in which universal suffrage is practised and various human rights are respected, democratic systems may be overturned by the military.

The Royal Institute of International Affairs (1996) has produced the 1996 Chatham House Forum Report, *Unsettled Times, Three Stony Paths to 2015*. The consensus of the contributors seems to be that the diffusion of democratic systems with a predominantly market economy worldwide is far from a foregone conclusion.

Three medium-term futures are summarised here:

- *Faster, faster* points to a world of starkly accelerating change, in which transformation is rapid and innovation is ceaseless.

- *The Post-Industrial Revolution* brings relative economic success, which creates conditions for purposeful change.

- *Rough neighbours* emerge as the industrial world (IW) falls into a period of general difficulty: 'The effect is ... a decade of muddled strife, from which the IW emerges fragmented and bruised, with any claim to global leadership compromised. It is confronted by an Asian economic region, revolving around Chinese predominance and answering to different ethical and political imperatives to those with which the industrial world feels familiar. A political centre of weight has developed around a number of the Islamic nations. The low-income world is cross-hatched with competing ideologies. Many of these alternative views find enthusiasts amongst the less capable within the industrial world, linked together by information technology.'

Of many adjectives applicable to people, the author particularly dislikes being called boring, naive, or gullible. He hopes that the reader who has managed to get through this book or has dipped into it has not found it too boring. Some parts may seem naive. He feels however that out there many people are gullible with regard to what they are told about prospects for the next fifty years and more. One reason, already noted at the beginning of the book, is that they lack a factual basis about both the world of the 1990s and trends and changes in the last 50 years. The main function of the present book was to help to put that right and to provide a basis for speculation about the next fifty years. No one has a monopoly here and everyone should be able to speculate if they wish.

For the last fifty years politicians have promised all kinds of bright futures, often, however, after huge sacrifices and strenuous efforts. Scientists and space agencies come up with assertions about possible advantages of space exploration, perhaps one reason being to obtain more funds for research. The development gap will go away if the poor educate themselves (e.g. Todd (1987)). Economists, many of whom, it seems, have never set foot in a really poor country like Haiti, Ethiopia, Tanzania, or Yemen, assert that the proper management of resources and the environment is all that is needed to raise such places to respectable if not dazzling heights. One American commentator, very out of touch with reality in the view of the author, proposed that the farmers of Kansas (who each grow enough food to support about 100 people) should sell food to Ethiopia where, given their very low productivity, farmers should leave the land and find better jobs. The ultimate answer to the problems of the development gap?

Centuries ago the cities of the Maya civilisation were abandoned, one explanation being exhaustion of their surrounding bioclimatic resources. At that time there were flourishing civilisations in many other parts of the world. The whole world is now faced with the situation of the Mayas. The prospect for humans over the next century or so has been likened to that of the Titanic, steaming towards an iceberg. This analogy might more appropriately be expressed in reverse as follows: the *Titanic* is the natural environment on which we all ultimately depend and the iceberg is 'manned' by humans, determined to sink it. Reverse thinking may, at times, produce dividends. The Trojans got it wrong in the expression 'Beware of Greeks bringing gifts.' This should have been 'Beware of gifts bringing Greeks.'

APPENDIX I

ANSWERS TO QUIZ ON PAGE xiii

1.   About 5,840 million a reasonable is answer 5,800 to 6,000.

2.   About 9,370,000 sq. km. (3,620,000 sq. miles).

3.   About 40,000 km. (25,000 miles).

4.   Saturn: about 10; Alpha Centauri: about 250,000.

5.   The Arctic is an ocean, Antarctica is a continent.

6.   About 11 per cent.

7.   India 340, Ethiopia 100.

8.   42.

APPENDIX II

DATA SETS FOR VARIOUS PROJECTIONS IN CHAPTERS 5-8
SHOWN IN FIGURES AS INDICATED

	Figure 5.1 Arable and permanent crops (hectares)		Figure 5.3 Forest and woodland (hectares)		Figure 5.4 Permanent pasture (hectares)	
	millions	per capita	millions	per capita	millions	per capita
1950	1,301	0.52	3,900	1.55	2,370	0.94
1955	1,370	0.51	3,900	1.43	2,480	0.91
1960	1,410	0.47	4,050	1.36	2,570	0.86
1965	1,420	0.43	4,060	1.23	3,050	0.92
1970	1,460	0.40	4,080	1.12	3,080	0.84
1975	1,460	0.37	4,120	1.03	3,120	0.78
1980	1,450	0.33	4,150	0.94	3,200	0.72
1985	1,470	0.30	4,130	0.85	3,200	0.66
1990	1,450	0.27	4,030	0.76	3,360	0.63

	Figure 5.5 Cereal production (tonnes)		Figure 5.5 Cereal area (hectares)		Figure 5.6 Livestock units	
	millions	per capita	millions	per capita	millions	per capita
1950	686	0.27	600	0.24	923	366
1955	836	0.31	650	0.24	1,166	429
1960	967	0.32	660	0.22	1,261	423
1965	1,054	0.32	687	0.21	1,396	423
1970	1,235	0.34	705	0.19	1,487	407
1975	1,407	0.35	740	0.18	1,570	391
1980	1,620	0.37	732	0.17	1,624	367
1985	1,791	0.37	716	0.15	1,672	345
1990	1,883	0.36	702	0.13	1,697	320
1995	1,970	0.35	685	0.12	n.a.	n.a.

n.a. = not available

	Figure 5.8 Fish catch		Figure 5.9 Fertilisers		Figure 5.10 Tractors	
	(millions of tonnes)	(kgs per capita)	(millions of tonnes)	(kgs per capita)	(millions)	(per 1,000 people)
1950	21.6	8.6	12.9	5.1	6.1	2.4
1955	28.2	10.5	18.9	6.9	8.6	3.1
1960	39.6	13.2	28.1	9.4	11.0	3.7
1965	54.2	16.4	43.1	13.1	13.4	4.1
1970	66.6	18.3	66.5	18.2	15.5	4.2
1975	68.1	17.2	91.3	22.7	17.7	4.4
1980	72.9	16.5	116.8	26.2	21.3	4.8
1985	87.0	17.9	134.0	27.6	24.6	5.1
1990	98.4	18.6	151.0	28.5	26.2	4.9

| | *Figure 6.1* Coal | | *Figure 6.2* Oil | | *Figure 6.3* Natural gas | |
	(millions of tonnes)	*(kgs per capita)*	*(millions of tonnes)*	*(kgs per capita)*	*(billion cubic metres)*	*(cubic metres per capita)*
1950	1,466	580	535	212	200	79
1955	1,605	590	770	283	320	118
1960	1,858	620	1,060	356	470	158
1965	1,968	600	1,525	462	710	215
1970	2,099	580	2,240	614	1,040	285
1975	2,355	590	2,815	700	1,270	316
1980	2,703	610	3,015	682	1,470	333
1985	3,129	650	2,850	588	1,650	340
1990	3,510	660	3,140	592	1,950	368

| | *Figure 6.4* All electricity production | | *Figure 6.4* Hydro-and nuclear electricity production | |
	(Billion kWh)	*(kWh per)*	Hydro-electricity *(billion kWh)*	Nuclear electricity *(billion kWh)*
1950	960	381	343	–
1960	2,285	767	686	3
1970	4,941	1,354	1,175	90
1980	8,154	1,845	1,740	714
1990	11,688	2,205	2,182	1,984

| | *Figure 7.1* Cotton production | | *Figure 7.2* Roundwood production | | *Figure 7.3* Cement production | |
	(thousand tonnes)	*(kgs per capita)*	*(million cubic metres)*	*(per capita cubic metres)*	*(million tonnes)*	*(kgs per capita)*
1950	7,820	3.10	1,490	0.59	141	56
1955	9,360	3.44	1,710	0.64	214	79
1960	10,153	3.41	1,800	0.60	314	105
1965	11,248	3.41	2,050	0.62	435	132
1970	11,954	3.28	2,350	0.65	574	157
1975	13,137	3.27	2,650	0.67	727	181
1980	14,226	3.22	2,930	0.66	859	194
1985	16,300	3.36	3,200	0.66	966	199
1990	18,503	3.49	3,460	0.65	1,142	215

| | *Figure 7.4* Aluminium production | | *Figure 7.5* Copper production | | *Figure 7.6* Pig iron production | | *Figure 8.3* passenger cars produced | |
	(million tonnes)	*(kgs per capita)*	*(million tonnes)*	*(kgs per capita)*	*(million tonnes)*	*(kgs per capita)*	*(millions)*	*(per thousand population)*
1950	1.4	0.55	2.5	1.0	131	52	8.2	3.3
1955	2.6	0.97	3.1	1.1	187	69	9.2	3.4
1960	3.5	1.17	4.1	1.4	241	81	11.5	3.9
1965	5.8	1.75	5.0	1.5	328	99	18.0	5.4
1970	9.5	2.61	6.3	1.7	428	117	24.3	6.7
1975	14.4	3.59	7.7	1.9	503	125	28.2	7.0
1980	18.0	4.07	8.1	1.8	509	115	29.3	6.6
1985	19.7	4.07	8.5	1.8	488	101	31.5	6.5
1990	21.9	4.12	9.0	1.7	536	101	34.5	6.5

APPENDIX III

SOME MISSED THEMES

Many big topics have received little attention in the book. Some have been given low priority simply because their predictability is poor; others depend on changes in topics discussed in some detail. Some are listed here as other themes for the reader to speculate about.

Ageing (or aging). A problem for the next few decades mainly for Europe, Japan and to a lesser extent North America, but a cause for concern also in China. As population growth slows down, ceases and is replaced by decline, the elderly section of the dependent population grows, relatively, while the young section decreases. Resources are shifted from education to healthcare. To some extent the question is a matter of definition and statistical conventions. If necessary (as during the Second World War) many people in their sixties and some in their seventies are perfectly able to work. One reason why most do not is that unemployment is fairly high and there are plenty of younger people to work.

Child labour. In the 1990s children below official school leaving age work full time or part time in many countries of the world. Child soldiers are used in East Africa, child prostitutes in Southeast Asia. In India (and elsewhere) children work long hours in factories and cottage industries. In Colombia their size and agility make them excellent coal miners. In Brazil they cut sugar cane and in Nepal they may be born into slavery. A situation that was largely eradicated in Western Europe and the USA by the end of the 19th century still continues in many developing countries and even in some developed countries.

Conflict. If 2000-2050 is at all like 1950-2000 there will be many regional conflicts and attempts at peace-keeping. Relics of previous conflicts, such as anti-personnel mines and of nuclear testing (Kazakhstan, Nevada, Australia, the Pacific) will still pose problems in 2050.

Education. Data on contrasting levels of educational facilities and of literacy are available in *UN Human Development Reports* and elsewhere. In developed countries education is continuously being extended to higher age groups. Is it really essential or is it a way to keep young people off the job market?

Gender issues. Numerous data are available in Human Development Report. The tendency is to emphasise gender issues prevalent in developed countries such as the right to vote, equal pay for the same work as men, positions in politics and management, access to education and healthcare. Unlikely to change much by 2050.

Healthcare. Much expenditure on research into and prevention and cure of various diseases goes to the populations of developed countries and to the well-off minority in developing countries. Sophisticated medicines and surgery contribute to prolonging life of the already elderly. A big increase on expenditure on the poorer half of the world's population might lower infant and child mortality rates and contribute to the population explosion.

Human rights. Largely those regarded as crucial or desirable in Western Europe and North America. Elsewhere they are widely ignored (Africa) or opposed with various degrees of vigour (some Islamic countries, China). Little change by 2050?

Languages. Behind the scenes, many languages with few speakers, like plant and animal species, are dying out (e.g. the last person to speak Cornish died in the 18th century). At the other end of the scale, English appears to be gaining on other languages as the second language in many parts of the world (mainly due to the US influence). Some change by 2050.

Overpopulation. This term has been avoided in the book. There is no universally accepted precise definition of the term. Density of population is certainly no more than a starting point for discussion.

Robotisation. On the experience of the second half of the 20th century there should be many new developments in this area before 2050 but, as with many other technological developments, the impact will generally be greater in developed than in developing countries.

Scientific progress. There is some disagreement as to whether all major scientific discoveries have now been made or whether scientific ends might not be simply new beginnings.

Unemployment. Only very rough estimates for most developing countries. There are great variations in developed countries (e.g. Japan, Switzerland about 3 per cent, Spain 15); it is a matter of definition. In developing countries many people are underemployed. In the former USSR there was officially no unemployment, epitomised by the 'key ladies' in hotels, one per floor, sometimes two. Little change likely by 2050.

GLOSSARY OF TERMS AND PITFALLS FOR SPECULATORS ABOUT THE FUTURE

Alpha Centauri The nearest star to our sun, actually a cluster of three stars, also referred to as Proxima Centauri

Anthropocentrism also **Anthropomorphism** Putting the human species at the centre of things in the world. Ascription of a human form and attributes to a (the) deity, or to anything impersonal

Arable land See *Cultivated land*

Back to the future A fashionable expression, at times vague, usually referring to the act of bringing something from the past to be used in the future, as for example, the restoration of the monarchy in Spain, the return to a (mainly) market economy in Russia after seven decades of Communist Party rule.

Berlin Wall was erected in 1961 to prevent people from migrating from Soviet controlled East Germany (including East Berlin) into West Berlin and thence into West Germany. See also Iron Curtain.

Bioclimatic resources The water, soil and climatic elements that support plant and animal life, as opposed to mineral resources including fossil fuels and metallic and non-metallic materials.

Biodiversity The variety of organisms considered at all levels, especially with regard to the communities that exist in given habitats, the physical conditions under which they live, and their interdependence. The biodiversity of a given habitat may be threatened by human interference.

Birthrate The number of births occurring in a given period (usually a year) in a given region (usually administrative) expressed in per thousand of the total population of the region. More specifically, the number of births may be related to the number of members (usually only female) in a given age group.

Borrowing time See *Buying time.*

Buying time Delaying the occurrence of a given situation, as for example by reducing emissions of pollutants, or carbon dioxide to 'improve' the environment or 'prevent' global warming. Similar to Borrowing time.

Central Europe A geographical term loosely applied to the area between Germany, the Baltic coast, Russia and the southern Balkans. Between 1945 and the 1990s the tendency was to subdivide Europe only into Western and Eastern blocs. Central Europe is back in fashion and roughly includes countries not in the European Union or the former USSR.

Circularity Projections that cancel out. For example, to grow crops to produce motor fuel to save oil (petroleum) and use oil to produce food to save agricultural land. You can't have your cake and eat it.

Cold War The ideological, cultural, political and economic confrontation between Western (capitalist) and Eastern (communist) countries, the main protagonists being the USA and USSR. It was at its most intense in Europe but was waged globally, in spite of the existence of a Third World of unaligned countries. Officially ended by M. Gorbachev in 1986.

Conspiracy syndrome The tendency to suspect some secret, behind-the-scenes, agreement on various scales from individuals to whole states. In 1956 the UK and French governments sent troops to protect the Suez Canal on the grounds that Israel was about to occupy it. Later it was revealed that it was a pretext to regain control of the 'vital' canal after Egypt had nationalised it. A case was seriously put that after Soviet-Chinese relations broke down publicly around 1960, in reality the two countries continued to collaborate in various ways. The idea that there is a conscious conspiracy among the rich countries and between them and rich people in the poor countries to keep the development gap as wide as it is would require too many people to keep it from becoming public knowledge.

Country A general term popularly used to refer to a sovereign (independent) state, a colony, even a subdivision within a sovereign state (e.g. Scotland in the UK, Tibet in China). Not synonymous with nation since many countries in the world have more than one nationally conscious group (e.g. former Yugoslavia).

Counter-factual A recent term referring specifically to the creation of alternative pasts, what might/could have happened if a given decision had not been made or event happened (e.g. if Hitler had won the Second World War in Europe).

Cropland See *Cultivated land*.

Cultivated land Land used to grow annual ('field') or permanent (tree or shrub) plants. Also applicable to temporary pasture as opposed to permanent, often natural pasture. *Arable land* and *sown area* refer usually only to crops planted annually. *Fallow* is land temporarily unsown or 'resting'. *Cropland* is broadly synonymous with cultivated land.

Deathrate The number of deaths occurring in a given region (usually administrative) expressed in per thousand of the total population of the region in a given period (usually a year).

Deforestation Clearance of forest, usually deliberately by human activities.

Delphi method An approach to speculation about the future referring to the consultation of a team of (usually) experts on a given subject, from whom a consensus (or lack of consensus) may serve as a guide as to what may be expected to happen.

Demographic Transition Model An empirically based model in which during an unspecified period of time the relationship between birthrate and deathrate changes, usually producing a period in which birthrate exceeds deathrate and population therefore grows. See example in Figure 2.2.

Dependency ratio The ratio of the economically dependent part of the population (usually under 15 plus over age 64) to the productive part (15-64).

Desalination The processing of sea/salt water to produce fresh water.

Developed countries The richer countries of the world according to a variety of criteria. Also referred to as Industrial, First (and second) World, North. See also *Developing countries*.

Developing countries The poorer countries of the world according to a variety of criteria. Also referred to as less developed, Third World and South. Third World originally referred to neutral countries in the ideological confrontation of the Cold War. South is geographically misleading, especially when extended to southern hemisphere, because some rich countries are among the most southerly, notably Australia, New Zealand and Argentina, and because most of the population in poorer countries, including India and China, is actually in the northern hemisphere.

Development A term widely used in the second half of the 20th century to refer to economic growth, industrialisation, modernisation, political and social change. A more neutral term might be transformation, which does not imply improvement. Development at times includes destruction, as of forests for their products or to make way for cultivation or reservoirs.

Development gap Sometimes used to refer to the difference, usually in economic or material terms, between the richest and poorest regions (especially countries) of the world.

Discovery Finding something hitherto unknown. It is patronising and inappropriate for the journeys of exploration of Europeans since the 15th century to lands already inhabited and, therefore known, to be referred to as voyages of discovery. A distinction should also be made between discoveries (e.g. how the solar system 'works') and inventions (e.g. the steam engine).

Doubling time (of population) The number of years needed for a given population to double its present size, assuming the current rate of population growth continues.

Drops in the ocean An apt description of many efforts to help the poor, especially in the developing countries (see Chapter 9 on official development assistance), and likewise to save materials and reduce pollution. Donations to private charities to help the poor are useful in a limited way but also ease consciences of the rich.

Ecocomic system The production, distribution and consumption of goods and services, with a contrast in organisation between a market economy, with most of the means of production in the private sector and a command (centrally planned) economy, with most of the means of production in the public (state) sector.

Ecosystem The organisms living in a particular environment and the physical part of the environment that impinges on them.

Emerging nations A term little used before the 1990s, now a common way of referring to developing countries, especially those with recent industrial growth.

Epidemiological Transition Model See also Demographic Transition Model. The ETM focuses on the causes of death, with contagious and parasitic afflictions keeping deathrate high in the early stages but (with improved healthcare) degenerative afflictions such as heart diseases and cancer gaining in prominence as causes of death as life expectancy increases.

Fallacies So-called Netherlands fallacy refers to density of population. The Netherlands is one of the richest countries of Europe. The density of population is more than 16 times as high as that of the USA. Therefore the USA could support 16 times as many people as it does now. The absurdity of such an assertion is shown if it is extended to Singapore, which has a density of population about 160 times that of the USA. In the present book the author refers to the idea that the world's problems will start to go away if and when zero population growth is achieved as the zero-growth fallacy. P. Ehrlich made the comment on a TV programme early in

June 1992: 'The idea that every country could become a net exporter of manufactured goods could only be taken seriously by dinosaurs and economists.'

Fallow land See *Cultivated land*

Fighting past battles Some individuals, institutions and whole countries may find themselves using past experiences as a pretext for dissatisfaction and unrest. The Irish have waited a century and a half for an apology from the British government for the way its predecessor handled the Irish potato famine. In Bosnia in the early 1990s Croats and Serbs turned on Muslims, the Serbs reminding themselves and the world of a defeat by the Ottoman Turks six centuries ago.

Fossil fuels Coal, oil (petroleum), natural gas, including different types such as anthracite and lignite, oil in shales and tar sands.

Fraud See *Hoaxes.*

Globalisation A term fashionable especially in the 1980s and 1990s referring particularly to the tendency for each transnational company to operate in many countries and even worldwide. Communications have facilitated and accompanied globalisation. Arguably the earliest global enterprise was the activity in the tropical world of the crowns of Spain and Portugal during 1580-1640 when they were united.

'Greenhouse' effect A process perceived by many scientists, resulting from the increasing amount of carbon dioxide and other substances in the atmosphere, caused particularly by the burning of fossil fuels and forests. The sun's rays are 'trapped' in the atmosphere causing warming. Expectations of what could happen from the process vary even among those who assume it is actually happening.

Gross Domestic Product (GDP) The total value of goods and services produced in a given period (usually a year). The total amount earned domestically. Gross National Product has a slightly different meaning since it includes income from abroad but excludes imports and property income paid abroad. For the purposes of the present book, the difference is not marked enough for it to matter which particular index is being used. Some publications (e.g. the World Bank), use GNP, some (e.g. UN Human Development Report) use GDP. Real Gross Domestic Product refers to the Gross Domestic Product of a given country after adjustments have been made to allow for distortions in exchange rates (usually in relation to the US dollar).

Gross National Product See *Gross Domestic Product.*

Gullibility The ease with which individuals and whole populations alike can be deceived into thinking that something untrue, preposterous or impossible is happening, such as the presence on our planet of anthropomorphic aliens or the prospect that the gap between rich and poor countries will disappear in a few decades time.

Hangover terms The use of terms that no longer have the meaning they originally had. Third World is now used to refer to the developing countries. Originally it referred to countries that were (or claimed to be) neutral with regard to the ideological conflict between the West and the East. When the British Labour Party was founded a century ago it contained many people who 'laboured' with their hands. Few do now.

Hoaxes The deliberate falsification of data or faking of material with the deliberate intention of producing an impact or for financial gain. Examples include the alleged invention of data by Sir Cyril Burt to support his views on intelligence, the Piltdown skull, Hitler's diaries, and much of the data published in Soviet (and other) statistical yearbooks.

Humpty Dumpty effect Events that change a situation irreversibly or irretrievably. For example, loss of virginity, once a disaster outside wedlock, now for many a great achievement. The loss of species, topsoil and minerals. A more marginal case is the extraction of water from boreholes into an (underground) aquifer (see Chapter 5). Such water will be replaced by rain falling over a wide area, but its level will drop if extraction exceeds replacement.

Iberia(n) Spain and Portugal, also Ibero-America, Latin America except for some small countries (Haiti, Jamaica, Guyanas).

Ice cap/Ice sheet The two terms are largely interchangeable but the former is generally used for Greenland, the latter for Antarctica. Ice sheets may cover sea areas as well as land. Ice corer, on individual mountain ranges outside Greenland and Antarctica is generally referred to as glaciers.

I'm alright Jack A British naval expression which in the broader context of future events might succinctly sum up the attitude of many people regarding prospects for people elsewhere or for future generations. My house is more than 100 metres above sea level. If sea level rises to 60 metres I will still be okay.

Indigenous 'Native' to a place, usually the earliest known settlers of a region, applied also to e.g. resources (i.e. local).

Industry Loosely used term, at one extreme covering virtually all economic activities, at the other referring specifically to processing and manufacturing. Generally the 'middle' of three broad categories of economic activity, agriculture (with forestry and fishing), industry (including mining) and services ('non-goods'). Post-industrial and de-industrialise are recent concepts.

Invention See *Discovery*.

Iron Curtain Not to be confused with the Berlin Wall. The Iron Curtain applied soon after 1945 to the heavily protected border between two Germanies, East (Soviet) and West (Western allies), preventing the free movement of people between the two except within Berlin itself, where the underground provided a leak until the Berlin Wall was erected in 1961.

Least developed countries A United Nations term, determined by the General Assembly (resolution 46/206), referring to about 30 very poor countries as determined by particular criteria.

Life expectancy The average number of years a person can be expected to live assuming a continuation of current mortality rates.

Migration A change of residence which is intended to be permanent and which involves crossing internal or international boundaries.

More of the same A useful expression which, however, has at least two possible meanings: a continuation of (recent) past trends, or a larger quantity of something (e.g. Mexico City in 1997 is very similar to Mexico City in 1967 but has twice as much of everything).

Nation See *Country*.

Natural gas Gas extracted from geological formations, not to be confused with 'town gas', extracted from coal (leaving coke and by-products).

Natural increase of population The amount by which a population increases (or increases negatively, i.e. decreases) in a given period through a difference in the number of births and deaths. The gain or loss is often expressed as a percentage of the initial total, e.g. the population of a given region is 100,000 in mid-1993, 102,000 in mid-1994, a natural increase of 2.0 per cent, there having been no immigration or emigration.

Needs and wants Assessing the needs of the poor in various regions and countries of the world is a major industry. Even absolutely basic needs differ from one region to another (e.g. clothing in the tropics and the Arctic). Most people want more than they need, some far more. In modern industrial societies, things that were at one time luxuries or non-existent, such as the car, have become necessities in new life-style conditions.

Oil A mineral fossil fuel, commonly referred to, especially in the USA, as petroleum, and also a vegetable product derived from plants bearing oil seeds (e.g. sunflower).

Peace Dividend The (financial) benefit of reducing expenditure on arms, the general idea being that the saving could be redeployed for example to assist poor countries and to protect the environment. A one-off rather than an on-going process, observed during the last decade or so as the superpowers cut military budgets, one effect being to raise unemployment levels in places depending on the arms industry.

Petroleum See *Oil*.

Per capita, per caput, per head, per inhabitant, per person All having virtually identical meaning. Per caput (singular) is strictly more correct than per capita, the Latin plural (nominative) of head.

Pre-Columbian World before the voyages of Columbus and other European explorers, which led to a global view of the world rather than an appreciation by different populations only of particular parts of it.

Primary Products Particularly products of cultivation, grazing, forestry and mining, often forming the ingredients for subsequent processing and/or manufacturing.

Proxima Centauri (star) See *Alpha Centauri*.

Psychopath A person with dissocial personality disorder, having a gross disparity between behaviour and the prevailing social norms and displaying callous unconcern for the feelings of others. (WHO Geneva ICD-10 Classification of Mental and Behavioural Disorders). Potentially lethal when in a position of great power.

Putting the clock back The expectation (or hope) that technologies and practices now largely or entirely replaced, if reintroduced or extended from a current limited contribution, can solve problems: organic farming, homeopathic medicine, ban the car.

Region This word is widely used in different subjects, with differing connotations. In a geographical or spatial sense, region can refer to a precisely or reasonably clearly defined area or territory, from a group of countries to a single country, a subdivision of country, or an area with distinct physical characteristics (e.g. a mountain region).

Scenario Generally used to describe a specific situation some time in the future resulting from particular decisions and events, created to illustrate or support the expectation of an individual or a team speculating about the future.

Second World War Conventionally it started in 1939 when Germany and the Soviet Union occupied Poland and the UK and France declared war on Germany, and it ended with the defeat of Germany and Japan in 1945. Italy entered in 1940, the Soviet Union, Japan and the USA in 1941.

Sown land See *Cultivated land.*

Supranational Refers to groupings of sovereign states in which each member is involved in an agreement with other states or actually renounces some of its sovereignty. Roughly in increasing degrees of involvement, the following types of supranational entity can be distinguished: military alliance, free trade area, customs union/common market, economic union (e.g. common currency), federal entity.

Sovereign state A state (or country) that is independent. Almost all the sovereign states are represented in the United Nations, but each is entirely responsible for its own internal affairs.

State See *Country.* As well as referring to sovereign state, is used to describe the major civil or administrative divisions of many sovereign countries, especially federal countries (e.g. USA, Brazil).

Surprise-free projection A term used by Kahn and Wiener (1967, p. 5), defined in a somewhat circular fashion: 'a surprise-free projection is one that seems less surprising than any other specific projection'!

Sustainable development A situation in which some kind of economic change is occurring, particularly with growth in material production and consumption, but without immediate or long term damage to the environment and excessive loss of non-renewable natural resources. Commonly used with reference to the possible improvement in living conditions of the poor in resource-poor regions of the developing world. Common sense alone seems to indicate that extractive activities that use up non-renewable natural resources are not sustainable in the long term.

System A interconnected set of elements that is coherently organised around some purpose. A system is more than the sum of its parts.

Things bite back An evocative expression used to highlight instances in which new inventions and technologies, while achieving intended goals, may also bring unexpected consequences, usually negative, as with the use of nuclear power, fossil fuels and chemical fertilisers.

Total fertility rate The average number of children each woman in a given region bears during her (child-bearing) lifetime. This statistic can only be calculated for women who have passed their childbearing period and its application to the estimation of the number of future births must be based on the assumption that there is no change in the observed rate.

Tsunamis (seismic sea waves) Often incorrectly refrered to as tidal waves, are actually caused by earthquakes under the sea, unlike tides, which are regulated by the gravitational attraction of the sun and moon.

White elephant A term originating in Southeast Asia in the unusual, rare birth of a white elephant, given as a useless gift intended to ruin the recipient. The sense has been transferred to projects that turn out to be excessively expensive, do not fulfil intended purposes, or are of little use. Brasilia, the Channel Tunnel and the Sydney Opera House are candidates.

Wilding In the area of wildlife and conservation the word refers to the process not just of leaving an area to revert to a natural state but of actively attempting to eradicate species and features not belonging to the original state.

Work animals Often referred to as draught animals, implying *pulling* loads. Work animals also *carry* loads and race for entertainment. They should be distinguished from animals producing milk, meat, hides.

Zero-sum game A term used in Game Theory in which losses and gains balance out, as for example in the card game of poker.

Zero population growth A population in equilibrium with a growth rate of zero, a situation reached when births plus immigration equal deaths plus emigration. In the view of the author such a situation is unlikely to last for a long time.

BACKGROUND READING

Background reading by topics. The full reference to each item can be found in References

Agriculture, water and food

Bender, W. (1997a), Bennett, J. (1987), Bongaarts, J. (1994), Brouwer, F. M. (1991), Brown, L. R. (1973, 1978, 1981, 1995), Canby, T. (1975), Falkenmark, N. (1992), Idyll, C. P. (1973), Micklin, P. P. (1977), National Geographic Society (1993), OECD (1996), Parry, M. (1990), Peixoto, J. P. (1973), Prosterman, R. L. (1996), Safina, C. (1995).

Data sources

Calendario Atlante de Agostini (annual), Novara, Italy, Food and Agriculture Organisation of the United Nations (FAO), Production Yearbook, Trade Yearbook, League of Nations (1929), OECD (1991), Population Reference Bureau (1997), *Statistical Abstract of the United States* (annual), UNDP (1996), US Bureau of Mines (1985), World Bank (1996), *WPDS 1996* (1996)

Development gap

Brown, L. R. (1997), Cole, J. P. (1981), Dasgupta (1995), Han Baocheng (1993), *Malaysia 2020* (1994), Morris, M. D. (1979), Sen, A. (1993), Thurow, L. C. (1987)

Energy

Attwood, G. (1975), BP (1997), Flower, A. R. (1978), Gibbons, J. H. (1989), Gregory, D. P. (1973), Kammen, D. (1995), Mounfield, P.R. (1991), National Academy of Sciences (1979), Nef, J. U. (1977), Shcherbak, Y. M. (1996).

Environment

Alexander, C. (1997), Bradley, I. (1990b), Colinvaux, P. A. (1989), Cohen, J. (1999), Collins, M. (1990), Core, R. (1995), Department of the Environment (1996), Elliott (1994), Erwin, D. E. (1996), Grove, R. H. (1992), HMSO (1996), Idyll, C. P. (1973), Karl, T. R. (1997), Lents, J. M. (1993), Malle, K.-G. (1996), Middleton, N. (1999), National Geographic Society (1997), Repetto, R. (1990), Revelle, R. (1982), Rice, R. E. (1997), Richards, P. W. (1973), Runnels, C. N. (1995), Schneider, D. (1997), Stanners, D. (1995), Thomas, D. S. G. (1993), Union of Concerned Scientists (1993), Zorpette, G. (1996)

Global views and strategies and future

Allen, R. (1980), Barney, G. O. (1982), Buckminster Fuller, R. (1969), *Caring for the Future* (1996), Dasmann, R. F. (1972), Ehrlich, P. R. (1972), Freeman, C. (1979), Goldsmith, E. R. D. (1972), Gorbachev, M. S. (1986), Kahn, H. (1967, 1977), Kates, T. R. (1997), Kennedy, P. (1993), MacNeill, J. (1989), Masser, I. (1992), Meadows, D. H. (1972, 1992), Mesarovic, M. (1975), Northcott, J. (1991), Pearson, I. (1998), Rostow, W. W. (1960), Sunday Times (1999), Timberlake (1978), Todd, E. (1987), Waddington, C. H. (1978), Wells, H. G. (1914, 1933)

Historical, timescales

Boorstin, D. J. (1975), Brunn, S. D. (1991), Burke, J. (1985), Calder, N. (1984), Cocker, M. (1998), Connor, S. (1996a), Driver, T. S. (1996), Ferguson, N. (1997), Gould, S.J. (1997), Hart, M. H.

(1993), Hawking, S. W. (1988), Horne, A. (1996), Kennedy, P. (1987), Mackinder, H. J. (1904), Morrison, P. (1982), Rostow, W. W. (1975), Toynbee, A.J. (1952), Wallerstein, I. (1983)

Materials and natural resources
Alexandersson, G. (1978), Alleman, J. E. (1997), Clark, J. P. (1986), Cloud, P. E. (1968, 1969), Eyre, S. R. (1978), Jensen, R.G. (1983), Larson, E. D. (1986), Livernash, R. (1998), Manners, G. (1981), Rees, J. (1985), Ridker, R. G. (1979, 1980), Sheldon, R. P. (1982), Simon, J. L. (1981, 1984), Smil, V. (1997)

Methodology of speculation about the future
Ayres, R. U. (1979), Clarke, I. F. (1979, 1985a, 1985b), Cole, H. S. D. (1973), Davis, W. (1996), Forrester, J. W. (1973), Guinness (1999), Hall, P. (1980), Harman, W. W. (1976), Kahn, H. (1967), Kennedy, P. (1993), McRae (1995), Naisbitt, J. (1984), Northcott, J. (1991), Nown, G. (1985), Rosen, S. (1976), Royal Institute of International Affairs (1996), Stillman, E. (1974), Strauss, W. (1991), Toffler, A. (1970)

Philosophical
Bradley, I. (1990a), Hawking, S. W. (1988), Horrobin, D. F. (1969), Sider, R.J. (1978), Swinburne, R. (1996), Vico, G. (1744)

Political and military
Amalrick, A. (1970), British Medical Association (1986), Cole, J. P. (1997), *The Economist* (1992a), Garreau, J. (1981), Harris, N. (1986), Lin, H. (1985), Schwarzbach, D. A. (1997), Smith, D. (1997), Webster, D. (1997), Whipple, G. G. (1996), White, D.W. (1996), Whittemore Boggs, S. (1940)

Population and healthcare
Anderson, R. M. (1992), Aviakan, A. (1996), Beier, G. J. (1976), Bien, M. (1997), Bogue, D. J. (1979), Bouvier, L. F. (1977), Bouvier, L. F. (1984), Caldwell, J. C. (1990, 1996), Calne, R. (1994), Chalkley, K. (1997), Conway, M. (1993), Cornish, E. (1986), Donaldson, P. J. (1990), Frejka, T. (1973), Gelfard, A. (1999), Haub, C. (1987, 1997, 1998), Hauser, P. M. (1971), Henderson, D. A. (1976), Langer, W. L. (1972), Lutz, W. (1994), McEvedy, C. (1978), Olshansky, S. J. (1993, 1997), Perls, T. T. (1995), Ravenstein, E.G. (1885), Robey, B. (1993), van der Tak, J. (1997)

Space
Gehrels, T. (1996), Gingerich, O. (1982), Luminet, J. (1999), Newbery, B. (1997), Roger, J. (1996), *Scientific American* (1999).

Technology
Forester, T. (1985), Geary, J. (1997), Gingerich, O. (1982), *Scientific American* (1995a, 1995b), Tenner, E. (1996)

Transport
De Cicco, J. (1994), *The Economist* (1992b), Gibbs, W.W. (1997), Porter, M. (1997), *Scientific American* (1997), Schafer, A. (1997), Sperling, D. (1996), Wouk, V. (1997)

REFERENCES

Acronyms are located alphabetically in their own right, which may not correspond to their position if they were spelt in full (e.g. EP, European Parliament). Note de in French is lower case d, De in Dutch is capital D. *Sunday Times* has pages numbered according to section - e.g. 1.3, 2.7. Note that in Italian Istituto does not have n after the initial I.

Adams, J. (1997a), 'MoD plans laster curtain against rogue missiles', *The Sunday Times*, 2 March, p. 1.5.

Adams, J. (1997b), 'Whole villages starve to death in Korean famine', *The Sunday Times*, 4 May, p. 1.24.

Ahuja, A. (1997), 'Voyage to Saturn', *The Times*, 13 Oct, p. 15.

Alexander, C. (Editor.) (1997), 'Our Precious World', Special Issue of *Time Magazine*, focusing on environmental issues including biodiversity.

Alexander, G. (1991), 'Old age: Japan's latest export', *Sunday Times*, 24 Feb., p. 1.19.

Alexandersson, G. and Ivar Klevebring, B. (1978), *World Resources, Energy, Metals, Minerals*, Berlin: Walter de Gruyter.

Alleman, J. E. and Mossman, B. T. (1997), 'Asbestos Revisited', *Scientific American*, Vol. 277, No. 1, July, 54–57.

Allen, R. (1980), *How to save the world, a strategy for world conservation*, London: Kogan Page (IUCN, UNEP, WWF).

Amalrik, A. (1970), *Will the Soviet Union Survive Until 1984?*, New York: Harper and Row.

Anderson, R. M. and May, R. M. (1992), 'Understanding the AIDS Pandemic', *Scientific American*, Vol. 266, No. 5, May, pp. 20–27.

Atwood, G. (1975), 'The Strip-mining of Western Coal', *Scientific American*, Vol. 233, No. 6, Dec. pp. 23-29.

Avakian, A. (1996), 'Gaza', *National Geographic*, Vol. 190, No. 3, Sept., pp. 28-53.

Ayres, R. U. (1979), *Uncertain Futures, Challenges for Decision-Makers*, New York: Wiley Interscience.

Back, K. and Sullivan, D. (1972), 'The decline of the ideology of growth', *Population Reference Bureau*, Selection No. 41.

Bairoch, P. *et al.*, 'The Working Population and its Structure', *Statistiques Internationales Retrospectives*, Vol. 1, Université de Bruxelles, Table A.2.

Barney, G. O. (Study Director), (1982), *The Global 2000 Report to the President*, Penguin Books: Harmondsworth.

Barraclough, G. (editor) (1979), *The Times Atlas of World History*, London: Times Books Ltd., pp. 158-9.

Bassett, P. (1996), 'Public sector puzzle casts shadow over job figures', *The Times*, 16 July, p. 27.

Beardsley, T. (1997), 'More gallons per mile', *Scientific American*, Vol. 276, No. 1, Jan., pp. 29-30.

Beeston, R. (1996), 'Thousands face evacuation as food and fuel crisis hits Russia's frozen north', *The Times*, 12 Oct., p. 15.

Beir, G. J. (1976), 'Can Third World Cities Cope?', *Population Bulletin*, Vol. 31., No. 4, Dec., Population Reference Bureau.

Beijing Review, weekly illustrated English language magazine on various aspects of life in China, subscription £19.50 a year at time of writing to China International Book Trading Corporation (Guoji Shudian), P. O. Box 399, Beijing, China.

Bell, S. (1997), 'Ecologists claim Chanel threatens rainforest trees', *The Times*, 2 July, p. 15.

Bender, W. and Smith, M. (1997a), 'Population, Food and Nutrition', *Population Bulletin*, Vol. 51, No. 4, February.

Bender, W. and Smith, M. (1997b), 'Feeding the Future', *Population Today*, Vol. 25, No. 3, March, pp. 4-5.

Bennett, J. and George, S. (1987), *The hunger machine, the politics of food*, Cambridge: Polity Press.

Bergamini, D. (1965), *Mathematics*, Time-Life International (Nederland) N.V.: Life Science Library, p. 146.

Bernoth, A. (1996), 'City forecasts 5% rise in share prices next year', *Sunday Times*, 29 Dec., p. 2.1.

Bernoth, A. and Smith D. (1995), 'Wary City expects little sparkle from shares in 1996', *The Sunday Times Business*, 31 Dec., p. 2.1.

Bien, M. (1997), 'Still planning our retirement', *The European*, 24-30 July, p. 35.

Binyon, M. (1997), 'Australia's stolen children were 'genocide' victims', *The Times*, 12 June, p. 16.

Blundell, N. (1991), *The World's Greatest Mistakes*, London: Hamlyn (first published 1980).

Bogue, D. J. and Tsui, A. O., (1979), 'Zero World Population Growth?'*The Public Interest*, Spring, pp. 99-113.

Bongaarts, J. (1994), 'Can the Growing Human Population Feed Itself?', *Scientific American*, Vol. 270, No. 3., March, pp. 18-24.

Boorstin, D. J. (1975), 'The birth of exploration', *The Listener*, 13 Nov., p. 633.

Bouvier, L. F. (1984), 'Planet Earth 1984–2034: A Demographic Vision', *Population Bulletin*, Vol. 39, No. 1, Feb., Population Reference Bureau.

Bouvier, L. F., Shryock, H. S. and Henderson, H. W. (1977), 'International Migration: Yesterday, Today and Tomorrow', *Population Bulletin*, vol. 31, No. 4., Sept., Population Reference Bureau. International migration in the third quarter of the 20th century and earlier periods.

BP (1996), *BP Statistical Review of World Energy 1996*, London: The British Petroleum Company plc. Also earlier years and 1997.

Bradley, I. (1990a), 'Greening of Christian theology', *The Times*, 29 Jan., p. 16.

Bradley, I. (1990b), *God is Green: Christianity and the Environment*, London: Darton, Longman and Todd.

Bragg, M. (1996), 'Did the cave man say it all before we did?', *The Times*. 11 Nov, p. 18, a review of S. J. Gould's *Life's Grandeur*.

Bremner, C. (1997), 'Russia sets sights on joining EU', *The Times*, 19 July, p. 15.

Brierley, D. (1995), 'Rush for oil in the "new North Sea"', *The European*, 10-16 Aug., p. 17.

Brierley, D. (1997), 'Death rattle of the Superphénix', *The European*, 19-25 June, p. 21.

British Medical Association (1986), *The long-term environmental and medical effects of a nuclear war*, March, London: the BMA Board of Science and Education (p. 8 quoted).

Brodie, I. (1997), 'Oil battle looms at Alaska sanctuary', *The Times*, 12 July, p. 14.

Brouwer, F. M., Thomas, A. J., and Chadwick, M. J. (1991), *Land Use Change, Environmental Transformations and Future Patterns*, Dordrecht: Kluwer Academic Publishers, (The GeoJournal Library, Vol. 18).

Brown, L. R. (1973), 'Population and Affluence: Growing Pressures on World Food Resources', *Population Bulletin*, vol. 29, No. 2, Population Reference Bureau.

Brown, L. R. (1978), 'The Worldwide Loss of Cropland', *Worldwatch Paper 24*, October, Worldwatch Institute.

Brown, L. R. (1981), 'World Food Resources and Population: The Narrowing Margin', *Population Bulletin*, Vol. 36, No. 3, Sept., Population Reference Bureau.

Brown, L. R. (1995), *Who Will Feed China?*, London: Earthscan Publications

Brown, L. R. *et al.* (1997), *State of the World 1997*, London: Earthscan Publications.

Brunn, S. D. and Leinbach, T. R. (Editors), (1991), *Collapsing space and time*, London: Harper Collins Academic.

Buckminster Fuller, R. (1969), *Utopia or Oblivion, The Prospects for Humanity*, New York: Bantam Books Ltd.

Bureau of Mines (1985), *Mineral Facts and Problems*, Bulletin 675, United States Department of the Interior, Washington: US Government Printing Office.

Burke, J. (1985), *The Day the Universe Changed*, London: British Broadcasting Corporation.

Burroughs, W. (1996), 'Wait for the big bang', *The Times*, 16 Sept., p. 14.

Buscall, E. (1994), 'Tighten the net to save the needy tomorrow', *The European*, 11-17, Feb., p. 11.

Calder, N. (1984), *Timescale: an atlas of the fourth dimension*, London: Chatto and Windus.

Caldwell, J. C. and Caldwell, P. (1990), 'High Fertility in Sub-Saharan Africa', *Scientific American*, Vol. 262, No. 5, May, pp. 82-89.

Caldwell, J. C. and Caldwell, P. (1996), 'The African AIDS Epidemic', *Scientific American*, Vol. 274, No. 3, March, pp. 40-46.

Calne, R. (1994), *Too Many People*, London: Calder Publications, Riverrun Press.

Campbell, C.J. and Laherrère, J.H. (1998), 'The End of Cheap Oil', *Scientific American*, Vol. 278, No. 3, March, pp. 60-65.

Canby, T. (1975), 'Can the World Feed Its People?' *National Geographic*, Vol. 148, No. 1., July, pp. 1-31.

Caring for the Future (1996), Oxford: University Press (subtitle: Making the Next Decades Provide a Life Worth Living. Report of the Independent Commission on Population and Quality of Life).

Catton, C. (1992), *Tears of the Dragon: China's environmental crisis*, London: Channel 4 Television.

Chalkley, K. (1997), 'Population Growth and Consumption', *Population Today*, Vol. 25, No. 4, April, pp. 4-5.

Channel 4 Television (UK) 29 Sept., 1997, 9.00pm 'Equinox: The Iceberg Cometh'.

China Map Press (1979), *Atlas of cancer mortality in the People's Republic of China*, Shanghai: China Map Press.

China Statistical Yearbook 1996 (1996), China Statistical Publishing House, State Statistical Bureau, People's Republic of China, p. 69. Also previous years.

Clark, J. P. and Flemings, M. C. (1986), 'Advanced Materials and the Economy', *Scientific American*, Vol. 255, No. 4, Oct., pp. 43-49.

Clarke, A. C. (1997), 'Why ET will never call home', *The Times*, 5 Aug., p. 16.

Clarke, I. F. (1979), *The Pattern of Expectation 1644-2001*, London: Jonathan Cape.

Clarke, I. F. (1985a), 'The course of human events, 1485-1785', (American anticipations), *Futures*, June, pp. 251-262.

Clarke, I. F. (1985b), 'A manifest destiny, 1782-1890' (American anticipations), *Futures*, Aug., pp. 390-402.

Clarke, J. I., Curson, P., Kayastha, S.L. and Nag, P. (Editors), (1989) *Population and Disaster*, Oxford: Blackwell.

Cloud, P. E., Jr. (1968), 'Realities of mineral distribution', *Texas Quarterly*, Vol. 11, pp. 103-126.

Cloud, P. E., Jr. (Editor) (1969), *Resources and Man*, San Francisco: W. H. Freeman.

Cocker, M. (1998) *Rivers of Blood, Rivers of Gold*, London: Jonathan Cape.

Cohen, J. (1999) 'A Mexican Warning', *Geographical*, Vol. 71, No. 5, May, pp. 34-39.

Cole, H. S. D. (Editor) (1973), *Thinking about the Future*, London: Chatto and Windus (for Sussex University Press).

Cole, J. P. (1963), *Geography of World Affairs*, Harmondsworth: Penguin Books, p. 295.

Cole, J. P. (1979), *Geography of World Affairs*, Harmondsworth: Penguin Books, p. 219.

Cole, J. P. (1981), *The development gap*, Chichester: John Wiley and Sons.

Cole, J. P. (1983), *Geography of World Affairs*, London: Butterworths, pp. 124-132.

Cole, J. P. (1987), 'China and the Soviet Union: Worlds Apart?', *Soviet Geography*, Vol. XXVIII, No. 7, Sept., pp. 459-484.

Cole, J. P. (1996), *Geography of the World's Major Regions*, London: Routledge.

Cole, J. P and Cole, F. J. (1997), *A Geography of the European Union*, London: Routledge.

Collins, M. (editor) (1990), *The Last Rain Forests*, London: Mitchell Beazley International Ltd in association with IUCN.

Colinvaux, P. A. (1989), 'The Past and Future Amazon', *Scientific American*, Vol. 260, No. 5, May, pp. 68-74.

Conan Doyle, A. (1912), *The Lost World*, John Murray, London, 1969 (first edition 1912).

Connor, S. (1996a), 'Dinosaur's death mystery solved', *The Sunday Times*, 10 Nov., p. 1.9.

Connor, S. (1996b), 'The Lonely Planet', *The Sunday Times*, 29 Dec., p. 1.11.

Conradi, P. (1997), ' Brussels seeks 62 mph car limit', *The Sunday Times*, 6 April, p. 1.26.

Conway, M. (1993), 'Tomorrow's Supercities', *The Futurist*, May-June, pp. 27-33.

Cook, R. C. (1958), 'Latin America, The "Fountain of Youth" Overflows', *Population Bulletin*, Vol. XIV, No. 5, Aug., Population Reference Bureau.

Cornish, E. (1986), 'Colossal Cities of the Future', *The Futurist*, pp. 2, 59, Sept/Oct., Bethesda, Maryland: World Future Society.

Dasgupta, P. S. (1995), 'Population, Poverty and the Local Environment', *Scientific American*, Vol. 272, No. 2, Feb., pp. 26-31.

Dasmann, R. F. (1972), *Planet in peril? Man and the biosphere today*, Harmondsworth: Penguin Books.

Davies, A. (1948), 'How man lives', chapter 1, in *Man and his life the world over*, London, Odhams Press Ltd., pp. 7-8.

Davis, W. (1996), *The Lucky Generations, A Positive View of the 21st Century*, London: Headline Book Publishing.

Dawkins, R. (1995), 'God's Utility Function', *Scientific American*, Vol. 273, No. 5., Nov., pp. 62-67.

De Bres, K.J. and Buizlo, M. (1992), 'A daring proposal for dealing with an inevitable disaster? A review of the Buffalo Commons proposal', *Great Plains Research*, Vol. 2., No. 2, pp. 165-78.

De Cicco, J. and Ross, M. (1994), 'Improving Automotive Efficiency', *Scientific American*, Vol. 271, No. 6, Dec., pp. 30-35.

De Koker, B. (1995), 'Going down', *Scientific American*, Vol. 273, No. 2, Aug., p. 25.

Department of the Environment (1996), *Review of the Potential Effects of Climate Change in the United Kingdom*, London: HMSO, March 1996.

de Soto, H. (1989), *The Other Path*, New York: Harper and Row.

de Tocqueville, A. *Democracy in America*, first published in 1835.

de Waal Malefijt, A. (1968), 'Homo monstruosus', *Scientific American*, Vol. 219, No. 4, Oct., pp. 112-118.

Dodds, F. (1997), *Way Forward: Beyond Agenda 21*, London: Earthscan Publications Ltd.

Donaldson, P. J. and Tsui, A. O. (1990), 'The International Family Planning Movement', *Population Bulletin*, Vol. 45, No. 3., November, Population Reference Bureau.

Dong Yuguo (1991), 'Looking Towards Modernization by the Mid-21st Century', *Beijing Review*, April 1-7, pp. 12-22.

Doyle, R. (1996), 'The Changing Quality of Life', *Scientific American*, Vol. 275, No. 1, July, p. 18.

Doyle, R. (1997), 'Threatened Mammals', *Scientific American*, Vol. 276, No. 1, Jan., p. 25.

Driver, T. S. and Chapman, G. P. (1996), *Time-scales and environmental change*, London: Routledge.

Drosnin, M. (1997), *The Bible Code*, London: Weidenfeld and Nicolson.

Duncan, A. and Hobson, D. (1995), 'Now we are all just prisoners of the state', *The Sunday Times*, 14 May, p. 3.7.

Durisch, P. (1997), 'Farmers tune into space to keep pesticides low and the yields high', *The Sunday Telegraph*, Sept. 21, p. 14.

The Economist (1992a), 'A survey of defence in the 21st century', 5 Sept.

The Economist (1992b), 'The car industry' (Survey), 17 Oct.

The Economist (1994), 'Back to the future', 8 Jan., pp. 19-21.

Ehrlich, P. R. and Ehrlich, A. H. (1972), *Population, Resources, Environment: Issues in Human Ecology*, San Francisco: W. H. Freeman.

Elliott, H. (1997), 'Safety pledges on new superliners', *The Times*, 26 June, p. 43.

Elliott, J. A. (1994), *An Introduction to Sustainable Development, The developing world*, London: Routledge.

Endean, C. (1997), 'Bridge to a brave future', *The European*, 18-24 Sept., p. 17.

EP News (1997), 'Ecu 75 bn Marshall plan', European Parliament, July, p. 1.

Erwin, D. E. (1996), 'The Mother of Mass Extinctions', *Scientific American*, Vol. 275, No. 1, July, pp. 56-62.

Espenshade, T. J. and Gurcak, J. C. (1996), 'Are More Immigrants the Answer to U.S. Population Aging?', *Population Today*, Vol. 24, No. 12, December pp. 4-5.

European Parliament (1996), *Public Hearing on Climate Change and Small Island States*, Luxembourg, 25 Sept., Directorate General for Research.

Evans, M. (1997), 'Bonn calls for 'Club Mad' missile shield', *The Times*, 23 July, p. 9.

Eyre, S. R. (1978), *The Real Wealth of Nations*, London: Edward Arnold.

Falkenmark, M. and Widstrand, C. (1992), 'Population and Water Resources: A Delicate Balance', *Population Bulletin*, Vol. 47, No. 3, Nov., Washington: Population Reference Bureau.

FAO (1950) *Yearbook of Food and Agricultural Statistics 1949*, Vol. 1, Production, FAO of the UN Washington D.C.

FAOPY (1995), Food and Agriculture Organisation (of the United Nations) Production Yearbook, various years.

Ferguson, N. (editor) (1997) *Virtual History: Alternatives and Counterfactuals*, London: Picador.

Fernandez-Armesto, F. (1995), 'Let's put our past in perspective', *The Sunday Times*, 3 Sept., pp. 10.8-10.9.

Flower, A. R. (1978), 'World oil production', *Scientific American*, Vol. 238, No. 3., March, pp. 42-49.

Forester, T. (editor), *The Information Technology Revolution*, Blackwell, 1985, especially Chapter 2, Artificial Intelligence and the Fifth Generation, Chapter 13, Long Waves of Economic Development.

Forrester, J. W. (1973), *World Dynamics*, Cambridge (Mass.), Wright-Allen Press (2nd edn.).

Franks, A. (1990), 'When one small thing leads to chaos', *The Times*, 4 Aug.

Frazer, G. and Lancelle, G. (1994), *Zhirinovsky, The little black book: making sense of the senseless*, Harmondsworth: Penguin.

Freeman, C. and Jahoda, M. (editors), (1979), *World Futures, The Great Debate*, Oxford: Martin Robinson.

Frejka, T. (1973), 'The Prospects for a Stationary World Population', *Scientific American*, Volume 228, No. 3, March, pp. 15-23.

French, T. (1997), 'Fear of gridlock as airports hit overload', *The European*, 27 March - 2 April, p. 25.

Gamini, G. (1997), 'Miners' invasion brings death to Amazon tribe', *The Times*, 28 Aug., p. 11.

Garreau, J. (1981), *The Nine Nations of North America*, Boston: Houghton Mifflin Co.

Geary, J. (Editor) (1997), 'The New Age of Discovery', Special Issue of *Time Magazine*, 4th December. Discoveries of the recent past and possible discoveries in the future relate to technology, changes due to computer technology, the world around us and the world inside us.

Gehrels, T. (1996), 'Collisions with Comets and Asteroids', *Scientific American*, Vol. 274, No. 3, March, pp. 34-39.

Gelbard, A., Haub, C., and Kent, M. M. (1999), 'World population beyond six billion', *Population Bulletin* of the Population Reference Bureau, Vol. 54, No. 1.

German, F. C. (1960), 'A tentative evaluation of world power', *Conflict Resolution*, Vol. IV, No. 1, March, pp. 138-144.

Gibbons, J. H., Blair, P. D., Gwin, H. L. (1989), 'Strategies for Energy Use', *Scientific American*, Vol. 261, No. 3, Sept., pp. 86-93.

Gibbs, W. W. (1994), 'No-polluting zone', *Scientific American*, Vol. 271, No. 6, December, pp. 12-13.

Gibbs, W. W. (1997), 'Transportation's Perennial Problems'. *Scientific American*, Vol. 277, No. 4, October, pp. 32-35.

Gingerich, O., (1982), 'The Galileo Affair', *Scientific American*, Vol. 247, No. 2, Aug., pp. 118-127.

Girling, R. (1997), 'Paddling down the A1 in the rush hour?' *Sunday Times Magazine*, 23 March, pp. 28-37.

Goldsmith, E. R. D. *et al.*, (1972), 'A Blueprint for Survival', *The Ecologist*, Vol. 2, No. 1, January.

Gorbachev, M. S. (1986), *The coming century of peace*, New York: Richardson and Steirman.

Gore, R. (1995), 'Living with California's Faults', *National Geographic*, Vol. 187, No. 4, April, pp. 2-35.

Gould, P. (1994), 'The guessing game', *Geographical*, Sept., p. 17.

Gould, S. J. (1997), *Questioning the Millennium*, London; Cape.

Grady, M. (1997), 'The uninvited guests', *The Geographical Magazine*, March, pp. 26-27.

Gramna (1997), Havana, Aug. 7, p. 14 (Cuban newspaper).

Green, D. (1995), 'Setting a course for development', *Geographical*, May, p. 18.

Gregory, D. P. (1973), 'The Hydrogen Economy', *Scientific American*, Vol. 228, No. 1, January, pp. 13-21.

Grimston, J. (1999), 'Nasa sets the controls for 'wormhole' space travel', *Sunday Times*, 18 April, p. 1.7.

Grove, R. H. (1992), 'Origins of Western Environmentalism', *Scientific American*, Vol. 267, No. 1, July, pp. 22-27.

Guinness Flight (1996), 'The 21st Century Belongs to Asia', London: Global Asset Management Ltd.

Guinness (1999), *Amazing Future*, London: Guinness Publishing. Under 12 headings, ranging from Lifestyles and Work to Space and Science Fiction, several hundred subjects are covered. Emphasis on new technology but very limited on basic needs such as Resources and Agriculture, each two pages. Sixteen contributors.

Hall, D. (1981), 'Put a sunflower in your tank', *New Scientist*, Vol. 89, No. 1242, 26 Feb.

Hall, P. (1980), *Great Planning Disasters*, Harmondsworth: Penguin Books Ltd.

Hamilton, D. (1968), 'Predicting technology's future', *New Scientist*, 11 July, pp. 67-9.

Han Baocheng (1993), 'Development Strategy for Central and Western Regions', *Beijing Review*, Apr. 19-25, pp. 23-26.

Hargrave, S. (1997), 'Global warming goes cold', *The Sunday Times*, 8 June, p. 5.10.

Harman, W. W. (1976), *An Incomplete Guide to the Future*, New York, W. W. Norton and Co. (1979 reprint).

Harris, N. (1986), *The End of the Third World*, London: I. B. Tauris and Co Ltd.

Hart, C. (1991), *Practical Forestry for the Agent and Surveyor*, Stroud: Alan Sutton.

Hart, M. H. (1993), *The 100: a ranking of the most influential persons in history*, London: Simon and Schuster.

Haub, C. (1987), 'Understanding Population Projections', *Population Bulletin*, Vol. 42, No. 4, December, Washington: Population Reference Bureau.

Haub, C. (1992), 'New UN Projections Show Uncertainty of Future World', *Population Today*, pp. 6-7.

Haub, C. (1995), 'How many people have ever lived on earth', *Population Today*, Vol. 23, No. 2, Feb., pp. 4-5.

Haub, C. (1997), 'New UN Projections Depict a Variety of Demographic Futures', *Population Today*, Vol. 25, No. 4, April, pp. 1-3, Washington, Population Reference Bureau.

Haub, C. (1998), 'UN Projections Assume Fertility Decline, Mortality Increase', *Population Today*, Vol. 26, No. 12, December, pp. 1-2.

Hauser, P. M. (1971), 'The Census of 1970', *Scientific American*, Vol. 225, No. 1, July, pp. 17-25.

Hawkes, N. (1997a), 'Pioneer spacecraft boldly goes to the final frontier', *The Times*, 2 April, p. 6.

Hawkes, N. (1997b), 'DNA scientists join war against malaria', *The Times*, 13 Aug., p. 7.

Hawkes, N. (1999), 'Planet discovery suggests we are not alone'. *The Times*, 16 April, p. 12.

Hawking, S. W. (1988), *A brief history of time*, London: Bantam Press.

HDR (1996), *Human Development Report*, United Nations Development Programme, Oxford, 1996 and earlier years.

Hedins, L. O. and Likens, G. E. (1996), 'Atmospheric Dust and Acid Rain', *Scientific American*, Vol. 275, No. 6, December, pp. 56-60.

Henderson, D. A. (1976), 'The Eradication of Smallpox', *Scientific American*, Vol. 235, No. 4, Oct. pp. 25-33.

Hirsch, P. (1990), 'Forests, forest reserve, and forest land in Thailand', *The Geographical Journal*, Vol. 156, No. 2, July, pp. 166-174.

HMSO (1996), *Review of Potential Effects of Climate Change in the United Kingdom*, UK Climate Change Impacts Review Group, London: HMSO, March 1996.

Holloway, M. (1994), 'Nurturing Nature', *Scientific American*, Vol. 270, No. 4, April, pp. 76-84.

Horne, A. (1996), 'What if Napoleon had won?' *The Times*, 19 Oct., p. 22.

Hornsby, M. (1997a), 'Green energy campaigners see red over wind farm', *The Times*, 20 May, p. 15.

Hornsby, M. (1997b), 'Cash carrot for farmers wishing to turn organic', *The Times*, 29 July, p. 8.

Horrobin, D. F. (1969), *Science is God*, Aylesbury: MTP.

Hulme, M. and Barrow, E. editors (1997), *Climates of the British Isles*, London: Routledge.

Hutchings, C. (1997), 'Down to the last drop', *Geographical*, Vol. LXXI, No. 8, pp. 23-31.

Idyll, C. P. (1973), 'The Anchovy Crisis', *Scientific American*, Vol. 228, No. 6, June, pp. 22-29.

INEI (1995), *Dimensiones y características de la pobreza en el Perú, 1993* (Dimensions and characteristics of poverty in Peru, 1993), Lima: Instituto Nacional de Estadística e Informática, July 1995.

Istituto Centrale di Statistica (1958), *Sommario de Statistiche Storiche Italiane*, Roma, p. 129.

Jabez, A. (1997), 'Commuting over traffic jams', *The Sunday Times*, 5 Jan, p. 3.19.

Jenkins, R. (1996), 'No cards and no presents, but the snow is guaranteed', *The Times*, 26 Dec., p. 5.

Jensen, R. G., Shabad, T., and Wright, A. W. (1983), *Soviet Natural Resources in the World Economy*, Chicago; University of Chicago Press.

Jiang Wandi (1995), 'Concern Grows About Increasing Disparity of Income', *Beijing Review*, July 24-30, pp. 12-14.

Jordan, R. P. (1968), 'Our Growing Interstate Highway System', *National Geographic*, Vol. 133, No. 2, Feb, pp. 195-219.

Kahn, H. and Wiener, A. J. (1967), *The Year 2000*, New York: The Hudson Institute.

Kahn, H., Brown, W. and Martel, L. (1977), *The next 200 years*, London: Associated Business Programmes (by the Hudson Institute). (subtitle A Scenario for America and the World).

Kaletsky, A. (1996), 'Good news for the economy but maybe not for politicians', *The Times*, 15 Feb., p. 27.

Kammen, D. (1995), 'Cookstoves for the Developing World', *Scientific American*, Vol. 273, No. 1, July, pp. 64-67.

Kane, F. (1997), 'Business too late to avoid havoc in 2000', *The Sunday Times*, 4 May, p. 3.14.

Karl, T. R., Nicholls, N. and Gregory, J. (1997), 'The Coming Climate', *Scientific American*, Vol. 276, No. 5, May, pp. 54-59.

Kates, R. W. (1994), 'Sustaining Life on the Earth', *Scientific American*, Vol. 271, No. 4, Oct., pp. 92-99 (quote p. 99).

Keens-Soper, M. (1996), 'Treadmill that we have to join', *The European*, 5-11 Dec., p. 4.

Kempson, R. (1996), 'United retain look of champions', *The Times*, 16 Aug., p. 36.

Kennedy, P. (1987), *The Rise and Fall of Great Powers*, New York: Random House.

Kennedy, P. (1993), *Preparing for the Twenty-First Century*, New York: Harper Collins.

Klepikova, E. and Solovyov, V. (1995), *Zhirinovsky, the Paradoxes of Russian Fascism*, Harmondsworth: Penguin.

Langer, W. L. (1972), 'Checks on Population Growth: 1750-1850', *Scientific American*, Vol. 226, No. 2, Feb., pp. 92-99.

Larson, E. D. *et al.* (1986), 'Beyond the Era of Materials', *Scientific American*, Vol. 254, No. 6, June, pp. 24-31.

League of Nations (1929), *International Statistical Year-book 1928*, Geneva 1929.

Leake, J. (1995), 'Astronomers predict faster than light travel', *The Sunday Times*, 13 Aug, p. 1.

Leake, J. (1997a), 'Water firms in drought-hit south turn to suppliers from the sea', *The Sunday Times*, 6 April, p. 1.26.

Leake, J. (1997b), 'Firms plan to import water by the bagful', *The Sunday Times*, 4 May, p. 1.26.

Lents, J. M. and Kelly, W. (1993), 'Clearing the Air in Los Angeles', *Scientific American*, Vol. 269, No. 4, October, pp. 18-25.

Li Rongxia (1996), 'Population decline promotes rising incomes', *Beijing Review*, Nov. 18-24, pp. 11-17.

Li Tan (1994), 'Population flow into big cities', *Beijing Review*, July 18-24, pp. 15-19.

Li Wen (1996), 'China and Eurasian Continental Bridge', *Beijing Review*, Sept 30- Oct 6., pp. 17-20.

Lin, H. (1985), 'The development of software for ballistic-missile defense', *Scientific American*, December, Vol. 253, No. 6, pp. 32-9.

Liu Zheng, Song Jian *et al.* (1981), *China's population: problems and prospects*, Beijing: New World Press.

Livernash, R. and Rodenburg, E. (1998), 'Population Change, Resources and the Environment', *Population Bulletin*, Vol. 53, No. 1, March.

Lorenz, A. (1997), 'Euro Pile Up', *The Sunday Times*, 9 March, p. 3.3.

Luminet, J., Starkman, G. and Weeks, J. R. (1999), 'Is Space Finite?', *Scientific American*, Vol, 280, No. 4, April, pp. 68-75.

Lutz, W. (editor) (1994), *The Future Population of the World*, London, Earthscan Publications Ltd.

Mackinder. H. J. (1904), 'The geographical pivot of history', *Geographical Journal*, April, Vol. 23, No. 4, pp. 421-2.

MacNeill, J. (1989), 'Strategies for Sustainable Economic Development', *Scientific American*, Vol. 261, No. 3, September, pp. 104-113.

Maddox, B. (1997a), 'Washington split on merits of North America's trade pact', *The Times*, 15 May, p. 29.

Maddox, B. (1997b), 'The disunited States', *The Times*, 15 Oct., p. 20.

Malaysia 2020 (1994), *Scientific American*, (Supplement), Vol. 270, No. 4, April, pp. M1-M82.

Malle, K.-G. (1996), 'Cleaning Up the River Rhine', *Scientific American*, Vol. 274, No. 1, Jan. pp. 54-59.

Malthus, T. R. (1798), *An essay on the principle of population*, 1970 edition Harmondsworth: Penguin Books.

Manners, G. (1981), 'Our planet's resources', *The Geographical Journal*, Vol. 147, Part 1, March, pp. 1-22.

Masser, I., Sviden, O., Wegener, M. (1992), *The Geography of Europe's Futures*, London: Belhaven Press.

Mather, I. (1997), 'Chirac retreats from Africa', *The European*, 31 July - 6 Aug., p. 23.

May, R. M. (1989), 'A Biologist's View of the Future', *Technology, Innovation and Society*, Vol. 5, No. 2, Autumn, p. 2-5.

McEvedy, C. and Jones, R. (1978), *Atlas of World Population History*, Harmondsworth, Penguin Reference Books Ltd.

McGinty, S. (1997), 'Think lucky and statistics prove that you will be', *Sunday Times*, 27 April, p. 1.7.

McNulty, S. (1997), 'Malaysia's Moment', *Newsweek*, Sept 1, pp. 24-28.

McWilliam, F. (1995), 'Meltdown theory challenged', *The Geographical Magazine*, Vol. LXVII, No. 8, p. 5.

Meadows, D. H. *et al.* (1972), *The Limits to Growth*, London: Earth Island Limited.

Meadows, D. H., Meadows, D. L., and Randers, J. (1992), *Beyond the Limits*, London: Earthscan Publications Ltd.

Mesarovic, M. and Pestel, E. (1975), *Mankind at the Turning Point*, Hutchinson: London, p. 69.

Micklin, P. P. (1977), 'Nawapa and two Siberian water-diversion proposals: a geographical comparison and appraisal', *Soviet Geography Review and Translation*, Vol. 18, No. 2, Feb., pp. 81-99.

Middleton, N. (1999), *The Global Casino*, an introduction to environmental issues, London: Arnold (2nd edition).

Mitchell, J. G. (1997), 'Oil on Ice', *National Geographic*, Vol. 191, No. 4, April, pp. 104-131.

Monmonier, M. (1997), *Cartographies of Danger: Mapping Hazards in America*, Chicago: The University of Chicago Press.

Morris, M. D. (1979), *Measuring the Condition of the World's Poor*, New York: Pergamon Press.

Morrison, Philip and Morrison Phylis (1982), *Powers of Ten*, New York: W. H. Freeman and Co.

Mortished, C. (1996), 'European domination in the pipeline for Russian gas giant', *The Times*, 21 Oct., p. 46.

Mosteller, F., Rourke, R. E. K. and Thomas, G. B. (1961), *Probability: a first course*, Reading, Mass: Addison-Wesley Publishing Co Inc.

Mounfield, P. R. (1991), *World Nuclear Power*, London: Routledge.

Mundzeck, T. (1995), 'Scientists issue urgent global warning over climatic change', *The European*, 3-9 March, p. 4.

Mundzeck, T. (1997), 'The poisonous legacy of Stalin's secret nuclear city', *The European*, 26 Aug - 3 Sept., pp. 18-19.

Murphy, E. M. (1983), *The environment to come: a global summary*, Washington: Population Reference Bureau.

Musto. D. F. (1996), 'Alcohol in American History', *Scientific American*, Vol. 274, No. 4., April, pp. 32-37.

'The More Species, the Merrier' (1996), *Scientific American*, Vol. 274, No. 4, May, p. 14.

Naisbitt, J. (1984), *Megatrends, Ten New Directions Transforming Our Lives*, London: Futura, Macdonald and Co.

Narodnoye khozyaystvo SSSR v 1989 godu, Moscow, Finansy i Statistika, 1990, pp. 550, 555.

Nash, J. M. (1997), 'Is it El Niño of the century?', *Time*, 18 Aug., pp. 46-48.

National Academy of Sciences (1979), *Energy in Transition 1985-2010*, San Francisco: W. H. Freeman, p. 1.

National Geographic (1997), 'The making of Canada', Sept. map.

National Geographic Society (1993), Special Edition: 'Water, the Power, Promise and Turmoil of North America's Fresh Water'.

National Geographic Society (1997), *Restless Earth*.

Naudin, F. (1997), 'Do great minds think alike', *The European Magazine*, 20-26 Feb., No. 354, p. 10.

Nef, J. U. (1977), 'An early energy crisis and its consequences', *Scientific American*, 237, No. 5, Nov., 140-151.

Nelson, F. (1999), 'Branson plans to go into orbit', *The Times*, 22 April, p. 29.

Newbery, B. (1997), 'The ultimate room with a view', *Geographical*, Vol. LXIX, No. 10, pp. 9-14.

Nippon (1993), *Nippon, a charted survey of Japan 1993/94*, Tokyo: The Kokusei-sha Corporation.

NkhSSR v 1958 godu (1959) (*Narodnoye khozyaystvo SSSR v 1958 godu, statisticheskiy yezhegodnik*), Moscow: Gosudarstvennoye Statisticheskoye Izdatel'stvo, p. 445.

NhkSSSR 1922-1982 (1982), *(Narodnoye khozyaystvo SSSR 1922-1982)*, Moscow: Finansy i Statistika, p. 271.

Norman, G. (1975), 'Introducing the hedonometer, a new way of assessing national performance', *The Times*, 26 May.

North, R. D. (1997), 'Out of the woods', *The Times Magazine*, 31 May, pp. 18-20.

Northcott, J. (Editor), (1991), *Britain in 2010 - the PSI Report*, London: Policy Studies Institute.

Nown, G. (1985), *The World's Worst Predictions*, London: Arrow Books, Hutchinson.

Nuttall, N. (1990a), 'Computers 'too unreliable' to deal with critical tasks', *The Times*, 15 May.

Nuttall, N. (1990b), 'Daily journey to the centre of the Earth', *The Times*, 6 Dec., p. 17.

Nuttall, N. (1996a), 'Deep-sea dump hailed as answer to world's waste', *The Times*, 6 March, p. 10.

Nuttall, N. (1996b), 'Scientists list 200 key wildlife sites', *The Times*, 2 Oct., p. 4.

Nuttall, N. (1997a), 'Earth at risk of collision with unseen comets', *The Times*, 4 Feb., p. 6.

Nuttall, N. (1997b), 'Drivers urged to plant trees to beat pollution', *The Times*, 12 June, p. 8.

Nuttall, N. (1997c), 'Death may lose its sting in 50 years', *The Times*, 7 July, p. 8.

Nuttall, N. (1999), 'Tide turns in favour of wave power', *The Times*, 26 Feb., p. 14.

OECD (1991), *The State of the Environment*, Paris: OECD (2 volumes).

OECD (1996), *The Agricultural Outlook, Trends and Issues to 2000*, Paris: Organisation for Economic Co-operation and Development.

Olshansky, S. J. *et al.* (1993), 'The Aging of the Human Species', *Scientific American*, Vol. 268, No. 4, April, pp. 18-25.

Olshansky, S. J. *et al.* (1997), 'Infectious Diseases - New and Ancient Threats to World Health', *Population Bulletin*, Vol. 52, No. 2, July. Population Reference Bureau.

Orwell, G. (1949), *Nineteen Eighty-Four*, Harmondsworth: Penguin Books.

Orwell, G. (1961) 'Notes on Nationalism' in *Collected Essays*, 1945, in edition by Secker and Warburg, London, p. 275.

Owen, R. (1996), 'Seventies dream of world with no hunger destroyed by conflict', *The Times*, 14 Nov., p. 16.

Packard, V. (1963), *The Waste Makers*, Harmondsworth: Penguin Books (first published in the USA in 1960).

Parfit, M. (1995), 'Diminishing Returns', *National Geographic*, Vol. 188, No. 5., Nov., pp. 2-37.

Parry, J. N. (1997), 'Coal falls into pit of despair', *The European* (Business), 12-18 June, p. 17.

Parry, M. (1990), *Climatic Change and World Agriculture*, London: Earthscan Publications Ltd.

Pearce, A. W. (1979), 'World energy prospects', *Esso Magazine*, Spring, No. 110, pp. 2-5.

Pearson, I. (Editor) (1998), *The Atlas of the Future*, London: Routledge. An attractively presented series of world maps with forecasts to various dates in the 21st century plus a Technology Calendar, World Table and brief notes on Forecasting Methods. Twenty five contributors.

Peixoto, J. P. and Ali Kettani, M. (1973), 'The Control of the Water Cycle', *Scientific American*, Vol. 228, No. 4, April, pp. 46-61.

Perls, T. T. (1995), 'The Oldest Old', *Scientific American*, Vol. 272, No. 1, January, pp. 50-55.

Popham, P. (1997), 'Parents are paid to have the daughters India lost', *The Independent*, 3 Oct., p. 5.

Popper, D. E. and Popper, F. J. (1987), 'The Great Plains: from dust to dust, a daring proposal for dealing with an inevitable disaster', *Planning*, Vol. 53, pp. 12-18.

Population Reference Bureau (1987), 'Human Needs and Nature's Balance: Population, Resources and the Environment', A Population Learning Series.

Population Reference Bureau (1997), World Population and the Environment (data sheet).

Population Today (1984), 'No Easy Answers to Poverty, Malnutrition', January, p. 3., Population Reference Bureau.

Population Today (1996), 'The Carrying Capacity Debate', April, p. 5., Population Reference Bureau.

Population Today (1998), 'AIDS, Population Growth Shape Sub-Saharan Africa's Future', Vol. 26, No. 1, January, pp. 1-2.

Porter, M. and Brierley, D. (1997), 'Has the car reached the end of the road?' *The European*, 18-24 Sept., pp. 8-13.

Prigg, M. (1999), 'Airship takes tourist to space', *Sunday Times*, 3 Jan., p. 3.12.

Profils Regionaux (1995), Commission of the European Communities, duplicated report only in French, September 1995, DGXVI-A4.

Prosterman, R. L., Hansted, T. and Li Ping (1996), 'Can China Feed Itself?' *Scientific American*, Vol. 275, No. 5, Nov., pp. 70-77.

'The Rainbow Majority', (1996), *Scientific American*, Vol. 274, No. 2, Feb., p. 11.

Ramesh, R. (1996), 'Warning: 20 years of gridlock ahead as new roads are axed', *The Sunday Times*, 8 Dec., p. 1.7.

Ravenstein, E. G. (1885), 'The Laws of Migration', *Journal of the Statistical Society*, Vol. XLVIII, Part 2, June.

Rayment, T. (1997), 'The lost world', *Sunday Times Magazine*, 15 June, pp. 46-51.

Raymundo, B. M. (1969), *Argentina 2000 una nacion semidesierta?*, Buenos Aires: Editorial Orbelus.

Rees, J. (1985), *Natural Resources, Allocation economics and policy*, London: Methuen.

Rees-Mogg, W. (1995), 'The end of nations', *The Times*, 31 August, p. 14.

Reid, T. R. (1995), 'Kobe wakes to a nightmare', *National Geographic*, Vol. 188, No. 1., pp. 112-136.

Repetto, R. (1990), 'Deforestation in the Tropics', *Scientific American*, Vol. 262, No. 4, April, pp. 18-24.

Revelle, R. (1982), 'Carbon Dioxide and World Climate', *Scientific American*, Vol. 247, No. 2, Aug., pp. 33-39.

Rhodes, T. (1997), 'Saddam joins the Queen on wealth list', *The Times*, 16 July, p. 14.

Rice, R. E., Gullison, R. E., and Reid, J. W. (1997), 'Can Sustainable Management Save Tropical Forests?', *Scientific American*, Vol. 276, No. 4, pp. 34-39.

Richards, P. W. (1973), 'The Tropical Rain Forest', *Scientific American*, Vol. 229, No. 6, Dec., p. 58.

Richardson, L. F. (1961), 'The Problem of contiguity', *General Systems* (Yearbook of the Society for General Systems Research), Volume VI, pp. 139-187.

Ridker, R. G. and Cecelski, E. W. (1979), 'Resources, Environment and Population: The Nature of Future Limits', *Population Bulletin*, Vol. 34, No. 3, August, Population Reference Bureau.

Ridker, R. G. and Watson, W. D. (1980), *To Choose a Future: Resource and Environmental Problems of the U.S., A Long-Term Global Outlook*, Baltimore: John Hopkins University Press.

Robey, B., Rutstein, S. O. and Morris, L. (1993), 'The Fertility Decline in Developing Countries', *Scientific American*, Vol. 269, No. 6, Dec., pp. 30-37.

Roger, J., Angel, P., and Woolf, N. J. (1996), 'Searching for Life on other Planets', *Scientific American*, Vol. 274, No. 4, April, pp. 46-52.

Rollnick, R. (1997a), 'Superphénix shuts down to rise again', *The European*, 2-8 Jan., p. 3.

Rollnick, R. (1997b), 'Toxic blight hits beaches of Normandy', *The European*, 24-30 July, p. 20.

Rosen, S. (1976), *Future Facts*, London: Heinemann. Covers a wide range of topics, focusing on probable innovations roughly to 2000. Ambitious to call them facts when they did not exist in 1976.

Rostow, W. W. (1960), *The Stages of Economic Growth*, Cambridge: University Press.

Rostow, W. W. (1975), *How it all began. Origins of the Modern Economy*, London: Methuen.

Royal Institute of International Affairs (1996), *Unsettled Times: Three Stony Paths to 2015*, RIIA: The Chatham House Forum.

Runnels, C. N. (1995), 'Environmental Degradation in Ancient Greece', *Scientific American*, Vol. 272, No. 3, March, pp. 72-78.

Ryan, S. (1995), 'Endangered whales return from edge of extinction', *The Sunday Times*, 5 March, p. 1.22.

Ryan, S. (1997), 'Jet-ship poised to shatter speed barrier', *The Sunday Times*, 5 March, p. 1.6.

Safina, C. (1995), 'The World's Imperiled Fish', *Scientific American*, Vol. 273, No. 5, Nov., pp. 30-37.

Schafer, A. and Victor, D. (1997), 'The Past and Future of Global Mobility', *Scientific American*, Vol. 277, No. 4., October, pp. 36-39.

Schneider, D. (1995), 'Global Warming Is Still a Hot Topic', *Scientific American*, Vol. 272, No. 2, Feb., p. 12.

Schneider, D. (1996), 'The More Species, the Merrier', *Scientific American*, Vol. 274, No. 5, May, p. 14.

Schneider, D. (1997), 'The Rising Seas', *Scientific American*, Vol. 276, No. 3, March, pp. 96-101.

Schwarzbach, D. A. (1997), 'Iran's Nuclear Puzzle', *Scientific American*, Vol. 276, No. 6, June, pp. 50-53.

Scientific American (1995a), 'The Computer in the 21st Century', A Special Issue.

Scientific American (1995b), 'Key Technologies for the 21st Century', Vol. 273, No. 3, Sept. (150th Anniversary Issue).

Scientific American (1997), 'The Future of Transportation', Vol. 277, No. 4, Oct., Special Issue.

Scientific American (1999), 'The Future of Space Exploration', Spring, Vol. 10, No. 1. Topics covered; I Spaceflight Today; II Exploring Mars; III Spaceflight Tomorrow; IV The Best Use of Space. About 20 contributors. Heavy emphasis on Mars.

Scommegna, P. (1996), 'UN Food Summit Tries to Focus World Attention on Hunger', *Population Today*, Vol. 24, No. 11, Nov., pp. 1-2, Population Reference Bureau.

Sen, A. (1993), 'The Economics of Life and Death', *Scientific American*, Vol. 268, No. 5, May, pp. 18-25.

Shcherbak, Y. M. (1996), 'Ten Years of the Chernobyl Era', *Scientific American*, Vol. 274, No. 4, April, pp. 32-37.

Sheldon, R. P. (1982), 'Phosphate Rock', *Scientific American*, Vol. 246, No. 6, June, pp. 31-37.

Showalter, W. C. (1916), 'How the world is fed', *National Geographic Magazine*, January, 29, No. 1, pp. 7, 24-25.

Sider, R. J. (1978) *Rich Christians in an age of Hunger*, London: Hodder and Stoughton.

Simon, J. L. (1981), *The Ultimate Resource*, Princeton: Princeton University Press.

Simon, J. L. and Kahn, H. (Editors) (1984), *The Resourceful Earth: A Response to Global 2000*, Oxford: Basil Blackwell.

Simonsen, M. H. (1969), *Brasil 2001*, Rio de Janeiro: Apec Editora S.A.

Smil, V. (1997), 'Global Population and the Nitrogen Cycle', *Scientific American*, Vol. 277, No. 1, July, pp. 58-63.

Smiles, S. (1986), *Self-help*, abridged from 1850 original, London: Sidgwick and Jackson.

Smith, D. (1997), *The State of War and Peace Atlas*, Harmondsworth: Penguin Reference, pp. 90-95.

Smith, M. (1974), 'When psychology grows up', *New Scientist*, 10 Oct., pp. 90-93.

Smith, S. (1997), 'Europe's 300 stateless 'nations' demand an independent voice', *The European*, 27 March - 2 April, p. 13.

Snape, T. (1996), 'EC energy tax plan ignites controversy', *The European*, 5-11 Dec., p. 17.

Snape, T. (1997), 'Customs set to become 'a formality'', *The European*, 1-7 May, p. 17.

Solovyov, V. and Klepikova, E. (1995) *Zhirinovsky The Paradoxes of Russian Facism*, London: Viking.

Spedding, C. R. W. (1988), 'The Future of Food Production', *Technology, Innovation and Society*, Spring, pp. 13-14.

Spengler, O. (1918) *Der Untergang des Abendlandes, Gestalt und Wirklichkeit*, Munchen: C. H. Beck'sche Verlagsbuchhandlung, English translation in two volumes, 1926 and 1928, *The Decline of the West, Form and Actuality* (1947 reprint), New York: Alfred A. Knopf.

Sperling, D. (1996), 'The Case for Electric Vehicles', *Scientific American*, Vol. 275, No. 5, November, pp. 36-51.

Stafford, J. V. (Editor) (1997), *Precision Agriculture '97*, Oxford: BIOS Scientific Publishers Ltd. (2 volumes, Vol. 1: Spatial Variability in Soil and Crop, Vol. 2: Technology, IT and Management).

Stanners, D. and Bourdeau, P. (Editors.) (1995), *Europe's Environment, the Dobris Assessment*, Copenhagen: European Environment Agency.

Statistical Abstract of the United States 1996, (1996), U.S. Bureau of the Census, Washington D.C.

Stelzer, I., (1994), 'An oil crisis knocks on recovery's door', *The Sunday Times*, 11 December, p. 3.7.

Stillman, E., director of study (1974), *The United Kingdom in 1980: The Hudson Report*, The Hudson Institute Europe, London: Associated Business Programmes.

Stix, G. (1995), 'Why Worry?' *Scientific American*, Vol. 272, No. 5, May, pp. 12B-13.

Stix, G. (1996), 'The Rainbow Majority', *Scientific American*, Vol. 274, No. 2, Feb., p. 11.

Stock, C. (1995), 'High Tidings', *Scientific American*, Vol. 273, No. 2, Aug., pp. 15-16.

Strauss, W. and Howe, N. (1991), *Generations, The History of America's Future*, New York: William Morrow.

Sunday Times (1999), Chronical of the Future, supplement of Sunday Times in five sections, decade by decade to 2050. A large number of specific scenarios (e.g. in 2003, nuclear strikes are used in Russia against rebels). Entertaining reading but already in 1999 one prediction for 2002, the resignation of England Football Manager, Glen Hoddle, has been disproved. It occurred in 1999! An illustration of the danger of being very specific about predictions.

Survival International (1998), *The Last of the Hiding Tribes*, London: Channel 4 Television.

Swain, J. (1997), 'Killing fields of Kisangani', *The Sunday Times*, 4 May, p. 1.21.

Swinburne, R. (1996), *Is there a God?*, Oxford University Press.

Tenner, E. (1996), *Why Things Bite Back, Technology and the Revenge Effect*, London: Fourth Estate Ltd.

Thomas, C. (1997), 'Car giveaway exposes lie of Indian boom', *The Times*, 22 July, p. 11.

Thomas, D. S. G. (1993), 'Sandstorm in a teacup? Understanding desertification', *The Geographical Journal*, Vol. 159, No. 3, Nov., pp. 318-331.

Thomas, M. (1989), 'Should we trust computers', *Technology, Innovation and Society*, Vol. 5, No. 2, Autumn, pp. 15-19.

Thomas, R. (1997), 'Measure for measure', *The Geographical Magazine*, Feb., pp. 18-20.

Thurow, L. C. (1987), 'A surge in Inequality', *Scientific American*, Vol. 256, No. 5, May, pp. 26-33.

Tilling, S. *et al.* (1997), *Tropical forests and human impact, Malaysian case studies* Preston Montford (Shrewsbury): Field Studies Council Publications.

Timberlake, L. (1987), *Only one earth - living for the future*, London: BBC Books/Earthscan.

The Times Atlas of World History (1978), ed., G. Barraclough, London: Times Books.

Todd, E. (1987), *The Causes of Progress*, Oxford: Basil Blackwell.

Toffler, A. (1970), *Future Shock*, London: Bodley Head, and London: Pan Books (also 1970).

Toth, N., Clark, D., and Ligabue, G. (1992), 'The Last Stone Ax Makers', *Scientific American*, Vol. 269, No. 1, July, pp. 66-71.

Toynbee, A. J. (1952), 'The World and the West', BBC Reith Lectures, *The Listener*, 20 Nov. - 25 Dec.

Tremlett, G. (1997), 'Africans risk death for a new life', *The European*, 3-9 April, p. 3.

Union of Concerned Scientists (1993), *World Scientists' Warning Briefing Book*, Cambridge Massachusetts: Union of Concerned Scientists.

United Nations (1949), *Mission to Haiti*, New York: United Nations.

United Nations (1963), *Industrial Growth in Africa*, New York: United Nations:

United Nations (1982), *Estimates and Projections of Urban, Rural and City Populations, 1950-2025: The 1980 Assessment*, New York: United Nations.

UNDP (United Nations Development Programme) (1996), *Human Development Report (HDR) 1996*, Oxford University Press, and earlier years.

van der Laan, N. (1996), 'HIV crisis in Belarus "worse than Chernobyl"', *The Daily Telegraph*, 2 Dec., p. 12.

van der Tak, J., Haub, C. and Murphy, E. (1979) 'Our Population Predicament: A New Look', *Population Bulletin*, Vol. 34, No. 5, Dec., Population Reference Bureau.

Verne, J. (1865), *Autour de la lune* (Round the Moon), Paris: Libraire Hachette, 1966 replica edition.

Vico, G. (1744), *The New Science of Giambattista Vico*, New York: Anchor Books, 1961 edition, p. 289-90 three kinds of government.

Waddington, C. H. (1978), *The Man-made Future*, London: Croom Helm.

Wallace, D. C. (1997), 'Mitochondrial DNA in Aging and Disease', *Scientific American*, Vol. 277, No. 2, Aug., pp. 22-29.

Wallerstein, I. (1983), *Historical Capitalism*, London: Verso Editions.

Washburn, S. L. (1960), 'Tools and Human Evolution', *Scientific American*, Vol. 203, No. 3., Sept., pp. 3-15.

Webster, D. (1997), *Aftermath, The Remnants of War*, London: Constable.

The Week in Germany (1995), German Information Center, New York, 24 Nov.

Wells, H. G. (1914), *Anticipations*, London: Chapman and Hall.

Wells, H. G. (1933), *The Shape of Things to Come*, 1984 Corgi Books, first published by Hutchinson 1933.

Whipple, C. G. (1996), 'Can Nuclear Waste be Stored Safely at Yucca Mountain?', *Scientific American*, Vol. 274, No. 6, June, pp. 56-65.

White, D. W. (1996), *The American Century, The Rise and Decline of the United States as a World Power*, New Haven: Yale.

Whittell, G. (1997a), 'Next stop, the Red Planet', *The Times*, Jan 6, p. 14.

Whittell, G. (1997b), 'Bob's Boys train their gunsights on Mexican border runners', *The Times*, 27 May, p. 11.

Whitemore Boggs, S. (1940), *International Boundaries*, New York: Columbia UP.

Williams, S. (1997), 'Oil Boom that can't get started', *The European*, 12-18 June, p. 4.

Windle, D. (1995), 'Bat plane swoops in to cut the cost of air travel', *The Sunday Times*, 5 March, p. 2.9.

Windle, D. (1996), 'Flying wing carries 1,000', *The Sunday Times*, 8 Dec., p. 3.10.

Woodcock, A. and Davis, M. (1980), *Catastrophe theory*, Harmondsworth: Penguin Books.

World Bank (1996), *The World Bank Atlas 1996*, Washington D.C.

World Bank, *World Development Report* (annual), Oxford: University Press.

World Resources Institute (1986), *World Resources 1986*, New York: Basic Books, Inc. (A Report by The World Resources Institute and the International Institute for Environment and Development).

Wouk, V. (1997), 'Hybrid Electric Vehicles', *Scientific American*, Vol. 277, No. 4, Oct., pp. 44-48.

WPDS 1996 (1996) and various other years, in full. World Population Data Sheet of the Population Reference Bureau, Washington D.C.

Wright, K. (1990), 'The Road to the Global Village', *Scientific American*, Vol. 262, No. 3, March, p. 58.

Wright, R. (1997), 'Liquid profits at a price', *The European*, 5-11 June, p. 22.

Yanagishita, M. (1992), 'Japan's Declining Fertility "1.53 Shock"', *Population Today*, Vol. 20, No. 4, April, pp. 3-4.

Zeeman, E. C. (1976), 'Catastrophe theory', *Scientific American*, Vol. 234, No. 4, April, pp. 65-83.

Zhou Xin (1997), 'Railway Fulfils Dreams of Affluence', *Beijing Review*, Feb 10-16, pp. 15-18.

Zich, A. (1993), 'The other China changes course - Taiwan', *National Geographic*, Vol. 184, No. 5, Nov., pp. 2-33.

Zorpette, G. (1996), 'Hanford's Nuclear Wasteland', *Scientific American*, Vol. 274, No. 5, May, pp. 72-81.

INDEX

Page numbers in italics signify tables, maps or diagrams